The Mystery
of
Crichel Down

1. Launceston Down and Crichel Down (skyline, left) from the South across the Tarrant Valley

The Mystery
of
Crichel Down

I. F. NICOLSON

CLARENDON PRESS · OXFORD
1986

Oxford University Press, Walton Street, Oxford OX2 6DP
Oxford New York Toronto
Delhi Bombay Calcutta Madras Karachi
Kuala Lumpur Singapore Hong Kong Tokyo
Nairobi Dar es Salaam Cape Town
Melbourne Auckland
and associated companies in
Beirut Berlin Ibadan Nicosia

Oxford is a trade mark of Oxford University Press

Published in the United States
by Oxford University Press, New York

© I. F. Nicolson 1986

British Library Cataloguing in Publication Data
Nicolson, I. F.
The mystery of Crichel Down.
1. Land tenure — Political aspects —
England — Wimbo (Dorset) 2. Crichel
Down (Wimborne, Dorset) — History
I. Title
333.33'5'0942334   HD610.W/
ISBN 0-19-827492-0

Library of Congress Cataloging in Publication Data
Data available

Phototypeset by Dobbie Typesetting Service, Plymouth, Devon
Printed in Great Britain
at the University Printing House, Oxford
by David Stanford
Printer to the University

Preface and Acknowledgements

This is the story of a great parliamentary and press controversy, culminating in 1954, which came close to splitting the Conservative government and party in the closing years of Winston Churchill's leadership. The uproar and crisis were resolved by the resignation of a previously (and also subsequently) widely respected and well-liked Minister of Agriculture, Sir Thomas Dugdale. He took much of the blame on his own shoulders, although a public inquiry had exculpated him, and others in politics, while blaming their subordinates. Those men, mostly civil servants, were condemned in the Inquiry report (Appendix 2) in language such as 'highly improper suggestion', 'regrettable lapse from the standard of conduct the public is entitled to expect from responsible civil servants', 'irresponsible attitude towards the expenditure of public money', 'lamentable exhibition of muddle and inefficiency', ' most regrettable attitude of hostility to a member of the public', etc.

Such charges could not be effectively gainsaid until, in 1984, under the 30-year rule, the official papers began to become available for study in the Public Record Office. Within the intervening thirty years a persistent myth of Crichel Down had taken firm root and spread far and wide (its main features are exemplified in Appendix 1).

This book is an attempt to establish the truth, to dispel that myth. It is hardly a matter for surprise or indignation that the politicians in the case should have fought hard for the survival of their party in office, and should have found, as well as sacrificial lambs, one conspicuous political scapegoat (Minister Dugdale) to bear away blame and guilt from a whole government and cabinet. It was a not unhappy outcome, for Sir Thomas Dugdale himself, to be released from the cares of thankless office, to be praised and remembered for the good if quixotic deed, shining out in the naughty world of politics, to have the opportunity to combine private country life with quieter, useful public service, and to be raised to the peerage, within a few years, as Lord Crathorne, by a Prime Minister (Macmillan) who appreciated his worth.

The immediate and lasting damage the 'scandal' did to the British civil service is quite another matter. Any remedial effect which the full story can achieve comes far too late for most of the Crichel Down officials. The vindication of them attempted in this book has been an unconscionable time in preparation. For good reasons, ingeniously argued, my request in 1979 to study the Ministry of Agriculture papers on Crichel Down, made with the help and encouragement of the then Head of the Civil Service, was courteously declined by the then Permanent Secretary, mainly because of the risk of hurt to the feelings of people involved in the affair, not all of them in Government service, who would be expecting that 'at least' the 30-year rule would apply.

The Ministry of Agriculture helped greatly later, by giving the many papers a flying start to the Public Record Office on the expiry of 30 years, and letting me have a list. By then I had ascertained that most of those who had been in political office at the time preferred not to rake over the ashes, and I had decided that it would be wrong to approach civil service survivors, not merely because of the Official Secrets Act but because they had every right to be left in peace. The study thus became perforce almost entirely documentary.

And what documents! The essentially simple story of Crichel Down — the pre-war acquisition of 725 acres in Dorset as an RAF bombing range, its post-war restoration for agricultural use and lease to a suitable farmer — was uniquely bedevilled with errors, legal, statistical, historical, and with repeated misunderstandings and differences of perception, even before political additives irretrievably spoiled the richly confused broth.

Without one lucky discovery in a Surrey attic in the summer of 1979 the detective work would have been even more difficult, even impossible. Mr Robert Crouch, Conservative MP for North Dorset left his bundles of Crichel Down papers with a friend, Dr Donald McI. Johnson, MP, who died in November 1978. In his memoirs Dr Johnson treated Crichel Down as a victory for his 'independently-minded' friend Bob Crouch over the Minister of Agriculture, recalling a 'pilgrimage' with Mr and Mrs Crouch to Crichel Down:

But the picture which I took of Bob Crouch with this temporarily well-known place as background scenery is one of the more forlorn exhibits in my photograph album. For there were to be no more Crichel Downs, and Crichel Down, far from being a landmark in political history, is but a dusty memory even these dozen years later. While Bob himself died in a diabetic coma within a year of that date. Prior to his death he had lent me his Crichel Down papers for research and they lie mouldering in my attic, not worth the undoing even for the purpose of this book. Nor, even at the mention of this fact here, do I anticipate any rush of demand from the archivists.

I am grateful to Mrs Betty Johnson, and to Dr Johnson's family, for permitting a search for the papers (the complete written evidence for the Clark Inquiry): my wife discovered them after several hours of warm and diligent search in the large, document-filled attic. They have now been deposited in the Library of Nuffield College, Oxford, by way of acknowledgement to the Warden and Fellows for hospitality and help in 1979. They may assist future students to make second and third guesses about the mystery.

My thanks are also due to Lord Crathorne for his help, both at Crathorne and at the House of Lords, and to Lady Crathorne; to Lord Inglewood for his recollections of the affair and of Sir Thomas Dugdale as Minister, from his point of view both as Parliamentary Private Secretary and as a friend (and, for good measure, as a landowner, a farmer, and a chartered surveyor); to Lord John-Mackie for help and advice from a radically different agricultural and political point of view; to Lord Carrington, Lord Nugent of Guildford, and Lord George-Brown for their courtesy in giving me their perfectly creditable reasons for preferring to add nothing to what they had said and written at the time—reasons which helped me not to do too much barking up the wrong trees; to Lieutenant-Commander Marten for permission to look at his papers, at Crichel, and for patient discussion of the affair with me, although aware from the outset that our viewpoints differed; to a score of civil servants in the Ministry of Agriculture and the Public Record Office who helped unfailingly, none of them betraying hooves, horns or other satanic signs of 'arrogant and unscrupulous bureaucracy'; to Mr Norman Cadge of the London School of Economics Library, for help in the location and interpretation of maps; and to Mr Desmond Roche of the Institute of Public Administration, Dublin, for a useful discussion and perceptive commentary.

None of those who have helped can be blamed for any errors or shortcomings in this work. It is probably too much to hope to escape error altogether, in a story so 'riddled with errors' in the past. The more serious difficulty, because of those past errors, has been to avoid exhausting the reader's patience whether by laborious detailed refutation of others' mistakes, or by tedious insertions of [*sic*] to bring them to attention. I have sought to achieve order, without inflicting pain, by completely rewriting the story in chronological order.

This should give the reader some advantage over the participants in the action, who were confronted with confusion throughout. None of them ever had orderly access to the facts, either before, during or particularly after the Inquiry which was supposed to discover the truth. Dramatic irony abounds, therefore, in this version of what can be seen either as a farce, as comedy, as tragi-comedy, or even, for some, as tragedy, dependent upon the reader's own prejudices, temperament, and sympathies. As for the decent and honourable citizens so freely, publicly, and unjustly condemned, whatever their errors and failings these were as nothing compared with the hostility, the irresponsibility, the arrogance, the complacency, and the 'lamentable exhibition of muddle and inefficiency' of those in press and in parliament and in academic life who hastened to condemn them. For journalists and politicians forced to act quickly there is some excuse for hasty judgements, but for those who claim scholarship there can be no excuse for not suspending judgement until the facts are known, particularly where there is 'injurious affection' of other men's reputations. If there are any serious errors left, in this latter-day version of the story, they are not deliberate or set down in malice—they are merely human errors, like those of the Blandford martyrs themselves.

Port St Mary,
Isle of Man,
Saint Andrew's Day, 1985

Contents

List of Illustrations

Plates (photographs: C. M. Nicolson, Michaelmas 1979)

Maps

2. Western boundary of the Crichel Down area,
showing thinness of soil over the chalk

Phase One: Story of the Land to 1949 and the Official Planning for its Future 1949–1951

The Land

When in 1937 the official scouts of the Air Ministry were urgently seeking sites for airfields, and for a much smaller number of practice bombing ranges (both badly needed), it was natural that their eyes should fall on the almost unnaturally empty Launceston Down/ Crichel Down area, lying conveniently within the sparsely populated north and east Dorset region, as a suitable site for a bombing range. For an airfield, in those days, fertile level land was sought, capable of providing ample grass cover, and there were of course many bitterly contested proposals for the pre-war acquisition and post-war retention of such land. (One such contest involving the same landowners as the Crichel Down case, the future use of the airfield at nearby Tarrant Rushton, went as far as the Cabinet for resolution, at the same time as Crichel Down: while not so complex a case, it was difficult enough, and the reader may be spared any further reference to it: the Crichel Down case itself is mystery enough for one book.)

For a bombing range, on the other hand (Map 2), what was sought was preferably open, empty waste land within fifty miles of a suitable airfield, with a clear field of view over the whole target area from one observation point, with little expense involved in compensation for dwellings or other buildings, or for arable land and crops, and no difficulties over clearing of valuable woods, or possible damage to power-lines, telegraphs, drains, or historic sites. Crichel Down fitted these requirements, except for the possibility of damage to Bronze Age relics buried under some eighteen barrows, small low mounds. Punctiliously, the Air Ministry, once the acquisition had been decided, paid for the Ministry of Works to undertake, with the landlords' agreement, an archaeological investigation, in August 1938. Mr (later Professor) Stuart Piggott reported finds 'of exceptional interest', showing human use of the Down from Neolithic times, through the early and late Bronze Age: 'Theoretically the earliest should be the low irregularly circular mound covering a crouched skeleton on the old surface with a leaf-shaped flint arrow-head of Neolithic type in its ribs.' (AIR 2/4326.)

There is much to follow which tempts one to see, in the dagger through the victim's ribs, a symbol of a 'Curse of Crichel Down'. And certainly, after the Bronze Age, the area became and remained empty. Even the Romans bypassed Crichel Down with their two roads intersecting nearby at the ancient stronghold of Badbury Rings, then proceeding, one straight to Bath, the other straight to Salisbury, both avoiding the Launceston and Crichel Down area.

The rational explanations for the emptiness of such chalk uplands (rising and falling about the 300 ft contour above sea level) include the thinness of the soil cover. Soil depth, when tested in 1954 for the Inquiry, showed that 217 acres of the contested 725 acres had 2½ in. soil cover or less, the rest mostly below 4 in. of soil; only 20 acres had soil 5 in. deep (MAF 236/4). With this thin cover over the porous chalk came dryness, in contrast with the better-watered, better-wooded, better-sheltered valleys between the downs. Over the centuries rain on the hills had sunk through the chalk, draining into the 'winter bournes' (or 'Wimbornes'), the streams, ponds and water-meadows of the valleys, taking with it much of the fertility of the uplands, leaving behind at best a few inches of leached soil over the chalk, affording summer sustenance to be shared by sheep and rabbits, barely adequate for cattle or for arable crops.

What is historically and administratively significant about the region, therefore, is not what was there but what was not: not much soil or soil fertility; not much water; not much shelter, so not much settlement; not many landed estates and farms, but large ones; not much 'public', so not much public opinion; few public houses; little local gossip; no local newspapers. In 1901 the parish of Long Crichel numbered 125 souls, the parish of More Crichel 334, according to the Victoria County History—hardly more than the figures in the 1801 census.

The nearest town, Blandford Forum, where the Clark Inquiry was held, is five miles to the West, on the main road (A354) running just to the North of Crichel Down, from Salisbury (18 miles NW) to Dorchester (20 miles SE). Blandford, however, was hardly a single centre of commerce and communication for the vicinity: it is one of several small country towns where country business might be done, and occasional markets might be found.

Within twenty miles or so, however, there are some of the more hectic holiday routes and resorts (ancient, medieval, and modern) of tourist Southern England. To the north lie Salisbury, Cranborne Chase, Shaftesbury, and busy roads to and from the west of England; to the east, close at hand, the New Forest; to the south, Bournemouth, Poole, Swanage, Corfe Castle, Lulworth Cove, and other seaside attractions. To the west (Blandford and beyond) stretches Thomas Hardy's Wessex, the Vale of Blackmoor, the Tolpuddle of the martyrs, and the county town of Dorchester.

Bournemouth, about fifteen miles to the south, is the largest town in the present county of Dorset, although it was only after the reorganization of local government in the 1970s that it was excised from Hampshire and tacked on to Dorset. It has therefore no traditional administrative connection with the predominantly rural hinterland of the county. Its closest connection with Dorset farming was probably the fact that Bournemouth was one of the two towns (the other being Blackpool) chosen for the wartime evacuation from London of hundreds of civil servants of the Ministry of Agriculture. Some of them were doubtless still serving in the Ministry when the storm over Crichel Down was raging in the 1950s, and might, if asked, have been able to put right from that experience and from local knowledge some of the misconceptions about the district which were proving so troublesome. One says 'might' because in fact several of those whose actions were bitterly attacked as interference by remote Whitehall bureaucrats — including Claude Wilcox, the most senior of them — were Dorset-born and -schooled, and some had lived and worked in Dorset for many years. Local knowledge did not help them in their troubles.

The peculiar remoteness, peace, and seclusion of east Dorset are not simply a function of being 'far from the madding crowd'. It is a border area, and those in history devising boundaries for landownership, for parliamentary constituencies, and for local government, found it convenient to run their boundary lines right through what became the Crichel Down bombing range (see Maps 1 and 2); it was empty, marginal land, not greatly valued.

On the larger scale, Dorset itself became a sort of Tom Tiddler's ground when administrative regions were established. Some ministries and departments included it in a general southern region. The

Ministry of Agriculture, however, dividing the country more on the basis of traditional farming practice, had lumped it together with the rest of the south-west, putting the farms of east Dorset under the care of officials at Taunton in Somerset reporting to higher officials at Bristol responsible to headquarters in London, while the Minister's personal Liaison Officer for the region in 1953–4 operated from Exeter in Devon. That was always inconvenient, and in the Crichel Down affair it proved worse than inconvenient. Dorset was later incorporated for agricultural purposes in the south.

Land Use

Traditionally, the use of the land, in counties like Dorset characterized by extensive uplands with shallow soil, and extensive heathlands, rough grazing and moorlands at the lower levels as well, and no particular mineral resources, was very susceptible to economic change. Sometimes, when 'corn' flourished, arable acres increased, in other seasons when 'horn' prospered, sheep, cattle, and pasture increased. Yet there was one basic, traditional pattern of downland farming (dictated more or less by the physical geography), based on sheep-rearing. The valley meadows yielded grass and hay for feed, while the chalk uplands provided grazing in the warmer months, and the arable and marginally arable fields in between the two extremes of hill and valley, manured by the sheep, and under very careful shallow ploughing and rotation, provided some winter feed, root crops, and grain. The ideal farm combined these three elements, and was of necessity fairly extensive, 'up hill and down dale'.

In hard times, when neither horn nor corn flourished — as in the depression years of the 1930s — there was a strong tendency (amidst great debate and disagreement about measures to improve the poorer pastures) for the poorer hill land to be used merely as a sheep-walk or cattle-walk, or to be left to its own devices as waste land. This was not necessarily neglect, nor deliberate conservation, nor necessarily misuse, given the realities of the international market.

In those years it had eventually become impossible for upland farmers in particular to compete unsubsidized with cheaper and plentiful imported meat, and grain, and dairy products other than quickly perishable liquid milk. And even dairy farmers had to rely heavily on imported feed and government assistance.

In such times the plough rusted disused, sheep and shepherds declined in numbers, and the older traditional pattern of downland farming was finally broken in the depression years. Rent-rolls fell also, and the great estates, some of them broken up, declined in importance as the local alternative to agriculture for rural employment. Depopulation and emigration therefore continued.

The Condition of the Land in the 1930s

Throughout the Crichel Down controversy there was a particularly bitter and poisonous misunderstanding over the state of the Crichel Down land before acquisition by the Air Ministry. Official references to low pre-war rental values, to lack of cultivation, and to the poor state of the land were taken to be false accusations of neglect made against individual landowners and farmers. Astonishingly, the objective facts were never firmly established, although they were on public record all the time. The truth was that the 725 acres taken for the bombing range were indeed bare, in poor shape, and of almost negligible rental value at the time when acquisition was first considered, in May 1937.

The clearest official record of the truth which did not prevail is contained in a dismal report dated 20 May 1937, by the Air Ministry Assistant Lands Officer first sent to reconnoitre and report on the suitability of the land for use as a practice bombing range, H. E. Bush. (His report can be followed with the aid of Map 2.)

Bush reported, in a newly opened file entitled 'Crichel Down Bombing Range, Acquisition of Land' (AIR 2/4326):

The area consists of very poor grass land which has recently been fenced off into fields, but there was no stock in any of these and there did not appear to be sufficient keep on the land for animals to graze. The well had a wind-driven pump fitted and a small boiler adjacent as a storage tank. Both these had fallen into a state of disrepair. The well was situated in the middle of two 16 point rifle ranges which had fallen into complete disuse. A certain amount of clearing and levelling will have to be done to the ranges.

Parts of six fields will have to be taken in on the High Farm side of the danger area. These fields were under cultivation.

In a supplementary report, on 15 June 1937, Bush mentioned that the greater part of the site was open downland, but 'certain fields on the East to South West are under cultivation', that Hyde Hill plantation 'contained little timber of any value', and that there were several tracks, but he had been unable to find out which were public rights of way. He then reported:

Messrs. Rawlence and Squarey, Land agents for Lord Alington informed me that doubtless Lord Alington would object because he did not wish to sell any part of his Crichel Estate and also because of the adverse effect of flying on the amenity of his country residence. Messrs. Rawlence and Squarey also act for Mr. Farquharson but it is doubtful if there will be much objection in this case.

(AIR 2/4326)

Much later, still serving in the Air Ministry, and sending to the Ministry of Agriculture on 9 April 1954 the gist of the evidence he proposed to give if asked at the forthcoming Clark Inquiry, Bush recorded his recollection of 'poor chalky downland with a tumulus and other earthworks, and an old rifle range. . . . At the time of my inspection I assessed the value of the downland for rental purposes at 5/- an acre.' (AIR 2/4326.) Nothing could be clearer than Bush's first-hand account, that at a time when the whole country was in poor agricultural shape, the part of it which became the Crichel Down bombing range was exceptionally little valued. It was not much coveted (apart from the needs of public defence), except for private seclusion and private sport. The large Crichel Estate of the Alingtons to which 328 of the acres belonged had been a famous sporting estate in the great shooting epoch which culminated in World War I. After Napier Sturt, the third and last Lord Alington, succeeded to the title in 1919, he was an absentee for long periods, and his sad story (and that of his estate) was a sort of rake's progress ending in his early death in Cairo in 1940. Appendix 5 gives some account of the changing fortunes of the three generations of Alington landlords and of their lands.

As to the other large estate, from which 382 acres of the range were taken, the Langton Estate, the trustees of that estate were in the process in 1937 of splitting it up and selling off the various farms comprised in it. And as to the small, third component of the bombing range, the fifteen Hooper acres, their owners, Hooper Bros. were substantial farmers with no fewer than ten farms in the region, breeding pedigree herds of cattle and sheep; they did not suffer from land hunger.

Bush expected a little difficulty with the farmers, but not too much: interviewed, Mr Hooper, of Manor Farm, Tarrant Hinton, had not welcomed the proposal ('but on the other hand, if an arrangement can be arrived at to leave his water supply reservoir undisturbed, I do not anticipate any undue opposition from Mr Hooper'). Messrs. Strange Brothers, of Tarrant Launceston (the tenants of the Farquharson or Langton Estate land) were on the point of purchasing from that Estate the portion which would be left after the Air Ministry acquisition. Bush also interviewed Lord Alington's tenant, Mr Spearing, noting that the acquisition would deprive his farm of about 105 acres of cultivated land, adversely affecting the remainder, which would be 'about 200 acres of cultivated land still available'. (AIR 2/4326.)

As Bush was an interested party, in so far as he was acting for and reporting to the acquiring authority, his picture of the land might be expected to be unflattering, but as Map 1 shows, there was already on record a detailed, quite 'unofficial' map of the land and its uses, dating from 1931–2, fully corroborating Bush's report of 1937, and showing that the poor state of the land was no very recent phenomenon.

It is a minor mystery in itself why this invaluable record, a modern Doomsday Book, was apparently never consulted or even mentioned in the great controversy. It was not secret, or confidential, but academically respectable, unique, public, and although quite overlooked in the 1950s it had been pretty well known in the 1930s, outside as well as inside governmental and agricultural circles.

It was an authoritative work, a land utilization survey of Britain, initiated by Professor Dudley Stamp of the London School of Economics, the most eminent geographer of his day, who was gravely concerned by the lack of information available as to the use and misuse of the land of Britain. That lack made informed discussion and resolution of a whole range of problems impossible—problems of town and country planning, of industry location, of transport, of agriculture and forestry, of conservation. If knowledge is the power base of bureaucracy, Stamp's efforts can be seen as tending by the increase of knowledge towards a bureaucratization of society; but that takes no account of a very human tendency to amnesia and muddle rather than to logical conclusions.

Of course, since the nineteenth century the British government had busied itself in the collection of farming statistics, but had always been so respectful of the privacy and the power of landowning and farming interests that it had been less than whole-hearted in collecting data, and decidedly secretive about the figures it did collect. The main reason for that was not any 'passionate love of secrecy inherent in so many minor officials' (Clark, Appendix 2, conclusion 4) but the actual statutory restrictions on the collection and dissemination of statistics without express authority. The understanding, the bargain on which farmers had been induced to provide any details at all of crops and yields was confidentiality for what they provided. Another (less respectable) reason for non-disclosure of statistics was the fact that little reliance could be placed on them, most farmers (until recently) having neither the time, nor the will, nor indeed the education, to deal competently with the complexities of the returns and their multiple overlapping categories. It was always a struggle to get the returns in at all, at least half the farmers in the country requiring expensive postal reminder, even in the days when the prospect of subsidies, guaranteed prices, and valuable free advisory services had somewhat enlivened farmers' interest in the work.

Such considerations of confidentiality could not apply to the extraordinary, amateur, unofficially organized (and to that extent 'unbureaucratic') land utilization survey instigated and guided by Dudley Stamp, resulting in maps showing the use of practically every useable acre. Difficulties there certainly were, of course, including the destruction in London, by war-time bombing, of much of the stock of six-inch maps prepared.

Through lack of the local financial support the Survey had enjoyed in other counties, the Dorset survey was one of the last to be published. But a patron was eventually found, the Lord Lieutenant of the county, the Earl of Shaftesbury (father-in-law and neighbour of Lord Alington, and grandfather of the future Mrs Marten). With this, and with the help of, amongst others, Mr T. R. Ferris (destined as County Agricultural Officer to play a part in the Crichel Down affair) it was possible to publish a smaller-scale (one-inch) Dorset map. Dudley Stamp recorded that the Survey was organized by the county's Director of Education and undertaken by the schools, between the end of 1931 and the end of 1932, when they had returned, completed, most of the six-inch maps issued to them: he was full of praise for the careful and accurate work the schools had carried out.

The charming, idyllic picture conjured up, of the local children let out in the springtime of 1932 to note the crops in the fields around Crichel Down, is rather spoiled by the fact that that particular map was prepared, not by children (there were few, locally), but by one of the teachers. It shows (see Map 1) the great bulk of the land not as arable, nor even as permanent pasture, but placed in category H, 'heathland and moorland'. The categorization of land presents notorious difficulties. It was the policy of the Survey to record as 'permanent pasture' much of the downland used for sheep and categorized in Ministry of Agriculture returns as 'rough grazing' — 'unless there is a considerable proportion of gorse, brambles or other rough herbage'. It is therefore reasonable to conclude, as the open downland that was to form the bulk of the Crichel Down bombing range was placed in category H, 'heathland and moorland', that it was very rough grazing indeed, and that its poor state in 1937 and later had nothing to do with rapid deterioration, whether before or after it passed from private ownership.

In other words, it is the Clark Inquiry version (Appendix 2, para. 27) which is 'quite untrue' and 'incorrect in fact', not the official reporting of the land's condition to which Clark applied these strictures. As to the controversy which raged about the actual acreage of 'arable' at any one time, the inaccuracy of farmers' returns, the lack of precision in measuring acres not particularly prized, nor tended, nor accurately surveyed, and above all the fundamental 'pre-bureaucratic' lack of agreement on the meaning of terms such as 'arable', 'permanent pasture', and 'rough grazing' — all these conundrums made the controversy itself barren, let alone the land, when worked over by eminent lawyers. One is reminded of the 'dirty boots' Wessex farmer mentioned by A. G. Street, the Wessex writer, who was asked how much of his land was 'arable'; he replied: "Orrible? It's all bloody 'orrible!'

And that can be the last word on the state of the Crichel Down land before the time of its acquisition, well before (see p. 21) the 1949 revolution in agricultural machinery and methods and in artificial fertilizer application which transformed both 'virgin downland' and 'marginal land' into indubitably arable land. Despite Dudley Stamp's being on the books of the Ministry during the controversy, as part-time Adviser on Land Use, there is nothing to suggest that his advice on Crichel Down was sought.

Acquisition by the Air Ministry, 1938

'Having heard the evidence and examined the documents' Sir Andrew Clark, QC, declared briskly in the preamble to his inquiry report

(Appendix 2, para. 3), 'I find the facts to be as follows' and then began what he called his 'factual narrative'—a narrative containing such basic errors that it is hard to see how they could have been honestly made, or how they could have gone so long without public exposure.

The most important later errors are touched upon at the appropriate chronological points, and this is the place to point out the misstatements about the Air Ministry's acquisition of the land. First, he asserted that 'in or about 1937' Crichel Down was 'compulsorily acquired' by the Air Ministry (Appendix 2, para. 4). The land was not acquired in 1937, not matter how 'abundantly clear' Clark found it (Appendix 2, para 26). Nor was it 'compulsorily' acquired, although that requires fuller explanation. Nor was it true to say (Appendix 2, para. 6) that after acquisition by the Air Ministry 'the land deteriorated rapidly becoming covered in places with gorse and infested with rabbits'. That could be a classic case of an observer seeing only what he wished to see, of Clark's undoubted conviction 'private property good, state ownership bad', but he must have had great difficulty in overlooking entirely the true story set in front of him in the pages of the (unpublished) bundles of correspondence laboriously prepared as documentary evidence to help him in his work of inquiry.

The land was acquired in 1938, not 1937. At the very beginning of 1938, on receipt of a letter from Lord Alington dated 31 December 1937 (after reconnaissance of several potential sites, selection of Crichel Down, negotiations with farmers, estimates of costs and of likely objections, and after obtaining Treasury sanction both for acquisition and for the use of compulsory powers if that proved necessary) the Air Ministry was made formally aware of the personal objection to the project of Napier Sturt, the third and last Lord Alington.

Alington's letter to the Ministry of 31 December 1937 read as follows:

Both Mr G. Farquharson and myself are strongly opposed to the Crichel area being chosen as a bombing practice ground and we are of the opinion that the waste down land at Pond Bottom would be more suitable as being further from any roads, farm buildings, and dwelling houses, also would not interfere with arable land, and thus put farmers and labourers out of employment.

The inconvenience to Blandford is purely imaginary. My agent Mr. Rawlence is trying to arrange a meeting with the Blandford Town Council and local residents on the spot. Would you find it possible to send an aeroplane over to drop bombs on Pond Bottom to satisfy them as to the harmlessness of the procedure, of which they seem to be entirely ignorant. Sorry that this trouble should have arisen.

The G. Farquharson mentioned in the letter was not the actual owner of the Langton estate, but a farming tenant, the estate being in the hands of the trustees of the large estate of a former Farquharson who died in 1871. Alington himself had formally ceased to be the actual 'owner' of the Crichel Estate under a marriage settlement of 1928 by which for complicated purposes of succession and estate duty he had become instead 'tenant for life in possession' of the estate, a distinction without a great deal of practical difference. One difference, however, of a practical kind, it had made, in the 1930s, which deserves mention, because of the light it throws on 'interfering with arable land' and on another of Clark's odd statements. A file in the Ministry of Agriculture (MAF 48/596: Agricultural Holdings Act, 1923, Higher Farm, Long Crichel, Dorset: *Lord Alington* v. *Messrs. Harding*) tells a story of arable being turned into pasture at great expense to the Crichel Estate. The file records a tenancy agreement of 1927 for the letting of Higher Crichel Farm — not the Middle Farm which lost acres in the bombing-range acquisition — for a term of eight and a half years. In 1935 the tenancy was duly determined, the Hardings vacated, and a sum of more than £2,000 was found to be due to them in respect of improvements, i.e. the laying down of about 410 acres of formerly arable land in permanent pasture, for which the tenants were entitled under their agreement with Lord Alington to payment at the rate of £5 per acre. Alington paid, then on counsel's advice sought an Order from the Minister of Agriculture to the effect that as the agreement had been made while Alington was still the fee simple owner of the estate, before the marriage settlement made him 'tenant for life in possession', he was entitled to repayment and interest payable by the Trustees out of trust capital. The Order was made, charging the estate with both the payment by Alington, and costs. None of this story of 'interfering with arable land' emerged in the Crichel Down palaver, which was tangled enough without vexations about the more metaphysical aspects of 'ownership' of the land, or about whether the Hardings, as asserted by Clark in Appendix 2 para. 5, occupied 'at all material times' the farm on the Crichel Estate from which 328 acres were taken for the bombing range. In fact, despite Clark's 'factual narrative' the Hardings appear not to have taken the tenancy of that farm, Middle Farm, until 1947, long after it was truncated by the Air Ministry acquisition.

The outcome of Alington's breathtakingly lordly letter of 31 December 1937 was inevitably delay while his alternative was considered. The Air Ministry had already taken action before Alington's own letter arrived. They had earlier been told, by Rawlence and Squarey, agents for both the Crichel and the Langton Estates, in a letter of 29 November 1937, of the objections to the Crichel Down proposal, and also that the Langton Estate was 'quite willing' that the Ministry take instead the 'the down known as Pond Bottom'. By 12 December 1937 the Minister had promptly inspected and considered Pond Bottom, decided to accept it as an alternative to the Crichel Down site (provided the Pond Bottom plantation was removed), and adopted for the new range the one-inch map name for the feature, Monkton Down, in preference to Pond Bottom, which was presumably more vernacular, and would certainly have been more confusing. In the same way, although the Crichel Down range had more Launceston Down in it than Crichel Down, there was clearly a need for the Air Ministry to avoid muddle with their existing installations at Launceston, Cornwall, no matter how 'harmless' the proposed bombing practice might be.

There followed the first real trouble—a good deal of angry protest by the citizens of Blandford, Pond Bottom being only about a mile from the town. There was a formal deputation to the Air Ministry in Whitehall, a meeting with the Under Secretary of State, and an eventual reprieve for Blandford, of a kind. They did not get a bombing range thrust upon them, but as often happened when alternative sites were 'volunteered' by their owners, Pond Bottom too was 'compulsorily' acquired, in the rather less disagreeable form, for a country town, of a military camp. It had been an RAF encampment at the end of World War I, and seems to be included in the 'Blandford Camp' of recent ordnance maps.

The Crichel Down acquisition was decided in May 1938 as a result of a crisp recommendation dated 5 May 1938 made by one of the most distinguished Royal Air Force commanders of World War II, the then Wing-Commander Portal (later Marshal of the Royal Air Force Viscount Portal of Hungerford, KG, GCB, OM, DSO, MC).

I ask your approval for the acquisition of the site at Crichel Down (Dorset) for the purpose of a practice bombing range.

2. We selected this site last year but at the request of Lord Alington and certain other local residents, we have been investigating since December 1937, an alternative site near Blandford.

3. The Blandford proposal raised considerable opposition and U.S. of S. saw a deputation. The position as he left it was that we were to try to get the people of Crichel and Blandford to settle it between them, and we held a bombing demonstration to try to convince them of the harmlessness of practice bombing.

4. Neither side, however, will give way and the conclusion we have reached, with which Professor Abercrombie agrees, is that Crichel has the weaker case. This case is really that they do not want to have aeroplanes flying about near their houses.

5. No Government department concerned objects to our taking the Crichel site.

C. Portal,

D. of O.

(AIR 2/4326)

(The Professor Abercrombie called in aid of the project by Portal was Patrick Abercrombie, 1879–1957, whose reputation in the fields of architecture and of town and country planning was as great as that of Dudley Stamp as a geographer. Lord Holford, in *The Dictionary of National Biography* said of him 'if any one man had a truly synoptic view of the physical planning problems of the British Isles, that man was Abercombie'. Apart from the many advisory reports and plans he had prepared by 1938, he had campaigned effectively for the Green Belt around London, and for the establishment of the Council for the Preservation of Rural England. His advice carried great weight, nationally and internationally, over the fifty years of his professional life, and must have been conclusive in the final, deliberate choice of Crichel Down as bombing-range, against Lord Alington's wish.)

The Air Ministry's next step, as the range preparation was 'considerably overdue', was to seek the permission of the tenant farmers (Messrs. Strange for the Langton Estate 382 acres and Messrs. Spearing for the Crichel Estate 328 acres), and of the landlords, for the Ministry's workmen to enter on the land, before formal acquisition, to erect fencing and the one or two sheds needed. The tenants readily agreed, subject to landlord consent, the Air

Ministry having made it clear to them that there would be no need to interfere with them 'at any rate before September the 29th' (i.e. Michaelmas, the traditional date in the locality for tenancy changes). Thus the tenants were still in possession until the end of the 1938 growing season, and able to use their sheep-walks and to harvest such crops as their threatened arable and marginally arable acres provided (MAF 236/1).

Rawlence and Squarey were asked by the Ministry on 23 June 1938 to obtain the landlords' agreement, the tenants having already consented. The agents wasted no time, passing the Ministry's request on to Lord Alington the following day, suggesting agreement, and adding, with an unusual trace of acerbity in their normally courteous style of correspondence with their aristocratic principal: 'failure to do so might look like deliberate hindering of national effort'. But whatever the cause of delay, it was not until 29 July 1938 that Rawlence and Squarey were able to convey Alington's agreement to the Ministry (MAF 236/1).

It was only after entry had thus been agreed that the Treasury Solicitor, in August 1938, served upon Lord Alington formal notice of the Air Ministry's intention to acquire, in the Solicitor's words, 'certain land in which it is understood you have an interest', with this explanation:

I would therefore explain that in serving upon you the accompanying Notice to Treat the Air Ministry is adopting a statutory procedure, rendered necessary by the emergency extension of the Air Force. In acquiring the land for defence purposes the Air Ministry has no desire or intention to act otherwise adversely to your interests, and they would not propose to have recourse to arbitration if terms of acquisition can be speedily agreed.

(MAF 236/1)

In the later storm over Crichel Down particularly heavy weather was made, unnecessarily, over the question whether the acquisition of land from the Langton Estate and the Crichel Estate was 'compulsory' or done 'under the threat of compulsion' or 'voluntary' or 'by agreement'. The actual conveyances (unlike the Hooper 15-acre compulsory conveyance), were in the usual form, recording nothing more than ordinary agreement as between willing seller and willing purchaser, signed for both parties.

Sir Andrew Clark (Appendix 2, para. 28) said it was 'quite untrue' that the two larger owners were 'not unwilling' to part with the land 'at a low price'. He maintained, instead, that 'they strenuously resisted the compulsory acquisition of their land, but without avail'.

It became a difficult topic, one thoroughly obfuscated throughout, and requiring detailed discussion later (see pp. 125 f.); but there was originally nothing very mystifying about the story, until strenuous efforts began to be made to fit the various transactions into one of three mutually exclusive categories, none of which fitted better than a left-hand shoe for a right-hand foot. If one takes the simplest transaction first, the Hooper 15 acres, Hooper declined the invitation to treat, so an arbitrator was appointed, who apparently was able to reach speedy agreement with him on the terms of compensation. A conveyance in the legal form appropriate to a compulsory purchase was prepared, referring to the exercise of the powers of the Secretary of State under the Defence Acts (and other Acts) to acquire and hold land, and to a certificate dated 20 December 1938 under the hand of the Lord Lieutenant of the County of Dorset, Anthony, Earl of Shaftesbury (Alington's father-in-law again) authorizing the taking of the property. Yet even that conveyance, making compulsion clear, speaks of agreement between vendor and purchaser as to the amount of compensation, £519 for the fifteen acres (MAF 236/34).

If on the other hand one takes the Langton Estate and the Crichel Estate conveyances together it is evident that what Clark called their 'strenuous resistance' did not go as far as the Hoopers'; they did not press the matter to arbitration by refusing to treat, and they stopped short of declining to sign a conveyance prepared as a voluntary agreement with no hint of either compulsion or any threat of compulsion.

It is idle to speculate about the reasons for their agreeing. So far as the Langton Estate was concerned, it was at the time in the process of being split up and sold off in bits, by rather distant trustees, and one may suspect that their unstrenuous association with Alington in his objection was from diplomatic neighbourliness rather than deep feeling, particularly as they were happily volunteering an alternative site for the range, not far away. So far as the Crichel Estate was concerned, Alington's lifelong activities were strenuous only in a very limited sense. No doubt the fact that his own father-in-law would have been obliged as Lord Lieutenant to authorize the compulsory acquisition of the land would have been some deterrent to further resistance. There was also the possibility, mentioned by Rawlence and Squarey, that further delay would look like hindering the country's defence effort. *Noblesse oblige*, in the last resort.

At any rate, compulsory powers were not used, and the conveyances of the Crichel Estate 328 acres and the Langton Estate 382 acres simply register that the vendors 'have agreed to sell the property', with the appropriate signatures for both parties, and with a covenant by the Secretary of State to erect and maintain stock- and rabbit-proof fences (MAF 236/34).

How did such preposterous confusion later arise and persist, over such a relatively simple matter? Given the importance of land, the primordial stuff of politics, war, law, and wealth, and given the overriding importance of public acquisition of land and resources in British domestic politics, it is astonishing to learn that until well after World War II universities and law schools taught students nothing of the 'multifarious powers by which governmental agencies of various kinds may interfere with the private ownership of land' with the result that most of the vast body of the relevant laws remained 'virtually unknown to private practitioners, both solicitors and estate agents alike, with consequent unfortunate and sometimes expensive results to their lay clients'. (Garner, J. F., *The Public Control of Land*, 1956, p. v.)

In the absence of formal teaching of lawyers in their youth about the public aspect of land law and conveyancing, and in the absence of textbooks, learning, for the few who did learn, was mostly by doing, in the service of public authorities, leaving others—Sir Andrew Clark and some others in the Crichel Down case included— strangely unshaken in an outworn creed, the belief in the sanc- tity of property under English common law, a belief based on ignorance, nothing less. It was a blissful sort of ignorance of the extent to which governments and parliaments ostensibly opposed to 'bureaucracy' had inevitably bureaucratized society with every step taken towards modernity. It was inevitable in that 'modernization and 'bureaucratization' are merely different ways of describing the same trend in organization. In reality, that process had not gone far enough, in 1938, to end the traditional English and obstinately pre- bureaucratic practice of 'muddling through' in a not very organized way.

By way of examples, because of the lack of accurate cadastral survey, the Air Ministry, after more detailed survey, had to alter the acreage recorded and to reconstruct fencing to accord with the

new line. Because of the lack of land registration they were late
in discovering that it was not the living Farquharson with whom
negotiations had been going on who 'owned' the Langton Estate
acres, but the trustees of the estate of an earlier Farquharson deceased
in 1871. Such compoundings of 'the law's delays' are part of the
price paid for too little bureaucratization rather than too much.
Judging the right amount, the extent of bureaucratization needed
to keep pace with requirements of modernity, is a problem not solved
by inveighing against bureaucracy, or officialdom, or the collection
of facts, or even by devising new bureaucratic organizations to
oversee and 'control' those already existing. The 'trick' is to have,
and to preserve, a 'tradition of civility' if it exists, as it did in the
England of the 1930s. That civilized tradition is reflected in the
reasonable and humane even if slightly muddled way in which the
government went about the desperate business of land acquisition
for the purposes of rearmament.

Between Michaelmas, 29 September 1938, when the Air Ministry
took possession of the land, and the spring of 1939, the eagerness
for 'speedy agreement' on settlement terms seems to have transferred
itself, quite understandably, from the Air Ministry purchasers already
in possession to at least one anxious seller, Lord Alington, whose
London solicitors (Tylee & Co.) were then writing to the Treasury
Solicitor, reporting that terms had been agreed and prompting him to
seek instructions for settlement from the Air Ministry. The Treasury
Solicitor was then told by the Ministry that the terms were 'not yet
definitely agreed by the Department'. This, conveyed to Tylee & Co.
towards the end of June 1939, brought an impatient response: their
client's agents still maintained that all the terms had indeed already
been agreed, so they could not understand why the matter could not
proceed (AIR 2/4327). Proceed it did; agreement was finally reached
by both sides' lawyers that agreement had finally been reached. But
by the time the conveyancing was completed it was 1940 (various
dates, the Crichel Estate first, 15 January 1940, the Hooper date
10 May, the Langton Estate last, 4 September: AIR 2/4329).

Clark's 'factual narrative' of acquisition 'in or about 1937' will
therefore never do—a margin of error of a year or more in a report
on which men's reputations and careers depended, in regard to
dates ascertainable from the evidence before him, seems excessive,
especially in a report so severely critical of others' (unproven)
mistakes and misdeeds.

Rabbits, in 1940

Clark was wrong about the rabbits, too. By the time of his Inquiry, in 1954, myxomatosis had almost done away with the British rabbit population, and the precise extent of previous infestations would not have been easy to establish, especially on land like Crichel Down, first fenced, then bombed, then regularly ploughed, with fences moved, and removed, and the whole pattern of land use revolutionized. Nevertheless, what the Air Ministry archives record of the life and hard times of the Crichel Down rabbits in the era of public ownership runs counter to Clark's twin assertions that before acquisition the land was not infested with rabbits (Appendix 2, para. 27) and that after acquisition 'it deteriorated rapidly becoming covered in places with gorse and infested with rabbits' (Appendix 2, para. 6). There is no certainty about the gorse (or about what being 'covered in places' might mean), but had there not been rabbits galore at the time of acquisition there would have been no need for the Air Ministry's covenant to erect a rabbit-proof fence to keep them in, or down. The evidence of the measures taken against them after acquisition seems convincing enough, and relates to the year 1940 chosen by Clark (Appendix 2, para. 27) for his guess about infestation.

In the spring of 1940 there were complaints about root-crop destruction by Air Ministry rabbits from Hyde Hill plantation at the western edge of the range. Years later, at the Clark Inquiry, old Mr Rawlence claimed the complaints had been made by him, but this seems not to have been known to the investigator appointed at the time. An already very busy man, in the spring of 1940 (the year of Dunkirk and of the Battle of Britain) a works superintendent of the Air Ministry was sent to inspect. In his perambulations he was exasperated to meet 'one of the tenants', who expressed great surprise ('failed to understand from whence such a complaint could have emanated') and agreed there was no ground for complaint. The Superintendent reported that there was more evidence of active depreciation by rabbits *outside* the boundary than *inside*, because the Air Ministry (as well as constructing a rabbit-proof fence) had employed a man to keep the rabbits down—which he had done 'very successfully' (AIR 2/4391). Whether Clark could be convicted of 'gorse error' as well as rabbit error, and serious errors about the state of the land before and after acquisition, and the date and methods of acquisition, is immaterial. Gorse had presented no real problem at any stage, whether to bombers, or bomb clearers, or farmers, and Clark's motive in making a point of it, fully conscious or not, was perhaps to bring public ownership and management of land ('state socialism') into ridicule and contempt.

The extent of his success was quite extraordinary; in the absence of detailed refutation of his version of the Air Ministry's acquisition of the land, whether in the press, or in parliament, or indeed in official statements by the departments concerned, Clark's story was accepted and later embodied in other accounts. The best example of the mythography to which Clark's account of the acquisition gave direct rise occurs in the very readable and lively guide or guide-book *The Battle of Crichel Down*, by R. Douglas Brown, journalist on the political staff of the liberal daily *News Chronicle*. It was published in 1955, but written, with commendable speed, in 1954. The writer's own close Dorset connections gave him a good start, and he had access at Crichel to the documentary evidence prepared for the Clark Inquiry, and to the shorthand transcript. But (as shown in Appendix 6) speed and a touch or two of journalistic and poetic licence, make for mistakes as well as for readability, and mistakes once detected arouse misgivings about the rest of the work.

Official Use of the Land, 1938–1949

This is R. Douglas Brown's account (op. cit., p. 20) of the immediate consequences of acquisition: 'The Air Ministry took over, the Down became a practice bombing range, the cottagers around grew used to the regular *clump* of exploding bombs and the roar of planes overhead, cultivation ceased, the land deteriorated, gorse began to spread freely and rabbits multiplied.'

This was splendid journalism. But cottagers within earshot were very, very few indeed. The assessment of the likely loss of amenity to the mansion of Crichel itself had been 'nil', partly, no doubt, because the planned use of the range was for smoke-bombs only, not high explosive bombs. Much later, once the Air Ministry had handed over to the Ministry of Supply, the range was used for experimental work on bombs, bomb-sights, bomb-release mechanisms, and other air-to-ground weapons, involving, apparently, occasional use of 'smaller' high-explosive bombs (MAF 140/41).

Even smoke-bombs explode, of course, but not with great noise —
and as for the roar of planes overhead, that was a sound which was
to become familiar to almost everyone in Britain, in town and
country, with no comfortable assurance that it presaged merely
harmless practice by friendly aircraft. The 'gorse' and the 'rabbits'
have already been dealt with.

There is in fact little more to record about the usage of the Down
during the war years, beyond the fact that in 1941 the Royal Air
Force decided that they had no further immediate use for it. It then
passed to the Ministry of Supply for use, without any formal transfer
of title.

Post-war Planning, 1945–1948

In 1945 the then Land Commissioner for the area reported the land
as 'Poor Down', Category C land, of rental value 5s. to 6s. per
acre — no advance in fact on Bush's 1937 figure of 5s. The Land
Commissioner in 1945 observed: 'This seems to be a range which
might well be kept in use if it is suitable to R.A.F. purposes.
L. H. Way 5.xi.45' (MAF 140/141).

In 1947 the (Ministry of Agriculture) Rural Land Utilization
Officer (stationed at Winchester) cited in his report Randol Ferris's
opinion that the land was below the general run of downland, that
retention as a range would not seriously interfere with farm units,
and that having regard to its relatively remote position and low
agricultural quality it might well be advisable to acquiesce in the
permanent loss of the land, in preference to the loss of other sites
which might be put forward. The Assistant Land Utilization Officer,
agreeing, noted a request by the local authority that the down be
returned to agricultural use, but noted also the fact that part of it
was already being informally grazed, while the remainder was 'pock-
marked and full of craters'. He thought that if a range was still
needed in that part of the country it could stay where it was: if not,
the land could be used for agriculture. On 30 May 1947, accordingly,
an inter-departmental working party agreed 'to recommend retention, without public local enquiry' (MAF 140/41). Nothing emerged,
in or from the Clark Inquiry, of this fairly detailed consideration
given to the Crichel Down range, in the heyday of post-war planning,
by the Ministry of Town and Country Planning, in consultation with
Agriculture, the service departments and others, and local authorities

(the Blandford Rural District Council and the Dorset County Council: MAF 140/1).

Nothing emerged either, from the Clark Inquiry report, of the most significant change which occurred 'in or about' 1949, transforming with remarkable suddenness first the experts' view of the land's potential and then the ordinary farmers' and landowners' appreciation of it.

The Agricultural Revolution, 1949

This was an agricultural revolution, no less, beginning about 1949. Its occurrence was firmly stated during the 1954 Clark Inquiry to have occurred, but there is no sign that Clark detected or accepted its significance. The change was the realization that by the use of the powerful modern machinery becoming available, together with intensive artificial fertilization, even poor marginal land could be turned into productive arable, at a time of continued food shortage, rationing, and public impatience with years of austerity and deprivation.

This coincided, more or less, with a decision by both the Ministry of Supply (who could after the end of 1948 use a new range at Imber) and the Air Ministry, that they had no further use for Crichel Down. Once that decision had been taken, the future use of the land had to be considered. No one could have guessed that the task of beating swords into ploughshares could cause such turmoil as it did, over the next five years.

The Official Plan, 1949–1951

The first, obvious requirement was to clear the land of bombs. On 29 March 1949, at the request of Squadron-Leader Boyle, RAF, Boscombe Down, Mr H. Dale, Assistant Agricultural Officer (Advisory) from the Dorchester office went with the Squadron-Leader to inspect Crichel Down and advise on the range's probable future use. The RAF needed that information. If the land were to be used for grazing only, 'clearance' would simply mean removal of visible bombs, and an undertaking to compensate farmers for loss of livestock from explosions. That sounds happy-go-lucky, until one remembers that the main use had been for smoke-bombs, and as the later use by Supply was mostly for experimental work, much of the buried material would not be suddenly lethal to man or beast. If, on the other hand, the land once cleared were to be designated as arable and ploughed, that would require a second phase of clearance, a process of mechanical metal detection to a given depth of ploughing, followed by laborious and careful hand-digging to unearth the objects detected — about a year's work for twenty men to clear to an eighteen-inch depth.

The RAF had hoped to be told that surface clearing for grazing livestock would be enough, but Dale had disappointing advice to give, being quite sure that arable use would be best 'because the existing herbage was extremely poor and of no value for pasturage. The stock-carrying capacity would be negligible.' (MAF 140/41.) This was the opening sentence of Dale's report, dated 7 April 1949, to the RAF, written after he had reported the meeting to his superior, Randol Ferris, the Dorset County Agricultural Officer. He had told Ferris that the RAF would report to the Air Ministry Dale's advice (he called it 'the fact') that the land should be used for arable purposes, in the interest of maximum food production: if there were any 'hesitation' concerning a thorough clearance, he understood that the RAF would again seek their advice.

Dale's report of 7 April 1949 went on more cheerfully, showing full appreciation of the great change in the land's potential value being brought about by the agricultural revolution already in train:

Practically the whole range could be ploughed and used for the growing of cereal crops, which is the proper course to take having regard to the necessity for maximum food production at the present time. After a course of arable cropping, the land could then be resown to ley, which would have a stock-carrying capacity incomparably greater than the present herbage.

Summer 1949 — Surface Clearance

So far, so good; but this was the first bombing range to be cleared by the Air Ministry and offered for agriculture. For the return to agriculture of airfields, a smoothly-working routine had been established between the two departments, Air and Agriculture, but over Crichel Down, as always, snags and misunderstandings arose. In September 1949, when the Air Ministry invited the Ministry of Agriculture to accept transfer of the land, subject to 'surface clearance' being completed before transfer, the Air Ministry's meaning was strictly literal—clearance from the soil surface of visible bombs. Before the end of 1949 more than 200 tons of live and inert bombs had been so cleared. The Ministry of Agriculture, on the other hand, took 'surface clearance' to mean clearance sufficient for safe ploughing, and accepted the land on that basis.

Winter 1949/1950: Snags

It was not until after transfer of the land had been accepted, effective from 9 January 1950, that the Ministry of Agriculture realized, indignantly, that neither the land nor the words had been clear enough, and that there had been no clearance below the visible surface. Action was being urged, through letters and visits, by the District Land Commissioner at Taunton, Lt.-Col. Norton-Fagge, who was keen to start the ploughing; the Ministry was placated by the Air Ministry's explanation and accompanying promise to clear the land as quickly as possible, to a depth of fifteen inches.

A second minor snag was the need to discover from the Ministry of Supply exactly what kind of bombs had been dropped (between 1941 and the end of 1948 when use of the range ceased) in order to ensure safe methods of clearance. A third difficulty arose over the sections to be cleared first. Norton-Fagge, when first confronted by the fact that the land was still unsafe for ploughing, had devised, with Ferris's help, a programme of clearance and ploughing, section by section, so that, as each section was declared clear, the big prairie-buster plough could move in straight away.

By typical Crichel mischance, however, in one of the small areas marked for ploughing first, the mechanical detectors revealed no fewer than 11,000 buried metal objects. Each such detection entailed cautious digging to discover the cause. Progress was slow until in co-operation with the RAF the ploughing programme was re-cast to leave the most highly-saturated areas (around the bull's eye of the target area) to be tackled last.

After that, clearance and ploughing went swimmingly, just about as fast as the plough could travel behind the RAF clearers. Although the spring sowing in 1950 (a few weeks only after the transfer) was not as extensive as had been hoped before the snags arose, there was extensive sowing, in the autumn of 1950, for the 1951 harvest, followed by further sowing in spring 1951—more than 600 acres in all (MAF 140/41).

A Minor 'Row', October 1949–February 1950

In a better world much credit would have been given to Lt.-Col. Norton-Fagge for his initiatives and cutting of red tape to get a start made on the productive use of the range, but instead of that a land-hungry member of the public had shot off, without precise aim, some wild accusations of 'sheer waste and negligence' and 'fiddling about'. If one counts the original 'row' between Blandford and Lord Alington over the siting of the range, in 1938, as the first, this in 1949 was the second Crichel Down row requiring ministerial attention, and the first occasion when the intervention of a Member of Parliament was sought by a farmer or landowner.

Captain D. W. Taylor, MBE, farming nearby Yarde Farm, Pimperne (140 acres) was the son of a man who had previously farmed many more acres, at Pimperne, land sold while the son was serving in the army. Captain Taylor, anxious for more land, confident that he had enough capital, machinery, livestock, and experience of the type of land to take it on immediately, began in September and October 1949 to show keen interest in the bombing-range, writing first to the Air Ministry's Works Directorate, then to the Air Ministry itself, then informing the county agricultural executive committee of his ambitions, and telephoning the county agricultural office at Dorchester. Prompt, but, unsurprisingly, slightly different replies came from the several sources.

The County Agricultural Officer and chief executive of the county committee, Randol Ferris, OBE, writing to Taylor on 3 October 1949 in response to the telephone message left with his secretary (and relying it seems on memory, without detailed knowledge or total recall of the 1938 land acquisition) said he understood the Air Ministry were considering release of the land (correct) from requisition (incorrect) and if so would no doubt release it 'to the person from whom it was requisitioned in the first place' (incorrect) — but that, if the land were handed to the county committee for agricultural use, Captain Taylor's 'wish to be considered in connection with it' had been noted. On 13 October 1949 the Air Ministry told him of the intention to hand over the range to Agriculture 'when it finally closes down' and suggested an approach to the county committee.

Somewhat prematurely exasperated, Taylor wrote to his (Liberal) constituency MP, Lt.-Col. Frank Byers, OBE, (later Lord Byers) on 5 December 1949, saying the range had not been used for four and a-half years, and that the Air Ministry had had 'two or three men fiddling about there for years, doing a little now and then and nothing most of the time'. Unless an immediate start was made it would be over six years after the end of the war (i.e. the 1951 harvest) before any grain could be harvested there — 'nothing short of sheer waste and negligence'.

In prompt responses to the MP both the Ministers concerned (Air and Supply) dealt personally with the complaints. The Air Minister (Arthur Henderson) told Byers the range had been handed over in 1941 to Supply, that Air, although still holding title, had no further interest in it, and that the complaint had therefore been referred to the Minister of Supply. The latter (John Freeman) wrote that his Ministry had used the range until the end of 1948, when a larger range (Imber) had become available, that in 1949 more than 200 tons of bombs had been removed, and that authority had been sent to the Air Ministry for transfer of the land to Agriculture.

The two Ministers' replies reached Taylor, through his MP, before the end of 1949, and the Air Ministry's letter confirming the 'outright transfer' of the range to the Ministry of Agriculture was dated 9 January 1950. Perhaps because of that juxtaposition of letter dates it was suggested in 1953, during the campaign for a public inquiry, by both Taylor and Marten (see Appendix 3), that Taylor's initiative had speeded up a discreditably slow process of bomb clearance. In fact such problems as arose over the transfer, the bomb clearance, the ploughing, sowing, and harvesting were, it seems, neither helped nor hindered by Captain Taylor's endeavours. The major credit for speeding things up must go to Norton-Fagge for his ingenuity, energy, and steady pressure on all concerned to take action.

Compared with the later example of an appeal by a Conservative MP (Crouch) to a Conservative minister (Dugdale) on behalf of a Conservative constituent (Marten) which takes a whole book to unravel, this earlier appeal by a Conservative voter through a Liberal MP (Byers) to Labour Ministers (Henderson and Freeman) could serve as a model of prompt, cool, and courteous response to an angry complainant with 'a regrettably hostile attitude'. The replies followed the twin proverbial principles honoured in the civil service of the time — 'a soft answer turneth away wrath' and 'least said, soonest mended'. It was just as well, too, that the accusations were not referred to the servicemen at 'the grass roots' engaged in bomb clearance: there might in that case have been a military rather than a civil reply.

As it was, when Taylor wrote to Ferris on 12 January 1950 citing the parliamentary correspondence and saying 'I do hope you may hear something soon as then some of it could be got ready for sowing in the Spring . . . ' Ferris was able to reply promptly that action was proceeding, that Taylor's name was being 'considered with others in connection with this land' but that letting was not in the hands of the Dorset County Agricultural Executive committee. To Norton-Fagge, in a letter of the same date, 17 January 1950, sending him a sketch plan for ploughing and sowing by sections, Ferris mentioned his knowledge that both Taylor and another named local farmer (H. W. Dibben) were interested in renting sections of the land, adding: 'In all probability some of the other adjoining farmers would be prepared to take further land but I have not actually been in contact with them on the matter.'

In reply, on 20 February, 1950, Norton-Fagge wrote to Ferris summing up the Crichel Down situation as he then understood it; the Ministry of Agriculture, having accepted transfer of the whole of the land, would doubtless hand it over for management to the body set up for that purpose by the 1947 Agriculture Act, the Agricultural Land Commission; but, almost certainly, recommendations from them (i.e. the Land Service and the county agricultural staff) would be required.

At that point, therefore, despite the allegations of waste and negligence by one local farmer, promptly dealt with, nothing could fairly be said to have gone far wrong. The local people of the Ministry had done all they could to get the land into production, to deal fairly with enquirers, and also (on Norton-Fagge's initiative) to have removal of electricity supply, demolition of buildings, wilful damage, and casual squatting on the land prevented or stopped so far as possible, and to give thought to the recommendations they should make, when asked, about the land's agricultural future.

1950—the Ryan Committee

Throughout 1950 a committee (the Ryan Committee) appointed by the Labour Minister of Agriculture Tom Williams at the end of 1949 to review the Ministry's organization grappled with its complexities, particularly the workings of county committees and decentralized activities generally, in fifty-two formal meetings. Many of the changes they favoured had already taken place before their final report was submitted in February 1951.

Their task had been to study the development of the Ministry since 1939, particularly its 'decentralized workings', and to make recommendations for any changes necessary. The Chairman, J. Ryan, was Vice-Chairman of the Metal Box Co., Ltd.: with him were three senior civil servants (2 Agriculture, 1 Treasury Organization and Methods), another industry representative, and an experienced Chairman of a County Agricultural Executive Committee. It was clear from the committee's composition and their terms of reference that what was sought from them was recommendations reflecting both business and civil service expertise in the management of large-scale, complex organization—'bureaucracy', in one sense of that word of many meanings.

What they found was complex indeed, and unique, the product of more than a decade of rapid expansion in a patchwork pattern, a pattern set by the need to be responsive to local feelings, and to the representatives of agriculture and its related industries, while respecting pre-existing agricultural traditions and practices. From its somewhat sleepy Whitehall hollow of 1939 (when only about 1,000 out of the 2,600 people in the Ministry were stationed outside London) the Ministry had spread and grown quickly. It had absorbed the agricultural staff (e.g. Randol Ferris in Dorset) and the functions of County Councils, setting up what was virtually a new form of representative local government for agriculture, in the shape of the wartime and post-war county agricultural executive committees, with functional subcommittees, and district committees, staffed and serviced by a new kind of civil service, with two new professional services for advice and technical help, the National Agricultural Advisory Service and the Agricultural Land Service. By 1950, the Ryan Committee found, there had been since 1939 a sixfold increase in Ministry numbers to more than 15,000, of whom barely 3,000 were at headquarters, the rest 'in the field' throughout England and Wales, mostly servicing the multitude of mixed official/unofficial activities. This was later described by the authors of a thorough and illuminating study as 'a close and pervasive pattern of co-operation between the Government and the principal agricultural organiz-ations'. (P. Self and H. J. Storing, *The State and the Farmer*, 1962.) So close had that partnership become that in 1951 a (Labour)

Parliamentary Secretary in the Ministry of Food was driven, before he resigned, to invent the new verb or usage 'featherbed' to describe the state's solicitous care for farmers' comfort and well-being.

After their fifty-two formal meetings, and their study of masses of evidence, and visits of inspection in the counties, and occasional admiring glances at simpler, tidier Scottish practices, the Ryan Committee came out with findings and recommendations which were far from faulting any tendency in the Ministry towards bureaucratic usurpation of power. Instead, their most important recommendations, some adopted in advance of their report, others requiring more time to achieve, were designed to sort out which of the myriad functions and duties which had sprung up since 1939 could and should be left entirely to civil servants to perform, without interference by the unofficial 'partners' of the state. They boldly stated the production of food to be 'the task of the Ministry' — 'a vital one at all times but never more so than in the circumstances of today'. The Committee placed great reliance on the organizational principles of the time, with their stress on simple, stark, single-word objectives such as productivity. (It was however the stress on productivity at all costs, since 1939, which had given such Byzantine shape to the Ministry in the succeeding years, and left little time or breathing-space for tidying up and taking stock.)

Ironically, given the great Crichel Down row that was to break out over arbitrary bureaucratic usurpation of power and high-handedness in the Ministry, the committee's first and most emphatic finding was of something very different — they were 'struck by the fund of goodwill the Minister commanded and could harness', 'the co-operation and wealth of talent which is voluntarily placed at the Minister's disposal and which is the foundation of the present partnership between the State and the Industry'. (para. 2, Ryan Committee Report, HMSO, 1951.) Their main recommendations were lightly disguised in diplomatic language, but above all they wanted the state's farmer partners to take the lead in disciplining their fellows who needed supervision, or the threat or actuality of eviction in extreme cases. They were the people to exercise these 'tough' functions, while the professional officers must not be drawn into these 'police' and 'judicial' duties — they must be and remain the farmer's trusted friends and advisers. And, again in the interests of productivity ('the national interest requires that all land must be made as fully productive as possible') the advisory officers must keep in the forefront of developments and purvey their advice 'as actively and widely as possible' without waiting to be asked. In other words, 'indirect rule' or 'divide and rule'; the tender functions, the making and tending of feather beds, would be done by civil servants, while any rude awakenings and tossings out of farmers should be done and be seen to be done by farmers themselves, as their part of the bargain. And both the farmers and the professional advisory officers should keep their noses out of routine 'administrative' business, the paperwork of applications, and the grants, subsidies, and accounts which were the proper concern of the 'ordinary' civil service applying the regulations.

Further ironies, given the Crichel Down difficulties to come over lack of facts, were the Committee's special praise for the care taken in the Ministry to see that direct collection of statistics did not extend beyond the Economic and Statistics Division, and their recommendation for the re-introduction of 'unofficial' Liaison Officers in Regions—not civil servants—to keep the Minister personally and directly in touch with farmer opinion. The appointed Liaison Officer for the West of England (in which Dorset was included) lived and farmed in Devon, near Exeter, and was not present at the Crichel Down Inquiry to defend himself because he knew nothing of the course of the inquiry until he saw its proceedings reported in the Press (Appendix 2, para. 94). The irony lies in the removal from the civil service of responsibility for keeping the Minister informed, presumably because the collection of political intelligence by civil servants would have been seen as a worse form of 'snooping' than collection and use of statistics. Instead, the work was given, in the Dorset case, to an honorary non-official, so placed geographically that the task was impracticable.

The Plan for Crichel Down, 1950

Nevertheless, there was no doubt in anyone's mind, from 1950 until the end of 1952, at least, that the imperative was the maximum production of food, i.e. grain from every possible arable acre, using the most productive methods. That dictated the plan prepared for the future use of Crichel Down, after a slight hesitation on the part of one of those whose advice was first sought, quickly changed into convinced support.

The initial doubter was Randol Ferris, when first asked for his ideas by Norton-Fagge in a letter dated 7 December 1949; Norton-Fagge, knowing the cumbersome nature of the machinery they would be expected to set in motion, wanted to get off to a flying start, a month before the transfer of the land to the Ministry of Agriculture and the subsequent transfer of management from that Ministry to the Agricultural Land Commission—another unofficial body (not within the Ryan Committee's remit) serviced by headquarters and field officers of the Ministry, and liable to become, if not handled with skill, tact, and good luck, an awkward set of wheels on the lumbering articulated waggon of Agriculture.

Ferris's prompt reply—Norton-Fagge had specifically said he did not want to put him to any trouble—was to suggest that 'each of the farmers' would be prepared to take over the occupation of the area formerly attached to the respective farms (overlooking changes which had taken place in farms and farm tenants since acquisition): 'I am quite sure that this would be a better method of dealing with the land, than by attempting to farm as a holding, as the land is not of any considerable fertility and production will be much higher if it is associated with established farms.' There was, later, a firm agreement and commitment at all levels, at headquarters and in the field, among the non-official members of the Agricultural Land Commission and their official advisers—including Ferris himself when he came to look more closely and discuss with others—that the best course in the interests of food production was to equip the range as a single holding.

On the whole, good progress was made in 1950, both in the short-term preparations for farming under the aegis of the Agricultural Land Commission (to which the Minister transferred the control and management of the land as from 1 April 1950) and in the long-term planning.

The short-term considerations included a fencing, ploughing, sowing, watering, and cropping programme. Because the Air Ministry had permitted neighbouring farmers to graze land on the range boundaries, at their own risk, without rent, Ferris and Norton-Fagge had to negotiate with them to bring that informal arrangement to an amicable end. In the process, Norton-Fagge established that both the farmers occupying land had gone beyond grazing and had actually cultivated nearly 100 acres between them. (In Appendix 2, para. 2 Clark refers contemptuously to 'some nebulous arrangement' with the Air Ministry over *cultivation*, but the only arrangements recorded with the Air Ministry were for *grazing*, not cultivation, and were with 'the Stranges' of 'Launceston Farm, Blandford', and 'the Spearings' at 'Long Crichel, Wimborne'. The Hardings, who had succeeded the Spearings as tenants in 1947, were not recorded as allowed to graze, but told Norton-Fagge they had been 'verbally authorized to go in and work the land'.) In a report dated 18 May 1950 Norton-Fagge recorded his impression of the very limited extent of the Hardings' interest in the land, of which, in May 1950, they were cropping 68 acres for barley:

With regard to the area occupied by Messrs. Harding and Messrs. Strange. The former have indicated that while they would quite like to continue the occupation of the 114 acres they do not wish to take on any larger area (i.e. none of the old downland pasture). I suggest that as these fields are on the best quality land, and conveniently situated, it would be desirable to retain them after Michaelmas next. Messrs. Strange have not yet been approached, but the 44 acres they now occupy are of relatively lesser importance, being poorer quality and remotely situated.

The short-term programme, therefore, for the 1951 harvest, had to include the clearing, from the maximum possible number of acres, of bombs, Stranges, and Hardings, so that the land could be prepared for planting.

Meanwhile, for the longer term, the equipping of the land as a single holding was beginning to seem the best way to fulfil the obligation of maximum production. It also seemed, to Ferris and Norton-Fagge, to preclude their asking any of the neighbouring farmers to undertake the cropping of the 600 acres expected to be available for the 1951 harvest, because there was no prospect of security of tenure to offer them. Norton-Fagge and Ferris therefore secured the agreement of the Chairman of the Dorset AEC to farm the land directly, using his committee's still ample reserves of machinery and labour.

For the rest of 1950 both short- and long-term projects marched forward together. With shortages of food and hard currency still acute, with the apparatus of the Agricultural Land Commission already in place (created by political consensus in the 1947 Act to manage publicly owned agricultural land), with no sign of hostile successors to deceased previous owners lying in ambush, waiting to strike, the way ahead was clear and uncontroversial—strenuous effort to increase food production. In the event, although good progress was made, there were the first difficulties with the Crichel Estate, over the necessary water supply for a mixed arable and dairy holding on Crichel Down; and at the end of the year, Norton-Fagge, the driving force behind the plan for Crichel Down, was transferred on promotion to Reading.

One of his worries had always been the security of water supply. Since 1939, by an annually renewable Licence from the Crichel Estate, the Air Ministry had obtained a metered, piped supply of water from the estate reservoir, conveyed, at first, across land not acquired, to a subsidiary reservoir. The subsidiary reservoir had been demolished, but the piping remained. The agreement was for a maximum of 1,000 gallons of water a day at a price of 2s. 6d. for each thousand gallons, with an acknowledgement rent of £1 a year payable in addition. The agreement being terminable and the supply limited, Norton-Fagge had considered it advisable to find an alternative source of water, but prospecting for it does not seem to have been pursued, after his departure, hopes being pinned on an agreed supply from the Crichel Estate until the farm could be connected with the public water supply system.

The Office of the Crichel Estate had shown on 24 March 1950 a very faint flicker of interest in buying (apparently) the whole bombing range, addressing to 'The Ministry of Agriculture and Fisheries, County Hall, Dorchester' the following rather languid letter:

Dear Sir,

Bombing Range, Long Crichel

I have been informed by Air Ministry Works Directorate, no. 14 Area, Launceston, that the department has no further interest in above, and that it has been handed over to the Ministry of Agriculture and Fisheries.
A few weeks ago I wrote to Air Ministry to enquire if the property was for sale, and if so, would they give us the opportunity of negotiating.
Will you kindly forward this enquiry to M. of A. as I do not know the address.

Yours faithfully,

N. O. Gilbert

More than four years later (Appendix 4, first paragraph) Lieut.-Com. Marten claimed that Gilbert's letter was an application by him (Marten) to buy back what had originally been part of his wife's property; but anyone receiving such an enquiry could be forgiven for not recognizing in it a serious proposal to negotiate with a government department for the purchase of hundreds of acres of land, whether the whole range of 725 acres was meant or merely the 328 acres of the former Crichel Estate area.

Norton-Fagge's reply, from Taunton, was prompt and courteous, although mistaken in one minor particular, a reference to the transfer of the land to the Ministry of Agriculture not being completed; that transfer had been completed, it was the Minister's own transfer of management to the Agricultural Land Commission that was not completed, although that too was authorized within a few days, with effect from 1 April 1950. But Norton-Fagge's main point was: 'Until the future of the land has been fully considered following completion of the transfer, it would be impossible for any definite reply to be given to your enquiry.'

Gilbert replied even more promptly, the following day, courteously but rather obscurely, thanking Norton-Fagge very much: 'May I ask you to please put on record to let me know when you are in a position to deal with this property as indicated in my letter of the 24th inst.' There was no suggestion, in that letter, of dissatisfaction that the letter of 24 March 1950 had not been 'forwarded to higher authority' as Marten maintained later that it should have been (Appendix 4) and there is no trace of any letter from Marten himself to Norton-Fagge asking for more definite news 'as soon as possible'. After this brief exchange, no more was heard from the Crichel Estate on the subject of purchasing land for more than two years (see p. 46).

It was water rather than land that seemed to be the only source of dispute with the Crichel Estate during the rest of 1950. Gilbert of the Crichel Estate wrote to Ferris a cross letter displaying no knowledge of the existence of a licence or provisions for its termination:

It has been reported to this office that in connection with your cultivations on Crichel Down, ex R.A.F., you are using water from the estate supply and I shall therefore be much obliged if you will please let me know if this report is correct. At the same time it would be interesting to know who gave you the authority for such use as when the R.A.F. people vacated the range the water supply to it was at once cut off.

Ferris called on the Crichel Estate Office and the rift was temporarily patched up, with a letter from Gilbert to Ferris:

With reference to your call here on Tuesday regarding water on the bombing Range, Long Crichel, I have authority to say that you can consume our water from the stand pipe that already exists on the site for use in tractors and watering some heifers. The period to expire on the 28th February 1951 and that you will pay the estate £5. 0. 0 for water up till 28th February next.

Ferris promptly and courteously acknowledged this letter, which amounted to notice of termination of the water supply, given in a rather haughty, high-handed manner. It must have been seen as a set-back to the prospect of building, equipping and letting an arable dairy farm for 60–80 cows by Michaelmas of the following year, 1951, with water required for farmhouses and cottages as well as for livestock and milking parlours.

At the end of 1950, however, apart from the unsolved problem of water, and the loss of Norton-Fagge's drive and knowledge, the production plan, short-term, was going well, and there was still hope for the long term. The progress made and the other noteworthy occurrences in 1950 are best set out briefly in a time-table of events in the year.

1950 — Timetable of Events

9 January   Transfer of range to Agriculture.

1 April   Minister transfers management of land to Agricultural Land Commission.

18 May   Norton-Fagge at Taunton submits cropping programme for 1951 and long-term plan for a single, equipped holding as the most suitable way of bringing the range into full agricultural production, to Provincial Land Commissioner Hole at Bristol; investment contemplated £18,000 for farmhouse, four cottages, farm buildings, new water-supply, and internal fencing.

1 June   Hole forwards Norton-Fagge's proposals to Agricultural Land Commission in London, agreeing that dividing the land in two or more holdings would be neither practicable nor economical, and that a set of buildings should be erected, details of lay-out to be dealt with later, once problem of water-supply solved.

20 June	ALC resolves one member (Hon. Geoffrey Bourke, eminent and experienced professional surveyor) should inspect and report 'as soon as convenient'.
10 July	ALC authorizes Norton-Fagge to 'go ahead immediately with the Prairie Buster at 50/- per acre'.
3 August	Further ploughing authority by ALC, for additional cleared land.
11 August	Inspection of land by Bourke, Edwards (ALC's Chief Land Agent) and authorization to Norton-Fagge to complete ploughing and follow on with cultivation programme, farming work to be supervised by Ferris, for County Agricultural Executive Committee. Recommendations that ALC:

    (a) farm for a year, from Michaelmas 1950;
    (b) let from Michaelmas 1951, if equipped;
    (c) approve Norton-Fagge's 'quite sound and adequate proposals' for buildings, etc.;
    (d) instruct Norton-Fagge to prepare plans 'forthwith'.

16 August	ALC approves in principle and resolves that the cultivation continue.
17 August	Edwards asks Norton-Fagge to reduce costs as much as possible, explaining that one ALC member felt prospect of 35*s.* to 40*s.* per acre was 'optimistic'.
19 August	ALC advises Agriculture Architect that Crichel Down buildings are their first priority for work on properties under their management.
9 September	Ferris reports to Norton-Fagge preparation of land completed earlier than expected, so proposes including wheat instead of oats, wheat being 'of very much more advantage from a National point of view'.
25 September	ALC agrees Norton-Fagge's detailed proposals for buildings.

Applications, 1950

Apart from Taylor's application in 1949 (p. 24), the note of Dibben's interest (p. 26) and Gilbert's enquiry about 'purchase' (p. 32), more enquiries about renting the land began to come in, between Michaelmas 1950 and the end of the year, as below, details being given in respect of the one enquiry which proved to be serious and sustained, that of Mr Tozer:

5 October   Mr Christopher Tozer, farming with father and brother a few miles away, at Woodyates, anxious to farm on his own, with request to see Ferris.

9 October   Request to Norton-Fagge from a Wareham (Dorset) farmer who had noticed the cultivation by the AEC and was interested in renting.

11 October   Formal application by Tozer, with references.

No other enquiries are on record in the correspondence prepared for the Clark Inquiry (MAF 236/1) so it seems justifiable to say that, without any public offer of land to let, the Land Service agents of the ALC had been made aware of two very keen local candidates (Taylor and Tozer), had a record of more perfunctory enquiry by two others, and the rather laconic enquiry from the Crichel Estate Office about buying an unspecified area. And contrary to what is suggested by Clark (Appendix 2, para. 14) and on pp. 38–9 of *The Battle of Crichel Down*, following Clark, no enquirer or applicant to buy or to rent had received anything so far by way of a 'promise' (whether of public tender, or of further particulars, or of careful consideration of any application they might make)—nothing beyond a statement, to those mentioning rental, that the land was not to let, but that their names were 'noted', or 'recorded', or would be 'borne in mind'.

1951—Slower Progress

The year 1951 began well enough with an authorization from the ALC headquarters to Hole in Bristol to 'go ahead, on the basis of the lay-out plan already submitted, have plans and specifications prepared and tenders invited with a view to completion by next September if possible'.

Other than the difficulty over water supply there is nothing in the correspondence which would account for delay in the plan, but the Clark report (Appendix 2, para. 15) and the Ministry archives agree that it was not until June 1951 that an agreement was entered into with the Crichel Estate, 8 June being cited by Ferris as the date on which he and Gilbert met and agreed (MAF 236/38).

Tozer and Taylor again

Meanwhile, the two earliest and most eager and persistent candidates for tenancy had asked again, Tozer on 15 January 1951 writing to R. G. A. Lofthouse, Norton-Fagge's successor, with apologies for bothering the Land Commissioner again, asking whether there were any developments, as he was 'most anxious' to start farming on his own. Lofthouse replied the next day, regretting he had nothing to add to Colonel Norton-Fagge's previous reply, but saying that Tozer's application was being borne in mind for the unit to be equipped and let.

Captain Taylor, the other eager candidate, wrote at greater length on 25 May to Lofthouse, saying he understood from Ferris and others that the land was to be let. Ferris had said he would support an application by him, and he gave other referees also, including Mr John Harding, the 'next door neighbour' of Crichel Down, as one of those who would be pleased to second his application. He went on to make it clear that he would be happy to have the land as it stood, without fences or buildings: 'Mr. Ferris has told me you are going to erect buildings cottages and fences there, but, should you decide against this, I should be very willing to rent the land as it stands or, alternatively, before they are completed.' Lofthouse in reply gave Taylor the first explicit assurance given to any applicant: 'I will certainly see that you are given the chance to make an offer for the farm, but the exact date from which it will be let has not quite been decided. I give you my assurance, however, that you will be kept in the picture.'

On 7 August Taylor wrote again to Lofthouse with 'many apologies' for troubling him again, for further news about Crichel Down, asking 'whether it will be let this Michaelmas' to which Lofthouse replied immediately on 9 August 1951 in terms quoted below in full to show what kind of 'promise' was made, before the unexpected event of the land being removed from the ALC's management and control, and before they had begun their usual procedure of public advertisement: 'I am in receipt of your letter of the 7th August and have to inform you that at the present moment the position is unchanged and as soon as the land at Crichel Down is likely to be available for letting it will be advertised in the public press, and any application you may make at that time will be carefully considered.'

In cheerfully undertaking to keep Taylor 'in the picture' Lofthouse had no reason to guess he might not himself be in that picture, that it would no longer be the familiar landscape, with the ALC letting land after public tender, but, instead, a new picture of a new Minister of Agriculture, in a new Government not yet elected, in an unprecedented step, taking, personally, the decision to sell the land to the Commissioners of Crown Lands whose centuries-old procedures for letting were not 'bureaucratic' public tender, but very different, more akin to those a wealthy private landlord would choose to follow.

28–31 August 1951 — Advertisement Deferred

Lofthouse, on 28 August 1951, sought the authority of Hole, the Provincial Land Commissioner based at Bristol, to advertise Crichel Down, observing that the water-supply from the Crichel Estate (pending public supply) seemed 'reasonably secure', that electricity supply was being negotiated, that the layout of house and buildings was substantially agreed, that boundary fences had been scheduled for repair, and essential internal fencing was being planned, adding:

I think we now seem all set to advertise, but before I went on leave you told me you were going to see Edwards and clinch the matter, and I wonder what happened at your interview.

I am sorry to trouble you on your well-earned holiday, but if you would scribble "Yes" or "No" or "Wait" on this letter, I should be very grateful.

Hole, replying by telephone on 30 August 1951, asked Lofthouse to speak to Edwards (the ALC Chief Land Agent in London). Lofthouse did so, and reported the same day (31 August) to Hole that Edwards felt the advertisement should be deferred until he had seen the Chairman, Sir Frederick Burrows, and found out his wishes. Meanwhile, Edwards agreed it had been right to authorize autumn ploughing, and that work must continue. It was clear that the farm could not be let from Michaelmas (29 September 1951) but Edwards thought it probable that the letting would be completed later that autumn, under arrangements drafted to show the farm as being on a Michaelmas tenancy.

31 August 1951—the Farmer's Weekly

Suddenly, without official advertisement, it became very widely known by farmers throughout Britain that a most attractive new farm—a very rare phenomenon indeed in an old country—might soon be available to let.

The *Farmer's Weekly* of 31 August 1951 carried a picture of as much of Crichel Down as could reasonably be displayed without aerial photography, and a photograph of Mr R. Farquharson, 'a neighbouring farmer', and Mr G. Malcom, 'in charge of Dorset A.E.C. Lands', discussing the very healthy crop being harvested. The caption read ONE WHEAT FIELD—530 ACRES and the commentary was enthusiastic:

Not the American wheat belt, but a picture taken on Crichel Down, Dorset, last week. The A.E.C. is harvesting what must be the largest wheat field in England, 530 acres—of which less than half is shown. A prairie buster was used for the cultivations: some chalk was brought up, but no weeds have appeared and over 200 tons of Bersee and Atle had already been taken off last week-end. The crops should be worth over £14,000. Recently abandoned as a bombing range, the land is farmed by the A.E.C. on behalf of the Agricultural Land Commission, who hope to let the land by Lady Day next. Plans for buildings have been prepared.

August–October 1951–More Applications

Within a week of the publicity there was a flurry of six enquiries, one of them dated the day *before* the *Farmer's Weekly* article appeared. One was from a Hampshire estate agent anxious to suit 'a very special applicant', one from Chichester, Sussex, one from a Yorkshire farmer who 'wanted a kinder climate', one from one of four brothers in Wiltshire, farming in partnership, who wished to 'divide out', two from Dorset farmers a few miles away, one at Beaminster, and one at Corfe Castle. There was one more enquiry before the end of September, making seven new names to be added to the four rental enquiries of 1950 (p. 36) including Taylor's proposal to buy or rent, but not including the Crichel Estate enquiry about purchase only. All these seven enquiries were answered in similar brisk fashion: acknowledgement, doubt about readiness by Lady Day (meaning 25 March 1952), and promise of particulars 'as soon as we are in a position to advertise'. Only one of the seven, the Corfe

Castle farmer, returned immediately to the charge, asking Lofthouse by return post, on 8 September 1951: 'Couldn't we come to a definite agreement now? I don't mind when I take over, either next March or next September but I would like something definite (subject to your plans being completed) to work on, I could rear some beef calves this winter and plan accordingly. I can give you references that I am sure would be to your satisfaction.'

It was to this frank bid for prior consideration that Lofthouse wrote the reply quoted in part by Clark (Appendix 2, para. 15) in such a way as to omit much of the writer's reasoning. Here is the full text of Lofthouse's letter, dated 11 September 1951:

Dear Sir,

Thank you for your letter of the 8th September. I can fully understand your desire to offer for the farm now, but I must remind you that I have on record a great many persons who are definitely interested and must be given the opportunity to make an offer. The plans for Crichel Down should be completed reasonably soon and it is wise to wait until I am in a position to tell intending offerers exactly how it is proposed to equip the holding.

I regret therefore that I must not negotiate with you in advance of any of the other offers.

Yours faithfully,

R. G. A. Lofthouse

October 1951–Tozer Tries again

So far as the records show, nothing had been heard from Mr T. Chris. Tozer since mid-October 1950 when Norton-Fagge had told him Crichel Down was not being offered to let at that time, but that his application would be borne in mind (p. 36). Tozer now wrote again to Norton-Fagge's successor, Lofthouse, on 1 October, 5 October, and 11 October, and after meeting Lofthouse at Dorchester at Tozer's own request ('I should very much like the opportunity of meeting you, so that I could become something more than just a name on paper.') on 8 November 1951. What emerged from the correspondence, on Lofthouse's side, was the by now usual undertaking to send particulars 'as soon as we are in a position to advertise the property' and a realization that Tozer, as he himself wrote 'did badly wish to obtain a farm'. For Tozer's part, he gained more knowledge than before of what was proposed in layout and buildings, which he thought very good: he also assured Lofthouse that he was prepared to take over the land from September 1952 'even though the building work would not probably be completed by then'.

Also in October there was one further enquiry, from Wimborne, dealt with in the usual way, doubt about Lady Day letting and promise of particulars 'as soon as we are in a position to advertise the property'. This enquirer, the last of 1951, made a total of thirteen recorded so far (including the Crichel Estate enquiry about purchase), of varying seriousness, from oral mention of interest through perfunctory letter to serious and persistent enquiries and proposals. Of these, only some (those enquiring in 1951) had received more than an acknowledgement that they were, as Tozer put it, 'just a name on paper'; they had received a promise of particulars as soon as the ALC was in a position to advertise the property to let — a position the ALC never attained.

31 October 1951

Two far more important events took place on 31 October 1951. That was the day on which Sir Thomas Dugdale was appointed Minister of Agriculture in the newly elected Conservative Government, succeeding the Labour Minister Williams, an old friend and former colleague in the wartime coalition government's agriculture department. (Agriculture was not yet an office in the Cabinet: Dugdale did not become a cabinet minister until 3 September 1953, when Winston Churchill abandoned his ideas of grouping junior ministries under senior cabinet ministers, the so-called 'Overlords', with Lord Woolton as the 'Overlord' of Agriculture.)

On the same day the Agricultural Land Commission conducted a full-scale inspection of Crichel Down. There is nothing to suggest anything but a fortuitous concatenation in these two events, and none of those present could have foreseen that their doings, that day, might set in train the events leading to a painful national scandal, the new Minister's resignation, and the eventual abolition of their own organization.

Those representing the Agricultural Land Commission were the Chairman, Sir Frederick Burrows, Mr E. Watson Jones, a highly respected, experienced and successful Shropshire farmer Member, the Chief Land Agent, Mr G. F. Edwards, and the Secretary,

Mr L. J. Smith. Also present were the Provincial Land Commissioner, from Bristol, D. A. Hole, the Land Commissioner for Dorset and Somerset, from Taunton, R. G. A. Lofthouse, and his assistant, D. S. Brown, the County Agricultural Officer, from Dorchester, T. R. Ferris, and H. G. Penfold, Architect, from the Ministry.

The conclusions reached were recorded by Hole:

1. That the homestead should be sited approximately in the position recommended by Mr. Ferris and not adjoining the road as originally proposed. This is subject to an inspection of farms by the Provincial Land Commissioner, and an assurance from him that similarly placed homesteads are more satisfactory than those on the road sides.

2. That the farmhouse should be sited adjoining the homestead in accordance with the draft plans submitted by the Architect.

3. That the cottages should be located on the road side near to the entrance to the farm but kept out of the low place originally occupied by the R.A.F. huts.

4. The C.A.O. should be asked to carry out the normal seasonal work on the boundary fences during this winter.

5. The internal fences to be constructed of timber posts, plain and barbed wire. The posts to be heat-treated with creosote. The erection of this fencing to be delayed until the winter of 1952.

6. The C.A.O. to be requested to continue to farm the land for two more seasons, but that it should be brought into a condition for letting not later than Michaelmas 1953.

7. The Commission approved the plans of the homestead except that a 30' Dutch barn should be erected having six 15' bays.

8. The Commission agreed that a shelter belt should be planted to the south west of the homestead, but should not be immediately adjoining it. They would prefer a gap of some 200 yards to the left.

Conclusion 6 is so clear on farming for two more seasons that it is hard to see why Clark reported (Appendix 2, para. 16) that the decision was to farm for one more season until Michaelmas 1952, and offer the tenancy from that date. Clark's list of those attending does not quite correspond with Hole's record, either, and Hole's conclusion 1 about farm inspections says nothing to support Clark's observation that 'certain local farmers, including the Hardings'

(Appendix 2, para. 16) were to be consulted as to siting and equipment. Nevertheless, as Clark stated, Hole did consult local farmers, five of them, including J. Harding and R. Farquharson, in the company of Lofthouse and Ferris. There is no evidence, in any of the papers preserved, of any of the farmers consulted displaying any resentment of the plans, or objection, or anything other than a neighbourly and friendly professional interest in the details of the proposals.

The End of the Year 1951

So, 1951 ended quietly, with the land ploughed again for the 1952 harvest, with a water supply from the Crichel Estate reasonably secure until a connection to the public supply could be made, and with the plans for the new farm having been shown to and amicably discussed with neighbouring farmers. One of them (R. L. Harding) had been given the shooting rights over the land, at £20. There was no hint of trouble from any quarter.

Later, the plan for a single holding was to be attacked in Clark's first conclusion as financially 'unsound' and in his second conclusion as having been persisted in because 'both the Lands Service and the Land Commission had become so infatuated with the idea of creating a new model farm that they were determined not to abandon the scheme for financial reasons'. (Appendix 2, conclusions 1 and 2). In short, there was a great 'rage over a lost penny'. Yet such a single holding, if it had been created, would have been a lucrative investment for its fortunate owners, bringing in millions of pounds in increased capital value and regularly reviewed rents, and in publicly financed support over thirty years or so. Of course neither Clark, nor the planners, nor anyone else could have foreseen such astonishing developments as were to occur between 1954 and 1984 in the financial support of agriculture, in the harvesting of subsidies, and in the debauching of the currency. Even without unexpected windfalls, however, the plan was a good and sensible one, made by experienced, public-spirited men, not at all 'infatuated' — a word better applied to their accuser than to them.

Had the plan been carried out a new farm would have been established at a cost of some £30,000 in buildings and equipment (farmhouse, cottages, barns, milking parlour, fencing, etc.). The land, cleared of bombs and valued at £15,000, would have been handed over by the Air Ministry at no cost. Thirty years later, the market value of the property, with vacant possession, would have been at least £1,500,000; so critics of governmental extravagance should look elsewhere for examples. They are, after all, not hard to find.

2

Phase Two: The Counter-Plan, Spring 1952–Autumn 1953: Confusion

Sheridan wrote: 'easy writing's vile hard reading'. If the opposite is true, this chapter should be easy reading, because it has been 'vile hard', in the writing and rewriting, to lay bare the simple outline of a campaign which brought about great confusion. The victorious culmination of the campaign can be precisely dated, 23 October 1953, when the Minister's decision to appoint a public inquiry was announced. The date of the opening shot in the campaign, the spring offensive of 1952, is more open to doubt and debate, because the chief campaigner, Lieut.-Com. Marten, who had married the heiress to the Crichel Estate in 1949 was afterwards to claim (Appendix 4, first paragraph) that he had made application in March 1950 to 'buy back what had originally been part of my wife's property'. In fact, the only enquiry from the Crichel Estate at that time was Gilbert's perfunctory letter of 24 March 1950 (p. 32) which can hardly be regarded as an opening shot, or even as a warning shot across the Government's bows. And after that, in Marten's own nautical words (Appendix 4): 'I formed the opinion that I should be merely spitting against the wind to try and get our land back under Socialist administration, and therefore decided to lay as low as possible.'

The First Shot, 26 May 1952
A better date for the opening of the campaign is therefore 26 May 1952, the date of a strangely amnesic enquiry to the Land Commissioner at Taunton, from the Crichel Estate agent Major Seymour. (Citations from documents in this chapter, as throughout, except where otherwise stated, are from the two bundles of evidence prepared for the Clark Inquiry, MAF 236/1 and MAF 236/2.) The letter is given in full:

Estate Office,
Crichel,
Wimborne.
26th May, 1952

Dear Sir,

As long ago as March 24th 1950 we wrote a letter about the Bombing Range at Long Crichel, to the Ministry of Agriculture at Dorchester and asked them to forward it to the correct authority, for at that time we did not know to whom it should be addressed. It appears that they never replied and for some unknown reason we then let the correspondence (which had been pretty lengthy and had been through the Ministry of Supply) drop. I enquired off Dorchester the other day and they say that they never received this letter, and so I am now writing afresh about the subject.

As you are no doubt aware this land (about 300 acres) was sold (I think compulsorily) to the Air Ministry on September 29th 1938, although the actual Conveyance was not signed until 12th January 1940. In 1950 we understood that the Air Ministry were selling it, or transferring it, to some other Government Department, but we were not certain which Department and so we wrote to find out whether this Estate could not be given first refusal, as it formed an important part of one of our tenant farmer's farms. As I have mentioned above this correspondence was apparently dropped before it reached the proper authority, which I gather is you. The matter, however, has lost none of its importance to us and our tenant farmer, and I should, therefore be most grateful if you could inform me what the present situation is and whether it would not be possible for us to buy the land back and thus restore it to that farm where it originally belonged, and to which it forms such an integral part.

Yours faithfully,

William Seymour (Major)

The Land Commissioner for Dorset,
4, Hamnett Street,
Taunton.

The new Land Commissioner, Lofthouse, had taken over from Norton-Fagge in November 1950, and spent no time on investigating the minor mystery of letters reported missing long before he took up his duties at Taunton. Instead, he sent an immediate acknowledgement and explanation that Seymour's letter was the first he had seen about 'the possibility of buying back some 300 acres of land sold to the Air Ministry in 1938', and that it was going to the Agricultural Land Commission for reply. He sent it the same day, 27 May 1952 to Hole, under a letter not in the least hostile to the Crichel Estate or its tenant farmers:

I had in fact heard a whisper that Major Seymour was interested to know whether there is any possibility of acquiring either the 300 acres formerly belonging to the Estate, or the whole 726 acres for which we are responsible. I believe, unofficially, that the Estate would add it to Messrs. Harding's farm at Crichel, and no new fixed equipment would be necessary because certain off-lying bare land would be taken from Messrs. Harding's farm, leaving a unit properly balanced as between buildings and acreage.

You will be aware that Messrs. Harding (you have met the nephew with Ferris and me) are first-class farmers and there is no doubt that if the land was sold to the Crichel Estate it would be well farmed. On the other hand, however, such an arrangement would not mean an extra holding being available for the farming community at large, except indirectly by freeing certain off land, now part of Messrs. Harding's farm.

It is clearly my duty to put Major Seymour's letter to the Commission, through you, and you will see that I have taken the liberty of asking the Commission to reply.

Hole at Bristol sent the correspondence back across the breadth of England to the Chief Land Agent of the ALC at their London headquarters, with equally commendable speed, on 28 May 1952, offering to go into the merits of Seymour's proposition if asked, and to find out how the Estate would propose to split it up, and 'whether the resulting units would be economic and fully equipped'.

On 10 June 1952 the Secretary of the ALC (L. J. Smith, Principal, on secondment from the Ministry of Agriculture) after discussion with the Chairman, replied (in two separate letters) to both Hole and Seymour, explaining to the former that the land was not the Ministry's to dispose of, that in any case the Minister's powers to sell land under the Agriculture Act were very limited, and they need not trouble Hole to go into Major Seymour's ideas for dealing with the land should it be sold back to the Estate. The reply to Seymour gave some details of the ALC's plans for the land, none about the limits of the Minister's legal powers:

As you know, the 300 acres of land in which you are particularly interested is part of a much larger area now managed by the Agricultural Land Commission, having been placed under our control by the Ministry of Agriculture and Fisheries. The Commission's function is to manage land to the best advantage, and they decided some time ago that the best use for this land would be to equip the entire 700 acres (odd) as a self-contained farm with sufficient accommodation for 60–80 dairy cows, together with farmhouse and necessary cottages. In the commission's view this would ensure the best use of the whole of the area on a long term. The provision of the necessary fixed equipment is now in hand. When equipped, the new farm unit will be advertised for letting by the Commission in accordance with usual practice.

Although the management of this ex-bombing range has become the responsibility of the Commission, the freehold is still owned by the Air Ministry, and so far as the Commission are aware there is no intention of transferring it to the Ministry of Agriculture and Fisheries.

Yours faithfully,

L. J. Smith

In Appendix 4 Marten seems to have jumbled the content of these two letters into one, calling that 'one' 'an extremely inept reply' and saying 'I immediately became aware that I was up against a body definitely hostile to my proposition. . . . ' There were no good grounds for such conclusions.

Amnesia at Crichel

The big puzzle about Seymour's letter of 26 May 1952 is the nonchalant lack of knowledge it displays of recent events and correspondence in 1950, the doubts he expresses on the matter of compulsory purchase in 1938, and yet his complete accuracy in regard to the earlier dates of acquisition and conveyance which were later to become so thoroughly confused.

Solving that puzzle requires a brief departure from chronological order. On the last day but one of the Clark Inquiry (MAF 236/8) Commander Marten, asked by his own counsel (Mr Melford Stevenson, QC) what had happened to Norton-Fagge's reply dated 28 March 1950 (p. 33)—the reply Seymour said had not been received—had this to say, according to the shorthand record:

'That had been filed in the normal way in our office file on this subject, and I took it off the file shortly after we got it in 1950 to show it to one or two people I was consulting about the possibility of taking up the qustion with the Minister direct. I did not get very much encouragement to do so from the people I consulted, and instead of putting the letter back on the file I put it in the waste paper basket and forgot about it.'

It was then adroitly but incorrectly suggested to Marten, and agreed by him, that the Land Commissioner also must have mislaid the same correspondence too. He had not; copies of the 1950 exchange of letters had obligingly been sent by the Ministry to Marten's solicitors before the inquiry without any apparent difficulty in tracing them. During cross-examination by the Hon. Charles Russell, QC for the Ministry of Agriculture, Marten was pressed a little harder, until rescued by the Commissioner, who was at pains to establish that under his terms of reference Marten's actions were not a topic of enquiry. The questions, answers, and interjection went:

Q. Your agent is saying: 'The matter, however, has lost none of its importance to us and our tenant farmer'. This correspondence was apparently dropped before it reached the proper authority. You go on to say: 'and I should, therefore, be most grateful if you could inform me what the present situation is and whether it would not be possible for us to buy the land back and thus restore it to that farm where it originally belonged, and to which it forms such an integral part.' Do you remember seeing that letter?

A. Yes.

Q. The earlier phrase is: 'For some unknown reason we then let the correspondence drop.' He is referring to the silence from 1950 onwards.

A. I do not think he is, actually, sir. I think what he is referring to is that when he looked at the file they had never had an answer.

Q. No, he has said that already, has he not? 'It appears that they never replied' he says, but we know that they did, and we know that you took it off your estate file and later put it in the waste paper basket?

A. Yes.

Q. It goes on to say: 'For some unknown reason we then let the correspondence drop.'

A. Yes. What he means is that we let the correspondence drop without getting a reply. At least that is what I take it to mean; I do not know what was in his mind.

Q. Obviously nothing was in his mind because he is saying that he did not know the reason. He says: 'For some unknown reason we then let the correspondence drop.'

A. Well, he could not remember, presumably, for what reason.

THE COMMISSIONER: What has all this got to do with anything in this
  Inquiry? How should this witness know what Major Seymour had in
  his mind when he wrote it? It is quite clear that the letter was written
  and the correspondence was not continued. Is it necessary to take up
  any more time on it?   (MAF 236/8)

The cross-examination then ceased, in deference to the Commissioner. Yet Clark could, perhaps should, have been corrected
on his own statement 'the letter was written and the correspondence
was not continued', because it was continued: not only was a reply
received, but it had also been acknowledged by Gilbert, and the
presumption must be that the record or copy of that acknowledgement must have disappeared too from the Crichel file; otherwise
it would have been plain to later readers of the file that a reply
acknowledged must surely have been received.

Another presumption may be that other correspondence about the
acquisition (including a lucid outline by Tylee & Co., the Estate's
London solicitors, sent in February 1950 at Gilbert's request) may
have been overlooked or gone astray. One need not wonder at the
Estate's defective memory of the pre-war events, because the agents
then handling the correspondence (Rawlence & Squarey) had ceased
to handle the Estate's business, and a certain loss of continuity in
wartime conditions and during the infancy of the orphaned heiress
was only to be expected. (An uncle and guardian, Lord Hardinge
of Penshurst, former Private Secretary to King Edward VIII and
King George VI, had lived at Crichel and had lent his help in the
Estate's business until Mrs Marten's coming of age in 1950, after
her marriage in 1949. But there is nothing to suggest he played any
active part in the Crichel Down controversy, or, apart from a letter
or two about building licences for cottages, that he had taken a hand
in that correspondence before he left Crichel in 1950.)

The Tylee & Co. explanation to the Estate of 27 February 1950
is important only in the advice given that it seemed 'doubtful whether
a claim to a right of pre-emption could be maintained in the event
of the Ministry selling the land', but: 'If, however, you can ascertain
that a sale is contemplated no harm can be done if the Ministry is
informed that the Estate is interested and would appreciate the
opportunity of re-purchasing the property in question.'

Tylee & Co. had also made it clear in the same letter that the
amount of compensation had been agreed, and 'paid and received

in full satisfaction of all claims by the Vendor in respect of severance, depreciation, injurious affection of adjoining Estate of the Vendor and otherwise however arising'. Marten may have been right, therefore, in thinking no claim in 1950 to re-purchase the 328 acres would have been accepted by the Labour Government then in office. Yet, as against that, it seems likely that a reasoned case for the purchase of the whole 725 acres, showing how the Estate proposed to divide and develop the land (rather than the perfunctory enquiry actually made) would have been received before Norton-Fagge completed his appreciation and proposals, and long before the Agricultural Land Commission (with slight misgivings about the costs involved) accepted those proposals. A timely alternative plan could and doubtless would have been examined by the professionals concerned on its agricultural and financial merits, not perhaps in complete disregard of the Labour party's known liking for public rather than private ownership of resources, but certainly with the professional considerations dominant in their minds.

What would have given Norton-Fagge more trouble than party politics or ideology in treating such a case was his knowledge that the Crichel Estate tenants were not so keen to extend as the landlords seemed to suggest; and the greatest trouble might have been occasioned by thorough examination of the qualifications and experience, at that time, of the new owners of the Crichel Estate, in landowning, farming, and estate (and office!) management.

Nevertheless, Marten's judgement in 1950 had been that it was best to lie low until there was a Conservative government which would give 'a sympathetic hearing' to his claim. It was, he said, 'a shock and a surprise' (Appendix 4) to get the Agricultural Land Commission's letter of 10 June 1952, and his immediate reaction was to fire a second shot, catching the Ministry between wind and water, and causing eventual damage utterly disproportionate to its actual calibre and potency.

The Second Shot, 12 June 1952

On 12 June 1952 Marten seems to have put pen formally to paper for the first time, in anger at what he called 'a very raw deal'. He wrote on that day a letter to his (Conservative) constituency MP, a Dorset man of farming stock and NFU (National Farmers' Union) background, Robert Crouch:

Crichel,
Wimborne.
12th June.

Dear Mr. Crouch,

I am writing to ask if you would be so kind as to take up with the Minister of Agriculture a matter of very great importance to this estate. I would have written to him direct, but not knowing him personally, and knowing of your great interest in the agricultural affairs of this district, I decided to approach you and ask you to lay our case before him.

The story is as follows:—

In 1938 the Air Ministry acquired, by compulsory purchase, some 300 odd acres of this estate as part of a bombing range.

In 1950 I heard that this land was to be disposed of. I wrote to the Air Ministry asking if we could buy it back. They said we should have to get in touch with the Land Commissioners as the land had been sold to them. I wrote to them and was informed that it was not the policy of the then government to dispose of this land. The Agricultural Committee started to farm it.

A few months ago I started enquiries again as to the future of this land and heard that, together with a further 400 acres of the bombing range, originally acquired from elsewhere, this land was to be turned into a new holding. I once again offered to buy the land back and enclose herewith the last letter we have had on the subject.

This is now how I see the situation:—

Our land was acquired compulsorily for defence purposes. It is no longer required for defence, but instead of being offered to the original owner, or put on the free market, it is being retained by the state for agricultural purposes. I should add that we are prepared to buy the whole 700 odd acres if possible.

The Ministry proposal for this area is I believe to build a farm, with its ancillary buildings, roads and so on. Water will have to be taken from *our* estate system as no other is yet available. The farm, which consists entirely of bare down, is then to be let. This is going to involve heavy capital expenditure, a considerable loss of land with roads and buildings, a loss of time, and then I venture to doubt if the rent that can be asked will be economic.

Our proposal is to let this land at once to the adjacent tenant, Robin and John Harding, who [*sic*] I am sure you know. They have done a wonderful job on the adjacent downland and I suppose their reputation is as high as any farmers in Dorset. They can take on this land with no additional buildings, except cottages which we have available without building any more. The land is adjacent to our woods and we can start at once to establish shelter belts, which is what this land needs more than anything.

I submit that it is not only right in principle that the land should be denationalized, but also that my proposals for its use are much more in accordance with the needs of the country.

We and the Hardings suffered a severe blow during the War because the Air Ministry took not only this land, but the entire Tarrant Rushton Farm, of which the Hardings were tenants, as well. This is now completely lost and we have heard that it is to be a R.A.F. jet training drome, of all unpleasant neighbours.

I hope you will agree that it all adds up to a very raw deal. No one can justifiably complain if it is for defence, but for state farming it seems so contrary to much that we had hoped for.

Yours sincerely,

George Marten

Leaving aside the Tarrant Rushton airfield, which is another story, the questionable reference to 'compulsory purchase', the minor discrepancies about the 1950 correspondence (already dealt with), the reference to returning the land to 'the original owner' (as if there were only one), the exaggerations about capital expenditure, the lack of understanding of the kind of mixed farming contemplated, and other minor points, there is no mistaking Marten's plea, which was simply that Crouch should take the matter up with the Minister and lay the case before him.

Bob Crouch, as he was generally known, was, by all accounts, friendly and unfriendly, not a clever man; he decided not to look into the case, as to the facts or the law, and not to take the matter up directly with the Minister, but instead, immediately, to send Marten's letter and its ALC letter enclosure to a man with whom he was rather better acquainted, from their shared NFU background, the Parliamentary Secretary to the Ministry of Agriculture in the House of Commons, Richard Nugent (later Lord Nugent of Guildford), under a covering letter supporting Marten but not mentioning his request that the matter go to the Minister:

House of Commons   13th June, 1952

Dear Dick,

I enclose correspondence I have had from Commander Marten regarding land at Crichel Down.

This is some good honest chalk land and the Crichel Estate is exceedingly well run. I would have thought it better to hand this land back to the former owners and allow them to let it to such tenants as they consider fit. The two men mentioned are really first-class farmers.

I do hope you will see your way to hand this land back. For your private information I would say the estate is owned by Mrs. Marten, a niece of Antony Head's, and the sole survivor of the Allington [*sic*] family. The Allington [*sic*] estate has been well run for generations.

Yours sincerely,

Bob

G. R. Nugent, Esq.,
Ministry of Agriculture

Crouch's and Marten's Suggestions Received

A hostile organization might have queried Crouch's assertion that the Alington estate had been well run for generations (see Appendix 5), but no one seems to have done so, the receipt of the Crouch correspondence being probably the first most Ministry officials had heard of that estate; and, very properly, there is no hint of any evidence that Crouch's mention of one of Mrs Marten's influential family connections affected the Ministry's or the Minister's deliberations and decisions one way or the other.

It was much later authoritatively stated that Marten's claim for the land was 'disregarded' (see p. 158), but that is the opposite of the truth. There arose, out of Marten's claim and Crouch's naïve suggestion as to future policy, not one but two interrelated issues, which were to rack the brains of many of the most senior statesmen of the time, and those of their lawyers, as well as those of civil servants, for more than two years. The mountain laboured to produce not one little mouse, but twin mice, a 'future policy' mouse and a 'Crichel Down case' mouse, the birth of both being left to the Minister of Agriculture to announce to the Commons in the same speech as his own resignation, on 20 July 1954, his own fifty-seventh birthday.

In this chapter the long gestation of twins is followed only as far as 23 October 1953, the date of the Minister's decision to have a public inquiry into the legitimacy of one, and only one, of the twins—the 'case mouse'—eschewing all consideration of the other—the 'policy mouse'. Already complex, the process, after that decision, was to become almost indescribably painful, noisy, and confusing.

The problem of policy—Crouch's simple suggestion that such land should go back to former owners—received repeated attention from the senior civil servants and lawyers of the Ministry of Agriculture, and from the Minister, and both the Parliamentary Secretaries, followed by references to the Law Officers, the setting up of interdepartmental consultations, and discussions in the Home Affairs Committee of the Cabinet leading to the appointment of a special cabinet subcommittee to advise on future policy, followed by repeated consideration by the Prime Minister and the full Cabinet.

The parallel process of considering Marten's case for acquiring Crichel Down was sometimes intertwined with the contemplation of future policy, and sometimes quite deliberately separated from it, to be decided on its own merits as an individual case which should not prejudice general policy. It too involved Minister, Parliamentary Secretaries, senior officials, legal and lay, the Agricultural Land Commission and its agents in the field, in Bristol, Taunton, and Dorchester; and, once the Minister decided to offer the land to them, the Commissioners of Crown Lands and their official and non-official agents — and then, once alarm began to spread among senior Ministers, the Home Affairs Committee of the Cabinet (another special Cabinet subcommittee, the Crichel Down subcommittee, being set up to consider the impending crisis). And once the decision to have a public inquiry was taken, there were more problems for the politicians, for the Law Officers, for legal and lay officials, and for the eminent lawyers briefed for the inquiry; and eventually, again, for the ageing Prime Minister (whose grasp of the subject and its significance was never good — see p. 160) and the full Cabinet, culminating in the Commons debate of 20 July 1954, the choice of a scapegoat, and the ritual slaughter of a few defenceless lambs.

None of this could conceivably have been foreseen when Crouch innocently catapulted Marten's letter into the senior and political levels of the Ministry of Agriculture, with his own suggestion. That approach acted as 'a spanner in the works' certainly, short-circuiting communications it would have been better not to disturb, because the cumbersome machinery could hardly work without reliance on them. One effect of the 'non-bureaucratic' approach by both Marten and Crouch was to skip the humbler, fact-finding and reporting levels of the civil service and to land the policy suggestion into the policy-making corridors of the Ministry. Marten's choice of the political line of approach (as he explained in Appendix 4) was because he (mistakenly) detected hostility to him in the 'machinery' — at the level of the Agricultural Land Commission and its Land Service agents in the field. So he exercised his political right to approach his MP, in the hope of a more sympathetic hearing at the political level if he could only gain access to the Minister's ear.

By inadvertence or ill-luck, it seems (although it is impossible to be sure) that it was the original of Smith's letter to him that Marten sent to Crouch, keeping no copy of it, or of his own letter to Crouch; and that Crouch sent both originals on to Nugent, keeping no copy of his own letter, or of the others sent with it. So much appears from the fact that neither Marten nor Crouch could later recall whether Marten had expressed willingness to offer for all the land, from the fact that the Ministry registry apparently did not enclose either Smith's letter to Marten, or Marten's letter to Crouch, in the Ministry file — doubtless because they were still the property of the recipients, not (as copies would have been) documents sent for retention. No copies (in this era before photo-copiers) were made in the Ministry, and the originals were eventually returned, in March of the following year, to Crouch, when Nugent sent him a definitive reply to his original letter (p. 82). This point is no more trivial than the loss of the nail that led to the loss of a horse, a battle, and a kingdom: its consequences were serious, and it explains two oddities: one, the fact that Marten and Crouch were not sure what their original letters contained (p. 69); and two, the fact that the need for a final reply from Nugent to Crouch came to be overlooked within the ministry, because the original letters by Smith to Marten and by Marten to Crouch would have stayed tucked away in an envelope at the cover of a file 'in constant action' (see p. 82). Once again, the moral seems to be that a lack of bureaucratic order can be rather worse than a sufficiency, worse even than too much bureaucracy; and that from the point of view of peace, order, and good government it would have been better for Marten to address his request for the Minister's personal attention through the more humdrum civil service channels. Such a request would have reached the Minister just as soon, but with an unhurried, un-hostile professional and factual commentary by Lofthouse, Hole, the Agricultural Land Commission, and the relevant Ministry staff.

As it was, when the correspondence ricocheted from Crouch into the corridors of power in the Ministry on 13 June 1952, it was promptly deflected away, by Nugent's Private Secretary, to the Agricultural Land Commission, and equally promptly returned by Smith, the ALC Secretary, to the Ministry for action, on 17 June, he realizing that it contained an appeal to the Minister against the Commission's action and against his own letter of only a week earlier, portrayed as a 'very raw deal'.

The speed of these transactions could hardly be matched in later decades. Only three weeks had passed since Seymour at Crichel had addressed Lofthouse at Taunton, Somerset, who had written to Hole at Bristol, who had written to Smith in London, who had replied to the Crichel Estate, who had, through Marten's letter, complained to Crouch, who had referred it to Nugent, whose office had dispatched it to the Agricultural Land Commission, whose Secretary had returned it to the Ministry, knowing that it would be improper for him to comment until invited to do so.

Crouch's and Marten's Suggestions Considered

For clarity's sake it is best to unravel the consideration of the Crichel Down instance from the consideration of general policy (which was in reality intertwined with it throughout) and to tackle the Crichel Down case first—that is, Marten's unwavering claim and campaign to get land, whether 328 acres or the whole 725 acres.

In any ordinary case finding out the action taken would require simple reference to a single file in a single Ministry's archives, but in this case there is no such luck. Many crucial documents are to be found in one of the composite files in the Public Record Office (now numbered MAF 142/148 and entitled Crichel Down Bombing Range: acquisition and transfer to ALC and proposed sale to Commissioners of Crown Lands). But as the plot thickened and the temperature rose, temporary jackets had to be opened, tagged 'main file constantly in action' and new files and folders were started, in the Minister's private office, in the main Permanent Secretary's papers, in the Land Division, and in the Legal Department (not to mention other Ministries, the Agricultural Land Commission, the offices of the Commissioners of Crown Lands and their agents, and the many other outlying offices in the counties). About the time of the inquiry and its immediate aftermath there were at least a hundred files in the headquarters of the Ministry of Agriculture alone dealing directly with Crichel Down in its multifarious aspects—quite apart from those in the outlying offices of that ministry, and the mass of other departmental papers relating to policies, procedures, and precedents considered directly or indirectly relevant. As an individual researcher is limited in access, within the Public Record Office, to one file or 'piece' at one time, it is very hard for a single researcher to gain a synoptic view of the whole. Even more so, at the time of the controversy, in the press of other public business, amidst the din of rumour and conflicting accounts, it must have been quite impossible for politician, civil servant, legal adviser, or journalist to master and hold in the head all the detail of a case of currently galloping complication.

Still, the examination of Marten's request began simply enough (MAF 142/148). In minutes climbing the ministry ladder towards the Minister the first point made was that the Air Ministry still 'owned' the land, and could sell it, not being bound by the restrictions imposed by the Agriculture Act. So the question was stated as whether to retain or to sell; and if there were to be a sale, how much—the whole, or just a part?

'A year ago' (Garside to Payne, MAF 142/148, 18 June 1952, in a clear enough reference to the change in October 1951 from Labour to Conservative government) the decision would have been to retain the land. 'On the other hand, in view of the present trend in policy towards selling perhaps the question of sale should be further considered.' It seemed a difficult question which could not be answered without the title deeds, so after considerable discussion an interim reply was drafted by Payne for Nugent to send to Crouch, which went to him on 10 July 1952:

I am sorry that I have not yet been able to reply to your letter of June 13th enclosing correspondence from Commander Marten about the land originally owned by his wife on Crichel Down.

I am afraid that I am still unable to give you a considered answer because the enquiries that I am having to make are taking rather longer than I expected. I can only assure you that I am going very thoroughly into this question and will write to you fully about it as soon as I can.

With hindsight, it is easy to see that the time-honoured practice of referring the whole appeal or complaint out and down to those complained against, after immediate acknowledgement, so that the facts could be examined, verified, or refuted at the lower levels, might have been better. Their feelings might have been hurt by the accusation of a 'very raw deal', but apart from the advantage of hearing both sides and having the basic facts correctly stated, there is in the old practice a recognition of the strong argument of natural justice for the persons whose actions have been questioned or complained against. At the time, however, there was no reason to suppose that Marten's sense of grievance could be so intense or incubated for so long. Had that been divined, there might have been more meticulous elaboration in the defence set up—more investigation of the acquisition, a fuller acknowledgement and report to Crouch of the investigations being made, etc. As things were, such elaboration would have seemed a tall and unnecessary order, a last straw on top of already heavy burdens.

Marten, however, had expected direct enquiries to be made about the estate's competence, and when they were not, and Crouch was unable to give him much information on progress, he first suspected, and then became convinced that the Crichel Estate had been portrayed to the Minister as 'indifferent landlords' (Appendix 4) waiting to buy a piece of land they had neglected before the war. So far as the official record goes, the consideration given to the suggested sale to the Crichel Estate included absolutely no adverse judgements on the estate's past or present management. But why on earth, then, did it take so long to process the case, the simple case it had taken Marten and Crouch so little time to prepare?

The Legal Difficulty

The first great difficulty was the state of the law, the Agriculture Act, 1947, the fruit of all-party deliberation and agreement during wartime coalition which had since then (pretty well on the whole, and with the support of the farmers) governed the work of the Ministry, enjoining on the Minister the prime task of increasing production of food.

The Act, which the new Conservative Minister was content to keep working as best he could, as the product of a wide consensus and the source of real improvement in agricultural performance and conditions, contained a provision in Section 90(1) enabling sale by the Minister of land acquired by him under its other provisions, and a mysterious proviso, limiting his power to sell, which both legal and lay minds found quite baffling. The proviso was: 'that the Minister shall not sell land acquired by him except where it appears to him that having regard to the use proposed to be made of the land, it is expedient that it should be sold by him.'

Until the Conservatives came into office in October 1951 the proviso had given no trouble, because the question of sale had not arisen under the Labour government. When the new Minister began the quiet 'trend' towards not acquiring more land if it could be avoided and towards selling if it could be done lawfully, one or two individual cases had arisen, and the established current interpretation of the proviso stood in the way of lawful sale. In those cases, both in England and in Scotland, the legal advisers of the Minister in London and of the Secretary of State for Scotland in Edinburgh had reached the same conclusions—that land acquired for agricultural purposes could not just be sold again, for agricultural use, without careful examination of the question whether it was 'expedient' or not, and that the problem should be referred to the Law Officers (Attorney-General and Solicitor-General) for advice.

The puzzle turned on the contrasting possible interpretations of the word 'expedient' (all of them, incidentally, finding authorization, definition, and apt illustrations of usage in the *Oxford English Dicitionary*). At one depreciative extreme 'expedient' could mean 'useful' or 'politic' as opposed to 'just' or 'right'. (As example, *OED* gives J. S. Mill, 1861, in *Utilitarianism* : 'The expedient, in the sense in which it is opposed to the Right, generally means that which is expedient for the particular interest of the agent himself'.) So, however attractive that interpretation might be at first sight to a Minister, acting upon it would be a sort of admission of wrong motive, and the proviso would be made pointless if it imposed no requirement to act in the public interest.

At the other, appreciative extreme, with nuances in between, 'expedient' could bear an opposite meaning, 'conducive to advantage in general, or to a definite purpose, fit, proper or suitable to the circumstances of the case' (with, as *OED* illustration, Hobbes, 1661, *Leviathan* : 'what he thinks expedient for the common benefit').

By any such interpretation as the latter, the Minister must be sure that selling the land was the best thing to do in the public interest: not easy, if one is Minister of Agriculture, if the purpose is simply agricultural use, if sale involves removal from management by the body set up by the statute to manage such land, if one is expertly advised on all sides that the best course is retention and equipment as a single unit (and then rental to an applicant chosen for farming merit, qualifications, experience, etc.), if the applicant purchasers have expressed their intention not to equip the land as one unit, if the legal advice is that no form of covenant or other means exists whereby a vendor can be reasonably sure that a purchaser will fulfil any promises given to provide equipment or to adopt particular farming methods.

Even the undoubted fact that the Air Ministry still had the freehold and could sell did not entitle the Minister of Agriculture to leave it to that Ministry to sell, without the restrictions of the Agriculture Act; he could not thus easily be relieved of his general duty and responsibility to ensure full production from agricultural land.

It was such matters as these, and their financial implications, which were the subject of conferences and minutes within the Ministry in the summer of 1952, while, in July, the process was begun of putting together, with the assistance of the Agricultural Land Commission, the full story of the acquisition of the land and its subsequent history. In the internal discussions in the Ministry the political heads — the Minister himself and his Parliamentary Secretaries — played a full part, in both future policy and Crichel Down itself.

Investigation by the Agricultural Land Commission

It was on 14 July 1952 that Payne addressed Smith, the Secretary, ALC, on the question of offering the Crichel acreage back to 'its original owner', soon after Nugent's first interim reply to Crouch indicating the need for further enquiry and promising to reply more fully as soon as he could. Payne in his letter of 14 July to the ALC called the question 'very difficult, and one that cannot be readily answered without some careful investigation', and asked for advice on 'several important points' — four points:

(1) If this 300 acres were sold would the remainder constitute a viable unit?
(2) Would the access to the remainder be more difficult and more costly to provide?
(3) Was the remainder originally in more than one ownership?
(4) If so, under how many and what were the approximate sizes of the different holdings?

Smith immediately put all four questions, identically worded, in a letter of 15 July to Hole at Bristol, adding in a postscript the answers to questions 3 and 4, in the form of a plan found in the ALC headquarters, while the letter was being typed, showing the original ownerships. He also told Hole he thought the Commission must give the Minister a considered opinion, not just on 'the approach by one of the owners to buy back her portion of Crichel', but on 'the whole question of sale *versus* equipment as one unit'.

The wording of his letter showed it was drafted just before the accompanying plan was found, because he would hardly have referred to 'some of the owners' if he had known as he wrote that there were only three altogether:

We ought to have a plan showing the various ownerships, to know what sort of people they are, and (if you are able to form a view without aproaching the people concerned) whether they would be both willing and able to buy back their various portions. Was the whole area purchased compulsorily, or were some of the owners willing sellers?

The very next day, 16 July, Hole sent on to Lofthouse at Taunton a copy of Smith's letter and the plan, referring in error to Smith's letter as one 'dated 15th June' and asking for an urgent reply: 'Would you consider this urgently and obtain all the further information you can without, of course, approaching the various owners and we can then discuss the form my report will take.'

The letter went on to advise and to stress the danger of delay to the building programme:

It looks to me as though Major Seymour's land is the better part of Crichel Down and that a satisfactory holding could not be made out of the remainder. Presumably, it used to go with Launceston Farm and if the owner were willing to buy it back it might be returned to that farm, particularly if there are adequate buildings there to cope with the increased acreage. You will have to consult Ferris I think, who may know the back history and you no doubt will be able to obtain from the Air Ministry Land Agent, information as to whether the land was purchased voluntarily or compulsorily.

You will appreciate that we must not delay on this question as I have asked Wood to proceed with the preparation of plans for the new buildings and I don't want him to put in a lot of wasted effort. On the other hand, if we hold matters up till this is settled then we may be in difficulties in getting the building completed by Michaelmas 1953.

Whatever the reason, whether overwork (see p. 184) or not, a fortnight elapsed before Lofthouse (then about to go on holiday) passed on at Taunton his detailed oral instructions to his Assistant Land Commissioner stationed at Dorchester, D. S. Brown, who later recorded them in a draft statement prepared for the Clark inquiry but 'cut to the bone' by the Ministry's solicitors (MAF 236/56). Brown was to send his draft report direct to Hole at Bristol 'so that he would be in a position to discuss the report with Mr. Lofthouse on his return':

I was informed that the matter was both very confidential and also urgent, that I was not to approach the Estate or make any detailed survey of the ground, and that I would have to rely largely on the County Agricultural Officer, Mr. T. R. Ferris' [sic] detailed knowledge of the area and any other information that I could obtain confidentially within the A.E.C. office organisation. I was also informed that papers on the subject were being forwarded to me but that in the meantime I should start to collect and assemble the information required.

I returned to Dorchester on the evening of the 31st and on Friday August 1st I made a start on collecting all the information likely to affect the subject that I could obtain from the A.E.C. office. I obtained the farm survey plans and record cards covering all the farmers bordering the boundaries of Crichel Down and copies of their latest agricultural returns. I obtained the relevant farm files and the A.E.C. file on Crichel Down.

It was on Saturday August 2nd that I received a copy of Mr. L. J. Smith's letter to Mr. Hole dated July 15th 1952 together with a plan showing the boundaries of the three original purchases made by the Air Ministry together with a schedule giving outline details of these three purchases.

Armed with these details I took the papers to Mr. Ferris on the morning of Saturday August 2nd, showed him Mr. Smith's letter, told him the general information that was required and the terms of reference under which the report was to be drafted and asked for his opinion and advice on the subject. Mr. Ferris thereupon dictated the following notes to me as a basis on which to build up the report:

(a) the sale of the area to the Crichel Estate would necessitate the sale of the whole of the land as the remaining area would not be economic to equip as one unit.

(b) the Crichel Estate area was generally the best part of the land.

(c) the Estate had not shown any real interest in the land until they had seen the crops grown by the Committee.

(d) the Hardings had a large area of rough downland adjoining the southern boundary of Crichel Down and a point should be made of that as there was no justification for adding extra land to the area farmed by the Hardings when there was an area still awaiting reclamation.

(e) the Estate in Mr. Ferris's belief were quite satisfied with the deal made with the Air Ministry in 1940, and he understood that the Air Ministry purchased by agreement. The same applied to the

Rev. Askew's land (now Strange) but the Hoopers refused to sell and the matter went to arbitration, and was completed by Compulsory Purchase.

(f)   apart from the enclosed fields on the eastern side of the Down no real intensive agricultural use was made of the Down before the Agricultural Executive Committee took it over and reclaimed it.

(g)   the buildings on Messrs. J. M. & R. L. Harding's farm were *inadequate* for the existing acreage.

(h)   the buildings on Mr. J. Strange's farm would be *adequate* for the increased acreage should he take over part of the Down.

(i)   that if the executors of W. K. Hooper purchased any *substantial area* of the Down their buildings would not be *adequate* for the *increased* acreage.
                                                                          (MAF 236/56)

Ferris's Recollections, August 1952

In Brown's draft statement for the inquiry, 'cut to the bone' by the Ministry's solicitors and so not revealed at the inquiry, Brown also recorded Ferris's reasons for his important change of mind about the land. At the outset (p. 30) Ferris had favoured return to previous owners/occupiers, but by 2 August 1952, by Brown's record of his discussion with him, Ferris no longer thought that would be the right course 'from a long term husbandry and estate management point of view':

because the farmers already had farms of adequate size and the addition of further areas of off-lying land could not be expected to produce the same return per acre as if the farm was properly equipped as one unit. In addition, should the prosperity of farming decline in the future, the condition of the Down would inevitably decline to the condition it was in when acquired by the Air Ministry.
                                                                          (MAF 236/56)

Ferris also recalled of the Hardings, when consulted by Norton-Fagge in May 1950, that, 'while they would have liked to keep the 114 acres enclosed on the Eastern side, they were not particularly anxious to take over any substantial portion of the open downland'. Of the November 1951 ALC discussions with five large neighbouring farmers to obtain advice on proposals for equipping the Down, Ferris was under the impression that the plans were not only favourably regarded in the district at that time, but were being watched with considerable interest.

Much of what was later called 'the Brown Report' was merely a preliminary draft in double spacing prepared by Brown for his superiors to consider and amend as they wished, on the basis of information given him by Ferris, who, as Brown said, 'had been a County Agricultural Adviser for 40 years in Dorset, and who I know had a most intimate and detailed knowledge of this part of the County'.

Ferris was not present at the Clark Inquiry: he had retired in 1953, becoming an agricultural consultant with a firm of produce merchants whose directors ordered him not to appear at the inquiry unless he received a *subpoena*. To compel attendance at a non-statutory inquiry would have required, according to the Ministry's legal advisers, a resolution passed by both houses of parliament. So Ferris did not attend, incurring the Commissioner's displeasure for that (Appendix 2, para. 31) but his implied approval (Appendix 2, para. 10) for his early suggestion that the land simply go back to the old occupants. Brown, who did attend, incurred more displeasure, for 'errors' which were either not errors, or not of his making, and in any case did not affect decisions taken. The cutting to the bone of his proposed evidence had been undertaken partly to remove 'hearsay' — evidence of what Ferris had told Brown, unsupported by evidence from Ferris himself. But Ferris, too, before his employers' objection to his voluntary attendance, had left a brief draft statement with the Ministry solicitors (MAF 236/57) which of course could not be produced in the circumstances of his absence. It contained nothing contrary to Brown's draft report, or to his draft statement, or to his actual evidence. In particular, it contained Ferris's memory of the poor condition of the land at the time of the Air Ministry acquisition: 'Much of the ground was rough, covered with poor quality grasses with some patches of scrub and gorse. Approximately six hundred acres were virgin downland.'

Brown Drafts a Report, August 1952

After this brief departure, in both directions, from strict chronology, one can rejoin Brown during his Bank Holiday weekend (2, 3, and 4 August 1952) as he busily prepares a comprehensive plan of the down (showing boundaries, owners and occupiers of all neighbouring farms) and drafts a report, deliberately putting everything in, as it was merely a first draft, rather than relying solely on 'the main issues without any secondary supporting information'. (MAF 236/56.)

This too was cut out of his later draft of evidence, as was his explanation (in March 1954) of 'the sole consideration' which had guided him in drafting, in August 1952 (MAF 236/56):

The sole consideration guiding the framing of the report was the question of what would be best in the national interest, and I had in mind particularly the terms of the 1947 Agriculture Act relating to good Estate Management and Husbandry and the Minister's wide powers under the Act. Outside the terms of the Act no consideration was given to private interests, and in fact at this time I was not aware that the Estate had made several applications to re-purchase their former ownership nor that in June 1952 Mr. Crouch had sent correspondence from Commander Marten to Mr. Nugent. The only papers I had affecting the issue were Smith's letter to Hole, Smith's letter to Seymour and Norton-Fagge's original report. (MAF 236/56)

(Another brief digression from strict chronology is needed here, to show the extent to which even insiders like Brown had by March 1954 become bamboozled, almost concussed, by the sheer force of rumour and repetition of incorrect statements. Thus, the Estate had not, in fact, by August 1952, 'made several applications to re-purchase their former ownership'. They had in 1950 sent one enquiry, destroyed the reply, and lain low for two years. In 1952 there was Major Seymour's enquiry, the reply to which, from Smith, Brown had seen. There was, therefore, little in the way of correspondence he had not seen, apart from Marten's letter of complaint to Crouch and Crouch's accompanying letter to Nugent. Had Brown and his superiors seen those letters too, they could have queried the errors in them easily enough, and so possibly saved truth from being the first casualty in the campaign.)

Brown's draft went straight to Hole, at Bristol, as agreed, with a copy to Lofthouse on leave, on 7 August 1952, under a letter confirming that 'this draft report' had been prepared 'in conjunction with Mr. Ferris who has studied the final draft and is in complete agreement with the information given and conclusions reached.' The main conclusion was stated thus, in the final paragraph of the draft:

In view of the fact that the whole area of land was in a marginal condition when it was purchased, that only rough off-lying land attached to large farms was taken, and all but 15 acres by agreement, I do not consider that there is any case for the sale of area B or any other part of the land and that the best course from both the national and the estate management point of view is for the existing scheme to go ahead.

Work held up, 6 August 1952

Ironically, the day before Brown's draft recommending 'go ahead' was sent, Hole had felt obliged to bring the scheme to a dead stop, despairing of an early decision. He wrote on 6 August to Ferris, telling him to delay the first job, the planned fencing, until it was decided whether the Crichel Estate land could be sold back to them ('Major Seymour's request' as he put it) and 'whether the remaining owners would also like to buy their land back', and, if not, whether the truncated portion on its own would make a satisfactory unit. It seemed also to be 'extremely difficult if not impossible' to complete the architectural plans and the building work for the new farm in time to let by Michaelmas 1953: he hoped therefore that if asked Ferris would be able to carry on farming for a further year—i.e. until Michaelmas 1954. Far from being 'disregarded' therefore, the Crichel Estate's request—quite apart from the stir it had caused in the Ministry in Whitehall—had brought the ALC's practical plans to a jarring halt.

Hole is asked to hurry, 8 August 1952

Within a day or two of ordering the field work to stop, Hole was asked to speed up the paper work. A letter of 8 August 1952 from Smith urged him to have the report in the ALC's hands in good time for the members to study it before they met on 20 August to consider 'the future of Crichel Down in the light of the approach to the Minister by one of the former owners'. Smith added: 'I expect you know that Watson Jones was there last week-end and takes the view that the whole area should be retained as one unit. However, we must have the necessary basic facts before making a recommendation to the Minister.'

Hole hurries, 13 August 1952

Hole's response was to send forward Brown's draft, as it stood, calling it ' a report prepared by Brown', explaining that there was no time before the meeting to discuss with Lofthouse (on leave till the end of the week), but that his own views were:

(a) that if this land is equipped as proposed, greater production both of crops and of livestock in the short and long terms are likely to be produced than if it is returned to the farms of which it originally formed part.

(b) to achieve this object however, will involve considerable capital expenditure of the order of £20,000. Taking a short term view I very much doubt whether the increase in production likely to be obtained justifies such a heavy outlay by the State. Whether it would do so on a long-term view depends, I think, on the general future prosperity of agriculture.

Hole referred Smith to Brown's report for answers to his two questions about former owners and about acquisition. On his first two questions (p. 61) about the effect on the remaining land of a sale to the Crichel Estate, he considered that if the *identical* land formerly owned by them were sold back, the remainder would not be viable, and access to that remainder would be more difficult and costly. But it seemed to be open, so to divide up the land, with the previous owners' agreement, that such difficulties need not arise: the Crichel Estate, for instance, could be offered a different 300 acres.

Hole was also far from 'infatuated' with the idea of the new farm:

Although the present proposal to create an additional 700-acre farm, fully equipped on modern lines, is most attractive from many points of view, the high cost of doing so does make me wonder whether the project should be undertaken at the present time if the land can be divided satisfactorily between adjoining owners without over-weighting the holdings concerned. Some additional equipment would obviously be required but the cost would probably be very much less than is at present proposed.

On the same day, 13 August 1952, Hole wrote to Lofthouse (just back from leave) explaining what he had done, saying Brown's report had 'dealt with the situation admirably', expressing the hope that Lofthouse would agree with his letter to the Commission, and ending: 'My hunch is that the Commission will advise the Ministry to go on with the equipment of the land as a separate unit.'

Marten writes to the Minister, 10 August 1952

Meanwhile there had been a first letter from Marten to the Minister, on 10 August, and a reply. Marten wrote:

Dear Sir Thomas,

CRICHEL DOWN BOMBING RANGE

I have been talking to Bob Crouch about the future of this area as he kindly took the matter up on my behalf a little while ago. In the course of conversation I found that he was not aware that we are prepared to make an offer for the whole area of 700 odd acres, and not merely the part that was formerly in the possession of this estate. I understand that this would overcome one of the main objections to letting us have it. It seems that I must have failed to make this clear in my letter to him, which he in turn forwarded to your Under Secretary.

He suggested I might write to you direct to clarify this point, as I believe you are personally interested in the future of the area.

Apart from this I do not think there is anything I can add to my letter to Crouch on the subject.

Yours sincerely,

George G. Marten

(Lieutenant-Commander G. G. Marten, R.N.)

After an immediate acknowledgement, the following reply went to Marten on 18 August 1952:

Dear Sir,

Sir Thomas Dugdale has asked me to thank you for your letter of 11th August about Crichel Down Bombing Range. He was, in fact, already aware that you are prepared to make an offer for the whole area of 700 odd acres. The matter is still being investigated, and I understand that, although Mr. Nugent will be writing to Mr. Crouch as soon as he can, he will not be able to give a considered answer to your original enquiry just yet.

Yours faithfully,

M. E. Vince

Private Secretary

The Minister was thus more aware of the content of Marten's and Crouch's letters, therefore, than they were themselves—until the originals were returned to them the following March (p. 82).

The Agricultural Land
Commission's Recommendations, August 1952

Hole's 'hunch' was correct. On the day he wrote to Lofthouse, 13 August 1952, making that prognostication, the Commission's most experienced farmer member, Watson Jones, was inspecting the land with Ferris and the Farms Manager (Malcom) and reporting that the whole area should be retained, because the type of farming to be followed on 'this second class chalk soil' required a large area 'to warrant high cost of complete new fixed equipment we have decided to build'. His report ended:

Crichel Estate have no farm buildings reasonably near this area and land could be better farmed from site on which we have decided to build. I am convinced area of land previously owned by Crichel Estate will be more fully and efficiently used with the buildings we intend to put up.

Mr. Ferris and the farm management staff are very anxious that the farm management of Crichel Down shall definitely cease in Autumn 1953 due to the reduction of farms in hand and we cannot reasonably expect them to continue after that date.

On 22 August Smith reported the Commission's deliberations of 20 August and their considered advice to the Minister, answering first Payne's four questions:

Q(i).   If this 300 acres were sold would the remainder constitute a viable unit?

A.   No.

Q(ii). Would the access to the remainder be more difficult and more costly to provide?

A.   No access from the public road to the remainder would be available. Rights of way would have to be negotiated.

Q(iii). Was the remainder originally in more than one ownership?

A.   Yes.

Q(iv). If so, under how many and what were the approximate sizes of the different holdings?

A.   Two owners—of 15.4 acres and 382 acres respectively.

The letter to Payne continued:

2. I must, however, dilate somewhat on these rather bald replies. You will see from the enclosed map, which I shall be glad to have back when you have finished with it, that the Crichel Down property of 726 acres was taken

from three farms and comprises the more remote and pre-war, generally speaking, the roughest portions of the farms concerned. Access to a great part of the land acquired by the Air Ministry was available only across the downland—pre-war there were no roads. It is the Commission's considered opinion that if the 328 acres purchased from the Crichel Estate were to be returned to that Estate as requested by them, the remainder of the land, some 400 acres, should not be equipped as a separate unit. It would comprise on the whole the worst of the Crichel land speaking relatively, and would not be of sufficient size to justify equipment. You will appreciate that the cost of equipping the 400 acres, though less than the cost of equipping 700 acres, would not be reduced *pro rata*.

3. If this is accepted it seems to the Commission that the only course reasonably open to the Ministry would be to offer the remainder back to the previous owners, who are the owners most conveniently situated to deal with the land. Certainly in the case of the land previously owned by the Reverend Askew, however, there is no doubt in the Commission's view that it would not be fully and efficiently used in the way in which it would be used if provided with equipment as part of the Crichel property. It would tend to go back to a sheep run, as it was in 1940, partly owing to difficulties of access.

4. Other factors which you may wish to have in mind when considering what recommendations to put forward to the Minister are—
   (1) The purchase from the Crichel Estate and from the Reverend Askew comprises almost the whole of the Crichel property and was by agreement.
   (2) The Commission understand that there is still on the Crichel Estate adjacent to the south-western boundary of the Crichel property managed by the Commission, an area of some 170 acres which is still rough unimproved downland. This is in much the same condition, we understand as the bombing range was when the Air Ministry took it over and before the Commission improved it, after its use for bombing.
   (3) Messrs. Hardings' farm on the Crichel Estate, to which we understand the 300-odd acres would be added in the event of sale by the Minister, already extends to nearly 1,300 acres. We are advised that the buildings on this farm are inadequate for the existing acreage.

5. Finally, I would say that the purchase and equipment of the Crichel property as one unit would be a satisfactory proposition from the financial point of view—certainly very much better than many other properties equipped by the Commission—and that its equipment as a self-contained unit is being eagerly awaited by a number of farmers who would be willing to pay a very satisfactory rent.

6. The Commission's advice to the Minister on this matter, should you think fit to convey it, would be that the whole area should be retained and equipped as a unit in the interest of full and efficient production.

The miscellany of minor 'other factors' in the fourth paragraph — later made into three bones of serious contention — could well have been omitted from the advice without weakening it. That apart — and the fact that serious exception *was* taken to it — Smith's letter would seem clear and unexceptionable.

More applications, 1952

So, too, another letter by Smith, on 3 October 1952, written to another applicant, at Salisbury, to rent Crichel Down (the sole application made direct to ALC headquarters), is a model of careful bureaucratic clarity which no one could construe as a promise later broken: 'Should this property become available for letting by the Commission, it will be advertised in the Local and National Press in accordance with the Commission's usual practice and it will be open to you to make an offer of rent for the property. It is unlikely however, that the Commission will be in a position to let Crichel Down for some time.'

By then there seem to have been three more inquirers to add to the thirteen registered at the end of 1951. Neither of the other two, one at Dulverton, one at Fordingbridge, was told much, except that the land was 'unlikely to be available before Michaelmas 1953 or 1954' and that they would be sent particulars when the land was available.

There had also been a surprising new offer from Captain Taylor at Pimperne to rent the whole down, as it stood, without any buildings or equipment, from Michaelmas 1952, for £2,000 per annum, reviewable every three years, with adjustments for later provision of buildings. This was thought to be an unrealistically high offer made in an exuberant mood, a rent of nearly £3 per acre for bare land being more than the experts at the time expected could be sensibly offered for the proposed new fully-equipped farm unit. Taylor's offer was rejected by the Commission in June 1952, on the recommendation of both Lofthouse and Hole, the latter being told the Commission were not prepared to let without equipment, that 'the Commission are anxious to get out of this as quickly as possible and they do not wish to farm after Michaelmas 1953. Will you please therefore take all steps to be ready to start the equipment in the early spring next year.' Clark thought the turning down of Taylor's offer 'strange' (Appendix 2, paras 18, 19 and 39), but it was the offer itself that was strange, not its rejection: Taylor's name was still on the list of applicants to be informed (in Lofthouse's own words to him) 'when we are in a position to receive offers to rent', so the 'turning down' was rather a polite way of declining to treat with him in advance. Nevertheless, it gave Taylor a renewed sense of grievance, the campaign some ammunition, and Clark an opportunity for criticism.

Autumn 1952

There was a year to go before the Minister decided to have a public inquiry, but the Ministry had already, by the end of the 1952 growing season, been thrown into serious difficulties — practical, political, legal, and financial — by the Crichel Estate's proposal to buy land.

At the practical level, Ferris had brought in another harvest, calculating the profit at just over £3,000 for the year, and done some planting for 1953, both cereals and leys; but in the absence of a decision on the Crichel Estate request he was being left responsible for farming the land, year in and year out, with 'no idea as to what is likely to be the future of the land' as he put it in a letter to Watson Jones on 30 December 1952. It was useless to sow further leys when there were no arrangements for fencing and water supply to the fields so that the leys could be grazed. It would not benefit the land to sow leys, make hay and sell the crop, and 'on this type of land we cannot go on cropping with cereals year after year without the land being depreciated'. Watson Jones agreed planning was impossible without a decision by the Ministry. 'I can only say that we cannot undertake Capital expenditure on water supply and fencing until we do get a decision. I agree that it is useless to put more land down to grass this Spring unless we get a decision.'

So both the short-term cropping plans and the long-term equipping and letting plans were held up. In the event, Ferris, who retired in 1953, was forced to plant cereals, taking a chance on the land standing up (with heavy fertilization) to a succession of white crop years; but the result was such depreciation as to abolish all the profits made in previous years, incur liabilities on the disposal of the land, and of course, further to discredit 'state farming'.

At the other extreme, on the wider canvas of national politics, 1952 had been a bad year — even the meat ration, nay, even ministers' salaries had had to be reduced. There was much back-bench grumbling about MPs' salaries, the gerontocracy of the overlords blocking advancement, and continuing failure to fulfil pledges to denationalize steel and road haulage. The health of several senior ministers had required hospital treatment, and the Prime Minister himself, in his seventy-ninth year, after a second serious stroke in July 1952, not publicly revealed, was not fully capable of continuing to work: he was very deaf, and deaf to advice most of all.

On the narrower front of Crichel Down the political difficulty of appearing to continue Labour government practice, by not immediately restoring private ownership of land, was obvious enough, and beginning to arouse impatience. In the absence of a full statement of the legal and other difficulties it was impossible for those of a Conservative turn of mind to see why there should be any difficulty or delay about selling land back to former owners if no longer needed for defence: if that was not the policy, it plainly should be.

The difficulty over policy was, however, beginning to be seen as including, but going far wider and further, well beyond Crouch's suggestion that one particular piece of agricultural land might be sold to successors of a former owner. The policy difficulty inhibited decision in the case. In September 1952 Payne, after discussion with Sir Frederick Burrows, decided to support the ALC's recommendations, and submitted to Nugent the case for retention of the land, with a long draft letter to Crouch explaining the reasons for refusing the Crichel Estate request. Nugent agreed a strong case against sale had been made, but had no wish to decide the matter himself; he wanted the Minister to decide; he knew the Minister's intention was not to purchase land unless there was an overwhelming case (MAF 142/148). Strictly this was an instance of retaining land rather than acquiring more, but Nugent seemed unhappy about the whole idea of state ownership of land, as well as about the particular case.

There followed, instead of the long letter of refusal, a further two interim letters from Nugent to Crouch, on 19 September 1952 and 27 October 1952, to assure him that the matter had not been overlooked and that he would be told the outcome 'before long'.

Neither Marten nor Crouch had pressed for a reply, Crouch's understanding certainly being that it would be better to wait for the desired change in policy rather than get a firm 'No' before the policy could be reviewed.

At that time the practice was for property no longer needed by a department to be 'hawked about' among other departments and public authorities, rather than put on the open market or offered back to previous owners. It was realized at the end of October 1952, after what was said to be 'a long discussion' between the Minister and his advisers, that the repercussions on other departments of a sale to the Crichel Estate should be examined.

Next, on 5 November 1952, it was suggested by Wilcox, supported by the Permanent Secretary (Hitchman) and Deputy Permanent Secretary (Franklin) that the recognition of a 'moral responsibility' to sell to a previous owner might be an embarrassing precedent for the Minister's colleagues, and that the Minister might refer the question of policy to the Home Affairs Committee to obtain other departments' views. The Minister agreed, and from that point on there was a sort of bifurcation in the paths of policy on the one hand and of the Crichel Down case on the other, with separate cabinet subcommittees eventually appointed to deal with each. An early decision on the Crichel Down case was needed, however, and could hardly await protracted interdepartmental discussions, so the Minister meanwhile asked Lord Carrington, the Parliamentary Secretary (Lords) to inspect the land and report to him (MAF 142/148). His report, speedily delivered, in November, resolved the dilemma, by the firmness of his conclusion (to which he adhered firmly throughout) in favour of retaining the single holding: 'I do not think that there can be any question that, from the agricultural point of view, the holding should remain as it is at present.'

The legal difficulty had been relieved in mid-November by a ruling given by the Law Officers and accepted (with some polite scepticism) by the Ministry legal staff as enabling the Minister to sell land acquired by him for the specific purpose of the efficient use of the land for agriculture, provided that each case was looked at separately, and provided all reasonable steps were taken to ensure the really efficient use of the land for agriculture (MAF 236/35). Partly because of the previous doubts, the Ministry had not sought the transfer of the freehold from the Air Ministry, but for all practical purposes the land had been 'acquired' by the Minister, by the Air Council's

direction, and the Ministry's agreement, in January 1951. The new
ruling gave an indication of the steps the Minister had to take before
disposing of land, and the considerations he should apply.

That left the financial problems — part of the steps required to
ensure efficient use of the land. The financial aspects of selling *versus*
retention, of selling the Crichel Estate part only, and the effect of
that on the viability of the remainder, the likely prices to be gained
by sale to the previous owners, or by sale on the open market, were
all considered conscientiously in the Ministry in consultation with
the ALC headquarters and with Land Service Officers, in October,
November, and early December, in very great detail (Clark's
reference in Appendix 2, paras 40 and 43 to an 'over-estimate' by
Hole is mistaken: Hole gave a higher and a lower estimate based
on former owners anxious to purchase and prepared to pay a full
price, as opposed to sale on the open market if the neighbouring
landlords were not keen to buy).

What emerged, by the end of 1952, was agreement that food
production would best be served by equipping the land and selling,
with vacant possession, by private treaty, to someone they had 'good
reason to think' would farm the land properly. Nugent was concerned
about possible queries, from the Public Accounts Committee or
elsewhere. Sale by auction had been suggested by the Finance
Division, to ensure the best price and disarm critics, but, as Franklin
had pointed out, sale by auction to the highest bidder would not
ensure the discharge of the Minister's obligation to make the best
use of the land, and so could not be seen as 'expedient', in the public
interest sense.

The Minister decides, December 1952

Before the year 1952 ended, the Minister had personally taken the
decision to do what the ALC had resolved to do in August 1950,
namely to build a new holding. What should happen to the new farm
was not yet clarified, but the decision taken seemed to dispose of
Marten's request to purchase, if only because he had freely expressed
strong views on the inadvisability of creating a new fully-equipped
farm.

The only record of the decision in the archives seems to be that
contained in a file note of 'vital dates' (MAF 236/17) saying that
no record of the date exists: 'There is no actual record of the precise

date on which the Minister reached a decision that the land should be equipped and farmed as one holding, but the decision appears to have been taken by the Minister at a meeting in December, 1952.' There is however no doubt that the decision was taken, and taken by the Minister himself. The best record is his own statement to that effect in Parliament. But no one told Crouch, or Marten, what had been decided, until much later.

The year 1952 therefore ended with everyone from the Minister down harassed by the problems of farming, fencing, water, and finance, and anxious, not to have 'fun' with a nice model farm, but to be rid of it quickly, so long as they did not fail in the process to discharge the requirements of statute, policy, and finance.

The Involvement of Crown Lands, January 1953

Enter, as Clark almost suggests (Appendix 2, para. 45), a *deus ex machina*, in the shape of the recently appointed Permanent Commissioner of Crown Lands, Christopher Eastwood, CMG, whose previous civil service had been in the Colonial Office and Cabinet Office. Like several others prominent in the Crichel Down story (the Minister himself, Lord Alington, Lord Carrington, the Hon. Geoffrey Bourke of the Agricultural Land Commission, Sir Andrew Clark, and several cabinet members, including James Stuart, the other Commissioner of Crown Lands) he had been schooled at Eton, but no particular significance need be attached to that. The fact that he came of a family of Sussex landowning squires had probably been of more significance in his selection as the Permanent Commissioner. The role and organization of the Commissioners of Crown Lands at the time (changed after Crichel Down) are concisely set out in the Clark report (Appendix 2, para. 45).

Soon after his appointment, in October 1952 (and therefore before the Law Officers' ruling making sale of land easier), Eastwood and Sir Reginald Franklin had had a discussion (on 20 October 1952, MAF 236/38) during which one topic had been the possibility of Crown Lands taking over management of lands situated near existing Crown estates which otherwise would be transferred to the Agricultural Land Commission for management: it was left that if any specific case arose, Franklin would get in touch with Eastwood.

It was natural enough, therefore, when Wilcox of the Ministry met Eastwood on 8 January 1953 over lunch to discuss relations between Crown Lands and the ALC and to arrange a meeting for Eastwood with Sir Frederick Burrows, that Wilcox should mention Crichel Down. It was natural enough for such business to be discussed at lunch, and natural enough for them to meet over lunch in a club of which they were both members. It was also, alas, natural enough for Marten's counsel at the Inquiry to make of this innocent routine matter a meeting 'at a luncheon party' and for the press to take it up, vaguely suggesting something either sybaritic or sinister about a workaday occurrence for civil servants which simply enabled them to devote their 'private' lunch hour to public duties, at no expense to anyone but themselves.

Sale to Crown Lands proposed, January 1953

It was left that Wilcox would look further into the possibility of Crown Lands purchasing Crichel Down, as they already owned property around Blandford, and had funds available (compensation, paradoxically, for the 'nationalization' of coal deposits on Crown Lands). With Franklin's agreement Wilcox arranged with Hole for Eastwood and Thomson, of Sanctuary & Sons, the Crown Lands Dorset agents, to see Crichel Down during a visit Eastwood was about to make to the Blandford area. Wilcox's letter about this to Hole, dated 13 January 1953, ended with a plea for confidentiality 'at the moment', ending:

Could you please treat this general question of sale of land as confidential at the moment as nothing has so far been said to the Agricultural Land Commission about it. The Minister is in fact seeing Sir Frederick Burrows on January 27th when he intends to let him know what he has in mind generally, and accordingly we do not want anything to get round to the Commission by indirect means before then.

Writing to Eastwood on the same day Wilcox asked Crown Lands similarly to treat the matter as 'very confidential for the time being', after setting out the financial position:

The land is at present without any buildings (I imagine the Dorset Committee have used their pool machinery for the cultivation); if we were not thinking of selling the land the Agricultural Land Commission would shortly be equipping it and letting it to an approved tenant.

I understand that the land in its present state is thought to be worth about £20,000. The provision of buildings and equipment might cost about £22,500 and we might just about expect to get this extra money back if we sold with vacant possession; if we sold the holding equipped with a sitting tenant we should of course get appreciably less. I would emphasise that the figures I have quoted above are just rough estimates that have been made for the purpose of the consideration we are giving here to the general question of the sale of Crichel Down; if you were interested the transfer would presumably be at a figure settled by, e.g. the District Valuer. If the idea of taking this land appealed to you then we for our part I think would prefer to transfer it to you as bare land in its present state.

The letter did not mention any previous applications to buy or rent the land, and as ill-luck would have it, Hole, who knew of them, was unable to accompany Eastwood on his visit: A. C. Middleton, newly posted to Taunton to take over from Lofthouse (who had moved to headquarters on promotion) was not so familiar with the past history, and might in any case have been inhibited by the temporary confidentiality imposed.

The confidentiality, originally for a few days, was in the event stretched to a few weeks, from 27 January 1953 until Minister and Chairman met on 17 February 1953. It placed the land service officers in the embarrassing position of being asked by one set of masters, the Ministry, to conceal information from the other set, the Commission. But the alternative was to hold up action by the Commissioners of Crown Lands until the Minister had cleared the proposed sale with the Chairman, and no one wanted that — except, of course, Marten, who would certainly have opposed the sale very strongly as soon as he heard of it. But, by an oversight in the ministry itself, not in the ALC or in the field, neither Crouch nor Marten had yet been told of the Minister's decision in December to keep the land as one unit and equip it, which ruled out or 'turned down' Marten's request, whether for 328 acres or for the whole 726 acres.

Sale to Crown Lands agreed, February 1953

So anxious was the Chairman of the ALC to be finished and out of the Crichel Down project by Michaelmas 1953 (whether by its sale to Crown Lands or by equipping and letting by themselves) that he readily agreed, when he saw the Minister on 17 February, insisting only that Crown Lands decide within two months to buy or not to buy. From the point of view of speed in action, therefore, it was just as well that the previous day (16 February 1953) a meeting of

Crown Lands and Ministry officials had agreed that as soon as Thomson of Sanctuary & Sons was advised of the agreed decision on sale he should start negotiations with a possible tenant he had in mind, Mr. T. C. Tozer of Woodyates, and see what rent he would pay and what buildings he would want. Thomson's opinion on price was definite: 'While I can make economies in my estimate, my opinion remains unchanged. We should not consider buying this land unless we can get it for £15,000 and we should still not commit ourselves until we have found the right tenant.'

As soon as Eastwood heard from Wilcox (on 19 February 1953) of the Minister's agreement with the Chairman, with the stipulation on sale within two months, he telephoned Thomson 'and authorised him to try and find a tenant for Crichel Down with the object of ascertaining the highest rent that could be obtained and the lowest amount that would be needed for equipping the farm in order to obtain that rent'. (MAF 236/38)

Thomson and Tozer agree Terms Quickly, February 1953

By 28 February, under the pressure of the two months' notice, by dint of telephone conversations, meetings to discuss equipment and rent, and visits to inspect farms, things had reached such a stage that Tozer wrote to Thomson:

Dear Mr. Thomson,

I thank you for your verbal offer of the tenancy of Crichel Down.

I have considered it with my Father and Brother, and would very much like to go forward with it, and I very much appreciate you giving me the opportunity. I am very interested in farm layout, and the construction of farm buildings.

Since the war I have been on several trips to study Continental Agriculture, and I have been 'fired' with the ambition to have at some time a holding as well laid out as one finds in many Scandinavian Countries.

It will be a great pleasure and experience in co-operating with you in the lay-out of this farm.

Yours faithfully,

T. Chris. Tozer.

So far as Tozer was concerned, therefore, he had eagerly accepted an oral offer made to him. Thomson had been told nothing, by Tozer or anyone else, about any previous applications to rent or buy the land. It was not until 31 March that he first heard mention of a Commander Marten, not until 23 July 1953 that he heard of Marten's request to buy the land—and even then he was unaware that Marten was the husband of the heiress to the Crichel Estate. In notes made on 29 October 1953 (MAF 236/38) Thomson recorded his assumption that when the Ministry suggested purchase by Crown Lands any previous owners expressing interest would have been notified that it could not be sold back to them: 'My own feeling in this case, had I known the wishes of the previous owner of the Crichel Estate, would have been to advise the Commissioners to wait until the whole question of the disposal of the land had been publicly settled, and all parties knew exactly where they stood.' By 19 March 1953, when he first heard of previous applicants, Thomson regarded Crown Lands as 'absolutely committed' to Tozer: 'It would have been deplorable if, because of statements which had been made by the Land Commission and which had not been communicated to the Commissioners of Crown Lands, any attempt had been made to go back on the agreements reached with Tozer.' (MAF 236/38)

Should Tozer, who knew, have told Thomson? There is nothing to suggest he should have done so, nor even to show that he knew Thomson did not know. Should the Land Service Officers have told Thomson sooner? Perhaps, but the temporary embargo on communication had prevented that, as it had never formally been lifted by the Ministry. And Tozer had settled the details with Thomson before Crouch and Marten received their refusal.

February 1953 had thus been a month unusually rich in dramatic irony. Early in that month, Ferris, answering a gloomy enquiry from Watson Jones about the prospects of further cropping if they had to continue farming, in the absence of a decision about the Crichel Estate land, said he hoped with heavy fertilizing 'down the spout and also as a top dressing' to produce one more profitable crop in 1953, but certainly not in 1954, when in any case he would not be there to superintend, being due to retire in 1953. (In the event, the 1953 harvest made no profit, and 'take-all' through over-cropping wiped out previous seasons' profit, leading to claims on Tozer's behalf for 'dilapidations'.) Also, during February, an order came to Hole to defer preparations for equipping, as a 'final decision' was hoped for from the Ministry within two months. And on 13 February Crouch wrote as follows to Marten, hinting at the prospect of a change of policy, to be achieved by the 'late summer or autumn':

13 February 1953

Dear Commander Marten,

I am sorry for not replying to your letter before, but I have been making discreet enquiries. Whilst I can get nothing definite from anyone, I should rather imagine that no alteration is going to be made in the ownership of the land this season. It appears that rather a long time is required to consider all the implications of this matter. It may be that we shall have to wait until late summer or autumn before we can get a full answer to our enquiry.

I am so sorry that this has been hanging on for so long but there are several Departments involved and that always takes longer.

Yours sincerely,

R. F. Crouch

The final stroke of irony in February 1953 was information by telephone just before the end of the month, from Hole at Bristol to Wilcox in the Ministry, of rumours in Dorset that Crown Lands were interviewing a candidate for tenancy of Crichel Down. Had the Crichel Estate been informed that their request had been refused? Wilcox's January had been a month of effort to keep sale of Crichel Down to Crown Lands a strictly confidential possibility: his February ended, once he discovered from the files that the letter drafted for Nugent's signature in the previous September had never been sent, with the hurried preparation of a reply to Crouch, and through Crouch to Marten, in the hope that it would reach Crichel before the rumours did.

Refusal notified to Crouch, March, 1953

The letter of refusal, dated 2 March 1953 is given in full below, because its disastrous consequences cannot be understood without the full text:

Dear Bob,

I am very sorry that I have not been able to send you earlier a final reply to your letter of 13th June, 1952, enclosing this one from Lt. Commander Marten but, as you will have gathered from my notes of July 10th, September 19th and October 27th it is a difficult case which we have had to go into with some care.

I will not deal at length with the point of principle to which Lt. Cdr. Marten refers but will only say that we could not in general accept an obligation to offer back to its former owners any land that had ceased to be required for the purpose for which it was originally bought. However, in this case, the history of which goes back for only a dozen years and in which all the facts are fairly well known, we have examined the matter purely on its agricultural merits.

You will appreciate that our concern is to see that this land, extending in all to some 725 acres, on which a great deal of trouble and money has been spent in the last two years and which has yielded in that time some first-class crops, should be used in future to the maximum extent for food production. The question we have had to consider was whether we could be reasonably confident that maximum production would be maintained if the land were sold back to its former owners and let as bare land in one or more blocks to neighbouring farmers to be absorbed into their existing farms. I am afraid we could not.

Lt. Cdr. Marten says that the 328 acres originally belonging to the Crichel Estate, if restored to that Estate, would be let to the Harding Brothers who now farm a neighbouring farm of some 1,300 acres. He says that the buildings already on that farm would be adequate if this additional acreage were added, but I am advised that this would not be so. I understand that there are still on this farm some 170 acres of rough downland which might well be reclaimed (as the bombing range was reclaimed by the Committee) and which would then provide the tenants with an appreciable increase in their arable land.

But apart from that we should still have to consider the possible fate of the remaining 397 acres of the area. They would not in themselves constitute an economic unit which it would be worthwhile to equip. We should be bound in fairness to offer them back to their original owners, who for their part could only let the land unequipped to neighbouring farmers. It would be almost inevitable that in such circumstances the land would tend to revert to something like its original state of rough sheep grazing.

In all the circumstances Tommy Dugdale has decided that the 725 acres should be equipped and let as a single farming unit in order to ensure the maximum possible use of the land. Discussions are now proceeding with the Commissioners of Crown Lands on the question whether they would be willing to take the land from us for this purpose, but failing that Tommy Dugdale has decided that the Agricultural Land Commission should be allowed to keep it under their management and proceed with their plans for equipping and letting it.

Yours ever,

G. R. H. Nugent.

Before this not at all 'curt' refusal reached Crichel, Thomson on 3 March 1953 had written to Tozer saying he was very glad indeed that he was willing to take the farm on the terms discussed 'last Sunday week' and that they must now get out a design for buildings, fences, roads, and water supply which would keep the total cost down to a reasonable figure. From that point on, Thomson quite properly regarded himself as morally committed to Tozer, with the moral obligation growing stronger each week as Michaelmas 1953 (the agreed commencement date) grew nearer. In that view he had the backing of the Permanent Commissioner, and of the Minister, and even Clark recognized (Appendix 2, para. 90) that 'a strong moral obligation' came to be established, although dating that as arising later than March. Nevertheless, it is plain enough that Crown Lands were committed to Tozer, from the beginning of March, if both sides went on with the purchase: if Tozer withdrew, Crown Lands too might withdraw without disgrace, but not otherwise.

The Third Shot, March 1953

Passing on the unfavourable correspondence to Marten on 3 March 1953, Crouch, with a possible change in policy in mind, counselled patience:

Dear Commander Marten,

I enclose the correspondence I have had from Nugent, and I am very sorry that it is unfavourable.

I will make some further enquiries quietly to see if anything can be done to alter this decision. I think at the moment the less put on paper may have the better result.

Yours sincerely,

R. F. Crouch.

The hint was not taken: Marten's reply was immediate, and angry, dated 4 March:

Dear Mr. Crouch,

Thank you for your letter enclosing Nugent's. This is a very great disappointment to us, and we are appalled at the Minister's decision.

The matter of principle is cast aside as of secondary importance. I simply cannot believe that this is the attitude of anyone in the government. Surely this is a department letter and decision. Of course we understand that this land must be used for full production. No one wants that more than ourselves, not only on this land but on our whole estate. We do what we can within the limits of the 1947 Act. I wish it was possible to do more.

As to the allegation that Harding has 170 acres of rough down land, this is utterly untrue and who ever gave this information should be made to answer for it. Frankly I must say there has been some underhand work here. In whatever enquiries have been made no one has asked us anything. Any information must presumably have come from the Agricultural Committee, and in view of the facts they give they are clearly prejudiced. Who, for instance says this area cannot be farmed without more buildings? Not ourselves who have planned to do it, but some arbitrary authority, who is strongly suspect of wanting it as their own baby. Really this one sided enquiry and refusal strikes me as a nasty business, quite unworthy of a government in whose name it is being carried out.

We have nothing to hide. If an independent man came down here we could show him everything, and lay down a plan which will see this land well farmed and won't cost another £50,000. We will buy, or at least bid, for our part of the range, or the whole range, either publicly or privately.

Can you possibly arrange for me to see the Minister? I can't sit down under this decision, and I'll bet he wouldn't either. I'm convinced we have the right answer both in principle and common sense and no axe to grind.

Best wishes,

Yours sincerely.

T. Marten.

This time Crouch did as asked, sending Marten's letter to the Minister and asking him to receive them both, adding: 'I am not at all surprised to hear that he refutes the suggestion that Harding has 170 acres of rough downland on his farm.' A curt, even frosty note to Crouch in reply might have nipped in the bud the fallacy that the decision had not been taken by the Minister himself, and could then have gone on to say that the accusations of prejudice against the Dorset County Agriculture Committee and other persons were entirely without foundation, as were the suggestions of prejudice, hostility, 'underhand work', 'nasty business', and untruthfulness. The difficulty of the Hardings' 'rough downland' would have needed the further investigation it was in fact given, but an immediate reply could have made also the fairly obvious point that different kinds of farming need different equipment, and that the planned mixed arable livestock and dairy farm capable of adaptation to changing circumstances needed more buildings, fencing and water supply than unbroken stretches of prairie all uniformly under the plough, farmed from a distance.

No such riposte was made. Instead, the Minister replied simply to Crouch:

Dear Bob

Many thanks for your letter of 6th March about the disposal of Crichel Down. As a first step I think it would be best if you would come and have a talk with Dick Nugent about the case, and possibly bring Commander Marten along with you. Nugent could then explain the matter at length.

If you agree I will ask Nugent if he will fix a time.

Yours sincerely,

Tom Dugdale.

The meeting between Nugent, Crouch, and Marten took place on 27 March. Payne, who had drafted the letter meant for Crouch the previous September, was also present, and explained the history of the mention of the Hardings' 170 acres of rough downland as follows:

The information that some land awaited cultivation was evidently correct when it was put into the draft submitted on the 10th September, 1952, and it only later became incorrect when the Harding Bros. tackled this area, with the aid, I believe, of a ploughing grant at the end of 1952 or early in 1953. The question was raised when Mr. Crouch and Commander Marten came to see Mr. Nugent on the 27th March 1953 when I offered that explanation. Commander Marten did not dispute it although he mentioned the matter again in his letter to the Minister of the 21st April 1953. (MAF 236/38)

It was not until after the meeting that a more complete explanation of the reference to 170 acres was received, in a letter from Hole to Wilcox the following day, 28 March 1953:

Dear Wilcox,

Thank you for your letter of the 24th March which I did not see until my return to the Office yesterday when I had a telephone conversation with Atkinson who told me that the meeting to which you refer was being held that day.

With regard to the 170 acres of rough downland on Harding's farm, which has been mentioned, I understand that Ferris has told Atkinson the position. It was reported to me when the question of selling off this land was first considered, that there was a large acreage of rough downland on Harding's farm which could well be reclaimed before more land is added to it and comprising approximately 170 acres. This report was passed on to the Land Commission. It appears that although the land in question could be seen from the boundary of Crichel Down, the exact area was not surveyed but as the tenant, Harding, showed 180 acres of rough grazing on his 4th June returns, it was assumed that this was the piece of land referred to. The C.A.O. informs me that some of this rough land has now been ploughed but without arranging for a detailed survey, I cannot give you more information than this. As you say, however, this is really not a material point. As I see the position, either the whole of the land should be sold or it should be equipped and any half-way policy would be a grave mistake.

Yours sincerely,

D. A. Hole.

Provincial Land Commissioner

(To this account can be added a report of 1 April 1953 to Middleton by D. S. Brown confirming that the figure of 170 acres had been derived by him from the Hardings' June 1952 census report, and that Ferris had since told Harding that as he signed the return he had only himself to blame: at the inquiry, Mr Robin Harding admitted the census return did contain the figure of 170 acres of rough pasture, but maintained that the rough downland had never been more than 70 to 80 acres, of which 53 acres had been ploughed in the winter of 1952–3, leaving the rest as a shelter belt of 'overgrowth' for cattle. He was not pressed further, presumably because of the statutory prohibition on publication of census details without the farmer's consent. So far as the Ministry was concerned, that remained an inhibition on public use of the Hardings' admission, and Clark ignored the admission altogether, simply blaming the officials (Appendix 2, para. 54).)

What about the Previous Applicants? March 1953

Something else happened in March 1953 which was to involve Eastwood and Wilcox in accusations and harsh findings against them, of 'dissembling', 'highly improper' behaviour, and 'grave errors of judgment' (Appendix 2, conclusions 12 and 14). Middleton, having received a copy of Nugent's 'final reply' to Crouch, and knowing that Crown Lands had approached the ALC, deduced that the confidentiality embargo was no longer applicable, and thought it safe to tell Ferris of the proposal to transfer the land as one unit. But he became concerned about the previous applicants, some of whom might feel the Ministry had 'to some extent broken faith with them' if Crown Lands bought the land and picked a tenant without their being given the promised notice of the land becoming available for letting. On 11 March he wrote to Hole asking: 'Do you think we ought to tell Crown Lands that we have already received a number of enquiries from people and send them a list of the applicants, when the main decision has been taken?'

Hole's reply on 16 March agreed 'this is an awkward one' and continued:

We really cannot say anything to the applicants concerned as we do not yet know definitely that Crown Lands will acquire this property. All I think you could do would be to send their names and addresses to Thomson and ask him if he is prepared to consider any of them. When the transfer is completed we could then inform the applicants of the position.

On 19 March Middleton wrote to Thomson telling him of previous applicants, most of them told they would have an opportunity to tender when the land was equipped, and suggesting Thomson 'give some thought to this' before making definite arrangements with Tozer. Thomson's immediate reaction was to reply to Middleton that there was little doubt that Tozer would get the farm if the transfer went through, and to write to Eastwood, in understandable annoyance, on 20 March 1953:

We enclose a letter from Mr. Middleton, the Land Commissioner.

We are afraid it is rather late in the day for this information to be given to us. We have already spent a great deal of time with Mr. Tozer inspecting recent layouts of farm buildings, and are now engaged in preparing an approximate estimate of the cost of equipping the farm. We hope to be able to send you our recommendations fairly soon.

In view of the rent which Tozer is prepared to pay, namely, about £3 an acre, we very much hope that this sale will go through.

Eastwood's reply, on 23 March 1953, is given in full:

I return Middleton's letter having kept a copy.

If these other applicants for the land have been promised a chance of tendering for it the position, as he says, does require 'some thought'. I quite appreciate that you have gone too far with Tozer to make it easy to give the land to anyone else and I am not suggesting that we should, in fact, do so. But I think it would be as well that you should ask Middleton to send you particulars of all those who have applied for the land and exactly what promises have been made to them. You may then be able to judge whether any of them are likely to have been serious competitors and we can then decide, in conjunction with the Ministry of Agriculture, what if anything we need to do, at least appear to, [*wording exactly as in MAF 236/2*] implement the promises made to them.

Meanwhile I do not think you need hold up your discussions with Tozer or recommendations to us on this account.

I am letting Wilcox at the Ministry of Agriculture know of this development.

(This letter is more fully discussed in the next chapter, at pp. 136 f., 142 f.; the very worst possible construction was put upon it at the inquiry, particularly the phrase 'at least appear').

Wilcox's fateful commentary of 25 March 1953, to Eastwood, which cost him a great deal of misery at the inquiry, was written in haste during a period of stress (p. 182).

25 March 1953

Dear Eastwood,

Thank you for your letter of March 23rd with a copy of correspondence with Thomson about Crichel Down.

It is of course a pity that Middleton did not let Thomson have earlier information about the promises given to various farmers on behalf of the A.L.C. that they would be given an opportunity for tendering if it were being let by the Agricultural Land Commission. Clearly if you buy a property then you are in no way bound by these promises, and I appreciate it may be too late for Thomson to go back on anything he may have arranged provisionally with Tozer but I am very glad that you asked Thomson to get hold of the list of names from Middleton so that we can consider whether there is anything that could be done with a view at any rate to appear to be implementing any past promises. I imagine that you and Thomson for your part will be anxious to avoid doing anything that may leave a bad taste in the mouths of any of the disappointed applicants, which might, e.g. prejudice your chance of getting them as tenants for other of your properties on your Bryanston Estate at some future date.

In the subsequent vilification of Eastwood and Wilcox for these letters it was overlooked that Eastwood was being very punctilious in asking Thomson to obtain and study the applications, and Wilcox equally punctilious in welcoming that suggestion. It had previously been put by Hole to Middleton that he should send the details to Thomson, but Middleton had not done that. That Clark said he had (Appendix 2, para. 56) merely illustrates Clark's own fallibility, even when examining correspondence he thought very significant.

In the event, apart from Marten himself, only one of the applicants (Taylor, p. 97) ever made any recorded complaint, but the campaign made, of the selection of a tenant without advertisement, 'unwholesome dealing' (p. 105). Paradoxically, through inaction, because no explanatory letter to the previous applicants was ever sent, what had been seen in early March as a slight potential difficulty, to be removed by an examination of the promises and an explanation of the changed circumstances, was allowed to become one of the chief grievances in the public campaign. There were many reasons of detail for no explanation being sent, but the only one worth mention is the fact that it was the Agricultural Land Commission on whose behalf any 'promises' given had been made, but at no stage between the revelation of their existence and the appointment of the public inquiry was the question of what to do referred to that Commission for resolution. It bounced about between the Ministry, Crown Lands, the Lands Service offices, and Sanctuary & Sons, until it was no longer necessary to send anyone a notification that the land had been let — the applicants could hardly have failed to see the press reports. The protracted absence of explanation gave the letting to Tozer a sinister and secretive appearance — it became another piece of smouldering combustible material which with hard blowing could be made to burst into flame. The campaign made use of it to increase the number of people with a sense of grievance and suspicion of underhand dealing, converting an originally private dissatisfaction with a decision into a matter of public concern.

Crouch and Marten meet Nugent, 27 March 1953

The same combustion was achieved with the other unimportant scrap of kindling, the 170 acres of rough downland. Marten took away from the meeting on 27 March a conviction of something more sinister than innocent error, a suspicion that Nugent had not been properly briefed, that he had been 'slippery' (Appendix 3) and that the facts had not been fairly presented to the Minister. He left behind with Nugent a new proposal, that the Crichel Estate take a tenancy of the whole of Crichel Down, for a trial period, to demonstrate ability to farm it well, the prospect of purchase to be considered after a few years. Nugent, not knowing that this idea came too late, because of the Crown Lands commitment to Tozer, said it would get 'sympathetic consideration'. But on 16 April 1953 that suggestion too was rejected, by Nugent, in a letter to Crouch, making it clear that it was the Minister's own personal decision, felt by the Minister to be right, Nugent's own opinion on it not being stated:

Dear Bob,

I have now had an opportunity of consulting Tommy Dugdale about the proposition Commander Marten put forward at our recent interview.

As you know from my letter of 2nd March it had already been decided that the land should be equipped and let as a single unit and discussions had been initiated with the Commissioners of Crown Lands to see whether they would be willing to take the land from us for this purpose. Tommy Dugdale still feels that this was the right course and I am afraid that in any case matters are too far advanced for us to go back on it now.

Yours ever,

G. R. H. Nugent.

Charge of Wastefulness, April 1953

Marten now added to the previous charges a criticism of wastefulness — not in his view only, but in that of others in the neighbourhood, in a letter to the Minister of 21 April 1953, the outcome of which was a meeting with the Minister on 5th May, attended by three local Conservative MPs — Crouch, Lord Hinchingbrooke, and John Morrison, later Lord Margadale.

Dear Sir Thomas,

Mr. Crouch has communicated to me your decision about the local bombing range at Launceston Down.

I feel quite sure that you would not have reached this decision unless you had very strong reasons undisclosed to me.

To ourselves and the few first class farmers on the spot who we have consulted, the plan is so clearly unnecessary and uneconomic that I feel justified in writing to you personally.

At the back of my mind is the thought that you cannot have had a fair presentation of the facts, and this is borne out by what I heard when Mr. Nugent kindly gave me an interview.

For instance he said that the Harding Brothers had 170 acres of rough grazing. This is utterly untrue and very damaging to our case, yet Lord Carrington must have carried this impression away from his visit here. I am extremely sorry we were given no opportunity to see him when he came down, for if he was so clearly misinformed on this point he may well have been on others as well.

Another objection was that there were at present insufficient buildings for us or anyone close to farm the land efficiently. I cannot agree — yet this point seems to have been decided without any enquiry as to the methods we should employ and the buildings we should use.

I am convinced that we can see this land properly stocked and farmed once water is laid on. Surely before very heavy expenditure is made we should be given an opportunity to show it?

We are doing an immense amount of work on this estate to raise production and improve housing and it is most discouraging to feel we cannot be entrusted with this job. If our farming operations were backward, or we were failing in our duty as landlords I should understand your hesitation, but I trust this is not so.

I am asking you to give a trial to the plan I put to Nugent. It should surely have sufficient safeguards. Your alternative will be considered locally as a monument to wastefulness, and rightly so because it involves very large expenditure with no corresponding gain in production.

Yours sincerely,

George G. Marten.

It is symptomatic of the growing confusion that what came out of this letter was not a formal 'bureaucratic' reply setting out the facts, but a political deputation and a meeting regarded by the Minister and the three MPs as 'private' or as 'a meeting in confidence' with no note taken, no officials present, and no statement issued.

What came out about it during the campaign was from the Martens (p. 131 and Appendix 3), and again at the inquiry itself, when Marten revealed that he had been told by two of the MPs that 'the Minister considered himself committed to the Commissioners of Crown Lands and for that reason could not consider our request, and I think that is all'. The intervention by sympathetic MP's had thus brought no immediate benefit to the campaign, but what he was told of it encouraged Marten to select Crown Lands as the next addressee or target.

The Clash with Crown Lands, May–September 1953

On 14 May Marten wrote to Crown Lands saying he understood they had not yet decided to buy the land offered to them, but he would like them to know he was anxious to buy it if the opportunity occurred: 'If, on the other hand, you decide not to buy yourself, I should be grateful if you would inform me so that I can again approach the Ministry.'

The letter was acknowledged, but not otherwise answered — strictly, no answer was being sought or to be reasonably expected, unless and until Crown Lands decided against purchase, which they never did. On 6 July Marten wrote again:

I wrote some weeks ago enquiring about the future of the land at Launceston Down, Long Crichel which the Minister of Agriculture had informed me you might be buying. I had an acknowledgement of my letter but no reply, and am wondering if you are yet in a position to give me any information about the business. The land adjoins this estate, and indeed was a part of it until compulsorarily [sic] acquired by the Air Ministry for defence purposes in 1939.

I have been attempting to buy it back now that it is no longer required for the purposes of defence, but have been unsuccessful. Nevertheless I have been keeping farm cottages clear for farm workers, should I have an opportunity to buy or farm the land, and am therefore interested in knowing of its disposal so that I can plan accordingly.

I should be glad to call at your office if it would be more convenient than writing.

There was an (unnecessarily) apologetic reply by T. J. Lester of the Crown Lands office, dated 9 July:

I am to acknowledge the receipt of your letter of the 6th July and to apologise for the fact that you had no full answer to your earlier letter of the 14th May.

The Commissioners are in negotiation for the acquisition of the Crichel Down Land, and in anticipation of completion of the contract for the purchase they are making provisional arrangements for equipping and letting it. Your desire to purchase the property if an opportunity occurs has been noted at this Office, but so far as can be foreseen at the moment it seems unlikely that the land will become available for re-sale.

The delay in answering your letter of the 14th May was due to the fact that the completion of the purchase by the Commissioner is taking longer than was anticipated owing to the need to settle certain minor details. The Commissioners have, however, no reason to suppose that the purchase will not be completed in due course.

Marten's response was immediate, again repudiating the idea of a separate new holding, on 10 July:

Thank you for your letter C.5228/53 of 9th July. I am most grateful to have a clear picture of the situation, but naturally dissapointed that land compulsorarily acquired from us for defence purposes in Wartime should not be returned to us when no longer required for that purpose. I note what you say about provisional equipment of the land. I should like you to know that in the hope of acquiring this land I have ear-marked four cottages in the adjacent village of Long Crichel to house farm workers and am fully prepared to rent or buy the land with no additional buildings whatever. Indeed this has always seemed to me the obvious and efficient means to dealing with the area instead of embarking on the expensive and unnecessary establishment of a separate holding.

I should be glad if you would lay before the Commissioners my proposition for farming the entire area with the minimum of capital expenditure, and I should be pleased to meet a representative, with my agent and farm manager, to lay rather more detailed plans before him to show how this can be done.

The letter was acknowledged and a further letter promised after enquiries had been made: they included reference of the papers to Sanctuary & Sons. Thomson wrote to Crown Lands on 23 July:

Commander Marten's Application

Both the Commissioner and Mr. Tozer are irretrievably committed to the present proposal. Only a few minor details have still to be settled with the tenant.

We should not like to express an opinion on Commander Marten's proposals without seeing his farm and him, just as we see likely applicants for Crown farms. Apart from this, we do not believe it is the correct policy to farm Crichel Down without equipping it.

By that time (late July 1953) it had been accepted by Thomson and by Eastwood that they had been morally committed to Tozer for four months, since March. Since then, the negotiations had gone on from agreement over the rent to be paid to detailed discussion of the design, cost and layout of farm buildings, and to agreement on the kind of farming to be practised, after examination of half-a-dozen modernized farms in the region. By mid-April, the Ministry, the Agricultural Land Commission and the District Valuer had agreed a price of £15,000 for the land, and the Minister had personally reaffirmed his conviction that equipping as one unit and sale to Crown Lands was the proper course of action (p. 91). At the beginning of May work had begun on the design of buildings, Tozer had been asked, and had obligingly agreed, to take over the the tenancy, without buildings, as from Michaelmas 1953, a year earlier than expected. By 21 May the Treasury had agreed to the transfer of the land to Crown Lands, on terms drafted by Eastwood and approved personally by the Minister in his dual capacity as Minister and as one of the Commissioners of Crown Lands. By the end of May a draft Memorandum of Terms was drafted ready for signature by Tozer, delayed only by difficulties of detail over dilapidations and valuation matters. So, before Marten's letters of 6 and 10 July were received, both parties were as Thomson's letter of 23 July said, 'irretrievably committed'. The reply to Marten of 27 July was clear on the point:

27 July 1953

Dear Commander Marten

I am writing to you about your letter of the 10th July regarding Crichel Down.

The position is, as you already know, that we are in process of buying the land from the Ministry of Agriculture. The sale was really virtually made to us on the understanding that we would equip the land with a farmhouse and buildings etc., and we are already committed to a prospective tenant.

I am afraid, therefore, that as far as I can see at the moment there is really no chance of our being able to re-sell the land to you. However, if you would like to come and have a talk please by all means do so. I am off on two or three weeks holiday at the end of this week, but anytime after that will be convenient to me. I expect to be coming down to Dorset myself before very long and if you would prefer we can meet down there.

It occurs to me that as you will not be able to take over this land you may not be needing one or two of your cottages. If that is the case and you were anxious to dispose of them conceivably we could come to an arrangement to buy them off you. But our present plans are to build new cottages actually on the land itself.

Yours sincerely,

C. G. Eastwood

Commissioner of Crown Lands

Marten's next step was to express his surprise and shock on hearing of the commitment to equip the land.

Crichel,
Wimborne
3 August 1953

Dear Sir,

Thank you for your letter of 27th July. I understand that the sale of Crichel Down is being made to you on condition that you equip the land with farmhouse and buildings. This comes as a considerable shock to me. A few months ago three M.P.'s for this district saw the Minister of Agriculture about the future of this piece of land. He informed them that his Ministry was negotiating to sell the land to you and that unless the deal fell through he would not consider another buyer. He said however that I might well

be able to buy or rent the land from you, and I understand that he more
or less gave his approval to my approach to you.

You can therefore imagine my surprise that you are committed to his
Ministry in any way. I feel that he may not be aware of this and I should
like to get in touch with him personally unless you prefer to do so yourself.
I will wait until I hear from you before doing this.

If you do build as you have in mind it is of course no business of mine
to whom you let the land, but I am naturally very disappointed that there
will be no opportunity to tender for it, as you are already committed to
a tenant. If it is not a breach of confidence I should like to know the name
of this fortunate man.

I shall be very glad to see you as soon as convenient after your holiday,
either down here or in London.

Yours sincerely,

G. G. Marten.

C. G. Eastwood, Esq.

In the event, Marten did not await Eastwood's return, but obtained
his holiday telephone number and telephoned him on 11 August 1953
(MAF 236/38). His chief complaint was that having first been denied
an opportunity to buy the land he had then not been given a chance
of renting it. He talked of trouble brewing locally in which he felt
he would have to take part. Douglas Brown (*The Battle of Crichel
Down*, p. 73) puts it more dramatically than the note in the archives:
'There was a long and lively conversation. Commander Marten
announced that the news about the tenant was out and he and a large
body of local opinion were very perturbed at what had happened.
Unless some action was taken to rectify the situation, *there would
be a row*.' Eastwood told Marten that arrangements were in train
for Marten and his MP (Crouch) to see the Minister, whose Assistant
Private Secretary (W. Gray) noted on the same day, 1 August 1953:

I was not able to discuss with the Minister until late yesterday evening this
question about the tenancy of the 700 acres at Crichel Down. The Minister
is quite clear that he gave no undertaking whatsoever about the tenancy of
the land, although he may have said to the deputation of three M.P.'s that
Mrs. Marten could apply for the tenancy if she wished to do so. He also
told the deputation that the question of another buyer could only arise if
the Commissioners of Crown Lands decided not to purchase the area. Now
that the Commissioners have taken over the land the Minister is completely
satisfied to leave the question of settling the tenancy to the Commissioners.

This, telephoned to Eastwood on his 'holiday' by the Crown Lands office, led to his advising a meeting between 26 August and 6 September, but when this was suggested to Gray on 11 August he said he was sorry a meeting had been suggested, as the Minister did not want to get involved (MAF 236/38). It was explained to Gray that Eastwood thought it better for Marten to air his grievances in discussion, rather than elsewhere. The Crown Lands note reads:

Mr. Gray saw the point but did not think it should be at the Minister's expense. He confirmed that the Minister took the view that the matter was entirely one for the Commissioners of Crown Lands to handle and that they were free to choose whoever they considered should be the tenant of property under their control.

As the Minister had by then already gone North and would not be back until Parliament had re-assembled it was consequently necessary for Commander Marten and Mr. Crouch to see Mr. Nugent. (MAF 236/38)

There was a certain illogicality about arranging for Nugent (not a Commissioner of Crown Lands) to deal with a matter the Minister (himself also one of the Commissioners of Crown Lands) had declared to be entirely at the discretion of Crown Lands, but that was what happened: a meeting was arranged for 4 September, in Nugent's room.

Meanwhile, Crown Lands had been made aware of growing discontent from several other quarters, including clear signs of Nugent's own lack of liking for the Crown Lands method of selecting tenants, in contrast to the Minister's readiness to leave it to them. Other members of the Government unhappy about what they had heard included the First Lord of the Admiralty, J. P. L. Thomas, who had written on 15 July 1953 saying that Mrs Marten, a friend of his, had asked him to help her and her husband get an early decision on their application to purchase the land. He had had a reply from Eastwood: so had Lord Hinchingbrooke, who had written, at Marten's request. Captain Taylor of Yarde Farm, Pimperne, had also written to Crouch complaining that the land had been let 'privately' by Crown Lands to 'a farmer who already farms, in partnership with his father, many hundreds of acres in Dorset'. Crouch was not satisfied with telephoned explanations of how the letting had come about. Nugent too had misgivings, and eventually his Private Secretary, Atkinson, was sent a long, lucid account of many pages by Crown Lands, on 31 July 1953, which contained the following lines in defence of not going always to public tender when selecting tenants:

Turning now to the question of our general policy on letting farms, the Commissioner, I know, is himself very much in favour of advertising in general principle—though it does not follow that one always takes the highest bidder. It is more important to get a good farmer who will respect the land than the last penny of rent. But I would like to comment on the assertion that the Commissioners, as a public body, are under an obligation to offer their tenancies publicly. I think that you will agree that we are not on quite the same footing as other Departments having a proprietary interest in land. We are by way of being trustees for the capital of the Crown and are under particular obligations imposed on us by the Crown Lands Acts. It is our endeavour to administer the Crown estates as good landlords. These principles applied to farms require, in our opinion, that our first duty is to obtain the right type of tenant and it does not follow that in all cases to do this it is necessary or desirable to let by public tender. In deciding what method to adopt we are guided by the circumstances of each case.

In preparation for the meeting in Nugent's office on 4 September 1953 Eastwood and Wilcox, who were both to be present, agreed in letters (Wilcox to Eastwood, 20 August) that the chief object was 'to ensure if we could that Commander Marten did not, by continuing his local agitation, prejudice the position of your new tenant'—or, as Eastwood put it in reply:

I quite agree with you that the main object in suggesting the meeting was to allow Commander Marten to 'let off steam'.

We are *most* anxious that we should not start off at Crichel Down in an atmosphere which would (a) cause us to have a bad reputation and (b) be very hard luck on Mr. Tozer, our prospective tenant. As far as I know, nothing has yet been said to Mr. Tozer about Commander Marten's agitation, but I expect he knows about it. If the agitation continues at all fiercely I think we shall have to give Mr. Tozer the chance of withdrawing altogether, and in that case we might not want to purchase the land at all.

However, I think there is quite a good chance that Commander Marten will be reasonable. I do very fully understand his being cross at not having got back the land that he (or his wife) owned before the War, and I feel that we should be quite sympathetic to him. But the plain fact remains that it is too late to do anything about it, and I do hope that we can persuade him of that.

The hope that Marten would be 'reasonable' seems to have been based on a supposition about what would be gentlemanly behaviour, and on a report Wilcox had received, from Brown, that Marten was 'a *pakka* gentleman'. Brown had visited the Crichel Estate several times in 1952/3 to advise and assist in various projects on the estate and its farms in hand, and considered himself to be 'on perfectly good terms' with both Marten and Seymour (MAF 236/38). But Brown had never really ventured to discuss with Marten the one topic — Crichel Down — likely to put his gentlemanly standards to the severest test. Wilcox had supposed from this estimate of Marten that 'once he realises that the game is up and that he has no chance of getting Crichel Down back then he is unlikely to prejudice Tozer's position' (Wilcox to Eastwood, 20 August 1953). The test came at the meeting on 4 September 1953 when diligent efforts were made to persuade Marten that he had no chance of getting Crichel Down.

Marten's own versions of what he regarded as an 'unsatisfactory meeting' are in Appendix 3 and Appendix 4. The official note of the meeting is more restrained, and is given below in full:

Crichel Down

Note of a meeting held on Friday, 4th September

Present

Parliamentary Secretary (C) — (in the Chair)
Mr. Eastwood	Commander Marten
Mr. Lester	Mr. Crouch
Mr. Wilcox	

Commander Marten thanked the Parliamentary Secretary for receiving him. The complaint he wished to make was that the Ministry and the Commissioners of Crown Lands had not made it clear to him in the course of correspondence and discussions he had had with them that they were too far committed to other arrangements for the disposal of Crichel Down to be in a position to accede to his wish either to purchase or to rent the land. In the first place it was not clear to him at the time he was negotiating for the freehold of Crichel Down that the Minister had already offered the property to the Commissioner of Crown Lands. Had he known this he could have taken steps to approach them for a tenancy. Secondly he deplored the fact that by the time it was clear that the Ministry were committed to the sale of the land to the Commissioners the Commissioners were themselves too far committed to Mr. Tozer, the tenant they had selected to give him an opportunity of applying for a tenancy. As a result Commander Marten thought that his wishes had been consistently thwarted. He did not allege lack of good faith so much as ineptitude on the part of the two Departments.

The Parliamentary Secretary replied that he did not consider it fair to suggest that Commander Marten had been left in ignorance of the Minister's commitment to the Commissioners. He referred to his letter of 2nd March to Mr. Crouch in which he had made it clear that commitments both to the Commissioners of Crown Lands and to the Agricultural Land Commission were in being. Commander Marten must therefore have known of the commitment.

Commander Marten then asked why neither the Ministry not [*sic*] the Commissioners had thought fit to give him an opportunity of applying for a tenancy before the Commissioners were too far committed to Mr. Tozer. In reply Mr. Eastwood explained that it was necessary for the Commission to find a prospective tenant and agree with him a rent and a standard of equipment so that they would be in a position to negotiate with the Ministry for the purchase of the land. All this had happened before it was known that Commander Marten was interested not only as a purchaser but as a tenant for the land. Commander Marten expressed himself dissatisfied with the course of events and Mr. Nugent expressed regret that he was not aware when he saw Commander Marten of the extent to which the Commissioners were already committed to Mr. Tozer, but explained that there was no reason why the Ministry should have been aware of that commitment at that stage. He agreed that it was unfortunate that no one had thought of Commander Marten as a possible tenant at an earlier stage.

Commander Marten and Mr. Crouch both deplored the Commissioner's action in selecting a tenant rather than advertising the tenancy of Crichel Down publicly. Mr. Eastwood said that he agreed in principle that it was better to advertise publicly rather than to select tenants but in the circumstances of Crichel Down the Commissioners had had no alternative but to open negotiations with a prospective tenant in order to determine what rent and what liability to provide fixed equipment would fall to them. Commander Marten then urged that the Commissioners should withdraw from its commitment to Mr. Tozer and proceed at this stage to advertise the tenancy for public tender. Mr. Eastwood replied that although no binding agreement had yet been executed the Commissioners were nevertheless morally bound to Mr. Tozer. He agreed under pressure to see whether in the light of local feeling Mr. Tozer would wish at this late stage to withdraw from the tenancy offered to him but made it clear that the Commissioners could not themselves withdraw from their undertaking to him. It was agreed that Commander Marten should be informed as soon as possible of the result of Mr. Eastwood's approach to Mr. Tozer.

Tozer 'Sticks to his Guns', September 1953

To the relief of the Ministry, Tozer did not hesitate when Eastwood put to him the facts, with, deliberately, no attempt to persuade him either way. His only anxiety was to get the agreement signed immediately, to give him a firm basis for entry on to the land by Michaelmas—in three weeks' time. He was not unduly concerned about the possible hostility of local landlords, considering friendly relations with neighbouring farmers more important, and being confident of his own good relations with the Hardings, and with others.

The Ministry's relief was due to the difficulties that would have arisen if Tozer had not 'stuck to his guns'. First, Eastwood had made it clear that if Tozer did withdraw, so would Crown Lands, and it would be back on the Ministry's plate to decide what to do with it. They could not let Marten have it without giving others a chance of bidding also. If the land were equipped and sold by public tender that would not meet the criticism that it was wasteful to build cottages when Marten already had cottages standing empty. (This was another misunderstanding: although Marten had referred to cottages having been 'left clear' and 'earmarked' it turned out that did not mean they were 'empty'.) The alternative, sell without equipment, by public tender, was ruled out by the impossibility of enforcing any covenant on the part of a purchaser to equip it properly. The Ministry saw Tozer's decision as a welcome end to the controversy:

Further to Wilcox's letter of 8th September you will be glad to hear that the result of Eastwood's talk with Tozer is that the arrangements for the sale of Crichel Down to the Crown Lands Commissioners and for the letting to Tozer will proceed. After speaking to the Parliamentary Secretary (Commons) Eastwood has told both Mr. Crouch, M.P., and Commander Marten of the decision. It looks therefore as if this long controversy is at an end.   (Hensley to Hole, 11 September 1953)

Eastwood wrote to both Crouch and Marten on 10 September 1953. His letter to Crouch read:

I enclose a copy of a letter which I am today sending to Commander Marten. It explains itself.

As I have said in the letter, we really had no other alternative.

The decision to go on with the letting to Mr. Tozer of course involves a decision to equip the 700 acres as a separate farm. After another look at the land, and after looking also at Commander Marten's cottages in Long Crichel (a mile or so away from the land) I see no reason to think that this will be a waste of money. There is presumably no question of the new cottages to be built being surplus to requirements (Commander Marten's are all occupied at present) and I cannot imagine that the whole 700 acres could have been farmed without any farm buildings. As to the new farmhouse, that I should have said would also meet an obvious requirement. Christopher Tozer is giving up Bockerley Farm, Woodyates to his brother George, and he will of course go to live in the new farmhouse.

I think I understand something of Commander Marten's feelings and I regret very much that our taking over of this land from the Ministry has caused this little bit of unpleasantness. I am much concerned now lest the incident should cause Tozer to start off at a disadvantage on a new venture, which is a very important one to him. I have every reason to suppose him to be a good farmer: he is keen and young, although already experienced in this kind of farming and it would be a thousand pities if troubles for which he had no kind of responsibility increase the very considerable difficulties which he will have to face. I shall be very grateful to you indeed if you will do all you can to see that this does not happen.

In a reply full of foreboding, Crouch thanked Eastwood for the trouble he had taken, saying he was sorry Eastwood could not alter the decision taken, and adding: 'I am afraid that so far as Commander Marten is concerned he feels very upset, and I cannot restrain him in anything he may say or do. We can only watch developments.' Eastwood's letter to Marten leaves little doubt as to his genuine sympathy for the recipient:

Since our meeting last week I have been giving much thought to the question of Crichel Down. I have also been down to Dorset and had a long talk with Mr. Christopher Tozer.

Mr. Tozer has entered into a great many commitments in the expectation of taking up the tenancy of Crichel Down at Michaelmas and he is most anxious to proceed with it. Our commitments to him are such that in these circumstances we could not possibly withdraw without a serious breach of faith to him.

This being so, I am afraid that, however sympathetic we might be, there is nothing that we can do to help you and the agreement with Mr. Tozer is now being signed.

I know that this letter will be a great disappointment to you and I am very sorry to have to write it, but it is the only course possible. I have spoken to Mr. Nugent before sending it.

Nugent, according to a letter of the same date from Eastwood to Hensley at the Ministry, had agreed the action taken: 'As we arranged yesterday I spoke to Mr. Nugent last night on the telephone and he quite agreed with the action I proposed about Crichel Down.' One wonders whether a diplomatic visit to the choleric Commander at Crichel (who had complained before about not being visited) might not have been worth the effort, but for a busy senior civil servant to write a sympathetic refusal instead of paying a possibly more placatory and flattering visit hardly provides material for a charge 'in a court of law or court-martial' — for either of which the Commander later considered (Appendix 4) the Clark Inquiry had been no substitute. His quick reply on 15 September fully justified Crouch's foreboding:

I have your letter of 10th September. In view of your attitude and that of the Ministry I intend, with local support to demand an enquiry into the business, which I am sure will expose many unpalatable facts.

I find that, contrary to your assurance at our meeting, Tozer applied for the tenancy of this land through the A.E.C., who must have passed it on to you. You will remember that you told me that he was on your waiting list of applicants for farms, which is a very different matter. In fact as I had suspected the tenancy was given to the A.E.C. nominee, and I can find no evidence of any other applicant being considered.

I have today laid the case before a group of local landlords, who are horrified at the methods employed in disposing of this land. I intend to take every available step to draw attention to this business and only regret that the name of the Crown, with which I was closely associated as equerry to the late King, should be brought into the matter.

Marten demands Inquiry and threatens Publicity, September 1953

The pace now became hectic: within a few days Marten had organized the protest to the point where he was able to send a threatening telegram to the Minister:

URGENT AND PERSONAL CRICHEL DOWN PROTEST COMMITTEE HAS BEEN FORMED TO PRESS FOR ENQUIRY INTO DISPOSAL OF THIS LAND RESOLUTION HAS BEEN PASSED TO REQUEST ENQUIRY FORTHWITH WITHOUT RECOURSE TO FULL SCALE PROTEST MEETING AND WIDE PUBLICITY WHICH WILL REFLECT ADVERSELY ON YOUR ADMINISTRATION STOP FURTHER REQUEST DISPOSAL OF LAND BE STOPPED UNTIL ENQUIRY COMPLETED MY ADDRESS CRICHEL WIMBORNE TELEPHONE 209 MARTEN CHAIRMAN OF COMMITTEE

The inevitable refusal (acceding to the demands would have been taken as guilty fear of publicity, as well as being a breach of both faith and a legal agreement with Tozer) came promptly and politely:

22 September 1953

Dear Sir

The Minister has seen your telegram of 19th September in which you ask for an enquiry into the disposal of Crichel Down and for the disposal to be stopped pending such an enquiry.

As has already been made clear to you, the Ministry could not withdraw from the present arrangements for the disposal of this land without a breach of faith, and in the circumstances he does not think that an enquiry into the matter would serve any useful purpose. He is sorry therefore that he cannot agree to your requests.

Yours faithfully,

J. Hensley.

Now it was Marten's turn to be left with no alternative to pursuing the chosen collision course with all speed: 'Almost immediately posters appeared on walls in all the villages around Crichel and every local landowner and farmer received a duplicated notice announcing a public meeting in the village hall at More Crichel' (R. Douglas Brown, *The Battle of Crichel Down*, p. 78).

The 'duplicated notice' was in the form of a circular letter dated 21 September 1953:

Dear Sir,

A meeting of landowners and farmers is being held at 7 p.m. on Saturday, 26th September, at More Crichel Hall to press for an enquiry into the disposal of Crichel Down. Mr. Ronald Farquharson will take the chair.

Briefly the history of the case is as follows.

In 1939, 700 acres of land were acquired by compulsory purchase by the Air Ministry for a bombing range. Several owners were effected by this order, including my wife's estate.

In 1950 when the land was no longer required for defence purposes the Air Ministry passed the land on to the Land Commission to be farmed by the A.E.C. When I heard of this I applied to buy back the 330 acres which had formerly belonged to this estate, as it formed an important part of one of my tenants farms.

After nearly eighteen months delay I was informed that we could not have it.

My protest at this treatment culminated in three local M.P.'s having an interview with the Minister, who, so I understand, informed them that it was then too late to reconsider the position, as some weeks before my case had been refused, the Ministry had started negotiations to sell the entire area to the Commissioner of Crown Lands. He said however that there was no obstacle so far as the Ministry was concerned to my acquiring the land from the Commission.

I immediately applied to do this and after a long delay was informed by the Commissioner that as a condition of the transfer he was committed to the Ministry to put up a farm house, cottages and buildings. Moreover although he had not yet bought the land he was committed to a prospective tenant.

To my own resentment as a Landowner must be added that of numerous local farmers who, because of this under-the-counter transfer of land were unaware of what was going on, and were therefore unable to tender for the tenancy. The prospective tenant alone appears to have received preferential treatment. I understand that he was informed two years ago by a member of the A.E.C. that he should apply to the Land commission, which he did. Another farmer who did likewise was informed in writing by the Commissioner personally that before being let the land would be advertised in the public press. NO such advertisement ever appeared. The first information he had was that the tenancy had been given to another man.

The result of this unwholesome dealing is that a holding is to be formed which bites deep into previously existing farms. It entails an extravagant and unnecessary expenditure of public money (about £35,000) on new buildings, when the surrounding farms already have sufficient to re-absorb the area.

Principles of vital importance to landowners and farmers, as well as the public interest, have been brushed aside in this affair, and though I have taken very considerable steps to obtain a fair hearing without recourse to a public meeting, I have had no success.

I most earnestly urge you, whether you have a personal interest in this land or not, to attend this meeting and join in asking for an enquiry, and I should be grateful if you would tell any of your friends who may be interested, of the meeting. Only by such action, it seems, can we safeguard our interests against the State.

I should like to emphasize that our grievance is not against the prospective tenant, but against the action of authorities.

G. G. Marten

Chairman of Crichel Down Protest Committee

Apart from the introductory paragraph, and the last sentence, there is hardly one statement in the circular to which objection could not be taken, on comparison with the correspondence and the facts.

The Last Days of September, 1953

In the last ten days of September neither the Minister nor the Permanent Commissioner of Crown Lands was in London, Dugdale being on holiday in the North of England and Eastwood on duty in Scotland; and there seems to have been one communication only to Crichel from either the Ministry or Crown Lands — a letter from the latter of 24 September pointing out Marten's mistake in suggesting that Tozer was the 'nominee' of the Agricultural Executive Committee, to which Marten replied: 'In my attack on the conduct of the Commissioners I will therefore omit any reference to this subject for the time being.'

Those days, however, were eventful. Apart from the business of calling and holding the protest meeting of 26 September, pursuing a vigorous press campaign, preparing and obtaining signatures for the petition of 26 September sent to the Minister with some sixty-six signatures, Marten suddenly had to be taken to hospital, where he spent some days with a mercifully mild attack of poliomyelitis, besieged 'by a powerful gathering of newspaper and radio reporters' as R. Douglas Brown described them. 'The persistence and persuasiveness of pressmen and patient', he continued, alliteratively, 'eventually overcame routine regulations and a party of journalists, suitably protected by hospital masks across their faces, was admitted to the bedside. Not only did Commander Marten answer their questions: he sat up to make a recording for a BBC news feature' (*The Battle of Crichel Down*, p. 81).

The public campaign for an inquiry was at its climax. In *The Times* of 24 September 1953 there appeared a letter in the name of Mrs Marten referring to the 'veiled nationalization of agricultural land', to the formation of a protest committee, to the demand for an inquiry, and to 'extravagance with public money' (see also p. 131). On 26 September the meeting took place at which Marten gave the Address reproduced as Appendix 3, and the petition itself was signed and dated 26 September also. It is given below, in full:

More Crichel Hall,
Wimborne.
26 September, 1953.

Sirs,

We, the undersigned, farmers and/or landowners of 167,748 acres and farm workers of this district request that you will institute a public and impartial enquiry into the disposal by the Ministry of Agriculture and the Commission for Crown Lands, of the area referred to as Crichel Down.

We have the following main reasons for making this request:

(1) The Land was compulsorily acquired for defence purposes in Wartime. Now that it is no longer required for that purpose and has been returned to Agriculture the previous owners and occupiers are being denied the opportunity to re-enter the land, for which they have adequate farmhouses, cottages and buildings already in existance. They are of high repute locally in their management of land.

(2) Contrary to a direct assurance in writing by the Land Commissioner that the letting of this land would be advertised in the public press, no such advertisement has been made. Farmers have therefore been denied the opportunity to farm the land except in the case of the prospective tenant, who appears to have had exclusive treatment.

(3) A very considerable sum of public money is being expended on creating a Holding which bites deeply into existing farms. We consider as experienced farmers and landowners in this district that this expenditure will not contribute one blade of grass to additional production.

Minister of Agriculture,
Whitehall,
London, S.W.

Commissioner of Crown Lands,
Cambridge Gate,
Regents Park,
London, N.W.1.

The petition carried the names of sixty-four individual signatories, with one additional set of initials and one name of a firm, an interesting collection, but hardly sufficient to impress or strike fear into the recipients. Six signatures were designated as those of farm workers, including, surprisingly, that of G. Malcom who as farm foreman had carried out the farming of Crichel Down under Ferris's supervision since it was reclaimed. Others included Lord Normanton, D. W. Taylor, one Farquharson, two Hoopers, two Stranges, and others identifiable as Crichel or other estates' tenant farmers and wives.

It went forward on 28 September 1953, the day before Tozer's tenancy began, to both the Minister and Crown Lands under the following letter from Marten:

Crichel,
Wimborne.
28 September 1953

Sir,

In view of your refusal to hold an enquiry into the disposal of Crichel Down, a public meeting was held on Saturday 26th September.

The attached petition is now forwarded setting out the views of local landowners and farmers, together with a few farm workers, and pledging their support to the request for an enquiry.

I also enclose a copy of my address to the meeting, which contains a complete survey of the facts as we know them, and our feelings in the matter.

This is being printed, together with the map, for National circulation. I am also taking advice about the legal validity of the written undertakings, over the signature of the Land Commissioner, to advertise the letting.

I shall be in London, and available on Thursday 1st October should any further information be required — Telephone Victoria 2360.

We most sincerely trust you see will your way to acceding to our request.

I am, Sir,

Your obedient Servant,

George G. Marten

The Minister replies, 9 October 1953

When the Minister returned to duty in early October and discussed the new turn of events with both Parliamentary Secretaries, it was not thought necessary for the Minister to use the press or the BBC to counter the campaign, but they agreed on the lines of a reply with the idea in mind that it might eventually have to be published. Previously, on 30 September, the Deputy Secretary had made a note of a discussion, before the Minister's return, with both Parliamentary Secretaries, the Permanent Secretary, and Eastwood's deputy at Crown Lands: 'We are all agreed that the right course is to stand by our guns and to refuse to give way to this agitation.' (MAF 142/148.)

They were to stand by their guns, until surrender was ordered, but they never opened fire, no matter how the propaganda war went against them. Adverse press comment was beginning to flow, and growing public unease was reflected in communications and warnings received in the Ministry from influential quarters — from Buckingham Palace and 10 Downing Street among them.

From Sir John Colville, Churchill's private secretary, the Minister's private secretary received a copy of Marten's circular letter calling the protest meeting, with a covering letter: 'I have no intention of bothering the Prime Minister personally with this matter, as Marten asks me to do, but I should like to send him a considered reply.' Colville's letter contained also an expression of the sort of misgiving and misinformed concern that was becoming general, in the absence of reporting of the Ministry's standpoint, and of the actual facts: 'Incidentally, is it really true that it has been Government policy not to sell back to its former owners land which had been compulsorily acquired for military purposes during the war?'

From the Palace, Lord Tryon, Keeper of the Privy Purse, let it be known that he was 'a bit concerned' about the association of the Queen's name with Crown Lands and Crichel Down, and was anxious that Her Majesty be kept out of it.

Letters reached the Minister from Conservative back-benchers, among them one from Crouch suggesting that an inquiry would be the best solution. Another serious kind of defection from the ranks of the Ministry's supporters and the traditional pillar of Conservative government seemed threatened when the President of the Country Landowners' Association saw the Permanent Secretary and the Deputy Permanent Secretary on 2 October and expressed the view that the government's position was not defensible on two points— the heavy expenditure, and the lack of advertisement of the tenancy. He (Colonel Burrell) told them some very restrained and sensible people on his Council were worried that the Crichel Down business might bring the Agricultural Land Commission, the county agricultural committees and the Minister's disciplinary powers under the 1947 Act into disrepute, with the Beaverbrook press only too anxious to use the affair.

So, even if the Minister and his team were prepared to 'stick to their guns' they were being made aware that many of their usual allies had no stomach for fighting on the Minister's side in a Battle of Crichel Down. There was an incipient split in the hitherto fairly cohesive élite of landowners, farmers, and their organizations and representatives—who included, after all, the Minister and both Parliamentary Secretaries.

As for the reply itself, carefully drafted for the Minister, mostly by Franklin, it satisfied neither Marten, who even after the inquiry was over thought it tricky, or artful, or deceitful (Appendix 4), nor

Clark, who thought it 'very unfortunately worded' (Appendix 2, para. 97). But the Minister's own view, when approving it after a few amendments, was that it was 'a good letter'. He wrote to Franklin in the file (MAF 142/148): 'Thank you very much. The fact that substantial payment for injurious affection was made at the time of purchase I think destroys any claim that Cdr. Marten may have had.'

The letter is reproduced below in its entirety, despite its length, so that readers may judge for themselves its goodness or badness:

9th October 1953

Dear Commander Marten,

I have given most careful consideration to the petition and statement about Crichel Down which you forwarded with your letter of 28th September, but I hope that for the reasons of which you are already aware from your two interviews with Mr. Nugent, one of my Parliamentary Secretaries, and which I shall mention in some detail, you will understand why it is not possible to meet your request.

When this area of some 726 acres of chalk down land was bought by the Air Ministry in 1940, partly by negotiation with the former owners, and partly by the exercise of compulsory powers, it comprised parcels of 328, 383 and 15 acres respectively. There were the more remote and generally the roughest portions of the three farms concerned, the land for the most part being a rough sheep run infested by rabbits and covered with scrub and gorse. Since the land ceased to be required as a bombing range, it has been managed for me by the Agricultural Land Commission, and after considerable capital outlay, was brought back into productivity by the Dorsetshire Agricultural Executive Committee who have secured good crops from it.

Your request over a year ago to purchase either the 328 acres previously owned by your father-in-law the late Lord Allington [*sic*], or, alternatively, the whole 726 acres received full consideration. The Government is under no obligation to sell back to the previous owners land acquired for a war purpose, whether by agreement or compulsorily, when that use comes to an end. In this case, I find that the late Lord Allington [*sic*] not only received a negotiated price for the land, but also a sum of £2,380 for injurious affection.

I have considered sympathetically the sentimental reasons for your proposal, but it is my first duty to take whatever course is most likely to produce the most food from the land. I must emphasize that I have been guided by the advice received from the Agricultural Land Commission, a body of experts who were appointed for their ability to manage and develop land. They said that if the 328 acres only were sold back to you, the remaining

398 acres would not be suitable to equip as a separate unit. There would be difficulties of access and fencing and the cost of equipment for the smaller area would have been virtually as great as for the whole 726 acres. If the 398 acres went back to the successors of its former owners, it was very doubtful whether it would have been practicable to farm it as if it were provided with equipment as part of the whole Crichel Down property.

The advice from the Agricultural Land Commission, which was confirmed by a subsequent visit of inspection by Lord Carrington (Joint Parliamentary Secretary to the Ministry), was that the best agricultural use of the land was for it to be equipped with a farmhouse, cottages and buildings, and the whole of it farmed as a self-contained unit, which was about the right economic size for this sort of down land. An important factor was that the land had been reclaimed for arable and ley farming by the A.E.C. and all my experts advised that it could not be properly farmed on these lines without its own buildings and equipment.

The normal practice would have been to arrange for the Agricultural Land Commission to equip the holding and for it then to be let or sold. Your proposal to purchase the whole area and farm it in conjunction with your own land without the additional equipment that my advisers considered to be necessary did not seem to be calculated to secure a maximum production from the land. In all the circumstances, I decided to explore the alternative course of transferring the property to the Commissioners of Crown Lands who already own a large estate in the district so that they, rather than the Agricultural Land Commission, might be responsible for its equipment and letting to a tenant of their choice.

It was agreed that if the land were to be acquired by the Commissioners of Crown Lands, it should be at the value placed upon it by the District Valuer of the Inland Revenue. Before the Commissioners could decide whether the purchase and equipment of the land would be a satisfactory proposition to them financially, they needed to ascertain whether they could find a tenant who would be willing to pay a rent sufficient to provide a reasonable return on their capital outlay; this is one of the obligations resting on them as trustees. It was in these circumstances (i.e. the need to settle the rent of the holding, and find a tenant willing to pay it, in advance of the acquisition of the land or its equipment) that the Commissioners decided to confine their enquiries to a few persons on their own list of applicants for farms rather than to invite tenders by public advertisement which they would otherwise have done.

The Commissioners of Crown Lands found such a prospective tenant and he has signed a Memorandum of Agreement to take on the tenancy of the farm from the 29th September 1953, and will enter into formal possession as soon as the necessary legal preliminaries have been completed.

Neither the petition nor your recent letter to the Prime Minister's Private Secretary have [*sic*] disclosed any new facts or considerations which would justify an enquiry into this case. I would add that throughout I have been actuated solely by a desire to carry out the obligation resting on me under the Agriculture Act 1947 to ensure that the best possible use of this land is made for producing food and I am convinced that this obligation will best be assured by the arrangements that have been made for the future farming of the land.

Yours sincerely,

Tom Dugdale.

Clark's, and to some extent Marten's, objections to the letter centred on the phrases about acquisition and the then condition of the land: they were groundless. A more serious objection to the letter would be that it was too placatory, too conciliatory, too civil; that it would have been better to take the petition itself as worded, with its three reasons for an inquiry, as the communication needing reply, and to follow the standard practice (after a brief acknowledgement) of giving those petitioned against the opportunity to comment and defend themselves. Since they included the Ministry, the Agricultural Land Commission, the Lands Service, and even the Dorset Agricultural Executive Committee, such a collection of accounts, comments and advice would have been an inquiry in itself, and would have taken some time, but would certainly have provided a sounder basis than the Minister in the event had, whether for refusing or for eventually granting the request for a public inquiry. It could indeed have provided a sound basis for a devastating indictment of the campaign, the misstatements made, the needless expense and waste of effort and of busy men's time that had been caused. Each of the three main 'reasons' given in the petition could have been pounded to destruction, systematically. Patient, complete refutation of the petitioners' reasons would have delayed the reply, of course, but the stage army of 'petitioners', as opposed to Marten himself, would not have objected to that. As it was, they received no reply, other than the eventual, 'partial' granting of the request for a 'public and impartial' inquiry.

Marten Replies Immediately, 10 October 1953

Marten's immediate reply of 10 October came from his hospital bed, and in fairness has to be given in full:

Dear Sir Thomas,

Thank you very much for your long letter of explanation in regard to the action you have taken over Crichel Down. I appreciate that you have acted in all sincerity on the advice you have received, and with the object of maximum agricultural production in mind.

I must assure you with equal sincerity that I believe you have been ill advised, and that the entire farming community of the district agrees with me. There is a widespread feeling that you have been not only ill-advised, but wilfully ill-advised, and your resistance to an enquiry can only deepen this impression and lead to a further deterioration of the relations between the farming community and your Ministry. If we see a grave injustice being done in our midst, and pushed to its conclusion in the face of constant representations, and in the teeth of the evidence, we can only expect the same treatment on National issues.

Your case for going forward with your present plan is based solely on the argument that greater agricultural production will be obtained. This was first put to me in March in a letter from Nugent. The reason then given was that our prospective tenants, the Hardings were not good enough farmers. As I immediately pointed out to you in a personal letter, that information was utterly false, and consequently the whole structure of the argument collapsed.

In your letter of yesterday you return to the same argument, but the previous grounds—the false allegation against the Hardings—are omitted. Instead you introduce fresh grounds for your decision, and these are just as false as the previous ones.

You say that the land was 'the more remote and generally the roughest portion of the three farms concerned'.

In fact in the case of the Hardings' farm some of the very best fields close to the house have been taken. The remainder is no more remote, and none of it is as rough as some of the portions of the farm that were left.

Such falsehoods, on which your case must have been based, drive me inevitably to the conclusion that you have been advised by people neither disinterested nor competent.

Your letter continues—' . . . the land being for the most part a rough sheep run infested with rabbits and covered with scrub and gorse . . . brought back into productivity by the Dorset A.E.C. who have secured good crops from it.'

This land was no better and no worse than thousands of acres of downland in this district, which since 1939 have been brought into production by local farmers, among whom the Hardings have been notable pioneers. Their land, next door to the bombing range is a much better example of good farming than the bombing range itself.

Again you say—'If the 398 acres went back to the successors of its former owners, it is [*sic*—the Minister's letter had 'was'] very doubtful whether it would be practicable to farm it . . etc. etc.'

To someone who knows and has consulted those successors the matter is in no doubt at all. In fact this statement has been produced without anyone ever going near them to find out their wishes, plans or capabilities.

Again you say — 'Your proposal to purchase the whole area and farm it in conjunction with your own land without the additional equipment that my advisers considered necessary . . . etc . . . etc.'

I do not recall making any such proposal. In March this year I propounded a plan for farming the land myself if it was only possible to rent it. Any plan which I have had in mind for *buying* the entire area has included other farmers, and has not excluded the necessary capital expenditure to make it a success.

Apart from this false and misleading web of words from your advisers, I should like to refer to Carrington's visit, which I presume clinched the decision so far as you were concerned. Perhaps I can best do this by asking some questions.

Was he aware that the men in the farms to which the bombing range originally belonged, were all first class farmers?

Did he know that they had all lost a great deal of land to various Ministries, and consequently had more than adequate buildings?

Did he know that their farmhouses were respectively 1, 2 and 3 minutes journey from their portion of the range?

Did he know that we had accommodation for 7 men in the immediate vicinity?

Did he know anything about ourselves as landowners? — the tremendous scale of work undertaken since 1946 involving the expenditure of £192,000 in excess of rents, on a 7,000 acre estate?

Did he invite the views of the A.E.C. husbandry or estate management committees, who were the only bodies who could possibly have the local knowledge to give certain advice?

Did he know that the three farmers referred to were, among others, all very keen to farm the land?

It is quite clear to me that he was totally unaware of any of these vital factors, with the result that the decision was taken at a high level without adequate knowledge.

To continue at this stage to maintain that that decision was correct, and to refuse an enquiry to establish the facts, will only be interpreted here as a desire to hush up, at all costs, the blunders and lack of thorough enquiry which led to the decision being taken in the first place. If you are personally convinced that you have taken the right course, an impartial inquiry can do nothing but good, in proving the fact publicly, vindicating your advisers, and showing the error of our ways. Have you anything to fear from an enquiry?

No one will be convinced by your explanation of the financial transaction. The land has been passed from one department of the state to another below the market price for reasons which do not bear examination.

I have written enough to make it clear your letter will give no satisfaction in Dorset. Indeed it underlines what we already know — your advisers have been grossly at fault. It will be a very severe disappointment that you personally are determined to perpetuate for all time the grave injustices which follow from their faults.

It has been my endeavour ever since March, when I first realized that you had been badly advised, to bring this business to your direct attention. I must tell you that I intend to continue to bring the matter not only to your attention but to that of the whole community. I am instigating a National campaign on this issue, which I already find has struck a responsive note in every corner of the country.

Yours sincerely,

George G. Marten.

P.S. Thank you for your kind sympathy about my illness. It explains this unbusinesslike letter written from my bed. Fortunately I have suffered no lasting effects, and my activities will be in no way affected.

Marten's letter reached the Ministry at the very time when the Country Landowners' Association (and the National Farmers' Union) were beginning to make public their views on the policy issue, in favour of offering back land compulsorily acquired or acquired under the threat of compulsion, when no longer needed by the acquiring authority, to 'the original owners or their successors'. The Crichel Down case and the policy issue were becoming intertwined again, as the Ministry's method of dealing with the publicly expressed concern of the Country Landowners' Association showed. That method was to send them a copy of the Minister's next letter to Marten, with an explanation of the preference for no publicity over Crichel Down, although it was made public that the Minister was proposing 'to consult his colleagues' on the principle advocated by the Association, that of returning land to former owners. Franklin's letter to the Secretary 'for his information and for the President' sent on 15 October a copy of the Minister's letter of the same date addressed to Marten, with this explanation.

I should add that we are not sending a copy of this letter to the Press because we do not think it is advisable to stimulate further publicity on this subject, and I hope that you will feel that the terms of the Minister's letter form the best way of dealing with the matter now that commitments as regards the future use of Crichel Down have been made and would be difficult to revoke. From your angle the more important question is the policy to be followed in the future and, as I have said, that is to be further examined.

The Minister's letter to Marten of 15 October foreshadowed possible changes in policy, although the Minister's chief concern was to reject the claim of injustice, very courteously:

15 October 1953

Dear Commander Marten,

First of all, let me say how glad I was to learn from the postscript to your letter of 10th October that your attack of poliomyelitis was slight and that you have suffered no lasting effects. I am sorry, however that you are not satisfied by my previous long letter in which I explained the reasons that led to my decisions about the future farming of the former Bombing Range on Crichel Down.

There are one or two points in your letter that I feel bound to correct. In the first place, I must reject completely your contention that a grave injustice has been done to you or to anyone else. The previous owners received a full and fair price for their land, including proper compensation for severance and injurious affection. Nor do I accept the suggestion that I was wilfully ill-advised whether by the Agricultural Land Commission or by the various officials concerned. I am satisfied that their advice, as always, has been entirely disinterested and designed to secure that this land is used to the best advantage.

I recognise, however, that as the Country Landowners' Association have pointed out in their statement in the Press of 14th October, this case raises a general issue of principle about the disposal of land acquired by the Government for a specific purpose, and I am ready to consider the issue of policy involved in consultation with my colleagues, many of whom are also concerned.

In your case, however, events have proceeded too far to be affected by the outcome of this consideration of the general policy of disposal of Government-owned land, and I am afraid that the decision to hand over the land at Crichel Down to the Commissioners of Crown Lands and their decision to let it to Mr. Tozer must stand.

Yours sincerely,

Tom Dugdale.

Cmdr. G. G. Marten, M.V.O., D.S.C.,
Crichel,
Wimborne,
Dorset.

The immediate response was a further catalogue of 'injustices' and a proposal whereby Tozer would be bought out from public funds, Crown Lands would withdraw, and the campaigners would possess the land:

Thank you very much for your letter of 15th October.

We very much regret your decision not to hold an enquiry to establish the facts of the case, but it will give wide satisfaction to know that you intend to consider, for future guidance, the issue of principle involved in the disposal of such land as this.

The issue of principle is not new. It has been the outstandingly clear feature of the case ever since you took office two years ago, and it is one that I have constantly been at pains to bring to your attention. Your readiness, even at this late hour, to consider the principle involved must mean that you are not happy that a just course has been followed in this case to date. Yet you completely reject my contention that a grave injustice has been done to me or anyone else.

May I draw your attention to some of the other injustices which we consider we have suffered.

(1) A written promise was made in your name as Minister, to advertise the land for letting. You have not done this, either as Minister, or in your capacity as a Commissioner of Crown Lands. We consider this unjust.

(2) As Minister you intend to sell the land to the Commissioners of Crown Lands, of which you are one, below the market price and below a better offer. We consider this unjust.

(3) Your reason for refusing my offer for the 328 acres that belonged to this Estate was that our prospective tenant had 170 acres of rough grazing on his present holding and was therefore unsuitable. This information was completely untrue, and very disparaging to one of the finest farmers of the South-West of England. Yet you based your decision on this misinformation. We consider this unjust.

(4) You have since given as a further reason for refusing our case the opinion of your advisers that the land was the more remote and generally the roughest portion of the three farms concerned. This is also untrue and very prejudicial to the case of the previous owners and occupiers. We consider this unjust.

(5) You have stated as a further reason for your decision that if the 398 acres that was not ours, was to go back to the successors of its previous owners, it is very doubtful whether it could be as well farmed as by the means you have in mind. This doubt has been cast on the ability of those concerned without any investigation of their plans, resources or capabilities. We consider this unjust.

(6) You have rejected my application to buy part or all of the land, and turned, unsolicited, to the Commissioners of Crown Lands who have no previous interest, no resources on the spot, and whose control is much more remote. This has the obvious implication that we are unworthy to own the land, although there has been no proper investigation of our capabilities, plans or resources. We consider this unjust.

No other reasons have been put forward for the decision you have taken and in view of the fact that all those we have heard are entirely inaccurate, you will surely sympathise with our contention that a grave injustice has been done. Failing any enquiry it must be left to the judgement of the community as to whether this misinformation was supplied disinterestedly or not, but if, in addition to your guarantee to examine the principles involved you can see your way to putting these injustices right, it might yet bring the affair to a happy conclusion.

I have every reason to believe that Mr. Tozer is a very fair minded man. He will be aware that his good luck is to others, with a much greater moral claim to the land, a very severe misfortune. Though this is not a situation of his making, it seems more than possible from what I hear of his character, that in the interests of justice he may be willing to forego this opportunity, provided he is reasonably compensated for his expense and trouble to date. I think it is likely that this compensation could be arranged without undue expense to the Commissioners or to the Ministry.

We feel sure that the Commissioners would not wish to press their claim to the land in the face of the widespread opposition that exists, and it would only remain for those concerned to have the opportunity, hitherto denied them, to satisfy you that their plans are in the best interest of full production.

I should be very glad to meet you or your representative privately to discuss the possibility of a settlement on these lines.

Yours sincerely,

George G. Marten.

Of all the possible ways of dealing with such a letter, the Minister chose the gentlest and most courteous one, ignoring the accusations of injustice (which could have been easily demolished) but agreeing to meet:

19 October 1953

Dear Commander Marten,

On reaching my office this morning I received your letter of 16th October and your telephone message. I think it would be a good idea if, as you suggest in your letter, you and I were to meet and talk the matter over, although, naturally, without prejudice. If you would care to get in touch with my Private Secretary he will make the necessary arrangements.

Yours sincerely,

Tom Dugdale.

The meeting took place on 22 October 1953: the only minute of the meeting, by the Minister's Private Secretary, G. L. Wilde (MAF 142/148) is a brief note of Marten having admitted that he had no legal title to the land, nor any objection to the appointment of a former public servant to conduct the Inquiry. The next day, the following letter went to Marten.

Dear Commander Marten,

I am writing to confirm what I told you at our talk on the 22nd October about Crichel Down.

As I stated in my previous letter of 15th October, I propose to consult my colleagues on the general question of policy with regard to the disposal of land that has been compulsorily acquired by the Government for a particular public purpose when the need to retain the land for that purpose has ceased to exist.

Also, in the light of further representations that I have received from various quarters, I have now decided that it would be desirable to hold a public inquiry into the procedure adopted in dealing with Crichel Down and into the arrangements made for the future farming of the land.

Yours sincerely,

Tom Dugdale.

Victory for the Campaign

Clark was to say (Appendix 2, para. 99) that it was 'as a result of that interview' (on 22 October 1953) that the Minister decided on a public inquiry, but Clark is not to be believed on this point either. As the Minister himself wrote in his letter to Marten, it was 'further representations' from 'various quarters' which decided him. Those quarters included the Conservative party's Food and Agriculture Committee, whose Dorset members told him at a meeting on 20 October 1953 'that the air was thick locally with all sorts of rumours of maladministration and even of corruption'. (Wilcox to Hole, 23 October 1953.) In his resignation statement on 20 July 1954 Dugdale explained his reasoning:

When in October of last year, I decided to arrange for a public inquiry, it had been brought to my notice that rumours of corruption and personal dishonesty were circulating. It was this information which finally led me to the conclusion that an independent inquiry should be held into the whole circumstances of the case. Sir Andrew Clark reported that he had found no trace of anything in the nature of bribery, corruption or personal dishonesty, and in the short statement I made in the House on 15 June I said that the Inquiry had thus achieved my main purpose.

As Clark, and Marten's legal advisers and Marten himself firmly maintained that he had never alleged corruption (despite his references to injustices, underhand dealing, deceit, exclusive treatment, dirty work, misdemeanours, etc.) it would hardly be in order for the campaigners to claim credit for an inquiry arising from unfounded rumours of corruption. Nevertheless, without the campaign for an inquiry there would have been no such rumours, and no Inquiry. It was certainly a victory for the campaign.

So the campaign ended, and phase two: a new chapter of accidents was about to begin, of even more formidable complexity. There were further brief exchanges between the Minister and Marten, in which Marten sought assurances about such matters as local holding of the inquiry, the supply of 'letters and documents', and that if the published findings favoured the complainants the land would be offered to them or put up for sale by public auction. The Minister decided that he could not give any assurances as to what he would do after the inquiry and the consultations with colleagues on policy, but agreed readily on supply of documents and public local hearings, informing Marten also that the person appointed to conduct the Inquiry 'will certainly not be a Civil Servant past or present'.

The last assurance was an ominous indication of a necessarily amateur approach, by a single investigator, to very complex professional matters. It was the Minister's personal decision, apparently uninfluenced by any person other than a senior colleague, the Home Secretary, himself an experienced lawyer and former Law Officer, Sir David Maxwell Fyfe, QC (later Lord Kilmuir). It was he who advised the appointment of a Chancery lawyer, and suggested to Dugdale that he invite Sir Andrew Clark, QC, a man without qualifications or experience in civil service, or government, or civil administration of any kind, or agriculture. Because Clark had a known hatred of anything even faintly resembling 'socialism', 'nationalization', or 'bureaucracy' it was like inviting a bull to do the stock-taking in a red-draped china shop. What he produced was a diabolical confusion, and great distress to honourable men, including the Minister who appointed him. There was doubtless a sort of rough justice in that, for the man who was made the scapegoat, but no justice at all for those who became the sacrificial lambs, 'the Blandford martyrs'.

3

Phase Three: The Inquiry, the Blandford Martyrs, and the Aftermath, 1953–1954: Confusion Worse Confounded

As soon as a Queen's Counsel was appointed to conduct the inquiry, adversarial procedure and the full, elaborate network of legal trip wires came into operation, supplementing the legal traps which had already caused trouble and embarrassment.

Those traps included the perennial difficulty caused by the ordinary provisions of official secrecy and the special statutory confidentiality of individual farm statistics. At a time of feverish public concern, a public presentation of the facts could have been an effective antipyretic, but once a public inquiry had been announced, there was the hazard of comment on pending proceedings which served to reinforce the traditional distaste for the art of public relations. It would have taken another, internal inquiry to establish the facts; but as it turned out, reticence was of no help to the officials under attack. This sort of routine difficulty apart, there were three particularly troublesome legal traps, peculiar to the Crichel Down case, which had had the effect of a strait-jacket on the Minister and his officials, from the time in June 1952 when the question of returning the land to previous owners was raised by Crouch's letter to Nugent (p. 53).

First there was the uncertainty over the nature of the Air Ministry's acquisitions of land, whether they were compulsory, voluntary, or mixed. Next, there was the conflict in legal advice to the Minister about his powers to sell land. And third, there was the binding force of the requirement on the Minister under the 1947 Agriculture Act to take the most productive course, with little or no discretion to take a politically more expedient course unless it could be shown to be also the most productively and agriculturally expedient.

Given also the undeveloped, almost 'pre-bureaucratic' state of English administrative law, lacking in statutory or other established rules, forms, and procedures for dealing with almost unprecedented and imprecise complaints, and rumours of corrupt behaviour by civil servants and others, a public inquiry by a sole Commissioner was a rather perilous venture without guides into unknown territory. Difficulties were only to be expected, particularly if the person appointed had no prior experience of such explorations. One thing, however, could hardly have been foreseen about the learned Commissioner: that was his inability or refusal to grasp, not merely the facts of the story, but the very provisions of the laws which had brought about the Ministry's difficulties.

It was Clark's mistakes concerning both the facts and the laws, in his public performance at Blandford, and in his privileged published report, which made an already complex story an almost indescribable tangle. It was eventually thought best by the authorities to put out the lights in the theatre and bolt the doors, to relegate the probably defamatory scripts and recordings of the proceedings to a publicly inaccessible place (the library of the House of Commons) and to resolve never to permit such a public performance again.

It is a sad breach of convention for a lay person to suggest that the eminent lawyers engaged in the inquiry were deficient in their mastery of the law: after all, there was a Queen's Counsel in the purported middle, and Queen's Counsel on both sides. One of them (the Hon. Charles Russell, QC) was the son of a Lord of Appeal and grandson of a great Chief Justice, and himself became a Lord of Appeal. Another, as Lord Widgery, was to be appointed Chief Justice; another became a High Court Judge, as Sir Melford Stevenson. During the inquiry both Russell and Widgery attempted politely but without avail to put the Commissioner right on several points. It is however essential for an understanding of the rest of the Crichel Down story to see how and where the Commissioner went wrong in his assumptions about the law, because it was from these misunderstandings that his condemnation of others stemmed. It is therefore necessary to interrupt the narrative of events from the autumn of 1953 to the denouement of Dugdale's resignation in July 1954, in order to unravel the three main legal knots—the puzzles over acquisition, over powers of sale, and over the policy of productivity. The last presented Clark with the least difficulty, in that he touched upon 'policy' matters only tangentially, in order to score incidental points against those loyally carrying out the policy: it is therefore best cleared out of the way first.

The Puzzle about Productivity

Clark accepted productivity as a question of policy outside the scope
of his inquiry; he accepted the Minister's chosen means to that end,
the equipping and farming of the land as one unit, as being a policy
matter (Appendix 2, conclusions 7 and 9). He therefore did not
criticize the Minister's decision, except by the highly indirect method
of criticizing the ALC's previous similar decision in 1950 as
'unsound' (from a purely financial point of view—conclusion 1)
while declining to say—as outside his scope—whether 'increased
production' outweighed 'financial disadvantages', yet praising the
Minister for finding, in sale to Crown Lands (conclusion 9) 'certainly
the best, and probably the only certain way' of assuring the policy
(productivity), while still suggesting (conclusion 10) it was 'not a very
sound one financially' for Crown Lands, but a matter of policy and
so outside his scope. This was an exercise in sophistry, enabling Clark
to criticize the ALC and the officials for the expense of their
proposals, while treating the policy justifications for that expense
as matters not proper for him to examine, and also excusing the
Minister from blame for his decision on policy on the (false) ground
that the 'true financial position' had never been brought to the notice
of anyone in the Ministry (conclusion 7).

Adversarial procedure ensured that the procession of expert
witnesses supporting the policy decision to equip and farm the land
as a single unit for productive purposes was confronted by expert
witnesses for the other side maintaining the opposite, with the
Commissioner coming down heavily and unfairly against the
Agricultural Land Commission (conclusion 21) and the Lands Service
(conclusion 22) for having been irresponsible, over-enthusiastic, less
than frank, and less than conscientious.

The merits of the proposal for a new farm as a means of
implementing the policy imperative of increased production (which
it was not Clark's business to examine) scarcely emerged clearly from
the adversarial arguments of the inquiry, but work of an expert kind
was being done in that era (begun in 1948 but not published until
1960, too late to save the Blandford martyrs) which produced
authoritative but unnoticed endorsement of the official plans for
Crichel Down. An exhaustive study sponsored by the Nuffield
Foundation sought to establish principles for agricultural policy: in
so doing the authors set out arrangements for farm management and

layout which bear a very strong resemblance to what was proposed for Crichel Down (see Map 3).

What the Nuffield study proposed (Williams, H. T., *Principles for British Agriculture Policy*, Nuffield Foundation/OUP, 1960) was, in summary, the general adoption in Britain, where possible, of a system of mixed farming, particularly ley farming, the keynote of which would be adaptability — 'adaptability to varying climatic and physical conditions and adaptability to changing economic circumstances' (op. cit., p. 196). For such a system, what was contemplated by the Agricultural Land Commission and Crown Lands in turn would have fitted exactly: 'The ideal arrangement is to have a compact farm with the farm-house and buildings conveniently placed on good roads near to the centre, and with rectangular fields of a size suitable for the type of farming practised.'(Williams, op. cit., p. 197.)

The conclusion of the study (p. 306) contained an estimate that a combination of the general adoption of the best scientific and practical knowledge would result in a 60 per cent increase in national output. At the height of the Crichel Down storm the Ministry of Agriculture was disbursing mostly unrequited largesse in aid to farmers at a rate of about £1m. each working day, with little prospect in return of direct benefit in greatly improved husbandry or estate management. It is therefore sad that the rare opportunity of a 'model farm' at Crichel Down, costing the Exchequer nothing, but pointing the way to better farming methods, was thwarted. Even if over-production at vast cost and the imperatives of conservation have replaced 'productivity' as major concerns in British (and other countries') agriculture, the Nuffield study's insistence was that their recommended mixed farming was adapted to all seasons and all circumstances likely to arise in Britain: 'Mixed farming has been shown in practice to be good husbandry. There is no better way of keeping land in good condition than by mixed cropping and stocking, together with the proper use of fertilizers.' (op. cit., p. 306.)

No wonder, then, that so many of the men given a share in the duty of planning Crichel Down's future showed, as Clark put it, 'eagerness'. In his condemnation of that eagerness, he showed little grasp of what might be at stake, of what was being attempted, or of what good husbandry and good estate management might include. In so far as the Minister and his officials were able to maintain any enthusiasm at all for their task, through all the torments inflicted on them, they deserved praise rather than blame for that, and for finding also what was—properly understood—as good a solution to the immediate problems of food production and of land disposal as could have been found. Put into effect, that solution would have ensured good husbandry and good estate management, and been a model and exemplar for more backward local landowners and farmers.

The Puzzle about Acquisition: 'That old Fallacy'

The fact that until well after World War II there was no formal teaching given to lawyers about the public aspect of land law and conveyancing (see pp. 16 f.) does much to explain the serious difficulty which Clark and others learned in the law had in understanding what processes had been involved in the Air Ministry acquisition. It does much in particular to explain the widespread inability—amongst the lay press, politicians and public as well as lawyers—to understand how there could have been any difficulty in establishing whether the acquisition had been by compulsion or not.

It was Clark himself who betrayed most dramatically the lack of understanding. On the very first day of the inquiry, before any witnesses had been called, while Russell was guiding the inquiry through the accumulation of correspondence in the case, Clark seized upon a phrase in the Minister's letter to Marten of 9 October 1953 (p. 110) in which the Air Ministry's purchase was described as 'partly by negotiation with the former owners and partly by the exercise of compulsory powers'—interjecting 'That old fallacy!' Eager to scotch the idea that there was any real agreement to sell the land, yet anxious to avoid criticism of the Minister who had signed the letter, Clark questioned Franklin, who had drafted it, refused to accept his defence of the statement, and described it as 'unfortunately worded'. Nevertheless, what Franklin had drafted was perfectly true, because even over the Hooper land there had been negotiation and agreement on compensation, as well as actual use of compulsory powers. In the Crichel Estate and Langton Estate transactions there had been no need and no use of compulsory powers, merely conveyances in the ordinary form of an agreement between vendor and purchaser. The documents in each of the two instances make no mention of compulsion, of the powers of the Secretary of State under the Defence Acts, or anything of that sort, but simply register that the vendors 'have agreed to sell the property' with appropriate signatures for both parties and a covenant by the Secretary of State to erect and maintain stock- and rabbit-proof fences (MAF 236/34).

The Ministry brief for Russell at the inquiry (MAF 236/38) showed that the Ministry was well aware of the difference between the Hooper compulsion over everything except the agreed compensation and the treatment of the other two owners who had not held out to the point of requiring compulsion: 'In the latter two cases the compulsory powers under the Defence Acts were in the background and could have been used if it had become necessary'.

The choice by Clark of 'compulsion' as a description of all three acquisitions occurs in the very first sentence of his 'factual narrative' (Appendix 2, para. 4). It confused the issue, but it enabled him as soon as the inquiry began to suggest that the officials not only went absurdly wrong themselves but that they seriously misled the Minister with an 'unfortunately worded' draft — a cardinal sin of which they were entirely innocent. Without the general ignorance of the law and practice of public land acquisition that finding by Clark could never have gained the bemused general acceptance that it did.

The Puzzle about the Minister's Power to sell Land

The third puzzle was something more complex, although both Clark and Melford Stevenson professed to find it so simple that even a child could have no doubt about the Minister's power to sell land. The matter was brought up by Melford Stevenson in his final address, on the penultimate day of the inquiry (MAF 236/8) while ridiculing what he called 'that remarkable piece of literature', D. S. Brown's draft report of August 1952 (pp. 66 f.):

Sir, it might be helpful to pause there and consider for a moment the very curious statements that have been made about a change of policy in this case. I feel some difficulty in dealing with them because I am not quite sure that I followed them, and I am not sure precisely what change of policy is alleged to have occurred and at what date. I understand that it is asserted that it is associated with some legal opinion which was given on the language of Section 90 of the Agriculture Act of 1947. I am delighted to know that some high placed lawyers were employed to answer a question as to what that language meant, but when you look at the language of the Section itself it is very difficult to imagine how even a child could have been in any doubt as to whether that Section, in fact, included a power to sell land.

Clark's response was one of hearty agreement, repeated emphatically: 'That is how it struck me. That is exactly how it struck me.' Encouraged, Melford Stevenson went on:

If it is not presumptuous to say so, I have an idea that between us we may be right, Sir. The first line says: 'The Minister may manage, farm, sell, let or otherwise deal with or dispose of land acquired by him.' Why it was necessary to ask anybody whether those words included a power to sell, is a matter which completely defeats me. How any such opinion could be associated with some change of policy is a matter at which my mind boggles, and I am content to leave it there.

THE COMMISSIONER: I have no doubt Mr. Russell will explain it to me.

MR. RUSSELL: I regret that I have failed so lamentably so far to get it across to my learned friend.

MR. MELFORD STEVENSON: Mr. Russell has the priceless advantage of the last word in this case.

THE COMMISSIONER: I am afraid, Mr. Russell, you have failed to get it across to me equally.   (MAF 236/8)

The following day Russell tried again, making the point that it was not Section 90 but its first proviso, not referred to by Stevenson, that was the source of the difficulty. What (as an intelligent child might have asked) does 'expedient' mean, if, by that proviso, the Minister can sell only if it is 'expedient' to do so? That the point was not fully taken by Clark is apparent from his report (Appendix 2, para. 21) where he pours scorn on the idea that the Minister did not have complete discretion to sell any land he had acquired. In fact, the Minister was left by the legislation with a 'ministerial' function to perform, one in which there could be little or no discretion as to the mode of its exercise. That public ownership of resources including land was a perennial issue between the major political parties conferred no right upon the Minister to interpret the law as his party might wish him to do, against the legal advice given to him.

Unknown to Clark, or Stevenson, the legal puzzle had recently been given a further, insoluble twist, in January 1954. The lawyers of the Ministry of Agriculture had then (tongue in cheek, perhaps) succeeded in flooring those 'high placed' lawyers, the Attorney-General and the Solicitor-General, with a further innocent enquiry concerning the purport of proviso (i) to Section 90.

What prompted the further reference to the Law Officers was the quandary the Ministry had found itself in over the consideration of Crouch's claim on Marten's behalf. It had been agreed in the Ministry that food production would be best served by equipping the land as a farm unit and selling it with vacant possession to some person they had good reason to think would farm it properly. That seemed to rule out sale by public auction (the more easily defensible way), and to suggest that sale by private treaty was the only way to discharge the obligation to ensure the best use of the land (MAF 236/5).

By the time the further reference to the Law Officers took place, the Crichel Down case had led to the establishment of two cabinet subcommittees, one examining the policy question of selling land back to previous owners, the other to consider the Crichel Down case itself. A complicating factor for the Ministry of Agriculture was not knowing what conclusions either subcommittee would produce, working in secret, or in what order. Any concession as a result of the Clark Inquiry might pre-empt the general policy deliberations. It also seemed prudent to establish that there should be no retrospective application to Crichel Down, or to any other land, of any procedure devised for the future, involving giving to former owners of land a prior opportunity to buy it back before disposal by public auction. So far as the Ministry of Agriculture was concerned, Section 90 of the Agriculture Act and its proviso (i) remained an awkward stumbling-block, making it more difficult for Agriculture than for any other department to agree to sale of land by public auction, particularly land acquired for the purpose of agriculture. No form of covenant or lease seemed adequate to ensure the proper equipping and subsequent farming of the land, and a host of minor problems would arise, in regard to keeping the land in one hand, and in regard to security of tenure. Covenants made with such objects in view would be either void, or, even if modified, unenforceable.

What was put to the Law Officers by the Ministry in January 1954 was therefore the peculiar difficulty of sale under Section 90, in the form of a question whether sale of land by auction would be in order. The Solicitor-General, Manningham-Buller, did not find the wording of Section 90 so 'unusually clear' and 'plain' as Clark was later to report (Appendix 2, para. 21). In a reply on 18 January the Solicitor-General wrote: 'I spent a great deal of time on this problem over the weekend and I have had a long discussion with the Attorney on it this morning.' Suggesting that if a piece of land had been transferred to the Minister under Section 88 the Minister might not be under an obligation to secure its full and efficient use for agriculture, he went on to say that, on the other hand, if Section 90 did not apply to Section 88 acquisitions there did not appear to be any powers in the Act for the Minister to deal with such land at all. He concluded: 'We both feel that having regard to the curious wording, Section 90 should be amended so as to make it clear at least in relation to land transferred under Section 88 that the Minister can sell by public auction or public tender'.

As it was clearly not the best of times to approach Parliament for a minor amendment to a major Act already considered to need more extensive changes, the Minister so reported to the Crichel Down subcommittee on 11 March 1954. He had been invited to set out 'in precise form' 'an administrative procedure for carrying into effect the proposals made by the Lord President for giving to former owners of agricultural land compulsorily acquired a prior opportunity to buy it back before its disposal by public auction was proceeded with'. (MAF 236/40.) His report included the following: 'I am considering whether Section 90 should be amended to give me greater freedom of sale but I suggest that any legislation of that kind should preferably be included in a measure amending the Agriculture Act in other respects and deferred until the next Parliament.'

So far as Crichel Down was concerned, the Minister recommended that there should be no retrospective application of the suggested procedure if it were approved, either to Crichel Down or any other land. None of these developments would presumably have been known to the Commissioner at the inquiry a month later, or to the lawyers appearing, so Clark and Stevenson, while finding all so clear and plain in the Minister's power to sell land, were moving about in a world of an obscurity they did not fully appreciate.

The Narrative resumed

Having adumbrated rather than illustrated the role of the three major legal puzzles in compounding the growing confusion, one can pick up the narrative skein again, from the beginning of the third and publicized phase of the case in September 1953. Unfortunately, it cannot be a coherent single thread of narrative. Not only were there the usual difficulties of onlookers seeing only what they were predisposed to see, there was the special difficulty, for all looking on, that only one side of the story was ever effectively presented to the public, the hostile version.

From the autumn of 1953 (when Marten's promised 'row' opened with a letter to *The Times*, a protest meeting and a petition) to the July 1954 surprise of the Minister's resignation during the Commons debate on Crichel Down, there had been scarcely a word written or spoken in defence of the civil service, except by the Minister himself and one or two speakers in the debate. Ordinary official reticence, cabinet secrecy, Crown privilege, and legal considerations of defamation and confidentiality combined durably to make it impracticable, in a growing 'lynch atmosphere' for perceivers of bureaucratic ineptitude to check their perceptions against reality, even if they had diligently sought to do so. In such an atmosphere it was easily overlooked that the civil servants (and those other unfortunates whose functions made it possible to mistake them for officials) were also citizens, with the rights of citizens to fair trial, on specific charges, with ample facilities for defence. Instead, they were perceived as some kind of alien oppressors of the citizen, upstart slaves who had arrogantly sought to usurp their elected masters' powers. With the choice of a less than impartial 'judge', a specific cabinet decision that the accused should not be thoroughly defended at the inquiry 'trial', and the decision that the public proceedings should be made inaccessible, the 'lynch' analogy becomes almost unavoidable, for the proceedings, if not for the actual punishment inflicted.

With some difficulty, because all three views of the situation were blurred (confused, in all senses of the word) it is possible to distinguish and to describe, for the purposes of the narrative, three somewhat dissimilar perceptions of what was being publicly enacted and discussed during the crisis of the row, the inquiry, and the denouement.

There was the general view, the version presented to the general public, the press view, the most consistently hostile view, which can be called the view from Printing House Square because it was *The Times* which led the pack more or less throughout, from September 1953. Then there was a partly distinguishable second view, relying largely on the first but containing further details from 'insiders'' talk. This was the view of the 'Top People' who, in the words of the advertisement 'take *The Times*', but had access to other sources as well, mostly around the parliamentary lobbies — it can be called the general view from Westminster, to distinguish it from the third view, the view of those under pressure and suspicion, mostly in the Ministry of Agriculture, which can be called the view from Whitehall Place, the perceptions of those most affected by the growing hostility to them of those outwith the departments under fire. They too were confused; no one was in possession of the full facts. No internal inquiry had established those facts before the appointment of a public inquiry effectively ruled out anything other than preparation of a discreet defence to be considered in public—an exercise involving not so much revelation of all the facts as meticulous avoidance of anything resembling the proverbially best form of defence—namely, attack (or, in this case, counter-attack). In the absence of an alternative story, it was the view from Printing House Square which was generally accepted.

The View from Printing House Square

The Times is singled out because its coverage was as extensive as any, because it was chosen by Marten as the prime vehicle of his press campaign, and because the tone of much of the rest of the press seemed to follow and depend upon reports and letters in *The Times*. 'The tone is taken from the top.'

It was in *The Times* of 24 September 1953 that the first impression on the national consciousness was made, by the letter (p. 106) bearing the name of Mary Anne Marten, referring to 'veiled nationalization' of land, and to acquisition of land in 1939 'by compulsory purchase', and going on:

As the area was no longer required for defence purposes I, as one of the previous owners, applied to the Ministry of Agriculture in 1950 to buy back the 330 acres which had previously been part of my estate and which formed an important portion of one of my tenant's [*sic*] farms. After a delay of nearly 18 months my application was refused, though neither then nor at a subsequent meeting with the Parliamentary Secretary were we told what was to be done with the area. At this meeting I offered to buy or rent the entire 700 acres and laid out my plans for doing so. I was told they would be given sympathetic consideration.

There followed an account of the Minister's supposedly 'private' talk with MPs on 5 May 1953, reference to an inquiry being sought and a protest meeting, to rights of farmers and landowners being involved, as well as possibility of 'extravagance' with public funds. Of course, there was a certain lack of warranted assertability in the statements made in the letter, particularly those about applications and letters by Mrs Marten, and delays in reply, but the fact that the Ministry chose not to comment publicly allowed the disastrous first impression to harden into indelibility in the minds of 'top people', and set the tone for most subsequent press comment. Once started on a false scent, the newshounds were soon in full cry.

On 28 September 1953 the headlines ran: FARMERS' CALL FOR INQUIRY—DISPOSAL OF LAND AT CRICHEL DOWN. There was an account 'From our correspondent, Wimborne, Dorset, Sept. 27' of the protest meeting and petition, with a note that 'Mr. Tozer, the prospective tenant, was not at the meeting and has declined to comment.'

On 3 October 1953, date-lined 'Wimborne Oct. 2' there was a quotation from Marten 'This situation would be a complete farce if it were not that it may mean tragedy for local men', and a report of a Ministry of Agriculture spokesman saying that the petition would have a reply 'soon'. On 8 October there was a reference to the Ministry 'still considering' and to Marten being in hospital and 'unable to make any comment'. On 12 October the headlines ran LAND INQUIRY REFUSED—MINISTER'S REPLY TO PROTEST, and Marten was quoted: 'The decision can only be interpreted as a desire to hush up at all costs the ill-conceived advice and lack of thorough inquiry which has led to the present situation.' and further: 'a grave injustice will be perpetuated in the teeth of strong evidence and earnest representation from sincere and honest people'.

On 13 October 1953 the headlines were DECISION ON CRICHEL DOWN CRITICIZED—NFU TO HEAR REPORT, with a report of concern expressed by the NFU and the 'very unfavourable reception of the decision' by farmers. On 14 October 1953, under headlines FURTHER PROTESTS ON CRICHEL DOWN—MINISTER URGED TO ALTER DECISION, it was the weakening of the Ministry's other main pillar of support that was announced, the Country Landowners' Association press release saying they were 'vehemently opposed to land nationalization in any form, and the fact that in this case the Commissioners of Crown Lands are to be the new owners does not appear to be sufficiently far removed from State ownership to mitigate this aspect'. The Ministry was said to have declined to comment. (This was a pity because the 'return' of the land to the 'private' royal estate could have been pointed to, in a jocular way, as an example of what the Country Landowners' Association was advocating so strongly, the principle of return of land to original ownership—what could be more 'original' than the Crown, the source of all holdings of land, particularly land in the old royal woods and forest of the South-West? It was largely compensation to the Crown for 'nationalization' of royal 'private' lands that was being used to 'privatize' Crichel Down for the royal estate—a transaction opposed with vigour only by landowners and others apt to number themselves—as the Martens did—amongst the royalists, the Crown's most supportive and loyal subjects. The point was never raised; there was confusion galore without it.)

On 16 October there was a report of cracks in the other main pillar, the NFU, in headlines FUTURE OF CRICHEL DOWN—PUBLIC EXPLANATION SOUGHT BY NFU. What the NFU executive was reported as proposing (because they recognized there were constitutional difficulties in a public inquiry) was that 'to end the confusion' the Minister or one of the Parliamentary Secretaries should visit Dorset and publicly explain, and answer questions. There was also another report, from Wimborne, 'from our special correspondent' predicting further trouble unless there were a public inquiry or public explanation, and announcing that Marten had written to the Minister declaring his intention 'to instigate a protest campaign on a national scale' (cf. p. 115).

On 17 October 1953 the headlines ran GENERAL POLICY ON LAND DISPOSAL—MINISTER'S REFERENCE TO CONSULTATIONS. The text outlined both the Minister's decision to consult with his colleagues on future policy (while adhering to his Crichel Down decision) (p. 116) and Marten's six 'instances of injustice' (p. 117).

On 20 October 1953 there was a report of the threatened buckling of the main foundation in Dorset of the governmental structure: the North Dorset Conservative Association had sent to the Minister a resolution viewing the situation 'with anxiety' and prophesying ' a detrimental effect on the Conservative cause'.

On 23 October the annual general meeting of the Country Landowners' Association provided the headlines: RESTORING FARMERS' CONFIDENCE—GOVERNMENT URGED TO GIVE STRONG LEAD. The story was of a unanimous resolution the previous day asking the Minister to reconsider his decision, of a deputation to him arranged for 24 October 1953, and of the Association's feelings about the decision: 'The Country Landowners' Association feel there is a strong moral obligation that it be reversed, and that the previous owners and occupiers be given an opportunity to prove that they can farm the land efficiently.'

On 24 October 1953 *The Times* announced the victory: DISPOSAL OF CRICHEL DOWN — INQUIRY ORDERED, quoting Dugdale replying to an arranged parliamentary question by Crouch, giving also, briefly, Marten's comments and treating the dispute at length in a leading article entitled A SORRY TALE. The writer began with the description 'a sorry and tangled tale' and went on to tangle the skein further. His version made the land ' a war-time acquisition', its subsequent sale to some 'Commissioners' a transaction 'behind the backs of former owners and sitting tenants', and Mrs Marten, mysteriously, a former occupant of the land, or of some of it. The writer accepted that the facts were not established, but already saw the Minister and the Ministry as clumsily guilty men, without waiting for either investigation, or charges, or trial, before reaching that verdict:

A SORRY TALE

The dispute over Crichel Down in Dorset is a sorry and tangled tale. It concerns farmland bought early in the war by compulsion, or threat of compulsion, for use as a bombing range. Subsequently, it passed to the Ministry of Agriculture, being managed by the Agricultural Land Commission and farmed by the local agricultural executive. The Ministry finally decided to sell the land, and the Commissioners agreed to buy it and build a new farm, provided they could first find a tenant farmer willing to pay a suitable rent. The tenant was found and the Commissioners promised him the tenancy. All this was done behind the backs of former owners and sitting tenants from whose farms the land was severed, although offers came from among them to buy or lease some or all of the disputed land. At some stage, it is alleged, a promise was given that the new tenancy would be advertised, but in fact the new tenant was found by other means.

These proceedings have not unnaturally caused indignation in the local farming community and the MINISTER OF AGRICULTURE has responded slowly and clumsily to their protests. Early in the month he refused a public inquiry into the protracted and involved proceedings leading up to the disposal of Crichel Down. A week later he conceded in a letter to LIEUTENANT-COMMANDER MARTEN (who has been seeking to regain the land his wife used to occupy and her father to own) that the case raised a general issue of principle about the disposal of land acquired by the Government for a specific purpose. While he wished to discuss this general question of policy with his Government colleagues, he insisted that 'in your case however events have proceeded too far to be affected by the outcome of this consideration.' Yesterday he told Parliament that a public inquiry is after all to be held, but only into the procedure to be adopted in disposing of Crichel Down, not apparently into whether the decision was wise or is still open to reversal.

This somewhat grudging concession will at least enable the facts to be established but the inquiry must surely be pressed further. Why must land acquired by the Government for a public purpose be retained in Crown possession when it is to be put to a totally different, and essentially private purpose? Is the principle of the 'dead hand' operating, or is it simply, as the Minister claims, that the land will be better farmed if the Crown is the landlord? The merits of that claim, which is hotly disputed, cannot be judged until the facts behind it are made public. Even if it were completely correct, would it be relevant? Are former owners and tenants, willing to pay as high a price or rent as anyone else, to be disregarded as actuated only by 'sentiment' (to use the Minister's own word) merely because the Government have no legal obligation to offer them first option of buying back what they parted with in time of national emergency?

After that clap of thunder, evoking no echo or reply from the Ministry, silence reigned, on the whole, in the columns of *The Times*, until the inquiry at Blandford opened in April 1954. It was broken only by the notification in November 1953 of the appointment of Sir Andrew Clark QC, the terms of reference, the place (the Corn Exchange, Blandford) and the proposed commencement. Later, in December 1953, there was notification of a joint application by both sides for a postponement, followed by Clark's agreement to that, accompanied by a characteristic observation by him that it was 'a little strange' that the Ministry had found it impossible to be ready. Russell, for the Ministry, had explained that it had not at first been appreciated by the legal side of the Ministry, not previously concerned with the detail, that there could be so much.

Both sides, indeed, needed time to master the hugh drifts of paper left with them after the blizzard of papers exchanged by the solicitors on both sides—mostly copies of official papers from the several departments. The collecting had been further complicated by questions of Crown privilege requiring Cabinet authorization (see p. 161).

The other side had had much less to contribute as material, but had 'no option but to concur' in postponement, as they needed time to sift through the documents received, to ask for more on certain points, to ask for named persons to appear as witnesses, to engage their own experts to contradict the Ministry's, and, like the official side, to coach and rehearse the cast in the speaking parts each should play, and to advise them where they would do better to remain silent. It was not to be a search for the truth, a heuristic exercise, but a fight, an eristic exercise of some sort.

On 21 April 1954 the headlines in *The Times* returned, CRICHEL DOWN INQUIRY OPENING TODAY—with the newspaper's 'special correspondent' delicately claiming credit for the newspaper, the inquiry being seen as 'the sequel to a dispute which first attracted national notice when it was outlined in a letter to *The Times* last September' (the letter in Mrs Marten's name, p. 131).

The first day of the hearing led to headlines on 22 April 1954: CRICHEL DOWN INQUIRY—OFFICIAL LETTERS 'ASTOUNDING'—CHAIRMAN'S COMMENT—thus giving prominence to the first of the juicy plums pulled out by Clark from the vast pile of correspondence being set before the inquiry by Russell. The letters thus singled out were those by Eastwood and Wilcox on their learning of previous applicants (p. 88 f.). Clark was reported as finding Eastwood's letter 'extraordinary' and Wilcox's 'even worse': 'It looks to me as if something is being cooked up to try and deceive people as to what the true position is.' Clark's ominous rhetorical question about Thomson's part was also reported: 'Why this soft-heartedness for Mr. Tozer, and his callous disregard for everybody else?' The very first public report was thus a highly unjudicial earmarking of the three who were to be the chief martyrs, preceding any opportunity of a word in defence or explanation by any of them, or by counsel. Worse was to come; these were merely the first swipes in what was to become a knockabout farce, a sort of Punch and Judy show played out in public, but with no word of press criticism of the absurd iniquity of the proceedings.

On the next day, 23 April 1954, there was a brief selection of points from the second day's hearing, under the headlines CRICHEL DOWN LETTERS—CHAIRMAN ON 'OLD FALLACY'—LAND COMMISSIONER'S EVIDENCE. Russell's response to Clarke's 'old fallacy' remark (p. 125) was mild—that the witnesses to be called included the person who had drafted the letter for the Minister (Franklin, the Deputy Permanent Secretary).

The next day, 24 April 1954, it was Nugent's turn to be trapped into a reluctant admission damaging to Wilcox. The headlines were: CRICHEL DOWN DISPOSAL — MINISTER'S VIEW OF OFFICIAL LETTER — I WOULD NOT HAVE AUTHORIZED IT. The report was about Wilcox's letter to Eastwood of 25 March 1953 (p. 89) already condemned by Clark: 'Asked by Sir Andrew CLARK about Mr. Wilcox's letter of March 25, Mr. Nugent inquired whether it was relevant to the inquiry for him to say whether he would have authorized the letter. Told by the Chairman that it was, he stated, "Well, then, I would not."'

In practice, no authorization by a Parliamentary Secretary of Wilcox's semi-official letter to a civil service colleague would have been necessary or appropriate, so Clark's question was an absurdly hypothetical one: but Wilcox himself was quoted on the same day as giving stumbling and embarrassed replies to Stevenson's questions on the same letter:

If I had reflected I should have appreciated that the only feasible cause [*sic*] was to tell them that the statements or undertakings about the property being tendered for letting had been on the basis of its being in the hands of the commission, but that the property had in fact been taken out of the hands of the commission and transferred to the land commissioners.

'Surely', Clark was reported as then asking Wilcox, it was his duty to say to the Commission (it is not clear which Commission was meant, reports differing on this point) that the promises would have to be implemented and the land put up for tender? In reply Wilcox said, apologetically: 'Yes, I think we ought to have given more consideration to it . . . it was an unfortunate letter.' (He would have done better to say that his job had been to implement the policy, agreed between the Minister and Sir Frederick Burrows, of sale within two months to Crown Lands, and not to put unnecessary obstacles in the way, there being no legal or other obligation on Crown Lands to follow the ALC's practices in letting land; but that, on the other hand, there was a more definite obligation on them to Tozer, and to the Ministry and the ALC, to conclude matters within the two months time limit given them.)

Of Lord Carrington's evidence all that was given was his conviction (actually expressed by him about ten times in answer to elegantly varied questioning) that from an agricultural point of view the land should be one holding.

In evidence on the 'old fallacy' Sir Reginald Franklin denied intending to convey the impression that Crichel Estate land sale to the Air Ministry had been voluntary: 'It was under the threat of a notice to treat, but the terms were negotiated. Unfortunately the conveyance is as if it was between a willing buyer and a willing seller.' The next report, on Monday 26 April 1954, was of the short Saturday morning session on 24 April, evidence by Eastwood, headlines SELECTING CRICHEL DOWN TENANT — INQUIRY WITNESS ON A MORAL OBLIGATION. The session was reported as ending with Clark promising 'a lot of questions' for Eastwood when the inquiry was resumed. Up to that point, Eastwood had denied that anything in the way of 'dissembling' had ever been done, that Crown Lands had incurred any moral obligation to anyone except Tozer, that he ever thought the Crichel Down enterprise would be 'rather fun' (this in reply to Stevenson). To a suggestion by Stevenson that moral obligations to other applicants arose from promises to them, Eastwood replied 'No doubt, but they were not promises made by us.' He conceded to Stevenson, however, that in correspondence with the Treasury it would have been more accurate to say, 'on the basis of a very considerable knowledge of the neighbourhood' when it came to Thomson's choice of a tenant, rather than 'after a good deal of inquiry'. Further challenged by Clark on the nature of Thomson's 'inquiry', Eastwood replied that it had presumably been Thomson's examination of applications for farms, but referred again to his earlier admission that the phrase was not strictly correct.

Oddly, *The Times* of Tuesday 27 April 1954 contained no account of what Douglas Brown called 'a quick-fire succession of one hundred and eighteen questions' (*The Battle of Crichel Down*, p. 27) from Clark to Eastwood, but there was probably nothing more sinister in the omission of what Brown also called 'the battle of the intellects' between Clark and Eastwood, than pressure on column space, or even a missed train and a reporter's absence. If *The Times* representative was not present, however, he was going against the trend of growing interest by the press. Brown described the inquiry as beginning almost unnoticed and ending 'in a blaze of headlines and a scurrying of excited politicians' with ' a stream of pressmen flowing from Fleet Street to Dorset', the last of them arriving an hour before the inquiry ended (Brown, op. cit. p. 86).

However it may have been, the view from Printing House Square was obscured by the omission; if the Monday's proceedings had been more fully reported, Thomson's ordeal on that day and the next would have been seen more clearly as victimization by Clark. For comprehension of Thomson's ordeal, therefore, the lack of an account of Eastwood's inquisition by Clark must be made good at this point, and it seems also as good a point as any to attempt some explanation of Clark's approach, in terms of his character and attitudes.

Brown (op. cit. p. 98) said of the Monday 26 April encounter between Clark and Eastwood: 'It went on for a long time, the constant pressure of questioning, the battle of intellects, but the witness was not to be flustered, as Mr. Wilcox had often been.'

Clark had already given on Saturday 24 April, during the course of Eastwood's evidence, the clearest display of intolerance and ignorance of the civil service. According to the shorthand record, on Eastwood's saying in the course of cross-examination that he thought he had heard the figure of 7s. 6d. an acre mentioned by Sir Reginald Franklin as pre-war annual rental for similar land, Melford Stevenson had asked: 'But how in the world would Sir Reginald Franklin know?' And Clark had joined in, apparently 'astounded': 'Surely you cannot mean Sir Reginald Franklin?' To this Eastwood's response was 'Yes indeed' and the following remarkable exchange took place immediately:

Stevenson: Was this another lunch?
Eastwood: No, it certainly was not. This is bare downland and I think it is generally known that was not worth anything more than that order of magnitude before the war.
CLARK: But Sir Reginald Franklin is a permanent Civil Servant holding a very high position at the Ministry. He does not know anything about agriculture, he does not know anything about Crichel Down. How could he have advised you in this?(MAF 236/6)

On Eastwood's responding that Sir Reginald Franklin might well know what was the order of rents of that type of land before the war, there was a good deal more nonsense, with Clark expressing the hope that Eastwood made very careful enquiries to ensure that the figure was not untrue before he put it in a letter, and saying that he (Clark) was not 'at the moment' contesting with Eastwood whether it was true or untrue, because he did not know, he was asking where Eastwood got it from. No doubt regretting having brought

Franklin's name into the silly business, Eastwood said: 'The answer to that is I cannot remember, but to the best of my belief it is true.' It was indeed true of the generality of such land, with Launceston and Crichel land being even less valued, but what was very far from correct was Clark's idea that a civil servant was necessarily an ignoramus.

That notion was not something recently conceived by Clark. As early as 1928, before his call to the Bar, in his first published work, a dreadful picaresque novel, *The Way of Lucifer*, he had put the following gem into the mouth of one of his characters: ' . . . a hard-working crew is just as necessary to the ship of State as it is to any other ship. They'll pick up all the knowledge they need as they go along and any knowledge beyond that is bad for them.' (The same applied to workers in general, rather than civil servants only): 'We've got to have workers, and an educated worker is a curse.'

It would be naughty to describe *The Way of Lucifer* as largely autobiographical, but the similarities are striking. The hero, Lucian Darrell Nation (D. Nation, or 'damnation'), ostensibly the son of a poor baronet (like Clark), educated at Eton (like Clark), is really the offspring of Lucifer himself, fathered upon the beautiful Lady Nation in return for a promise of limitless wealth and worldly success. The horror and shame of this secret lead to the baronet's suicide, and his lady's early death, leaving Lucian an orphan boy, immensely wealthy, handsome, endowed with supernatural abilities ensuring academic success at Eton and Trinity College, Cambridge, and absolute worldly success at the gaming table, particularly at Monte Carlo (the reputed source of Clark's wealth also). A whirl of Mediterranean yacht cruises and seductions with vodka and 'priceless hock from long blue Venetian glasses' lead to murder, by Lucian, and then attempted murder of Lucian himself by an avenger of one of the seduced innocents, many of these events being accompanied by 'mirthless laughter', by the strains of Lohengrin or Götterdämmerung, and by thunder and lightning. Finally, the fiend hero Lucian disappears with his assailant in a flash of lightning, to the sound of more mocking laughter, leaving behind no trace, 'only a great cabuchon ruby, like a drop of blood, and the broken blade of a long, keen knife'.

That was the first of Clark's two works of melodramatic fiction, the second taking the shape of a diabolical Command Paper (Appendix 2). If Sir Thomas Dugdale had read the novel, it may be doubted whether he would have accepted Maxwell Fyfe's advice to appoint the bold, bad, melodramatic baronet Sir Andrew Clark for an inquiry better suited to the more humdrum attention of worthy civil service knights.

Clark's flamboyant, swashbuckling activities during his week at Blandford were a seven days' wonder to the people of the county. R. Douglas Brown marvelled (op. cit., p. 88) at a demonstration given by Clark to the High Sheriff of Dorset and guests at a dinner party, of the shooting out of dining-table candles at fifteen paces with an eighteenth-century flint-lock pistol, and of the shooting of a hole in the mahogany dining-room door with a candle 'bullet'. As Brown said, Clark was indeed a 'card'. 'Flash', the word used of him by legal colleagues, seems to fit as neatly as doubtless did his 'magnificent collection' of 'fancy silk waistcoats . . . including one in silver-blue satin, embroidered with pink rosebuds, which he designed himself' (Brown, op. cit. p. 87).

Clark had been an unsuccessful Conservative candidate in the 1945 general election, and because of his own wealth, reputedly gained on the Stock Exchange and at Monte Carlo (Brown, op. cit. p. 87) as well as by his Chancery Bar earnings, his sympathy with both the wealthy and what might loosely be called the Conservative interest could be relied upon. Being wealthy, and a martyr to surtax and supertax, Clark was happy to waive a fee for his inquiry services, accepting instead untaxed reimbursement of hotel and other expenses. Understandably enough, he was hostile both to heavy taxation and to the bureaucratic apparatus which collected and expended the revenue. In his obituary notice in *The Daily Telegraph* of 22 May 1979, his uncompromising views expressed nearly twelve years before were quoted: 'I am sick to death of being the complete slave of the Inland Revenue. I am killing myself working nine days for them for the pleasure of keeping my tenth day's earnings to myself.' In the same obituary his Crichel Down finding of 'no trace of bribery, corruption or personal dishonesty' was cited, but with a significant later addition attributed to him: 'But he added that he had had to make the best of his way through an impenetrable tangle of secrecy, prevarication and inefficiency.'

With this, the nearest Clark ever came to an acknowledgement of failure to uncover the truth, one can return to the unlikely Commissioner's inquisition of Eastwood, the 'quick-fire succession of one hundred and eighteen questions' on Monday 26 April 1954, bearing in mind that on the previous Friday Wilcox, similarly martyrized by Clark and Stevenson, had proved himself to be — as Russell was to say in his summing-up — 'a hopeless witness'. He had been unable, although innocent, to defend himself from slurs such as 'dissembling', 'cooking something up' against Marten, and prying, from malice against Marten or at best from idle curiosity, into matters which were none of his business.

On 26 April 1954 Clark seemed determined to establish that when Eastwood and Thomson were made aware of previous applicants, there was no definite obligation to Tozer, that the idea that a commitment existed emanated from Thomson, and that Eastwood was 'completely dominated by Thomson' (Appendix 2, conclusion 15, 'obviously a strong character and determined to the extent of obstinacy in upholding his own views'). Clark's questioning of Eastwood therefore took the following line:

Q. Do you really ask me to believe that that was so definite that, when you found that a Government department (the head of which was one of the Commissioners) was much more deeply committed to 14 other people, you thought that little talk overrode the interests of those 14 other people and made a greater moral obligation? You are trying to be so fair: now do think!

A. Yes: I was trying to recollect my thoughts at the time. I think I must say that I did, yes.   (MAF 236/7)

(Clark was wrong to say there had ever been a 'deeper' commitment to others; some early applicants, *including* Tozer, had had routine letters from the ALC, but the deeper later commitment by Crown Lands was to Tozer and no one else, arising not from a 'little talk' but from an offer to him and an eager written acceptance by him, in the midst of meetings, negotiations, joint planning and inspections of properties, conducted on the authority of the Permanent Commissioner with the blessing of the Minister.)

Clark next quoted Eastwood's letter to Thomson of 23 March 1953, including the phrase 'at least appear to' (pp. 88 f.). Eastwood said 'I do not seek to excuse that sentence' and Clark gave a most condescending reply: 'One may write all sorts of very silly things on the spur of the moment which one regrets afterwards. We are all liable to that: no doubt I have done it myself on many occasions.' Clark went on:

If you are a gentleman with such high moral standards that you cannot back out of a tentative offer made to Mr. Tozer which he tentatively accepts and which you know is to be in no way binding, it seems to me to be incredible that a person with such high moral standards as that could think for one second of inventing a story to deceive fourteen other people.

Although Eastwood replied 'I must agree'—meaning, one has to suppose, that the suggestion was indeed incredible—Clark went on, by his reference to Eastwood being 'the serpent in the garden' and 'poor Mr. Wilcox' 'a very willing Eve' to declare his belief in the incredible. He next put forward a disingenuous solution of his own for the difficulty of inviting tenders for an equipped farm, when there was nothing visible but bare land:

But let me put it this way: you go out to one tenant and you say to Tozer: 'Look here, if we put up certain buildings, what sort of rent are you prepared to give?' and he says 'Well if you put up those buildings I will give you a rent of £3 an acre'. You say 'We are a public body: we cannot just take it, but provided that is at least near the best rent—we are not bound to go to the highest offer—we shall be prepared to take you as a tenant, but we have got to put it out to tender, specifiying the buildings you have agreed.' You consider the tenders. Everybody then has a chance to tender and you can judge whether Tozer's is a fair one or not.

Eastwood's response to this unfastidious suggestion was 'Yes. I think that would have been possible', and the exchange continued:

CLARK: If you had done that it would have been quite possible and we might probably never have had to hold this Inquiry.
Eastwood: Yes.
CLARK: Everybody might have been satisfied. I do not say they would have been, but they might have been. It is very, very unfortunate. You see, I cannot understand why you had this extraordinary feeling that you were so bound to Mr. Tozer. Really, it seems to have emanated from Mr. Thomson of Sanctuary and Son: they felt they were bound and you really relied on them, I think.
Eastwood: Yes, I am bound to confess that I did not consider the proposition you have just put, that we might have gone out to tender on the basis of buildings agreed with Mr. Tozer but not yet built. We did not consider that one at all, and I think that would have been a possible course.

'Possible' it might have been, but it might have led to more objections, moral, legal, and practical, than anything that was ever contemplated. Morally, the objection would have been that it involved 'cooking up' a 'dissembling' story to deceive other people into thinking a fair process of selection was going on when in reality the farm was being tailor-made to suit one particular applicant 'behind the backs', as *The Times* would have said, of 'previous owners and tenants' and 'local men'; had the obvious deception been exposed, real credibility would have been given to all sorts of rumours of dishonesty and corruption. Legally, the objection might have been that the real point of sale to Crown Lands was that they were best placed to carry out the legal requirement on the Minister to see that the land was farmed by someone he had good reason to think would farm the land properly; that could scarcely be achieved by the process of public tender so simply as by the method used, the selection, honestly carried out, of a tenant on the basis of known agricultural and financial competence, experience, and other qualifications. The practical objections would have included the fact that the process could not have been completed within the time Crown Lands had for decision, unless everything went more smoothly, without obstacles and objections, than anyone had any right to hope, given what had gone before in the story of Crichel Down.

Having disposed of a difficulty to his own satisfaction, Clark next turned to an overt attack on Thomson for his views on Marten as a possible Crown Lands tenant, and to a hectoring of Eastwood for defending him. The questions and answers went, in the shorthand record (MAF 236/7):

Q. Do you agree with that statement, that Commander Marten had behaved in such a way that you could not possibly have him as a tenant? Do you agree with that?

A. I think I would have found him rather a difficult tenant to deal with if the question had arisen.

Q. Why? (No answer)

Q. Why? What had he done? (No answer)

Q. 'After the way he has behaved.' What had Commander Marten done?

A. I think it was shortly before this — I am afraid I cannot remember the date — that I had had a very long conversation with him on the telephone when I was away on holiday in Cornwall, from which I certainly got the impression that he would be — what shall I say? — rather a difficult man to deal with.

Q. But you do not write that about anybody who may be difficult to deal with. I expect 90% of your tenants are difficult to deal with — tenants always are difficult to deal with.

A. Yes: I did not write this letter.

Q. I know that you did not. All that I am so surprised at is that you are trying to defend it now. When I put this letter I expected you to say to me: 'I cannot think what Thomson wrote that for. I expect I was thinking he was going away on holiday and that is why I did not answer it'. I expected you to say: 'If he had not been on holiday I should have said he seemed to be mistaken about Commander Marten'. I should have expected you to say that. I am going on with this because I am amazed that you support this letter and say you agree with it.

A. No, I do not entirely agree with it. I would not go as far as he is saying.

Q. I thought so. I am sorry you did not say so as soon as I put it to you. It would have saved a good deal of time and given a much better impression.

This marinading of Thomson for martyrization on his appearance must have given Stevenson the clearest possible indication of the line which the Commissioner would find acceptable in the cross-examination of the next chosen victim, and the way was thus prepared for Thomson's ordeal. Yet, from the accounts in *The Times* on Tuesday 27 April, under the headlines LAND AGENT'S EVIDENCE and SPEAK CAREFULLY ADVICE AT INQUIRY, no reader could have derived any clear idea of what was alleged against Thomson, except that he had shown hostility to Marten, and incurred the Commissioner's wrath.

On 28 April the headlines were UGLY STORY OF INTRIGUE and COUNSEL'S CLAIM AT INQUIRY. A diligent reader would have gained from the text the perplexing ideas that the Commissioner had said no evidence had been given to suggest corruption, that Stevenson had charged general incompetence by people who were prepared to embark on 'petty deception and intrigue', that Thomson had publicly apologized to Marten, and that Marten 'honestly believed that if his name had not been blackened by the local officials the land would have been returned to him'. So far as they went, the reports were not seriously incorrect in any single particular, but they were incomplete to the extent that even the most careful and reasonable reader might have been left feeling that there must have been some fire somewhere in the midst of all the smoke. What was not detectable from the reports was that the smoke rose from the 'cooking up' of burnt offerings from sacrificial animals: but so it was.

Much of the unpleasantness in store for Thomson on 26 and 27 April arose from his letter to Eastwood of 13 August 1953, the letter Eastwood had amazed Clark by supporting, rather than instantly disowning. The letter in question was peripheral to the main story and it was wrong to imply that it contained improper hostile allegations against Marten rather than honest professional advice, sought and given in confidence, on the consequences of Marten's declaration of war. Briefly, after Marten had threatened a 'row' (p. 96) Eastwood sent the papers to Thomson for his 'observations' (MAF/38). Immediately, in a prescient two-page letter, Thomson, about to go on holiday the next day, replied, giving the requested observations, which in any ordinary circumstances would have remained private, covered not by official secrecy but by the qualified privilege of professional advice. At the beginning of his letter, Thomson said:

From the correspondence alone I should say that Commander Marten was the last person we should want as a tenant.

I can only repeat that we are committed to Tozer. The row which Commander Marten is determined to make is clearly going to be very unpleasant for Tozer, and, to a less extent, for ourselves, and there is no doubt that everything possible will be done to embarrass both of us.

That was true enough: in a postscript Thomson developed his argument:

P.S. I do not wish to be misunderstood when I suggest that Tozer should be given an opportunity of withdrawing. The matter would not of course rest there. If you carried on with the proposal to acquire Crichel Down you would have to find a tenant, and you certainly could not have Commander Marten after the way he has behaved. We should have to find someone else as a tenant who combined Tozer's farming ability with a very thick skin. The new tenant would also have to have the same plans for farming Crichel Down as Tozer, otherwise we should have to modify the details of our lay-out but not, of course, the main outline.

This would not make matters any easier with Commander Marten, and my own view is that if you decide to carry on with the purchase of Crichel Down everything should be done to persuade Tozer to accept the tenancy which has been negotiated with him. This does not mean that he should not be told about what is going on.

It boils down to this:—

If you give way to Commander Marten's campaign, I think you should abandon altogether the proposal to buy Crichel Down, and leave the Ministry to get themselves out of the difficulty which has now been handed on to you.

Out of this frank letter, rather more hostile to the Ministry than to Marten (the references to the latter being quite restrained, given the circumstances, and the fact that Thomson was not bound by civil service rules and practices) Clark and Stevenson seized on the two offending remarks about Marten being 'the last person we should want as a tenant' and 'you certainly could not have Commander Marten after the way he has behaved'. Between them they gave Thomson as hard a time as they could, repeatedly and heartily inviting him to do what he had not done and did not do, i.e. make allegations against Marten.

The grilling of Thomson on 26 April 1954 began with Stevenson asking him to say what was the very worst thing Marten had done, at the time of the letter of 13 August 1953. 'Do not mince words' he said (MAF 236/7). The Commissioner had not yet ruled that the inquiry was not concerned with Marten's conduct. He did that later, when Russell was cross-examining Marten ' . . . it does not seem to me that this is an inquiry into Commander Marten's conduct one way or the other' (MAF 236/9). Still, it might have been wise for Thomson to decline what was an invitation to walk the plank. Instead, he merely said that, never having met Marten, all he knew was what he had seen in the press and in correspondence—that Marten was starting a public campaign to prevent the letting to Tozer: so, to accept Marten as tenant, in place of Tozer, would create a bad impression among other Crown tenants. They should always think that a local landowner had only to make a 'scene' and Crown Lands would give way, regardless of their commitments to their tenants.

Stevenson then tripped Thomson up, on the minor point that up to 13 August 1953 there had been nothing at all in the press. It was then also that Clark intervened to deliver to Thomson a solemn warning: 'You are not on oath and therefore I do ask you to remember that you should try, as a professional man, to speak as carefully as though you were. Please give careful consideration before you answer.' Asked by Stevenson to show any letter which would suggest Marten would be an unsuitable tenant, Thomson made no reply, and Clark enthusiastically took over the attack:

> You wrote this extraordinary letter. Do you usually write letters making allegations like that against people of eminent standing in the county and saying that they are not fit to be tenants without having any reason for making such allegations? I should imagine that you know very well why you made a statement such as that about a figure such as Commander Marten.

Thomson: I am sorry I cannot say anything on that all [*sic*]. I have no recollection of the correspondence.

CLARK: You will have an opportunity of looking at it tonight, and if you wish to correct that tomorrow and you would like to come back and point out to me when you have had time to look through all the correspondence, just what the letters were, I shall be delighted to give you an opportunity because I should not like to go away with the impression in my mind that you are the sort of man who makes these allegations without any foundation whatsoever. Therefore if you can find any foundation . for them I should like my mind disabused of the impression which I have at the moment that these allegations were made without one shred of evidence. I want to give you every possible opportunity to show me what were the grounds on which you made these two extraordinary statements. In that connection will you remember that the first one is made 'from the correspondence alone' so I want to see letters and letters only on that, and that the second one is that if you carried on with the proposal to acquire Crichel Down you would have to find a tenant and 'you certainly could not have Commander Marten after the way he has behaved'. That is an allegation of behaviour, and I want you to tell me the exact details of his behaviour which make you make that allegation. At the moment my impression is that both those statements were made out of pique and because you were cross, that you were afraid Commander Marten might thwart your own schemes. That is the impression I am left with. It may be a quite untrue one and I should hate to go away and report under a wrong impression, so I should like to give you every opportunity for finding out what the grounds were so that you can come to me tomorrow morning and show me what they were and disabuse my mind of the impression I have at the moment, which I shall be very sorry to go away with.

> If you cannot find out anything, then I shall be reluctantly left
> with the impression with which I am left at the moment.

Thomson: Yes, sir.

The Times report on 27 April of the same proceedings was even
more damaging to Thomson than Clark's allegation against him,
of 'an allegation of behaviour' against Marten, because Clark's
allegation was not reported: what was reported was an allegation,
by Stevenson, of 'a lie', in another letter by Thomson:

> What you wrote in that letter was a lie, was it not?
> Strictly speaking, it was not true (Laughter).   (MAF 236/7)

The occasion for this was nothing more serious than the wording
of a routine acknowledgement of a new application to rent Crichel
Down sent to Thomson: he wrote in acknowledgement (19 May
1953): 'It seems likely that this land will be handed over to the
Commissioners of Crown Lands, in which case your application will
have to be considered together with the others which have already
been received. At the moment we regret we can say no more than
this.' Stevenson had contended that by that date Thomson was
determined to consider no one but Tozer, and his offensive question
about 'a lie' followed directly on Thomson's explanation of the
reason for the dispatch of his non-committal routine letter: at that
date there was no certainty that Crown Lands would buy, or that
Tozer might not withdraw, or that Crown Lands would go on if
Tozer did withdraw. Nothing appeared in *The Times* to show either
the trivial nature of the allegation or Thomson's explanation of the
circumstances.

The next day, 27 April, the baiting and humiliation of Thomson
continued. What was reported in *The Times* the following day,
28 April 1954, under the headline 'UGLY STORY OF INTRIGUE' was
a very mixed bag, too mixed and condensed to enable a reader
to judge where any blame requiring apology might lie. There was
a report that Thomson had made an apology to Marten for using
'intemperate language' and that Clark had given the apology his
approbation, with the words 'I think that is a very proper attitude
to take.'

This brief mention was confusingly sandwiched between reported
statements by Clark (that no evidence had been given to suggest
corruption), by Stevenson (that there had been general incompetence

by people prepared to embark on 'petty deception and intrigue') and by Marten (of his honest belief that if his name had not been blackened by the local officials the land would have been returned to him). In fact what had emerged from Clark's mountainous Monday tirade against Thomson, alleging 'allegations of behaviour', and 'pique', and being 'cross' and 'afraid that Marten might thwart his schemes' was a brief explanation by Thomson that the 'correspondence' on which he had based the remarks in his letter of 13 August was the bundle of papers sent to him for his observations by Crown Lands, containing a file note of Marten's telephoned intention to call for a public inquiry if he did not get his way. Thomson then said: 'I should like to add, if I may, that I think now my language was intemperate and I should like to take this opportunity of apologizing publicly to Commander Marten for it' (MAF 236/8). And Clark said: 'Thank you very much: I think that is a very proper attitude to take. I am sure Commander Marten will think so too.' There is no record of what Marten may have thought, at this, the high point of irony in the whole Crichel Down story, but Brown (*The Battle of Crichel Down*, p. 100) says: 'Commander Marten rose in his seat and bowed to the witness.' The public apology for intemperate language, in the presence of Clark, Stevenson, and Marten (all three of whom had used far less temperate language) was doubtless made on legal advice, to bring the wretched proceedings to an end, but it stands out as too chivalrous, an apology where none was deserved.

On 28 April 1954 *The Times* recorded the ending of the inquiry on the previous day, and Clark's expressed intention to return the following day to London to work on his report 'at the weekend' and deliver it to the Minister the following week. Russell's and Widgery's rejections of Stevenson's accusations of intrigue and undue secrecy were recorded, with Russell's comments on them as 'quite unjustified' and containing 'cheap jibes' — and, a final puzzle, Clark's acceptance of Widgery's contention that there was 'not the slightest suggestion' of any improper motive on the part of Mr Thomson. This was odd, because Clark himself had added to Stevenson's suggestion of 'ugly intrigue' his own suggestion against Thomson of 'schemes', clearly in the dictionary sense of 'plans made in a secret, underhand way'. There had been frequent far from temperate suggestions of improper motive on the part of Thomson and others, never satisfactorily and clearly withdrawn, with or without apology.

After the inquiry nothing of significance appeared in *The Times* until 28 May 1954, when Dugdale was reported as having given a House of Commons reply to Crouch, the previous day, to the effect that he had had Clark's report for a fortnight and hoped to publish it soon. The first report of the contents came on 16 June 1954, and was even worse for the Government than anyone could have feared. Clark had taken longer than he had expected, but not long enough to eradicate grievous errors. The headlines ran: OFFICIALS CRITICIZED IN CRICHEL DOWN REPORT — DETERMINATION TO FOLLOW OWN PLANS — M.P.'S DISQUIET — MINISTER QUESTIONED ON ACTION TAKEN. The story was of indignant cries in Parliament of 'Robbery!' (because there was to be no sale to 'former owners') and of disquiet and incredulity among Conservative MPs over Sir Thomas Dugdale's 'bland conclusion' that in view of the nature of the mistakes and errors of judgement and the public way in which they had been exposed he need take no further action in relation to them. Crouch was reported 'hardly able to believe his ears'. Dugdale's statement was given, referring to Clark's final conclusion (Appendix 2, conclusion 25) that there was no trace of bribery, corruption, or personal dishonesty, and no legitimate complaint about the sale to Crown Lands or their subsequent letting: 'The inquiry has thus achieved my main purpose, which was to deal with any rumours and suggestions of this kind.'

On the same day, 16 June 1954, *The Times* published an editorial (titled, inappropriately, NABOTH'S VINEYARD) which perfectly illustrated the intoxicating effect of drinking from the poisoned well of the Clark report, the contents working as a hate-potion against the civil service:

Inquiry, detailed, acute and objective, has thrown disquieting light not only on how bureaucracy, left to itself, is capable of acting, but on the limits of a Minister's knowledge and control . . . The cruellest and most irresponsible maker of gibes against the arbitrary incompetence of bureaucracy could scarcely have invented Crichel Down.

The writer was wrong in every particular: cruel and irresponsible gibes, and *lack* of 'detailed, acute and objective' enquiry *had* 'invented Crichel Down'.

On 18 June 1954 the news was headed 'M.P.S' STORMY MEETING' and 'MINISTER CRITICIZED ON CRICHEL DOWN'. The story was of a two-and-a-half-hour meeting of 150 Conservative members of the party's *Agriculture and Food Committee*, strongly critical of the Minister and making many points of which the Minister undertook to take note, while making it clear that he felt it would be wholly improper for him to discuss with the Committee the actions of individual officials. A statement after the meeting said the Minister had 'stressed to the Committee his desire to accept, as Minister, full personal responsibility for the actions of his department'. It was a straightforward, proper and manly attitude which Dugdale was to maintain quite consistently throughout. His honesty was never questioned, although his cleverness was: the honesty was thought by many to be quixotic, or over-chivalrous to his officials, and the paradox was achieved of belief in the complete honesty of the man and yet some disbelief in the veracity of his words.

On 26 June 1954 Commander Marten reappeared in the news headlines: 'CRICHEL DOWN CHALLENGE — CDR MARTEN WRITES TO MINISTER', making a renewed claim for the land and expressing preparedness to buy it. (His views at that time are set out in Appendix 4.) There was also in the correspondence columns of *The Times* a lively series of letters to the editors uniformly hostile to the ministry, except for one on 28 June 1954, from Leonard Buxton, former Chairman of the Association of First Division Civil Servants, making two points. The first asked how civil servants could be expected to express their views with confidence to those responsible for decisions if what they wrote was not to remain confidential to those amongst whom it circulated, but could be sent *in toto* to an inquiry probing below the level at which the decision was taken. The second point was the danger of having only one person to conduct such an inquiry — 'I do not know Sir Andrew Clark, but can it be that more than one person could have signed the report as it stands?' — better, if such an inquiry occurred again to have at least three persons conduct it.

On the same day, 28 June 1954, there was a third editorial in *The Times*, titled STORM-SWEPT DOWN, saying: 'The Minister owes Parliament and the public (and COMMANDER MARTEN) an exhaustive explanation of the present entangled legal situation . . . '

As the climax approached, the parliamentary debate on Crichel Down, on 20 July 1954, Dugdale's fifty-seventh birthday, the view from Printing House Square had developed over the months from the first letter in *The Times* on 24 September 1953 into one of growing public suspicion, surprise, disquiet, and even alarm, particularly among the government's supporters. It built up (in the absence of satisfactory explanations or denials of what seemed an inexorable continuance of state socialism under bureaucratic dominance) into a crescendo of annoyance, exasperation, even rage. And yet, even when Clark's report was public, nothing much had been attempted, in the field of public relations, to calm things down.

The General View from Westminster

Those inside government and politics at Westminster, but outside the small circle of politicians and civil servants who had actually seen and worked on the increasing number of Crichel Down files, had had little more to go on than did the general public—the columns of *The Times* and other journals, some radio and less television, and a spate of uncontroverted rumours and gossip, most intense in Westminster, in parliament and its lobbies. A simple system of internal reporting of the facts to other departments, without despised public relations or propaganda skills, would have helped, at least to ensure better-informed preparation in these other departments of briefs and memoranda for cabinet and cabinet committee discussion, better-informed discussions between Ministers, and better understanding and recording of their discussions by the cabinet secretariat.

For illustration of the mischievous spread of misinformation, at the very centre of government, one has merely to look at some other departments' contributions to cabinet committees' Crichel Down discussions. Wider internal circulation of the facts would have prevented such errors: once made, they could have been corrected only through wider internal circulation of the cabinet papers containing them, and the lucky chance that they might have been seen by some official with the necessary knowledge to detect errors and the courage, tactlessness, or pedantry to insist on their being brought to notice. As there are in the index to Cabinet papers in the Public Record Office a couple of dozen references to Crichel Down submissions to cabinet committees or to the full cabinet, the risk of error and of confusion was great.

One group of cabinet papers goes some way to explaining the aged Prime Minister's confusion over the Crichel Down case. Even a much younger, fitter statesman than Churchill then was, and one less preoccupied with great, global issues, would have had difficulty in grasping the problems as put to the cabinet on 29 December 1953.

The preparation of that submission had really begun in September 1953, just before Lord Woolton relinquished his 'Overlord' role in Agriculture. Woolton, one of the first of Churchill's ministers to become aware that the inquiry was to be what he 'called 'a troublesome affair' (MAF 236/12) appointed a subcommittee of the Home Affairs Committee to go into it, consisting of the Home Secretary as chairman, with the Law Officers, the Minister of Agriculture and the Secretary of State for Scotland as members. Subsequently, because of his increasing concern 'with the political aspects' (MAF 236/12) Woolton himself joined the subcommittee. He became satisfied there had been no corruption, but there would be criticism of the departmental handling of the matter 'with consequent embarrassment for the Minister' and the Law Officers were 'much concerned' over the question of privilege and the possible calling for and examining of minutes passed inside the department. So Woolton asked Dugdale to prepare a memorandum for the Home Affairs Committee, which came before them on 15 December 1953. In it he gave the history, making no mistakes beyond an insignificant passing reference (CAB 134/912) to purchase by the Air Ministry 'at the outbreak of war', before going on to make perfectly clear his support (despite practical difficulties) for 'a moral claim' by former owners, a right of pre-emption not dependent on whether the land was acquired in war or peace, or whether it was agricultural land or not: 'In his view, although the former owner had no legal right, he had a strong moral claim to be allowed to have back his land where it was no longer needed for the purpose for which it was originally taken from him against his will. Such a view would, he thought, be consistent with general Conservative philosophy' (CAB 134/912).

Then the fun started, according to the minutes. The Solicitor-General opined there was no strong claim to a pre-emptive right, merely a claim to an equal opportunity to buy on the open market. The War Office representative (Parliamentary Secretary) suggested limitation to agricultural land. The Minister of Works (Eccles) said it was not unreasonable for the government to keep land for a new 'good purpose' and there was no reason to think that other public authorities accorded such rights to previous owners. The Ministry of Supply representative (Parliamentary Secretary) agreed with the War Office view that the idea should be confined to agricultural land. The Lord Privy Seal (Crookshank) doubted whether distinction could be made between agricultural and industrial property. The Lord Chancellor (Lord Simonds, a very distinguished lawyer and judge) said it would not be possible to establish a right to buy back without so hedging it round with so many reservations that the right would be largely meaningless; so he supported further examination by a subcommittee. As chairman, Woolton came down in favour of a subcommittee to examine further the matter of principle, leaving the only urgent case, Crichel Down, to be decided in the light of its particular circumstances, while the general principle would be considered at more leisure.

Thus Dugdale, although himself in favour of the principle so strongly urged upon him by organized pressures, not only from the Marten campaign but by the Country Landowners' Association, the National Farmers' Union, and by MPs of his own party, was getting insufficient support from his colleagues to carry the day. He tried again, according to the minutes of the same meeting of 15 December 1953 (CAB 134/912):

The Minister of Agriculture said that the Crichel Down case presented special difficulties which it would be easier to resolve in the light of such a general principle as he had suggested. He had a duty under the Agriculture Act, 1947, to see that if agricultural land belonging to the Government was disposed of, the new owners were in a position to farm it adequately in the interests of maximum food production. In the case of Crichel Down he had come to the conclusion that this duty would best be discharged if the land were transferred to the Commissioners for Crown Lands. They had agreed to co-operate and had found a very suitable tenant. In view of the confusion which had arisen, however, and of suspicions which had been aroused that there had been irregularities in its disposal, he had announced on 11th November the appointment of a Committee [*sic*] of Inquiry to examine the circumstances in which it had been decided to dispose of the land to the Commissioners of Crown Lands. The inquiry was due to open on 4th January. If the Committee agreed that as a general principle, and subject to the safeguards he proposed, a pre-emptive right should in future be given to former owners, this would give him some room for manoeuvre in trying to devise a solution to the Crichel Down problem which would have regard to the moral claims of the former owners.

What that solution might have been was not revealed: the minutes go straight on to record the Solicitor-General's observation that 'if the Committee of Inquiry was proceeded with' (the word 'Committee' being altered rather than corrected to 'Court', in manuscript, in the PRO records), it would be necessary for the government to decide whether Crown privilege should be claimed. The minutes also recorded his fundamental objection (the word 'only' in the following extract is a manuscript addition to the PRO typescript minutes): 'The giving at this stage of an opportunity to the former owner only might give occasion for criticism that the Government had bowed to pressure in the Crichel Down case.'

On that objection, the Chairman closed the discussion, making a suggestion 'generally acceptable to the Committee' that the case raised issues of considerable importance and that a subcommittee of ministers should be appointed 'to examine the question of according a pre-emptive right to former owners on the lines suggested by the Minister of Agriculture, with particular reference to the Crichel Down case'.

The formal wording of the conclusion was:

The Committee:—

Invited the Chancellor of the Duchy of Lancaster to arrange for the appointment of a small Committee of Ministers:—

(i) to consider further, in consultation as necessary with other Ministers departmentally concerned, the changes proposed by the Minister of Agriculture in M.A.(53)137 in the present policy governing the disposal of land compulsorily acquired for public purposes, and to make recommendations thereon;

(ii) in the light of their recommendations under (i) above, to review the arrangements made for the disposal of Crichel Down, Dorset;

(iii) to consider the implications of the Court of Inquiry into the procedure adopted for the disposal of Crichel Down.

Thus by December 1953, responsibility for Crichel Down had been collectivized in three cabinet committees, or one committee (the Home Affairs Committee) and two subcommittees. Before the end of the month the full cabinet made a fourth collectivity caught up in the thicket of problems. Woolton suggested, to the Law Officers, that they circulate a cabinet paper on the question concerning them, crown privilege in the inquiry; to Dugdale, that the Prime Minister would like a report from him; and to the Prime Minister, a request for early cabinet discussion. Time was short when Woolton put his request to Churchill on 23 December 1953, with Clark due to hold a preliminary meeting on 29 December and to open the inquiry on 4 January 1954. Churchill decided on 26 December 1953: 'This seems to raise some most important issues. It should come before Cabinet on Tuesday.' (MAF 236/12, 'Tuesday' being 29.12.53.) With this collectivization of responsibility in the full cabinet and three of its committees, and the imminent 'individualization' of responsibility for inquiry in the hands of a sole Commissioner, neither the Minister, nor his officials, nor Crown Lands, nor the Agricultural Land Commission, nor the Lands Service, had much left to contribute. Power to decide was now in the hands of people with insufficient time and knowledge to make sense of what had been a simple bucolic dispute but had now become Byzantine in its metropolitan ramifications.

On 29 December 1953, between Christmas and New Year celebrations, Churchill and his cabinet had before them (just after a railway strike item and just before one on Somali grazing rights in Ethiopia) the Law Officers' paper on crown privilege (CAB 129/54, memo C(23) 61) beginning, in the gloomy tone suited to Crichel Down: 'A difficult and embarrassing question has arisen in connection with the public inquiry.'

The difficulty was the terms of reference, regarded by the Law Officers as so widely drawn that any attempt to comply literally with them must involve a radical departure from the established practice (evidenced by leading cases cited) whereby crown privilege had always been claimed in respect of disclosure of official minutes and briefs for ministers, and in respect of oral evidence by officials of such kinds of advice. To set a precedent of disclosure would make it difficult to refuse a similar demand at every future public inquiry affecting any department:

We understand that it is proposed to call as witnesses the two Parliamentary Secretaries and several senior officials of the Ministry of Agriculture and Crown Lands Commission, and, in view of certain unfortunate passages in the correspondence already disclosed, there is bound to be cross-examination as to the exact course of events. Failure then to insist upon Crown Privilege in relation to documents and to oral evidence would create a very dangerous precedent, as already explained. On the other hand, insistence upon privilege would be open to damaging criticism, both as being unfair to officials who ought to be entitled to defend themselves, and also as being inconsistent with the terms of reference.

This dilemma must however be resolved on grounds of policy, and Counsel instructed accordingly, unless the inquiry is to be abandoned and some form of confidential investigation substituted for it.

The dilemma was thus designated one of policy rather than law, on which the Law Officers eschewed recommendations. The cabinet also had before it, instead of the more usual departmental memorandum, factual information (of unstated origin) later incorporated in the minutes, containing one seriously misleading error to add to the prejudicial effect of the phrase in the memorandum about 'certain unfortunate passages in the correspondence'. The new error had to be added to the now standard error about the acquisition date ('at the outbreak of war'); it was the false idea that Commander Marten and others had made applications which had been 'disregarded'. In any ordinary use of the word that put the Ministry pervasively in the wrong: that 'disregarded' itself disregarded the phenomenal amount of ministerial and official work, trouble — and, unfortunately, time — put into the only applications to buy ever made, those by Taylor and those on behalf of the Crichel Estate. Even the former, although thought unrealistic, had not been 'disregarded'. The Cabinet record, including the errors, was as follows:

The Cabinet were informed that about one third of the former Crichel Down bombing range had previously belonged to the father-in-law of a certain Commander Marten. It had been acquired at the outbreak of war under threat of the use of compulsory powers and on payment of a suitable price together with a substantial sum for 'injurious affection'. When the range was no longer required by the Air Ministry, the land had been handed over to the Agricultural Land Commission, who had farmed it on behalf of the Ministry of Agriculture. At a later stage the Ministry had decided to dispose of the land and had been advised that, in the interests of food production, it should continue to be farmed as a single unit and for this purpose should be equipped with buildings at substantial expense. Commander Marten and others had asked for an opportunity to buy the land, but their applications had been disregarded and it had been decided to sell the land to the Commissioners of Crown Lands, who had subsequently entered into a binding contract with a certain Mr. Tozer, who had taken possession of the land as a tenant. These proceedings had given rise to local accusations of malpractice by officials, and in these circumstances the Minister of Agriculture had announced in the House of Commons on 11th November that a public enquiry would be held by Sir Andrew Clarke Q.C., with the detailed terms of reference reproduced in paragraph 2 of C (53) 361.

The Minister of Agriculture said that, at a preliminary hearing that morning, Sir Andrew Clarke had agreed to adjourn the opening of the enquiry from 4th January to 21st April. This would give the Government more time in which to consider, not only the difficult questions raised in C (53) 361, but the wider possibility of modifying the present policy governing the disposal of land compulsorily acquired, but no longer required, for public purposes.

The Home Secretary said that a Sub-Committee of the Home Affairs Committee, over which he had presided, had considered the implications of the forthcoming public enquiry into this matter. They had felt no doubt that the Government must adhere to the decision that a public enquiry should be held, in spite of the difficulties described in C (53) 361. On the question of Crown privilege it was his view that the Government should stand by the disclosure of interdepartmental correspondence which had already been made, but should try to avoid making available additional documents, including Departmental minutes and advice from officials to Ministers. He recognized, however, that it might be necessary for the Government to indicate their readiness to consider on its merits any request for further information that might be made as the enquiry proceeded.

The Lord Chancellor said that the terms of reference for this enquiry were unusually wide and would make it exceedingly difficult for the Government to attempt to withhold information without exposing themselves to the criticism that they were stultifying the enquiry which they had themselves ordered.

The Attorney-General said that, at the preliminary hearing that day, Sir Andrew Clarke had indicated that he would expect to be provided with all information necessary to enable him to conduct the enquiry effectively.

On the question of the policy governing the disposal of land compulsorily acquired for public purposes, the view was expressed, and found support, that, while no hard and fast rule could be laid down, it should be generally recognized that, unless there was some clear reason to the contrary, a former owner of land or his representative ought normally to be given an opportunity to recover his land when it was no longer required for the purpose for which it had been acquired.

The Cabinet—

Invited the Home Secretary's Committee, with the addition of the Lord Chancellor, to continue their investigation both of the policy governing the disposal of land compulsorily acquired for public purposes and the extent to which advantage could properly be taken of the doctrine of Crown privilege in the forthcoming Crichel Down Enquiry, and to submit their findings and recommendations to the Cabinet before Parliament re-assembled.   (CAB 128/26)

The confusion over the terms of reference, their breadth or narrowness, is explained later (p. 165 f.) but the degree of confusion in the mind of the Prime Minister who presided over the cabinet meeting on 29 December 1953 may be judged from the record of a conversation with him, the following morning, 30 December 1953, made by his physician, Lord Moran, in his diary entry for that day, and published in his memoir *Winston Churchill: the struggle for survival 1940–1965* (p. 517 f.). If one accepts Moran's record, and if Churchill was speaking candidly, little room is left for doubt that the Prime Minister had been quite unable to grasp the problem which the Crichel Down affair presented; and that the errors in the cabinet papers were partly to blame for the muddle he was making of it:

I went into his room with his breakfast. Before I could say good morning he barked out what was in his mind. Government, he grumbled, has become more complicated than it used to be.

'You mean Labour is difficult and has more say in things?'

'Oh no, it's worse than that, we have to consider intricate matters, valuations and that kind of thing, which never came before the Cabinets I can remember. For example, some agricultural land was requisitioned during the war as a bombing range. Now for some reason they no longer want it as a range.'

'You mean Crichel Down?'

'Yes. It would seem proper in the circumstances to return it to its owner, who is asking that his ancestral acres be returned to him, with of course such compensation as may be agreed. But not at all—the government department concerned wants to take it over as Crown Lands, though nationalization of land is against Tory policy. It seems to me all wrong. The land was taken for military purposes in a national emergency; it is no longer needed, and cannot be retained for some other purpose.'

He yawned noisily. 'I get very tired when I do anything. My back aches, and I don't want to tackle a difficult job. No zest. No energy.'

Moran's response was to remind his patient that when he last saw him he had some thoughts of retiring, and to record Churchill's reaction to that suggestion:

'Oh,' he answered in an off-hand way. 'I'm not thinking of that. I don't want you to think I'm in a bad way. Yesterday I was as clear-headed at the end of the Cabinet as I was when it began. I sleep well: it is a great blessing. Nature ought to make some provision that as we get older we sleep more and more. A time would come when we might sleep eighteen out of the twenty-four hours, though when we were awake we should be nearly as good as ever.'

When the cabinet considered on 18 January 1954 the findings of the Home Secretary's committee (C54/16) they had before them the committee's unanimous recommendation that no statutory right of pre-emption should be accorded to previous owners. Instead, the 'general view' of the committee was in favour of the adoption in future of an 'administrative practice', in regard to agricultural land acquired by a department possessing compulsory powers (whether used or not), of notification to the owner or successor in title to the whole or part of the land, if traced without undue difficulty. Such persons should then have an opportunity of purchasing it in competition, the preferable methods being by public auction or public tender. Even this practice should be announced with 'all due caution', making it clear that departure from what was intended to be normal administrative practice might be unavoidable in particular cases, and that it would not apply to land which had been 'developed' by putting up buildings other than purely agricultural buildings. Once again, a point of legal difficulty having been referred to the lawyers to be straightened, it had returned from their workshops subtly wrought into a delicate, double-edged weapon. Dugdale and Stuart did not consider a former owner's strong moral claim would be adequately met by an equal opportunity with others, but only by 'first refusal'; but the general view was against this as tending to give a former owner a financial advantage, like a pre-emptive right, to which he was not entitled, and there would be pressure to make it a statutory right. The general view was also that there should be no retrospective application to Crichel Down, although Dugdale was recorded as considering it 'regrettable that Cdr. Marten should be able to derive no advantage from the change in Government practice which will have been brought about in part as a result of his representations'. (CAB 128/27)

The outcome of the cabinet meeting of 18 January 1954 was a further deferment of decision on the questions of 'a statutory right of pre-emption' and of 'no retrospection', but specific approval, in regard to Crichel Down, of recommendations that there should be full disclosure of evidence to Clark, for him to decide on grounds of relevance (rather than Crown privilege) what additional documents should be made available; further, that the Minister of Agriculture should take no initiative towards securing a withdrawal of the inquiry or a limitation of its terms of reference, or restriction of its scope in practice; that the Minister should arrange for Mr Russell to be instructed that his general approach to the inquiry should be on the lines that he was appearing on behalf of the Minister, who desired him to assist the conduct of the inquiry in every possible way. (On this last point, the actual recommendations made to the cabinet had included the sinister old idea of 'not defending the indefensible': 'The Committee considered that it would be right that Mr. Russell should put his cards on the table and not attempt to defend those actions of officials revealed in the documents already disclosed or to be disclosed, which were clearly indefensible.')

Already, therefore, before the inquiry, the general viewpoint of those in government, from the Prime Minister down, was blurred and wrapped in gloom. When even senior members of the cabinet were misinformed of the Crichel Down facts and unable to agree on future policy in land transactions, they could hardly explain the problem convincingly to back-benchers, who became increasingly impatient and exasperated, and more inclined to accept both the hostile propaganda and the persistent rumours of 'something worse than inefficiency' on the part of the civil service. The unpleasing impression the cabinet itself had been given was one of bad work by officials which it would be prudent to cover up — not exactly a case, in Clark's phrase, of 'cooking up a story to deceive other people' but one of belief that there was much to hide, of regret that an inquiry with such a wide scope had been appointed, and of hope to limit the publicly visible damage likely to be suffered.

The View from Whitehall Place

Out of the 12,000 civil servants in the Ministry of Agriculture, in Whitehall Place and other London and provincial offices, perhaps not more than 100 or so would have learned anything of Crichel Down before the public controversy. The vast majority, in the absence of full internal reporting of the facts, had little more to rely on than the press, tempered by professional knowledge that allegations of authoritarian behaviour could scarcely be true of a departmental civil service dedicated, perhaps more than any other department, to helping, advising and co-operating with their clientele of landowners and farmers. Persistent rumours of inefficiency, insensitivity and even corruption, going far beyond the usual run of music-hall banter, were particularly damaging to reputation and morale throughout the period of the campaign. By the time the Clark report was published, manifestly hostile to the civil service, the resentment was such that one of the first steps taken by the Permanent Secretary (Hitchman) was to report to the Minister in a secret minute of 17 May 1954:

I feel I ought to put before you at this stage certain considerations relating to the morale of the Ministry's staff.

2. In the first place, the propriety of a public — as distinct from a private — enquiry is being challenged by the staff here, and will perhaps be challenged by the Civil Service as a whole. There is an undoubted case to answer here, not only because it is obvious that the normal strict practices governing the secrecy of documents have gone by the board, but because there are important precedents for private enquiries.

3. I must also report to you that, in my opinion, there has been a feeling that the staff of the Ministry did not receive fair play at the enquiry. This arises no doubt to some extent from a belief that it was unfair that the proceedings should take place in public. But there is certainly a strong impression that Mr. Melford Stevens [*sic*] treated certain witnesses in an unfair way. And I must also say that, in my opinion, there is a feeling that Sir Andrew Clark himself did not display complete objectivity and lack of prejudice. I realise that it may well be answered that such a feeling is natural bias resulting from a proper loyalty to colleagues under criticism. Indeed, it is a bias I myself may well share. Nevertheless, I feel that I must bring this view of mine to your notice.

4. This could all be dealt with reasonably well if Sir Andrew Clark's report itself is regarded by the staff as fair and presenting a reasonably fair and true picture of, and commentary on, what happened; or alternatively, if they can be brought to feel that a true and fair assessment of it is reached by Ministers and made public. Such a true and fair assessment cannot be reached until the persons criticised in the report have had an opportunity of explanation and defence and until these comments have been reviewed in a proper way. In view of this, it would be wrong for me to attempt to comment on Sir Andrew Clark's report at this stage. I feel, however, that it is not a foregone conclusion that Sir Andrew Clark's report presents a reasonably fair and true picture of, and commentary on, what happened. In order to avoid, if I can, any appearance of bias, I should perhaps say that in my opinion Sir Andrew Clark in his Conclusions might have criticised the Ministry's Headquarters more than he did in at least one particular.

5. I would much have preferred not to put these points to you at this stage. I feel I must do it for the following reasons.—

    (i) If justice is to be done, and seen to be done, to the staff of the Ministry and to the Agricultural Land Commission (not to mention Crown Lands and their agents, for whom I have no responsibility) proper time must be given for an adequate review of Sir Andrew Clark's report. There will no doubt be much pressure for early publication and a quick expression of the Government's views. I do most earnestly beg that this be resisted, although naturally, in everyone's interest, the matter must be dealt with as quickly as possible.

(ii) To explain why I recommend that nothing should be done at any stage until a final view has been reached which would imply either approval or criticism of Sir Andrew Clark's report.

6. I propose, if you agree, to let Sir Edward Bridges have a copy of this minute.   MAF 236/16)

There seems to be no written evidence of the Minister's response. But despite the clamour for early publication he did resist that pressure, as Hitchman had begged him to do (i above), and, as Hitchman recommended (ii above), he resolutely did nothing meanwhile to imply approval or disapproval of the Clark report, until there had been a review and a decision, by himself, against further punishment of officials. Dugdale at that period must have felt that practically every man's hand was against him, or, if not against him, against any conceivable course of action that might be suggested. There was no way of meeting the conflicting wishes of Prime Minister, cabinet colleagues, party, agricultural, and landowning pressure groups, lawyers, complainants, and petitioners. Such measures as sale to Crown Lands, and the later appointment of a public inquiry, had merely sown more dragons' teeth.

Dugdale's relatively few defenders and real sympathizers seemed to be limited to those who had themselves served in Whitehall Place. These included, paradoxically, the Opposition's agriculture spokesmen such as Tom Williams (later Lord Williams) the Minister of Agriculture in the previous Labour government, and George Brown (later Lord George-Brown) who had been Parliamentary Secretary. For a Conservative minister under repeated attack and angry criticism by his own party, the friendliness of the opposition, like the well-meaning efforts of his dedicated but discredited officials, could be the kiss of death.

From the announcement of the public inquiry in November 1953 until the Clark report was received by the Minister and comments on it were sought by him, there had been quite remarkable restraint shown, by the Minister himself and by all the officials concerned, in their references to their tormentors. The very worst thing on record in an official file written by a civil servant about Marten (who had believed his name had been 'blackened' by officials) was a harmless, half-puzzled, half-jocular remark.

The author of the remark was Middleton, writing to Hole on 21 September 1953: 'I cannot understand Commander Marten's alleged remarks and can only infer that the mention of the cottages was rather a swift one.' It arose from a triviality, a perfectly natural misunderstanding of Marten's own statements that the Crichel Estate had 'ear-marked four cottages' at Long Crichel to house farm workers (p. 93), and earlier that they had 'cottages available without building any more' (p. 52) which they had 'kept clear' (p. 93). Wilcox, taking this to mean that cottages needing a government licence to build and attracting a government grant were standing empty (which turned out not to be so), had asked Hole whether he could 'throw any light' on how a licence could have been obtained in 1950 for building them, and Hole had passed on the enquiry to Middleton for reply. Clark used this minor matter of Wilcox's Treasury-minded or audit-minded query in order to level at Wilcox an accusation (Appendix 2, para. 91) of trying to bring up something to Marten's detriment. As Marten was in 1950 still a serving officer in the Royal Navy and had nothing to do with the building and licensing of the cottages there could have been nothing to his discredit about the licensing. Wilcox's only faults lay in believing, from Marten's words, that the cottages were empty (not in asking why) and in being trapped and bullied by Clark into an admission of 'idle curiosity' which did him less than justice and which he afterwards bitterly regretted (p. 183). Middleton's remark apart, and a few acidulous comments which the legal department permitted themselves when the question of costs came up, the records show remarkable official sympathy with Marten's claims and feelings rather than hostility, from the Minister down, throughout. The highly unofficial comments of the Minister's unofficial liaison officer Colonel Trumper about 'a long tale of woe from one Commander Marten' were in a different category (Appendix 2, para. 94), and merely serve to underline the restraint and patience exercised by the Minister and his officials.

Thus, when the senior men in the Ministry drafted the terms of reference, within the Ministry, at a meeting on 22 October 1953, with the Parliamentary Secretary (Lords), Lord Carrington, they were not worried about any accusations of hostility or lack of sympathy or fairness; their concern in drafting was not about rumours of corruption either, but to ensure that the inquiry did not stray outside the Ministry's business into the wide policy question of a possible future right of pre-emption by former owners (MAF 236/12). That wider policy question was already being considered in the cabinet committee system and it would have been quite out of order for the Minister of Agriculture to ordain an inquiry trenching on it. The early draft produced was quite clear, and was approved the same day by the Minister, subject to consultation by him that afternoon with the Home Secretary, Sir David Maxwell Fyfe, the same eminent lawyer-politician who had advised Clark's appointment:

To inquire into and report upon the procedure adopted in reaching the decision that land at Crichel Down should be sold to the Commissioners of Crown Lands and in the selection of a tenant by them, excluding consideration of whether the policy should have been to give preferential treatment to any particular applicant on grounds of previous ownership or occupation.

Maxwell Fyfe transformed the final version from horse into camel: it emerged from the consultation with him enormously stretched by the addition of the phrase 'and the circumstances in which those decisions were made' and intendedly narrowed by the exclusion of all policy questions, until it read (as in Appendix 2, para. 1) as follows, with the material changes from the earlier version shown here in italics:

To *enquire* into the procedure adopted (a) in reaching the decision that land at Crichel Down should be sold to the Commissioners of Crown Lands; (b) in the selection of a tenant by them; *and the circumstances in which those decisions were made*, but excluding from the enquiry *all questions of governmental policy and, in particular, any question of* whether preferential treatment should have been given to any applicant on the ground of previous ownership or occupation of the land.

The deletion of the requirement 'to report', in the second version, is a mere oddity: it did not, alas, prevent Clark reporting. But the addition of instructions to inquire into the circumstances in which decisions were made but to exclude all questions of policy made nonsense of the original, through exclusion of all the circumstances of agricultural law, policy, advice, and information without which the decisions were inexplicable. The earlier version, excluding only the one consideration of preferential treatment for previous owners, but confining the inquiry to procedure, would have been more realistic, despite the notorious difficulties of an agreed dichotomy between policy and procedure.

The terms of reference once decided, the punctilious course was for the laymen to leave the preparations for the duel in the hands of the lawyers on both sides to arrange: and this was done. There followed a laborious dredging through and copying of all the documents, a process which revealed early to both sides that evidence of corruption or anything like it was completely lacking. The inquiry, therefore, looked unnecessary and undesirable; but it was unstoppable, after the cabinet decision on 18 January 1954 that the Minister should take no initiative to stop or modify it (p. 161). To one side at least, the Ministry's legal department, the lack of evidence of corrupt behaviour was neither a surprise nor a disappointment, but they were less happy to find in the official papers statements and details which they took to be mistakes. They then set their minds, and Counsel's briefs, defensively, not to concealment—the other side had the documents too—but to a strategy of minimizing reference to them in discussion, as matters of unimportant detail. It is not clear how many people apart from Counsel were made aware of the cabinet's decision not to 'defend the indefensible', but the general strategy adopted was passive resistance.

Until the 'unfortunate passages' surfaced, and the horrid complexity of the case was appreciated, the Ministry's legal department had regarded the proposed inquiry as one of no great importance, which could be handled with the aid of junior counsel engaged at the Treasury's usual daily rates. The appointment of Clark and of an eminent Queen's Counsel by the other side forced them to change their minds and to seek an unsympathetic Treasury's approval for unprecedented extra expense, a discomfort only partly relieved by Clark's readiness to act on the basis of expenses only. The other discomfort, the 'unfortunate passages', was more lasting. The 'mistakes' were believed to occur mostly in Brown's draft report (p. 65 f.), so the legal department, correctly believing that his report had not had the great influence which the other side attributed to it, took action to cut his prepared evidence about it 'to the bone', in the erroneous belief that he had gone wrong over the poor state of the land in the 1930s, over the conveyances 'by agreement', and over the Hardings' uncultivated land. Brown himself, although understandably losing confidence in the correctness of some of the points in his report derived from his notes of Ferris's recollections, had been quite anxious to give full and frank evidence, and was afterwards so angry at his treatment by all concerned before and at the inquiry and in the report that he resigned (in June 1954, even before the Minister did), justifiably incensed about his treatment by friend and foe alike (MAF 236/68).

The Ministry's lawyers were also inhibited in presentation of the defence by the unfortunate fact that the protracted consideration of Marten's application had so upset plans and so delayed equipment and water supply that Ferris had been left with no alternative but to go on, for one harvest more than the land could stand, producing 'white straw' arable crops, without rotation, so bringing on 'take-all' damage, wiping out the profit of previous years, and exposing the government's farming to ridicule. Attacking the other side, over that, given the Commissioner's evident sympathies and antipathies, and the state of public opinion, and the cabinet's growing anxieties about the extent of political damage, would have been hazardous: 'least said, soonest mended' seems to have been the view taken by the Ministry's legal department in preparing the evidence, in briefing counsel, and in advice to the prospective witnesses.

It is therefore mildly surprising that when Marten's solicitors on several occasions took the initiative of suggesting the abandonment of the inquiry, the Ministry's solicitors did not leap at the chance. There may have been some failure to communicate to the Ministry's solicitors the exact terms of the cabinet's decision of 18 January 1954, that the Minister should take no initiative towards a withdrawal of the inquiry (p. 161), but the record (by the most senior of the Ministry's lawyers, A. R. Astley Weston, MAF 236/38) is one of initiatives by Marten's Bournemouth solicitors, Preston & Redman:

On the 11th December Commander Marten's solicitors had written without prejudice indicating that he would be ready to withdraw his opposition if Mr. Tozer, the Crown Lands tenant, could be persuaded to give up the land and if then the land was put up for sale by public auction. In that event, Commander Marten, it was stated, could see no necessity for the holding of a Public Inquiry (see GEN 451/2 dated 15th December 1953, paragraph 13). It was not at that time possible to answer that letter and Commander Marten's Solicitors have revived the suggestion in a letter of 15th February.

What seems to have happened (MAF 236/39) is that between December 1953 and February 1954, in various letters and telephone conversations, Marten's solicitors had stated that their client had never alleged corruption, and was prepared to agree a formula for publication to the effect that, although he considers a muddle was made of the whole matter he has found no evidence of corruption, and as the land is to be sold by public auction [*sic*], he has achieved his object, and can see no necessity for the inquiry to be held — please tell us frankly if the suggestion which eminated [*sic*] from us is impracticable.

Their client was prepared to pay, £15,000 for the land, £2,000 towards getting Tozer out, and also tenant right, and for fertilizers applied since 29 September 1953; he was also prepared to let Strange and Hooper and Harding have such areas as would ensure best distribution of land from the point of view of maximum production. And if there was any possibility of a settlement on these lines, Mr Neville-Jones of Preston & Redman 'would be pleased to come up to London provided he can talk to someone who is in a position to take decisions'.

The last exchange of letters in this abortive scheme of settlement was the solicitors' letter of 15 February 1954 and the legal department's reply of 19 February 1954 to the effect that the procedure and practice for release of lands acquired for defence purposes were under the consideration of a committee, as stated in the House of Lords by the Lord Chancellor, and that the Legal Department had no instructions which would enable them to reply to the suggestion. In other words, there was no one 'in a position to take decisions', and so far as the Ministry of Agriculture was concerned the proffered olive branch was rejected.

There is some evidence, however, of a later and strictly confidential suggestion made by the Law Officers to Melford Stevenson, counsel for Marten, early in April, 1954. According to that evidence (a brief note in the papers at Crichel House recording a telephone conversation between Marten's solicitors and counsel) Melford Stevenson had been sent for by the Law Officers, and the suggestion was put to him that if Marten could arrange with Tozer some reasonable consideration for giving up the land, the government 'would put pressure on Crown Lands to find an alternative farm for Tozer', but that short of something of that sort being arranged there was nothing that could be done for Marten in connection with getting the land. Once again, nothing came of the suggestion, and the inquiry proceeded as if no such remarkable ideas for dispensing with it had ever been conceived on either side — if indeed there could be said to be only two sides, not the three that the final proposal seems to suggest. So the government's trumpet, or trumpets, made a highly uncertain sound as their champions prepared, not so much for battle as for a meek form of passive resistance, without weapons, going like lambs to the slaughter.

The Inquiry Record

The shorthand record of the seven days of the inquiry runs to many hundreds of pages — never published. Clark himself supposed that both the documentary evidence and the transcript of the proceedings would appear with his report. In the typescript of the report presented by him to the Minister, both are shown as proposed Annexures for printing and publishing with it (MAF 142/271). That would have made a massive volume of great controversial potential which would have provided fuel and ammunition for years of legal, political, and press mischief, damage, and revenge. While the report itself was a privileged document presented to Parliament by Royal Command, the publication of the full correspondence might have led to a spate of actions for defamation by some of those accused of incompetence, dishonesty, and the rest, which might in turn have reflected badly on those, in the cabinet and elsewhere, whose involvement would otherwise remain unknown.

Other alterations before publication, in Clark's first typescript, were insignificant, but not without a certain charm. For instance (Appendix 2, conclusion 18), where he had previously put 'Wilcox's snooping enquiry' (about the cottages) that was changed to 'Wilcox's unnecessary enquiry'. 'Snooping' was a word much used in the period of wartime and post-war controls, in resentment of the civil service instruments of their political masters' will to control so many of the citizens' activities: the stereotype of the civil servant as a prying, snooping busybody, lacking in proper respect for 'persons of eminent standing', was strong in Clark's mind.

Enough has been quoted in earlier pages, from the transcript, to show where Clark's sympathies and antipathies lay. From the first two days, during Russell's conducted tour of the correspondence, Clark's interventions had been prejudicial in manner as well as matter. Douglas Brown, present at the press table, says in *The Battle of Crichel Down* that Clark 'sat up sharply and snapped' when voicing his suspicion on the first day of something being 'cooked up to try and deceive people'; that on the second day he joined in 'the roughest handling' of old Mr Watson Jones, including the remark 'He is giving us a lecture' when Watson Jones took 'nearly two minutes' to explain the arguments for equipping the downland as a single unit; that on the third day Clark 'broke into' a cross-examination of the very adequately qualified and knowledgeable witness, Brown, to say, with an apparent mixture of pity and scorn, 'It is not his fault. It is no good blaming him. How could he make a report?' On the same third day, Friday, in what Brown called 'the most painful episode of the week', Clark was described by him as becoming 'stern and forbidding' in his 'grilling' and 'grim exchanges' with a nervous witness, Wilcox; on the fourth and fifth days Clark was described as having 'rapped out' his 'quick-fire succession' of questions to Eastwood; on the fifth day, Thomson's attempt to explain to Stevenson the difficulty of offering for tender an equipped farm unit when all that existed was bare land 'brought an explosive interruption from Sir Andrew Clark: "The most absolute nonsense I have ever heard." ' (R. Douglas Brown, op. cit. p. 89 ff.).

The contrast with the treatment of the other side's witnesses was extreme: no harsh cross-examination, no 'judicial humour', no bullying, all seven witnesses heard the same day, the sixth day of the inquiry, leaving the rest of the day and the next day for Counsel to make final submissions. These included a request for costs by Stevenson, on Marten's behalf, on the basis that he had 'done a great public service in causing this matter to come to the attention of a public from whom most of it was designed to be hidden'. Clark's response was:

I am afraid it is wholly outside the scope of my authority to do anything of the sort. What I can do, and what I can properly do, is to put in my report, as this will be on the shorthand note, a note that you have made that request through me and that that is a matter which the Minister may wish to consider. It is quite beyond the scope of my authority to express any opinion on it. I can only say I naturally have sympathy for your client and the costs he has expended. I cannot say more than that.

Russell, asked by Clark whether he wished to say anything on the question, said merely: 'No sir. It is nothing to do with me.'

It was a very restrained reply: Russell had just demonstrated by polite cross-examination of Marten that his main purpose throughout had been the private one of land acquisition. In the circumstances, there was a good deal of irony in the closing exchanges in Russell's cross-examination of Marten and Clark's sympathetic intervention on Marten's behalf when his hostile motivation was becoming too clear:

Marten: [of the 1950–1 situation] . . . I thought about it a bit and I came to the conclusion that the A.E.C. were farming it and were probably quite enjoying farming it and with any luck would go on farming it for several years, until they had extracted what they could out of the land, and then wonder what they were going to do with it, and I rather hoped that during that period there might be a change of government and then I could slap in again for the land with a considerably better chance of my views being accepted.

Russell: That does not fit in with the proposal of a farmhouse and equipment, that they were just going to go on farming?

Marten: No, but it is what they did do, you see. In fact, I did catch them bending, in the end, because they went on farming.

Russell: You did what? I am sorry I did not hear.

Marten: I caught them bending, was what I said.

Russell: I am sorry, I still did not hear

THE COMMISSIONER: Let us leave it, Mr. Russell; I think I did. It does not matter. He thought he caught them out.

Russell: You thought you caught them out?

Marten: I beg your pardon?

Russell: You thought you caught them out doing what? This is my version of what is reported to me of your last answer.

Marten: Yes, well they were still farming the land in 1952 in spite of the fact that they had other plans for it: there were still no buildings there; nothing had happened, and the situation which I had hoped would develop had, in fact, developed and there was the bare land still available, I hoped, for purchase, and a new government in power. I therefore made another approach and I honestly believe that if my name had not been so successfully blackened by the local authorities the land would very likely have been returned to me.

Russell: I am always sorry to disappoint, but having regard to the limits of the terms of reference, Commander Marten, I regret I have no more questions to ask you.   (MAF 236/8)

The Post-mortem

The immediate reactions to the Clark report, in the Ministry of Agriculture, Crown Lands and the Agricultural Land Commission, were shock and horror, followed by detailed analysis of almost every point, undertaken in separate files opened for the purpose in the Minister's private office, in the main department, in the legal department, and in the other offices. One of the legal department's folders was actually titled 'post-mortem', without precision as to whose death was under examination. Those accused by Clark were given the opportunity to express views: others not accused were set to analysing the report and separating grain from chaff, others to preparation of the Minister's defences against political attack. Nothing in the official comments reached the high point of vituperation later achieved in the Commons debate of 20 July 1954 when Sir Richard Acland was rather mysteriously quoted in Hansard (column 1220) as asking: 'How can it happen that a trained Q.C., a leader of Chancery, can release a pent-up organism of vilification and abuse over civil servants . . . ? (*The Times* of 21 July 1954 quoted Acland as referring, less mysteriously, to 'a pent-up orgasm of vilification and abuse.') In the same debate George Brown described the report as 'a very partial Report, full of partiality from the beginning, very prejudicial and very argumentative where it is supposed to be factual, and inaccurate', and gave apposite illustrations.

Commentary by the civil servants was still very much more restrained. In what follows an attempt is made to piece together, from the piles of paper the various commentaries produced, the jigsaw puzzle that the adversarial process had further scattered rather than assembled.

Reimbursing Marten's Costs

One of the first questions tackled, even before the report was received, was that of reimbursement of Marten's £3,270 costs (less than the ministry's costs in counsels' fees alone). The early legal advice to the Minister was unanimous, that the request should be refused; the agitation for public inquiry had not really been from disinterested public motives; before the inquiry Marten's language had been unrestrained; during the inquiry the presentation of his case and the way civil servants had been cross-examined had not commended itself to either the Ministry's lawyers or counsel presenting the official case, who had been moved to comment on the 'cheap gibes' of the other side; it would be a mistake to create the impression that Marten was in the position either of a successful litigant or of one who had performed some valuable public service; but that the Minister might wish to wait for the report before reaching a decision. Nevertheless, it was decided by the cabinet on 2 June 1954 that payment of costs would help to counter any accusation of unfair treatment; the Ministry's lawyers were instructed to settle the claim for costs, and did so.

The Blandford Martyrs: Thomson and Eastwood

The first of the martyrs to comment to the Minister on the Clark report, Eastwood, wasted no time in doing so, his immediate and very proper concern being not the attack on himself, but the accusations against the Crown Receiver and agent, Thomson, whom Eastwood regarded and reported (MAF 236/15) as 'a completely frank, honest and upright man'. Eastwood's reaction, on his first sight of the Clark report on 19 May 1954, was to seek an interview with the Minister 'at once'—an unusual phrase for a civil servant to put to Ministers, more often used by Ministers to civil servants:

One thing in particular I should like to talk about at once is the position of Mr. Thomson. He is coming to London this morning when I will hand him the report, and he will be here all day today and tomorrow. I should like to have had a word with you before he leaves.

I enclose some rather hurried notes about the references to him. . . . I will leave it to him to comment in detail on the criticisms of him. I am quite horrified at them. I am not by any means under his domination, as Sir Andrew Clark says, but I do have the highest opinion of his integrity and of his professional ability.

The report was still in typescript. Eastwood suggested that, if there was any chance of Clark agreeing, the omission in the printed version of a very few words would take a great deal of the sting out of the objectionable passages: e.g. at para. 66 'an explanation which I cannot accept' and, at para. 83 'and I was not satisfied that Mr. Thomson was being truthful about it'. It was a forlorn hope, not, apparently, taken up, but in later comments dated 25 May 1954 Eastwood listed six more 'unjustified statements' by Clark on Thomson, saying: 'It is to me fantastic that he should be accused of any untruthfulness. . . . I am perfectly convinced that Mr. Thomson is the soul of uprightness and integrity.'

Eastwood's tenacious defence of Thomson led to the appointment in early July 1954 of a more expert inquiry into the very technical problem of dilapidations, by a valuer, Mr Charles Walmsley, recommended to the Minister for the purpose by the President of the Royal Institution of Chartered Surveyors. In three days he produced a thirteen-page report, finding that Sanctuary & Son had shown 'a high level of competency' except for two bits of 'faulty judgement' and one 'lapse'. Not content with that finding, Eastwood straight away pointed to errors in Walmsley's own report, and it was then promptly accepted that they were indeed errors, in a supplementary report which 'exonerated Sanctuary & Son from any criticism on grounds of competency'. A year later, in June 1955, a report (Cmd. 9483) of the Trustram Eve Committee on Crown Lands appointed by the Prime Minister in December 1954 (part of the aftermath of Crichel Down) administered the *coup de grâce* to Clark's unfounded comments against the work of Thomson and his firm (Cmd. 9483, para. 30):

These comments arose in connection with the work of Mr. Thomson, a partner in a firm of high repute (Messrs. Sanctuary and Son) who acted for the Commissioners of Crown Lands; and appear to have arisen from Mr. Thomson's handling of a claim for dilapidations and the initial estimate of the firm's fee. Except on these two points we do not read the report as implying that the use of a salaried agent would have made a material difference to the course of events. Subsequent enquiries have however been made into these two points and no criticism of substance was sustained against Mr. Thomson or his firm by the report of either enquiry. We are therefore satisfied that there was no such dereliction of duty on the part of Mr. Thomson or of his firm — a duty owed by them to the Commissioners of Crown Lands and to the Commissioners alone — as to bring discredit on the method of employing private firms of land agents. We have not therefore thought necessary to change or qualify our general conclusions about the use of firms because of the particular instance of Crichel Down.

Eastwood's vigorous defence of Thomson had therefore achieved as much vindication of him and his firm as possible, little enough compared with the ordeal of highly publicized calumny Thomson had undergone, but more than Eastwood himself received, with no such doughty defender to fight his corner. His own part as Permanent Commissioner was considered by the Trustram Eve Committee in a more ambivalent and somewhat muddled way: they appreciated that the Permanent Commissioner, as head of department referring at his discretion to one or other of two ministers, was 'out on a limb', with 'a wide and lonely responsibility', 'his own chairman, management board, general manager and finance officer'. They favoured, and recommended, the (more elaborate, expensive, and formally bureaucratic) structure of a Crown Estate Board. ('Boards are screens', said Bentham.) Their recommendation was adopted, and Trustram Eve appointed as the first Chairman.

The Committee's mistake lay in accepting some of Clark's criticisms (Appendix 2, conclusion 23) and using them to support the case for a Board: the ambivalence lay in finding that such 'failings' were not 'widespread', when in fact they existed only in Clark's mind:

> Our general review has not shown that those failings were widespread but we are confident that a board of trustees would be free from any weaknesses of this kind which may have existed. Indeed the findings of the Crichel Down report appear to us to provide a good illustration of the weaknesses that might result from the lack of a board of trustees. The isolation of a recently appointed Permanent Commissioner and the dual position of the Minister are particularly noted in the report.

The three inquiries after Clark (including the Trustram Eve Committee itself) finally disposed of Clark's charges of 'lack of adequate control' and 'a tendency to leave everything to the Crown Receiver and to accept without question everything he says or does'. Given the Minister's instruction to the Permanent Commissioner to get the purchase decided in two months, and his clear delegation of the choice of a tenant, it was the inherent efficiency of having a single full-time Commissioner operating through the principal of a private firm which enabled the Minister's purpose to be effected so quickly that the commitment was in being before the Agricultural Land Commission with their 'Board' were fully alerted. Any weaknesses lay, not in the simple landlord–agent combination in Crown Lands, but in the cumbersome Ministry–Board–Land Service structure of the Agricultural Land Commission, whose complexity permitted the headquarters and the field officials inadvertently to keep each other in ignorance of developments affecting both of them. Had the ALC been the responsibility of a single Commissioner, not of a Board, the worst complications of Crichel Down might never have arisen.

As for his own part, Eastwood went patiently through the report, in his detailed commentary to the Minister on 25 May 1954, correcting some mistakes, denying all serious accusations against him, and calmly admitting insignificant errors. He denied, for instance,

Clark's assertions (Appendix 2, para. 60): 'Mr. Eastwood admitted that he had not made any enquiry and did not know at all how far Mr. Thomson had gone when he wrote this letter.' Eastwood denied making any such admission, noting there was nothing of the sort in the record; he pointed out that at the time he already knew that Tozer had agreed to the rental proposal, and that Thomson and Tozer had together visited farms in neighbouring counties. Similarly, Eastwood categorically denied Clark's suggestion (Appendix 2, para. 69) of financial laxity, explaining that there had been no need to check a preliminary estimate, and that the actual calculation of the fee payable would have been scrutinized in the department, in the usual way, when the work was done and the first draft account was sent in; he commented further: 'Sanctuary's have always been most reasonable in the fees charged for work not covered by their management fee and scrupulous in the preparation of their accounts. The words "it may well be that" are less than fair to Sanctuary's. "No doubt" would be all right.' (MAF 236/16.)

Eastwood's further denials and corrections included demonstrations that whereas Clark (Appendix 2, para. 74) had said a letter was never answered, it had been; whereas (Appendix 2, para. 75) Clark said Wilcox had approved a letter to the Treasury, it was the Minister himself who had agreed the draft; he denied 'absolutely' Clark's statement (Appendix 2, para. 78) that he had answered Treasury questions about rents in a 'light-hearted' manner, and also Clark's strange assertion (Appendix 2, para. 77) that he had admitted making no enquiries about pre-war rental value. He did not comment at length on tenant right valuation and dilapidations (Appendix 2, paras. 79–84), observing merely, and, as it proved after the three further inquiries, correctly: 'There are no grounds whatever for believing that Mr. Thomson acted improperly or was not being truthful.' (MAF 236/16.)

Clark had commented (Appendix 2, para. 90) that Eastwood had been 'quite unable to give any satisfactory explanation' of his 'somewhat strange attitude'—i.e. Eastwood's idea that Crown Lands might not go on with purchase if Tozer withdrew. Eastwood's report to the Minister was: 'I cannot find that I was ever asked to give any explanation of my attitude. It was a perfectly straightforward one. It was obvious by now that there was going to be trouble about Crichel Down and we should have been very glad not to be mixed up in it.' (MAF 236/16.)

Turning to the 'Conclusions' portion Eastwood contested Clark's conclusion 13 of 'no commitment' to Tozer, his conclusion 14 (that Crown Lands could have advertised the tenancy without difficulty), his conclusion 15 (that Eastwood was 'completely dominated' by Thomson), and conclusion 24 (about a 'most regrettable attitude of hostility to Marten' evinced by Eastwood, Wilcox, Thomson, and others unnamed.

On the commitment to Tozer, by late March 1953, thought 'wholly unjustified' by Clark, Eastwood wrote: 'I do not agree. I am quite clear in my own conscience that by this time if we decided to buy the land at all there was some moral commitment to take Mr. Tozer as a tenant. We were not, of course, bound to buy the land at all and a possible course would have been for us to withdraw altogether.' (MAF 236/16.)

On what Clark called (in conclusion 13) 'Mr. Eastwood's improper suggestion' Eastwood wrote: 'I do not seek to excuse the sentence in my letter of the 23rd March to which this refers. It should never have been written. A few moments' thought would have shown me that, quite apart from other obvious considerations, it would have been quite impracticable to mislead effectively. No attempt was, in fact, ever made to do so.' (MAF 236/16.)

Since Wilcox's concurrence with Eastwood's view was thought by Clark to be 'even worse' or 'equally improper' it has to be considered further in the case against Wilcox, in which Eastwood was characterized by Clark as the serpent and Wilcox as a very willing Eve (see p. 143).

On conclusion 14, Eastwood wrote:

I contest this. We had not decided to buy the land because we did not yet know how much it would cost and whether we could make an economic proposition of it. How then could we have invited tender? I suppose that as soon as we knew the cost of the land and the approximate cost of equipping it we could then have invited tenders, in the knowledge that we were assured of a rent from Mr. Tozer that would have made the proposition economic. It would have been impossible, however, to do all this within the time limit imposed, and it would not have been, in any case, very satisfactory. It is an exaggeration, therefore, to say that there would have been 'no difficulty whatever' in advertising.   (MAF 236/16.)

On his being 'completely dominated' by Thomson (conclusion 15) Eastwood wrote:

I am interested to learn this. I have the highest opinion of Mr. Thomson's professional ability and, being rather new to my job, I naturally leaned rather heavily on his advice, but it is certainly news to me that I am under his domination. My officers tell me that none of our Crown Receivers, whether our whole-time employees or private firms, are more ready to accept criticisms of their proposals than Mr. Thomson, and that is certainly my own experience in the 18 months I have been in my job.   (MAF 236/16)

On conclusion 24, alleging 'hostility' to Marten, without excuse, 'irritation' etc., Eastwood wrote a complete denial:

I deny this absolutely as regards myself. In point of fact my sympathy was very much with Commander Marten. I thought (and think) that it is right that previous owners should have the first chance of getting requisitioned land back when it is no longer wanted by Government. I realised that he felt very strongly about Crichel Down and I took particular pains in my letters to him to be friendly and courteous. The Commissioner, indeed, recognized this. He said 'all your letters seem to have been most friendly. You were writing to him in a most friendly strain.' (Day 5 p. 13.) Apart from letters my only contact with Commander Marten was a very long telephone conversation while I was on holiday in Cornwall, in which I went out of my way to be as helpful as I could, and the meeting in Mr. Nugent's room on the 4th September.

I can only think that the Commissioner takes this view because I did not rap Mr. Thomson over the knuckles for statements in a letter of the 13th August (Corres. p. 394) that 'Commander Marten was the last person we should want as a tenant' and because in examination by him (Day 5 p. 12) I conveyed the impression that I would not have wished to have Commander Marten as a tenant of the Crown. This is, indeed, true enough. Commander Marten by this time (middle August) had made it clear that he was going to make a row and would probably press for a public enquiry and it was sufficiently obvious that he would be a difficult customer to have as a tenant.   (MAF 236/16)

So far as the strictures against Eastwood himself were concerned, he had thus rebutted them all, in a restrained and dignified way, except for the accusation of being the serpent in the Garden of Eden, the satanic embodiment of evil, tempting Wilcox to sin. And in that there was nothing that would have justified disciplinary action: no sort of sustainable charge could have been framed on the basis of the puzzling phrases about 'appearing' to keep promises used by both Wilcox and Eastwood — phrases they could neither of them explain or excuse, except to deny there was any intention or attempt to deceive, or to 'dissemble' in the discreditable sense of that word. It is strange that Clark himself, having found that there had been no trace in the case of personal dishonesty, should not have realized that he had been dealing throughout with honest men acting with complete propriety, but without complete infallibility.

The Blandford Martyrs: Eastwood (continued) and Wilcox

Except for the alleged 'dissembling' in a letter to Eastwood, Clark's criticisms of Wilcox amounted to very little. There was the fulmination about the cottage licences (conclusion 18) when Wilcox, misled partly by Marten's wording, merely asked for a check to be made. As much of the Crichel Down trouble arose from hesitations to check information, whether by 'snooping' or otherwise, it was ironic for Wilcox to incur such blame. His enquiry was no 'regrettable lapse from the standard of conduct the public is entitled to expect from responsible civil servants': the public is 'entitled to expect' them to make such enquiries, and to blame them for slackness or worse if they do not. That incident seems to have been Clark's sole justification for suggesting hostility to Marten on Wilcox's part (conclusion 24). It was insufficient. Other charges, such as not telling Nugent that Crown Lands were committed to Tozer (Appendix 2, para. 70) can be dismissed, because Wilcox at the time did not know the degree of Crown Lands commitment to Tozer, which was in any case a moral commitment, not a legal one (and one whose very existence at the time Clark himself had denied). And Crown Lands, at the time, had just become aware of the previous commitments by the ALC and had undertaken to examine them.

What was really left, therefore, for Wilcox to answer, was the business surrounding his letter of 25 March 1953 to Eastwood (p. 89). The clearest and lengthiest statement of his position comes from a confidential letter he wrote on 23 July 1954, just after the denouement of Dugdale's resignation, to Robert Vile, then Chairman of the Association of First Division Civil Servants. (Wilcox had then recently completed a three-year term of office as a member of the Association's Executive Council.) In 1970, after retirement from the civil service (in the same rank as he occupied before Crichel Down) Wilcox came across the letter among old papers and sent it to the Ministry of Agriculture asking for it to be placed among the other

Crichel Down papers so that it should be available with the rest for public inspection in 1984 (MAF 236/69). When this was done, he wrote to the Ministry thanking them and saying: 'It is nice to feel that when the papers are open in 1984 to the earnest research workers (Crichel Down would make quite a good subject for a Ph.D. thesis), this will be available for their inspection also.'

Wilcox's letter of 23 July 1954 is reproduced in full, because it shows the essential honesty and modesty of this, the meekest of the Blandford Martyrs, writing at a time of great trouble, his career and reputation blighted:

23 July 1954

My dear Bob,

Now that the Crichel Down debate is over it may be helpful if I send you this note with my reflections on some of the issues which have arisen.

First of all you will have noted that Sir Thomas Dugdale at the end of his speech said:

'I have no regrets at having ordered a public inquiry, for I am
certain that good will come of it,'

and the Home Secretary in his reply by implication defended this sort of inquiry. I hope this will not cut across too much the confidential and informal discussions which you have been having at National Whitley level about future inquiries of this nature. Ministers obviously had to defend their decision to hold the Crichel Down inquiry, but the consequences have been such that clearly everyone concerned is going to think very carefully indeed before authorizing any similar inquiry in future.

The documents disclosed at the Crichel Down inquiry showed clearly that the Minister had ordered it because of local rumours of corruption, e.g. that Tozer had been bribing Thomson to get the tenancy. It was not I think appreciated at the time how much wider than this the terms of reference went.

If there are to be any public inquiries in future, or for that matter private ones, the terms of reference would need to be very carefully considered.

In the Debate George Brown and Sir Richard Acland amongst others drew attention to alleged examples of bias, inconsistency and inaccuracy in Sir Andrew Clark's report. Some of these criticisms were exaggerated or perverse, but looking at the matter as impartially as I can, I would say that both in the conduct of the inquiry and in his report Sir Andrew Clark did display very considerable bias and prejudice (no doubt quite unconsciously). In saying this I am not thinking of the references to myself, and I have some reason for thinking that this view is fairly widely held among those who have been dealing with the matter in this Department and who are not personally implicated in the case: obviously, I cannot quote you any names.

It is pretty clear, however, that Ministers must have had very much in mind the Prestwick case of December 1949 (referred to in paragraph 5 of F.D.Gen. 1/54) where the present Home Secretary led the attack on [*sic*] the House of Commons on Lord Packenham [*sic*] who had been sticking up for the civil servants in his Department and rejecting some of the findings of the K.C. who had held the inquiry.

I am not suggesting that the Crichel Down case was in all respects a parallel with Prestwick. I have read the Parliamentary debates of 4th and 8th December 1949 on Prestwick. The questions seemed to turn on some very technical considerations of the amount of meteorological information which the ground staff should have wirlessed [*sic*] to the aircraft and there were apparently good reasons for saying that the ground staff had in fact done all that their instructions and the situation required of them. At Crichel Down there were admitted mistakes, muddles and errors of judgement. Nevertheless, in general Sir Andrew Clark seemed to be determined to place the worst construction he could on the acts of the civil servants and of Thomson, though I must acknowledge that he was to some extent prepared to give me the benefit of the doubt as regards my letter of 25th March, 1953, and in this respect I was luckier than some of my colleagues. However, the whole handling of the matter shows that while Ministers may have wanted to reject some of Sir Andrew Clark's conclusions (and Sir Thomas Dugdale in his speech came as near as he dared to rejecting the strictures in paragraph 21, page 31, on the Agricultural Land Commission, which is a body he clearly couldn't afford to offend—think of the to-do if the Chairman, Sir Frederick Burrows, had offered his resignation)—yet Ministers were evidently very much afraid of appearing to reject explicitly any of Sir Andrew Clark's conclusions.

I do not want to burden you with a long account of my own case. As I told you at the outset, I had no wish at all to ask for any F.D.A. intervention on my behalf and in fact throughout I have received the greatest consideration and kindness from Hitchman and everybody else here. I need, however, to tell you my own position very briefly in order to draw the morals from it. It is, incidentally, of course, rather galling that one cannot make public one's own side of the case, though I realise that this is inevitable in the circumstances.

The case against me rests essentially on my letter to Eastwood of 25th March, 1953, quoted in paragraph 61, page 17 of Sir Andrew Clark's report (Cmd. 9176) and the enquiry at the end of my letter to Hole of 8th September 1953 about the building licences mentioned in paragraph 91, page 25. My letter of March 25th was written at a time when I was working under considerable pressure arising to some extent from the fact that Franklin, and also one of my Assistant Secretaries, had been switched onto other work connected with the East Coast floods. For example, I had at short notice to take over from Franklin the chairmanship of a Committee on a subject rather outside my normal work which had instructions to report by Easter. My letter of 25th March was written immediately on return from a two-day visit to one of our Agricultural Research Stations and is something I must have dashed off in a hurry in an attempt to reduce the pile that one always finds in one's in-tray when one returns from a short absence from the office.

In that letter I committed an error of judgement in assuming without due thought that it was too late to go back on the arrangements we had so far made with Crown Lands and in not appreciating all the implications of the promises made to the other applicants. Also, without due thought I took up and repeated Eastwood's unfortunate phrase about 'appearing to implement the promises'. Looking at those words in cold blood afterwards Eastwood and I found it very difficult to say what we could have really meant by them, but we could not deny that on any natural construction they must be taken to imply the possibility of 'dissembling statements'. I think I must have had in mind the possibility of the negotiations with Tozer breaking down, in which case it might have been feasible to give some of the others an opportunity to tender. In short, my letter of 25th March was hastily written and ill-conceived and sent off without appreciation of its implications.

Sir Andrew Clark sprung on me his questions about building licences after I had been through a pretty gruelling cross-examination on other matters, and I was so taken aback at the suggestion that I made the enquiries in the hopes of being able to blackmail Marten that I am afraid that I gave my evidence on this point very badly. What I really had in mind was that the Dorset committee officers might well have been lax in sponsoring an application for building licences before there was a real need for the accommodation. One thing that I clearly couldn't say at the inquiry was that Mr. Ferris, the former C.A.O. for Dorset, had not got a reputation for being amongst the brightest of the C.A.O.'s as an administrator whatever his virtues were on his main task of technical adviser. I did in fact on reflection suggest to our legal people afterwards that I should go into the box again to make a supplementary statement on this point of the building licences, but they advised against this as they felt that it would only serve to draw attention to the point.

I mention these points not only because I think it is right that you should know my side of the case but because the first incident, that of my letter of March 25th, illustrates what I feel is an important point made by Walter Elliot in the Debate (Hansard Column 1249), namely, the strain under which Ministers and civil servants are working.

Hitchman, since the Debate, has very properly enjoined on us the importance of seeing that all letters that we send out whether to the public or to other Departments are cast iron and, in particular, when in any doubt we should refer the case to Ministers, and I imagine that this will be a fairly general attitude now in other Departments. All this is going to put a greater strain on administrative officers, and particularly our minds must be always alert to spot at the outset anything which unless very carefully handled may turn into another Crichel Down. All this I think has a bearing on the general question of hours and leave and more particularly on staffing complements. If a civil servant is to have the constant mental alertness necessary, if he is to be certain of spotting all potential sources of trouble he must not be overworked too much.

It is possible, incidentally, though I have not enquired into the facts, that this factor of overwork may have been responsible for another of the slips in the handling of the Crichel Down case, namely the fact that after Hole had written to Lofthouse on 16th July, 1952, passing on Smith's request for a report (see paragraph 24 on page 8) Lofthouse was apparently not able to do anything on it for the next fortnight and then unloaded it on to the unfortunate Mr. Brown. I repeat, I have not enquired into all the facts: the officers concerned in any event are not administrators, but it does occur to me that this is possibly a symptom of overwork in Lofthouse's office at the time.

Yours ever,

C. H. M. Wilcox.

(MAF 236/69)

This was a remarkably mild letter from a man whose career was in ruins, expressing little hostility towards Clark, and none towards Marten, and seeing overwork rather than malevolence as the main source of trouble. Lofthouse, incidentally, whose overwork Wilcox thought might have contributed to one of the 'slips' in the case, was one of the few criticized officials (perhaps the only one) whose careers were not permanently blighted by Crichel Down: he became the Ministry's Chief Surveyor in 1973. The fact that Wilcox wrote nothing about the alleged 'authorizing' of Eastwood to 'ignore' or 'disregard' the earlier applicants merely underlines the absurdity of that charge, and of the quite undue importance attached to it by Clark and Stevenson during the inquiry. Wilcox had merely expressed gratitude to Eastwood for the action already taken by him to investigate the promises made to previous applicants, although clearly under no obligation to do so. Clark and Stevenson made of Wilcox's statement of the obvious 'Clearly if you buy a property you are in no way bound by these promises' (p. 89) something more sinister:

CLARK: That seems to be the key to it.
Stevenson: I agree.
CLARK: Those words are the key. Mr. Eastwood, rightly or wrongly,
            took the view that Mr. Wilcox's letter was complete authority

from the Ministry to go ahead and disregard the former
applicants.

Stevenson: Yes.

COMMISSIONER: I certainly would have read it in the same way myself.

Stevenson: I agree.

CLARK: That, I believe, is the clue to the whole of this trouble.

Stevenson: Yes. (MAF 236/6)

This was nonsense: had the Permanent Commissioner of Crown
Lands thought further authority necessary he would have sought it
directly from Dugdale, not in his ministerial capacity, but in his
capacity as Commissioner of Crown Lands, and certainly could not
have taken a passing remark in a semi-official letter from a civil
servant of equal rank to his own, with no suggestion that it conveyed
any message from political masters, as authority to do something
he was not in fact intending to do—'to go ahead and disregard the
former applicants'. He had already told Thomson to go ahead, but
to find out more about the other applicants to see what could be
done—with, clearly, 'letting them down lightly' in mind. To
compound the confusion, Clark characterized the suggestion of a
tactful letter to the various applicants turning down their offers as
'a perfectly correct view' (Appendix 2, para. 66) and said it was
unfortunate that advice was not followed. Had it been followed, it
would have involved doing what Clark himself had criticized—i.e.
disregarding the applications, the step for which Eastwood and
Wilcox were blamed, but had not taken. Wilcox's own criticism of
his own part, that he had not proposed to the Minister that he
abandon sale to Crown Lands and revert to equipping and letting
by the ALC, was misplaced also. Marten, opposed root and branch
to the policy of a single equipped unit, could scarcely have been
chosen as an ALC tenant, ahead of Tozer; Wilcox's plan if adopted
would therefore have achieved the same result as sale to Crown
Lands—i.e. a 'row'. A shrewder man than Wilcox, not necessarily
a less honest one, might have immediately 'passed the buck' of past
commitments, as soon as he heard of them, to the Secretary of the
Agricultural Land Commission, in writing of course, whether that
Board already knew of them or not, and so would have cleared his
own yardarm, thus, perhaps, saving his own skin and career.
Whether that would have furthered the public interest it is impossible
to say: but at least the existence of possible previous 'promises' would
have brought to the attention of those on whose behalf they had

been made—if indeed any of them could be accurately described as 'promises' or 'commitments'.

The Board of the Agricultural
Land Commission declines Martyrdom

The Chairman and members of the board of the Agricultural Land Commission gave an apt illustration of Bentham's aphorism 'Boards are screens' by angrily rejecting Clark's charges against them, declining martyrdom, and coming close to threatening action for defamation. That threat must have helped to consign the Crichel Down documentation to the limbo of the House of Commons library's secret papers for the next thirty years.

In three pages of 'preliminary reactions to Sir Andrew Clark's strictures' on 25 May 1954 (MAF 235/16) Sir Frederick Burrows made it clear to the Minister that the members felt their credit and reputation so closely touched that they needed time to consider what they should do to defend themselves if necessary, but would probably want to see how Parliament disposed of the matter before deciding what action they should take.

Meanwhile they rejected Clark's findings. He had no business (conclusion 1) to comment on policy: no one else, from any quarter, had ever criticized the ALC policy of investing in food production and such essentials for it as good farm buildings and good housing. Words such as 'infatuated' (conclusion 2) were unjustified and offensive, and the accusation (conclusion 21) of being 'very anxious to gain experience' was 'little short of grotesque to anyone who takes the trouble to identify these expert members and examine their record'. Clark's allegation of lack of frankness with the Ministry was baseless, and it was impossible to leave his charge of an irresponsible attitude to public money unchallenged. The commission worked in the closest possible contact with the Ministry, but their decisions were made in their own discretion, on their own responsibility, in the exercise of their statutory powers—including the decision to equip Crichel Down as a single unit: 'The Commission holds firmly to the view that their decision was right.' (MAF 236/16).

In short, the commission, as a body, was 'not for burning'; its board was a fire-proof screen. Instead of being burnt at the stake, therefore, the commission was allowed over the years, as a result of ministry reorganization, to become less used and less important, and finally to fade gently away.

The Blandford Martyrs:
the Servants of the Agricultural Land Commission

The civil servants attached to the commission, or acting as its field agents, were not so well protected, although the commission itself took steps to defend the former secretary (L. J. Smith) in his absence abroad from January 1954, on secondment to the Greek ministry of agriculture. They described him as ' a very able and conscientious official', and were certain that he had not deliberately withheld information (Clark's suggestion, in conclusion 21). It was left to Smith himself to return to England, at his own expense, to defend himself in detail, with the other accused, before the Woods Committee.

The Woods Committee was an ingenious product of one of the many cabinet sessions devoted to considering the problems of Crichel Down in the hectic last weeks before the Commons debate on 20 July. The cabinet were still discussing and making alterations to the draft speech of the resigning Minister on the morning of that day, and still failing to reach complete agreement on policy for the future. But the Woods Committee had been conceived at an earlier meeting on 1 July 1954, when Churchill was absent abroad, in the United States and Canada, and the chair was taken by the Deputy Prime Minister, R. A. Butler, a politician with a reputation, even amongst his colleagues, for craftiness. Dugdale had made a statement in the House of Commons which had caused great anger among government supporters: he had intended to say that he took 'a more favourable view' of the civil servants' part in Crichel Down than Clark had done, and that he continued 'to have full confidence in the Agricultural Land Commission'. But when that statement had come, in draft, before the cabinet meeting on 2 June 1954 an extraordinarily ungenerous suggestion was put forward, and agreed, that Dugdale's warm words 'more favourable' should be changed to 'less unfavourable' and that 'I continue to have full confidence in the Agricultural Land Commission' should be changed to 'I consider that the Agricultural Land Commission continues to fulfil a useful function'. Even with these niggardly alterations the Minister's statement on 15 June 1954 had met with noisy disapproval.

Butler's suggestion to the cabinet of a small committee to consider whether any civil service transfers were necessary was a belated and blatant public relations effort, a sop to those indignant at Dugdale's decision that the civil servants for whom he was responsible had been punished enough. In putting the suggestion forward, Butler gave his reasons with frankness: on the one hand, public opinion would not be satisfied if no action were taken, but on the other hand it would be ill-received by the civil service if it came to be thought that the Minister's previous decision not to punish was being reversed. The appointment of the committee should be made on the personal authority of the absent Prime Minister, if only because one of the civil service appointments under question (the Permanent Commissionership of Crown Lands) had been made on the Prime Minister's own recommendation. But the announcement of the committee's appointment should be made at once, in the Prime Minister's name, in anticipation of his approval. The cabinet agreed, and so, on his return, did Churchill—having, one must suppose, little alternative (CAB 128/27).

The report of the Woods Committee was submitted to the cabinet in the morning, just before the Crichel Down debate (20 July 1954) together with the remaining contentious Crichel Down business, and the announcement by Churchill of a *fait accompli*, Dugdale's resignation. He said that Dugdale had decided, 'in view of the strong feelings aroused among Government supporters by the Report of the Crichel Down Inquiry', that 'the only dignified course for him to follow was to resign his office'. The resignation having been submitted to the Queen, there was nothing left for the cabinet to do, except to express polite regret at 'the loss of a loyal colleague' as the Prime Minister put it, to agree that Dugdale should himself announce his resignation in his speech that afternoon, and to busy themselves going through the draft of that speech, including the proposed references to the Woods Committee report on the transfers considered necessary 'to maintain public confidence'. The unease felt by the cabinet can be judged by the detailed attention given not only to the form of words in which Dugdale should announce the committee's recommendations, but to the precise timing of the release of the report to members of parliament. The Prime Minister's own oral suggestion was adopted, that copies should be available in the vote office only at the conclusion of Dugdale's speech, and 'no special steps need be taken to make the text of the report available to Opposition spokesmen in advance of the debate (CAB 128/27/51st meeting conclusions). The stratagem of the Woods Committee was about as successful as it deserved to be, not really satisfying to either side, but receiving some polite applause in the press.

Those investigated by the Committee, apart from Eastwood (who was to return to his old department, the Colonial Office) and Wilcox (who had been moved already to other duties in the Ministry of Agriculture and was to remain there), were L. J. Smith, D. A. Hole, and R. G. A. Lofthouse. D. S. Brown, having already resigned in May 1954, was not of the number. He had been angered by the restrictions placed upon him in making his draft report, and in giving evidence, and by the tone of the Clark report, and by the damage to his reputation and prospective career, and was unable to accept assurances by the Permanent Secretary and others that there was no danger of Crichel Down being used against him. His bitter words of farewell to the Permanent Secretary, after substantial but unsatisfying correspondence with the legal department, were: 'I can only hope that you will take what action is necessary to ensure in the future that no junior officers are placed in a similar predicament.' (MAF 236/68.)

L. J. Smith was not better pleased than one would expect at the attacks made on him by Clark during his absence abroad, regarding it as most unfair that he had not been better defended. He disposed of Clark's accusations easily enough, one by one, including the point that Clark in expressing 'regret' at Smith's absence from the inquiry should have acknowledged that it was in no way his fault — no one had asked for his presence, since the presence of the Chairman himself had been thought quite sufficient. The Woods Committee regretted his absence too, but were less than generous in repairing the damage done: 'We share that regret and consider that his absence was detrimental to his interests. As Mr. Smith was in London during our sittings we were able to interview him. Having read his observations and heard what he had to say, we are satisfied that there is no occasion for any action with regard to him.'

This was grudging, and negative; Smith had shown Clark's accusations to be without merit. What Smith had said about the Air Ministry retaining the freehold (para. 22) was correct. As to Clark's para. 23, what Smith said about the acquisition of the land was more correct than Clark's own version. As to Clark's para. 37, what Smith sent was not a personal view but the ALC's formal advice. As to the idea (conclusions 6 and 21) that Hole's doubts should have accompanied Brown's report, the fact was that neither went: what did go was the ALC's considered advice, as sought. Understandably dissatisfied with his treatment throughout, Smith protested heartily and resigned from the service immediately.

D. A. Hole, Provincial Land Commissioner with twenty-four years' service, and R. G. A. Lofthouse, also Provincial Land Commissioner at the time, were given a grudging sort of acquittal. The committee did not think Hole's actions could 'properly escape all criticism' but they 'were not such as to impair his usefulness as an officer of the Agricultural Land Service in his present post', so they recommended no action, no transfer in his case, or in the case of Lofthouse, who had been transferred to London in December 1952 as Provincial Land Commissioner. The only matter alleged against both jointly was Clark's charge (para. 18) that their treatment of Taylor's offer to rent the bare land at £2,000 per annum was 'a little strange'. It was the offer itself that was strange, rather than the way it was treated. Against Lofthouse alone, Clark had alleged (para. 25) that he had given 'somewhat extraordinary' instructions on confidentiality to a 'young and comparatively inexperienced subordinate', Brown, and did not pass on to him an order to consult the Air Ministry land agent. The advice about confidentiality was defensible enough, with Crichel Down showing clear signs of becoming troublesome. Most inspections and reports—the overwhelming majority of planning procedures and the like—have long been done quietly, as 'second gear' inspections in most cases, in order to avoid just what Lofthouse sought to avoid, the stirring up of hornets' nests by well-meant investigations interpreted as 'snooping' by over-zealous or inexperienced officials. And there was simply no need for Brown to consult the Air Ministry land agent (Launceston, Cornwall) because he had recently obtained, studied and reported on all the Crichel Down conveyances, a fact which had emerged at the inquiry and should have been noted by Clark.

In the circumstances, the Woods Committee seems, in its treatment of the civil service citizens referred to it, scarcely to have lived up to its own bland and sanctimonious precept, cited and welcomed in the press at the time: 'It is the more necessary that the Civil Servant should bear constantly in mind that the citizen has a right to expect, not only that his affairs will be dealt with effectively and expeditiously, but also that his personal feelings, no less than his rights as an individual, will be sympathetically and fairly considered.'

Clark had also seriously criticized the Deputy Permanent Secretary for drafting a 'very unfortunately worded letter' (para. 97), and, less directly, in his criticisms of the presentation of matters to the Minister (conclusions 7 and 8) questioned the actions of the Permanent Secretary himself, who bore the chief responsibility for advice to the Minister. If the reasons for the existence of the Woods Committee had been less disingenuous than they were, and the same rules had been applied to the senior men as were applied to those of the rank of Under Secretary and below, both the Permanent Secretary and the Deputy would have been on the mat with their juniors, faced with the choice of either repudiating the Clark report in their own defence, or taking part dutifully in the public relations exercise of 'maintaining public confidence' in the administration. One wonders whether they would have chosen the latter course as the cynical path of peace and duty, rejecting the temptation to demolish the Clark report once and for all. To pursue the analogy of sacrificial animals and burnt offerings, the fat would then have been in the fire; but the embarrassment was successfully avoided.

The Denouement

Dugdale's statement in the House of Commons on 15 June 1954 had claimed achievement of disproof of corruption, disclaimed need for disciplinary action against civil servants, accepted personal responsibility 'wholly', reimbursed Marten's legal costs, notified the decision not to sell the land to the previous owners' successors, but instead to honour the obligations to the Crown Lands tenant — and set the House in an uproar. It had in it ingredients not to tranquillize but to excite, depress, and infuriate parliament, all parties (but the government party most of all), press, and public. The reports and editorials of *The Times* in the second half of June 1954 (p. 151 ff.) were not untypical of the general press comment of the time.

On the evening of 17 June 1954 there was an excited meeting of the Conservative parliamentary party's agriculture, fisheries and food committee 'to consider the problems arising' out of the Crichel Down report. It was after this that the Woods Committee was appointed in the Prime Minister's name, and the Crichel Down debate postponed until 20 July 1954 to enable him to be present, on his return from America. The delay gave more time for tempers to sour, for press speculation, and for moves such as Marten's address at the National Liberal Club in Whitehall Place on 30 June 1954, with allusions to 'deep and dirty roots' still to be unearthed (Appendix 4).

As a result of the party's agriculture committee meeting, there were in June and July three meetings of the back-bench 1922 committee, attended by various ministers attempting with little apparent success to explain and justify the government decisions (R. Douglas Brown, *The Battle of Crichel Down*, pp. 116 ff.). These meetings culminated in an 'angry' meeting on 15 July 1954, at which Maxwell Fyfe attempted 'to turn the tide' running against the government, but failed; and the ministers present left the meeting, according to Brown (op. cit., p. 119 f.): ' . . . with the knowledge that the government could not control its own supporters unless it made some further gesture. It was their responsibility to pass that information to the Prime Minister.

Four days after the meeting, Sir Winston Churchill discussed the situation with Sir Thomas Dugdale. At that meeting the scapegoat was selected.'

It may well have been so, but a decision to resign on seeing the Crichel Down affair through to its end must have been in Sir Thomas Dugdale's mind for a long time. How could it not have been, after such an ebbing away of support for so many months, a troublesome inquiry, appointed by him, a consequent muddle for which he had accepted responsibility, and vociferous demands for his resignation, from his own party? A simple, honourable resignation, once the crisis was reached, carried with it the attractive prospects of ending the party row, saving the government, and restoring to himself some leisure, country peace, and family life. With such a plethora of good and sufficient reasons for departing, it need not have been a difficult decision for a not over-ambitious man to take.

Which of the reasons was dominant is less certain. In the ritual exchange of letters before the debate, neither the Prime Minister nor Dugdale went into detail. Dugdale said merely that it was done 'in view of the criticisms which have been levelled at the handling of the Crichel Down case, for which as Minister of Agriculture and Fisheries I accept responsibility', while Churchill's reply the next day, the day of the debate, 20 July 1954, said, after a tribute to Dugdale's work and an expression of 'keen regret': 'The reasons which have led you to tender your resignation do not at all detract from the value of the work you have done and I think that your decision to sacrifice your office will be regarded as chivalrous in a high degree.'

Dugdale had originally intended to say more in his letter of resignation, but what it was is not revealed in the official archives, and must remain a mystery. He seems to have preserved in his private papers (at Crathorne, in his heir's possession) only two documents which throw any light, however indirect and tantalizing, on his resignation. The first is a record of the stormy meeting just before his resignation, with the party's agriculture committee, some demanding his resignation, others asking him not to resign but to punish the civil servants severely, as an example and as proof of Conservative rejection of 'bureaucracy'. The second was a brief, cryptic note of advice to him from a friend and colleague in the cabinet, James Stuart, Secretary of State for Scotland (later Viscount Findhorn) written on Prime Minister's Office notepaper (Stuart being then at 10 Downing Street) suggesting that the resigning Minister's draft letter to the Prime Minister be re-drafted 'to *resist* going into detail' concerning the '*underlying* causes' for the resignation. (It is quite typical of the complexities of Crichel Down that the source of this advice to Dugdale should have been James Stuart. Stuart had been a close friend, since their Eton schooldays, of the third Lord Alington, had indeed been one of the executors of Alington's will. But that gave Stuart no special knowledge of the Crichel Estate; that large estate of some 17,000 acres had ceased to be 'owned' in any ordinary sense by Alington, on his marriage, when he became 'life tenant in possession' of the estate for the purposes of the Settled Lands Act, 1925; and a 'statutory owner' only. The Crichel Estate was therefore legally separate from the personal estate of which Stuart was one of the executors, and there would have been no identifiable conflict of interest set up for Stuart in relation to decisions about it.)

Dugdale, an easy-going man, usually accepted friendly advice, and did so on this occasion. What was deleted from the draft is anyone's guess, but it may well have been very close to what Churchill had said in cabinet on 20 July, that it was party anger over his decisions that led Dugdale to conclude that resignation was the only dignified course open to him (cf. p. 188).

The Debate

A few minutes before the debate opened in the House of Commons on 20 July 1954 Dugdale called George Brown, the chosen leading speaker for the Opposition, 'behind the Speaker's chair' and said to him 'George, don't be too rough, because when I come to speak I'm going to tell you that I've resigned.' (Lord George-Brown's memoirs, *In My Way*, 1971, p. 152 f.) Brown tells how he had 'a terrifying speech' prepared, demanding the Minister's resignation, but threw it away and started again, emphasizing in his speech that the Clark report denied civil servants the protection they should have, and that responsibility should not be 'shuffled off' on to them. He therefore in his memoirs heartily approved both Sir Thomas Dugdale's acceptance of responsibility and his resignation: 'Whether the incident really demanded the resignation of a senior Minister is another matter, but Tommy Dugdale's self-sacrificing defence of the doctrine of ministerial responsibility was a noble one. I am sure that it is the right doctrine and that we ought all to defend it.'

Brown himself later in the debate came in for praise from a rather unexpected source, Maxwell Fyfe. The Home Secretary gave the closing speech in the debate, calling Brown's contribution 'a remarkably skilful and magnanimous speech', before going on to show less sympathy with one of his own side who spoke in the debate than he had for one of the opposition who refrained:

My most vivid memories of the ensuing debate were of Tom Williams, who had declined to take part out of his personal friendship for Dugdale, sitting alone at the end of the Opposition Front Bench, and the impatience with which the House listened to Mr. Crouch, the Conservative Member for North Dorset who had started the whole business.

(*Political Adventure: the Memoirs
of the Earl of Kilmuir*, 1964, p. 227.)

In his own memoirs, Tom Williams (later Lord Williams of Barnburgh), who had been Labour's Minister of Agriculture, had been at pains to pay tribute to Dugdale, confirming that he and Dugdale had enjoyed ' a pleasant relationship' since 1929 when Dugdale entered the House of Commons, and that he had been pleased to see Dugdale take over from him as Minister, but: 'Sir Thomas did not reign long: he was hounded from office on the wholly fictitious issue of Crichel Down, a case almost as shameful as the dismissal of W. S. Morrison sixteen years earlier. The resignation of Sir Thomas was not an issue out of which I was prepared to try to make Party capital.' (Tom Williams, *Digging for Britain*, 1965, p. 182.)

Although these quotations give an impression of rather unusually non-partisan and generous attitudes in both the major parties, that was not the atmosphere of the debate itself. After some six hours of what one of the speakers, Walter Elliot (another former Minister of Agriculture) called 'rough, raw and odious debate' the House divided at ten o'clock in the evening on party lines, giving the government a fairly comfortable majority of thirty-one. There had been a very full attendance, with 563 members voting, and fifteen speaking, not counting the frequent interjections, questionings, points of order, and what Elliot had described, early in the debate, as from time to time 'a note of almost hysterical laughter in the House'.

Dugdale's carefully prepared, cabinet-approved opening statement took three-quarters of an hour to deliver. Those who heard it had also had a few days' access to the inquiry transcript and the documentary evidence, as well as a month to study the Clark report. They were in a position—as Walter Elliot said—to know of the subject 'as much as, and perhaps more than, any of the people who were handling it at the time'. But that did not prevent most of the speakers and the interjectors from reproducing, in their wilder condemnations of the Crichel Down muddle, a further plenitude of the kind of hostile mistakes of fact and inference which had appeared in the press.

Even the Minister's opening statement, so careful, so laboriously prepared and vetted, the product of many hands and minds, legal and lay, was not free from 'old fallacies'. Clark's error about the date of Air Ministry acquisition, 1937 instead of Michaelmas 1938, was still there, as was the acceptance as revealed truth of another Clark error—his rejection of the truth that before acquisition the land was in rough, poor condition. A third error was less correctable—that was the erroneous belief that the Minister had been misinformed when told that the Crichel and Langton land had been sold 'voluntarily'. The Minister's statement contrived to put all three errors into one simple, compendious error about the position at the end of 1952 when he decided to equip the land as one farm: 'It is true that at that time both the Land Commission and I were under certain misapprehensions about both the condition of the land when the Air Ministry acquired it in 1937 and the form of acquisition of most of it.'

It was not true: the bad condition of the land led to its selection in 1937, and its acquisiton in 1938, and the form of acquisition of most of it was in law voluntary—as indeed the Minister went on to recognize in another sentence beginning 'It is true', intended to show that he had not been under any real misapprehension:

It is true, as I have said, that I was told incorrectly that the land from the Crichel and Langton Estates had been sold voluntarily, but I did not at the time regard the difference between voluntary and compulsory purchase as decisive. I recognised that the landowners concerned would have known that, failing agreement, compulsory powers could be exercised. Indeed, I knew that Mr. Hooper's 15 acres had been compulsorily acquired. Accordingly, I weighed this claim against the agricultural case.

Believing in Clark's statements led Dugdale to believe in what his statement called 'the fact that mistakes and grave errors of judgement were made which undoubtedly merited severe censure and reprimand'. That was a tragic error. The real mistake lay in believing Clark: the tragedy, for civil servants and for Thomson, lay in the Minister's consequent inability to embark on a vigorous and complete defence of them. A final effort of concentration may now be required of the reader, to appreciate the paradox that the real mistake of the civil servants (Thomson made none) lay in accepting Clark's mistakes, and in not preserving the Minister, the Law Officers, the Prime Minister, the Cabinet, the Parliament and the Press from the grave apostasy of belief in Clark. The evidence to disprove him, after all, was there in the ministry's own files, and in its own library, and in the Air Ministry's files. If no one else thought of doing the necessary research, the Permanent Secretary should have ordered it, from a mixture of scepticism (in Clark) and faith (in his own service).

Speaking of the Agricultural Land Commission itself, Dugdale did his duty by them without reservations, stressing the members' high reputations, their full regard to financial and agricultural considerations, absolving them completely from the charge of withholding information from him. In other words, he cleared the Commission's members of all charges by Clark, without openly repudiating Clark.

Yet here again, there was error; innocent, inadvertent error: in giving the Chairman and Board the clean bill of health they sought, without which they would have considered 'action' (p. 186) the Minister absolved himself with them, in connection with the promises which were not quite promises given by the ALC and not implemented. All he said on the subject was:

I admit at once that it was most regrettable — and I make no attempt to excuse it — that the promises made on behalf of the Land Commission to previous applicants for the land that their applications would be considered in due course were not brought to the notice of those handling the matter until after Crown Lands felt that they were under a moral obligation to the prospective tenant. Had Crown Lands not taken this view, it would have been possible, even at that stage, to have advertised the tenancy, although such a procedure would have been unusual, because Crown Lands had not at that time decided to buy the land.

It seems genuinely never to have occurred to anyone, neither Dugdale, nor Sir Frederick Burrows, nor anyone else, that if any blame was to attach to any individual for the muddle over 'breach of promise' it certainly could not be pinned on anyone but the Minister and the Chairman themselves jointly. First the Minister had decided on sale to Crown Lands but had given strict orders on confidentiality until he cleared the proposal with the Chairman, at a meeting which took place later than expected. By the time they met and agreed and gave Crown Lands a very tight time limit for action, and a clear delegation as to selection of a tenant, that efficient combination of civil service and private enterprise, Eastwood and Thomson, had found not merely a tenant but probably the best available tenant. The work was accomplished before the field officers of the ALC had learned of the proposal and reported the snag of previous commitments innocently made by them. It was a classic example of men at the top 'cutting red tape' and deciding matters without full knowledge of the implications, without consulting those at the lower levels who did know them, and without lively *Angst* enough to wonder whether their decisions might not disappoint the legitimate expectations of individuals and cause difficulties to their subordinates following previous instructions. It happens every day in large organizations, and is often praised as 'decisiveness'. Certainly there was little wrong with the decision to sell to Crown Lands, apart from the unintended (because unanticipated) consequences of cutting red tape and enjoining speed of action. It is the embarrassment of the situation produced which is reflected in Eastwood's and Wilcox's 'obnoxious' letters — private ruminations by men landed into difficulties not of their making, difficulties later incapable of really satisfactory solution. Had Dugdale thought the matter through, it would have been entirely in character for him to have taken on the minor additional burden of defending more vigorously what his colleagues had called indefensible.

For the rest, the statement announced decisions of varying importance, the most dramatic being left to the last: (a) Sanctuary & Sons to be relieved of management of Crichel Down, despite the accepted propriety of their actions (b) Woods Committee's recommendations accepted (c) Crown Lands and (d) Agriculture Department to be reviewed (e) future sale of all agricultural land possible, rather than ALC management (f) agricultural land acquired 'by compulsion or threat of compulsion' to be sold, when no longer required, unless so altered as to be unusable for agriculture (g) such land for sale to be considered, each case on its merits, for offer to former owner or successor at a price assessed by the district valuer as the current market price (h) as to Crichel Down, although the Minister's carefully considered decision against Marten's claim was right at the time, when maximum production was essential, the better 'food situation' and the 'new procedure' in (g) would be applied to Crichel Down retrospectively, were it not for the 'practical difficulties' that the land was already let to a tenant who could not properly be evicted, so it could only be sold 'subject to the tenancy', so long as the tenant was unwilling to surrender the tenancy, and 'clearly' only to one individual rather than three successors of former owners: if the three successors could agree on one among them to purchase, the Minister would be prepared 'to sell the land, subject to the tenancy and the obligation to equip'; (i) that he had resigned his office as Minister: 'Having now had this opportunity of rendering account to Parliament of the actions which I thought fit to take, I have, as the Minister responsible during this period, tendered my resignation to the Prime Minister, who is submitting it to the Queen.'

That was that. George Brown followed, saying Dugdale had been 'hunted and harassed' by his own party, that it was a very sad moment, coming after a 'very sad and very sorry tale'; that the new policies were 'a sad sell-out for agriculture'; that 'a long story of delay, indecision and muddle' had culminated in 'perhaps the most curious public inquiry that has ever been set up in circumstances of this kind'. Then George Brown too, one of the sharpest and most intelligent politicians of his time, went wrong: 'I am now accepting the view of Commander Marten and of other gentlemen concerned

about the condition of their land when it was bought from them.'
But his comments on the 'one-man inquiry', the partiality and
contradictions of the Clark report, the lack of protection for civil
servants, the 'messing about' of Tozer, and the lack of adequate
direction in a department which 'muddled, delayed and messed
about over a long period' were both sharp and shrewd. They infuri-
ated the government side, but contained no personal attack on
Dugdale.

Of the other speakers, the one to mount the most eloquent attack
on Clark and his report was a fellow baronet, Sir Richard Acland
(already quoted, on p. 173), who combined that with a blistering
reference to the press reporting of the Clark report:

Since its publication, I believe that it has done great damage because of the
sustained onslaught which has been released upon the public service, whose
servants have been castigated in all the journals of middle-class and upper-
class opinion as incorruptible tyrants, secretive conspirators, and discourteous
nonentities, contemptuous alike of the rights of individuals and of the real
public interest.

I believe that great damage has been created by the resulting ill-odour
which has been spread upon every organ of public control, especially in
relation to land.

Of his fellow-baronet Sir Andrew Clark, Acland spoke with utter
disrespect: 'He was a very remarkable Conservative candidate. I
believe that it was said locally at the time that he was the only man
who could perform the miracle of losing Barnet for the Conservative
Party . . . ' Yet Acland too went wrong on the facts, when making
a point on 'the sad complaint of our defeated Tory candidate Q.C.'
(that the ministers were not told the truth about compulsory
acquisition):

Whose fault was that? . . . I say that it is the fault of Ministers. . . . The
drill is this: you get a complaint, you look at it, you pass the complaint
to your staff and ask for a report. Then what? You get the report and you
look at the complaint *vis-à-vis* the report and you look at these two for the
purpose of spotting whether there are any contradictions on fact. If you
find any contradiction on fact, you write a polite letter to the complainant
and an almighty rocket to your own Department asking for 101 per cent
confirmation of the point on which there is contradiction. If the head men
do not do that piece of elementary administrative work, it is no use blaming
the underlings because the Minister did not know.

Correct on the need to verify the facts, Acland had gone wrong in not 'spotting' the contradiction in the Crichel Down acquisition story just revealed in the Minister's statement — a contradiction which in a perverse way was no real contradiction at all. Dugdale had said he had been told, incorrectly, of voluntary sale of Crichel and Langton land. Yet there was no real contradiction; he had also made it clear that he knew, at the time of his decision — as did the landowners at the time of acquisition — that if they did not agree compulsion could be used, as in Hooper's case. So they 'volunteered', in the same sense that a man knowing the alternative is conscription may volunteer, and be accurately called a volunteer, whereas the man actually conscripted cannot.

In general, Labour speakers more in favour of public ownership (although none chose to speak of land nationalization) were less hostile to the civil service and the ALC than Liberal or Conservative speakers. Liberals were greatly concerned with individual rights and the dangers of 'bureaucracy'. The Conservatives had at one extreme men like Crouch from Dorset and Lord Lambton from Berwick-on-Tweed, while the other end of their spectrum was represented not by extremism but by the moderation of Walter Elliot.

Crouch talked of battles won against past oppressors, of King Charles's head, of 'the battle against the bureaucrats, who must also be beaten', of the Tolpuddle martyrs, and of Mrs Marten's great-grandfather on her mother's side, the seventh Earl of Shaftesbury, 'the greatest friend of the working classes'. That was a Dorset contribution to confusion: from the other extreme of England, Berwick-on-Tweed, came an even more bizarre view, from Lord Lambton, who out-Clarked Clark himself, loosing off about 'speeches' by Wilcox and Eastwood which 'completely condemn the civil servants for, at the very least, deceit'; about 'a deliberate untruth' by Smith; about Hole, Wilcox, and Eastwood 'conniving . . . in preventing applicants from knowing what had happened to their applications', and about the unwisdom of retaining in the service 'men who have practised deceit and chicanery' — with more in the same strain to show that the civil service had not been treated 'nearly severely enough on this occasion'.

Walter Elliot spoke only because the other former Ministers of Agriculture present, ironically enough, either could not (the Speaker, W. S. Morrison, later Lord Dunrossil) or would not (Tom Williams). He made the point that both ministers and civil servants were working under great strain—it was a case of 'There, but for the grace of God, go I'—one slip, and you might be saved 'by the skin of your teeth', or you might not: 'The Minister has paid forfeit with his political life. I do not believe that he could have carried out those disciplinary steps unless he had been willing to resign when he had carried them through. This was the duty of the man at the top—to clear up the mess and then to say, "My responsibility is also overriding, and with that I go." '

The psychological insight, in the last sentence, seems accurate, but the Minister's worst troubles with the party had stemmed not from taking but from steadfast refusals to take the 'disciplinary steps' against civil servants that were being loudly and persistently demanded; confusion again.

Herbert Morrison (later Lord Morrison of Lambeth) was the last opposition speaker, charging the government with administrative incompetence, with succumbing to pressure by their own back-benchers 'happy that they have the scalp of a Minister', and with ceasing to put production first, but 'putting doctrinaire Tory politics first' instead. By way of introduction for the last speaker in the debate, Maxwell Fyfe, the Home Secretary, Queen's Counsel, former Law Officer, and Lord Chancellor-to-be, Morrison suggested that the fact that he was to reply to the debate was proof of the weakness of the government's case: 'Merely because he is, or was, a distinguished lawyer, the Government perpetuates the mistake that he can, therefore, defend any rotten case of the Government.'

Maxwell Fyfe was defending himself as much as the government as a whole, and chose to escape into empty generalities, 'three thoughts': first, sorrow for Dugdale's departure and gratitude for the magnificent way he had handled 'the problems of increasing production and harmonising guaranteed prices with a freer economy'; second, 'the prime concern of all of us', 'to see that what had taken place in regard to Crichel Down does not happen again'; and third, the need to state fairly and fully the doctrine of ministerial responsibility in regard to the civil service.

Maxwell Fyfe had been closely and personally associated with Crichel Down throughout the trouble, and would have done well to accept and declare his own responsibility for error, in the same manly fashion as Dugdale himself. He had, for instance, advised Clark's appointment (p. 120), made nonsense of the terms of reference of the inquiry (p. 166), and had had the closest connection with the affair throughout the 'collective responsibility' phase in cabinet committee and subcommittee. What he actually said boils down to a vacuous statement that with a few exceptions civil servants hold office at pleasure and can be dismissed 'at any time' by their Minister, with an outline of the following unexhaustive categories:

(i) Where a civil servant carries out an explicit order by a Minister, the Minister must protect him.

(ii) Where a civil servant acts properly in accordance with the policy laid down by the Minister, the Minister must protect and defend him.

(iii) Where an official makes a mistake or causes some delay, not important or seriously involving 'a claim to individual rights' the Minister acknowledges the mistakes, accepts responsibility although not personally involved, and takes corrective action without exposing the official to public criticism.

(iv) But where action has been taken by a civil servant of which the Minister disapproves and has no prior knowledge, the Minister is not bound to defend it, but 'he remains responsible to Parliament for the fact that something has gone wrong' and 'he alone' can 'tell Parliament what has occurred and render an account of his stewardship'.

By that simplistic set of rules, the Crichel Down civil servants should have been absolutely protected under (i) and (ii), and should not have been exposed to public inquiry and criticism under (iii). And (iv), whether it applied to Crichel Down or not, is a covert admission that public inquiry was wrong: the Minister should have inquired in private—no public inquiry, no White Paper laid on the Table for debate—and, presumably, no cabinet committees and subcommittees, merely the Minister, 'he alone' rendering to Parliament an account of his stewardship. This was not so much a set of rules as an adroit way of suggesting what was false: that no blame for Crichel Down could lie with Prime Minister and cabinet, but might well lie with civil servants, for actions which might not have been known to ministers, 'indefensible' actions, in breach of individual rights, which ministers would (of course) never have approved had they been told of them. It was the last word in the debate, and went unquestioned, both in parliament and in the press, becoming eventually authoritative text-book material.

The Aftermath

It is difficult to answer, in regard to Crichel Down, little Peterkin's question about another 'famous victory' of another Churchill, at

Blenheim in 1704: 'But what good came of it at last?' So far as Sir Thomas Dugdale's belief was concerned, that good would come in the end from the inquiry, in that a tendency to 'bureaucracy' and 'bureaucratic behaviour' in the civil service would be reversed, the end is not yet.

Certainly, in repute, in morale, in discipline, in loyalty, in patriotism, in incorruptibility, in dedication and selfless service, in peaceful staff relations, and in freedom from strikes and other disputes, the history of the civil service in Britain was, in the thirty years from Crichel Down, a story of a fast and accelerating fall from a previous state of grace when 'not only inflexible but fastidious' standards of conduct were the accepted ethical norm. That is not meant as a wholesale condemnation of the modern service: it means only that in the Crichel Down era there was still an imbalance in the situation, when politicians, parliament, and press were getting a civil service better than they deserved, a service with higher standards of duty and ethics than prevailed in the rest of public life. After Crichel Down, and in part at least because of Crichel Down, the country began to get the worsening civil service that it deserved, and the process of deterioration was to continue. In the previous years of the century, cases of corruption, real or merely imagined and rumoured, were scarce: thirty years later large police bureaucracies of full-time fraud investigators throughout the country (a squad of thirty in the Metropolitan and City police areas alone) were kept very busy examining hundreds of cases of suspected corruption in the public sector. That such investigations should be undertaken 'in private' and 'bureaucratically' is no doubt necessary, and a considerable advance on the Crichel Down method of inquiry, but it is hard to see in it any reversal of what Max Weber feared — a probably inevitable, universal spread of bureaucratic domination of human life, made more pervasive by attempts to reverse the process. What happened to both the Ministry of Agriculture and to Crown Lands in the aftermath of Crichel Down provides apt but contrasting examples of that process.

The Ministry of Agriculture, one unarmed civil vessel in what must be called a convoy rather than one single ship of state, had been holed by Commander Marten's torpedoes and raked by Brigadier Sir Andrew Clark's shore batteries, and had to be patched up at sea. The Arton Wilson committee (expanded to five members from the two mentioned in the debate, with Wilson himself the only career civil servant) deliberately chose a strengthening of the bureaucracy, in their report (Cmnd. 9732, presented April 1956, the committee having been appointed in December 1954). What they had found was bureaucratic anathema, 'a formidable array' of organizations in the department, ' a patchwork of organizations, often unco-ordinated, and working within 22 different sets of boundaries', trying to discharge, in relation to its main industry, agriculture, 'almost all the functions of Government', creating its own 'local authorities' (the County Agriculture Executive Committees), extensively using its professional and technical staff for executive work.

The remedies they proposed were mostly accepted: they amounted to the application of the classical principles of bureaucratic organization: 'clear lines of command, along which precise instructions should flow from the centre to the furthest out-station'; 'Ideally, no officer should be in doubt about the definition of his own responsibilities: or answerable for executive action to more than one superior'; 'The Ministry's local organization is riddled with divided loyalties and dual control.' There must be no 'perfectionism', none of the 'bureaucratic touch'—yet the first strong recommendation made was that the 'unofficial' county committees should cease to participate in routine administration or 'in any way to supervise the civil servants engaged on this work'. The whole trend was to strengthen the bureaucracy with better regional co-ordination (Dorset, for example, ceasing to be grouped with the south-western counties controlled from Bristol, and becoming part of the southern region around London). There was to be a new Lands Service with a small group of 'expert professional staff for full-time duties as managing agents' to whom responsibility would be transferred from the Agricultural Land Commission—for whose retention, indeed, the Committee could 'see little reason'. In sum, although the 'bureaucratic touch' might be deplored, it was to be ended, tactfully, by putting a simpler, hierarchical bureaucratic pyramid in place of the cumbersome combinations of civil servants and representative institutions which had served well in emergency, and by abandoning the 'tough' functions which public opinion had turned against. So the Ministry, in its more, not less, bureaucratic form, with its sharp teeth of sanctions against poor farming extracted, 'ploughed' on. The reorganizers of Crown Lands, finding a very simple, monocratic bureaucracy whose only fault had been too speedy response to ministerial direction (p. 176) took a view opposite to the Arton

Wilson committee, and created a cumbersome but protective board structure requiring a larger and more expensive bureaucratic infrastructure to service it. 'Bureaucratization' can take many forms, if the monocratic form is rejected.

Even Sir Thomas Dugdale's own efforts, after his resignation, were not to lead away from bureaucracy; he worked for the cause of European union, involving massive not wholly foreseen or intended increase in the numbers and influence of bureaucracy, in agriculture in particular, in the monstrous shape of the Common Agriculture Policy and its instrumental bureaucratic organizations.

As to the people in the Crichel Down story, Dugdale was deservedly raised to the peerage as Lord Crathorne in 1959, by Harold Macmillan, not long after he became Prime Minister. That can be seen as an act of recompense for the party's ill-treatment, and of respect. Lord Carrington, his offer of resignation with his Minister refused as unnecessary, by the Prime Minister, suffered little check to his political career, filling with distinction many important ministerial offices until his own resignation as Foreign Secretary on the outbreak of hostilities in the Falklands in 1982 — a resignation on the honourable Dugdale model, and the third occasion, in fact, when he had felt obliged to offer his resignation from political office. It was followed by an important 'bureaucratic' appointment as Secretary-General of NATO.

Nugent also, his proffered resignation similarly declined, was raised to the peerage in 1966 as Lord Nugent of Guildford. In 1971 his appointment by Carrington, then Minister of Defence, to chair a committee to advise and report on future policy in regard to land acquired for defence purposes may have given both a kind of ironic satisfaction. Neither, then, could be said to have suffered in their careers from association with Crichel Down. Nor did Maxwell Fyfe suffer, soon attaining, in October 1954, the office of Lord Chancellor which he had long coveted, and becoming Earl of Kilmuir.

Sir Andrew Clark's satanic gifts for reproving sin were not used again on official business. The unnamed journalist of the *News Chronicle* (possibly Douglas Brown) who described Clark in the issue of 20 July 1954 as 'a demon for work in the most complicated cases' was much nearer the mark than he could have meant or guessed. Clark did not pursue any further political ambitions. Nor did Commander Marten. The land itself went to the Crichel Estate, at the district valuer's price of £15,000, together with a substantial sum paid to Tozer by the estate, to buy him out, and other costs which made Marten first hesitate over purchase and then, in vain, seek arbitration over the price. Finally, given by Crown Lands a time limit for decision he agreed 'under protest' to buy at the official price (*The Times*, 16 February and 19 February, 1955). Tozer found another farm, and Crichel Down remained under cultivation as arable land, farmed partly 'in hand' by the Crichel Estate, and partly by tenants.

Whether or not the old adage is true, that 'the best fertilizer is the farmer's feet', no one can yet say for certain whether it would have been better to have persevered with the proposed equipping as one farm, whether for productivity or for some other cause more appropriate to a time of over-production. Certainly, the land was kept in good condition under more remote control—no gorse, no scrub, no poor pasture, but large, rolling arable fields, an emptier landscape than a new mixed farm would have provided, but profitable and productive enough for the times, so far.

Many commentators have attempted to identify a real lesson of Crichel Down, but the one that was thoroughly learned and inwardly digested by the government was that clearly marked in July 1954 by one of the Ministry of Agriculture lawyers (F. P. Mallows) when invited by the permanent secretary to comment, in preparation for a meeting called by the head of the civil service 'to consider the lessons of Crichel Down'. Mallows made brief suggestions, ending sardonically (MAF 236/36): 'Of course, *the* lesson of the Crichel Down Inquiry is, never under any circumstances in future to have such an inquiry again.' A scandal it certainly was: it was the inquiry itself and the treatment of the Blandford martyrs during and after the inquiry which constituted the scandal, not anything the martyrs did, or meant, or did not do. And year in and year out, the scandal persisted, with the uncanny persistence demonstrated in Appendix 1. Crichel Down was often the cruellest stick at hand for critics' exaggerated comment, e.g.: 'The handling of such notorious cases as Crichel Down, and the Stansted Chalk Pit, threw a glaring light on the chicanery and crookedness of which Departments are capable in seeking to cover up blunders and injustices at the expense of the private citizen.' (Nicholson, Max, *The System: the Misgovernment of Modern Britain*, 1967, p. 189.)

To call victims of such vilification martyrs may itself seem an exaggeration; after all, they lost, not their lives, but merely good name, livelihoods, or career prospects. Worse things happen, at sea and on land. But the Tolpuddle Martyrs were not put to death, either, and restitution was eventually made to them. Because the Blandford martyrs behaved, like their Minister, very respectably throughout, and very admirably and with dignity in adversity and political persecution, they too, however belatedly, should be accorded the respect and admiration which are their due as — like their Minister — honest English gentlemen.

Paralipomena

Containing (in roughly chronological order of publication, from English language sources only) some of the louder reverberations, over the years, of the Crichel Down storm, taken from the press, and from later writings by politicians, academics, and others; these extracts show stages in the establishment of the myth of Crichel Down as a classic example of abuse of power by civil servants, the pathology of a bureaucracy become high-handed and unresponsive. As time passes by the facts seem more rather than less blurred, with little 'self-correcting' tendency in the considerable literature visible. Excerpts 28 and 29, from 1982 to 1983 commentaries by senior civil servants show the myth being taken to heart as truth by the civil service itself, and used as an authoritative cautionary tale for the young.

1. 'Storm-swept Down'
'There is no sign of a lull in the high winds that have blown across Crichel Down since the publication of the shattering Clark report and they will reach gale force in the Commons debate when it comes. . . . ' (Editorial, *The Times*, 28 June 1954.)

2. 'The success of our campaign for an Inquiry owed a very great deal to the Press, whose nose for dirty work seems to have been so much more acute than the Minister's.' (Address by Lieutenant-Commander G. G. Marten to the National Liberal Club, 30 June 1954. For full text see Appendix 4.)

3. 'The details of this shabby affair do not matter. What matters is that private citizens were apparently pushed around, misled and steam-rollered — simply because they had the nerve to question the acts of a Government Department.'
'The only way Dugdale can carry the can for his arrogant bureaucrats in this business is by resignation.'
'This is not a Party dispute. It is the case of the ordinary man against the bloody-minded bureaucrat.'
'And the public wants to know that — for the tinpot Napoleons concerned — Crichel Down was their Waterloo.' (From the *Daily Mirror* editorial, 20 July 1954.)
(In an editorial on the following day reporting 'Dugdale quits — another blow for Churchill', The *Daily Mirror* proudly reproduced the previous day's demand for his resignation and commented: 'The minority Right-wing group which has fought the Premier on these two issues (Crichel Down and M.P.s' pay) is open in its desire to force Sir Winston's resignation.'

'He could have carried the majority of the Party with him had he fought to protect his Minister. It is this second sign of weakness that has so dismayed the Premier's usually loyal supporters.')

4. 'What has been disturbing is the revelation of how, under the immensely complex bureaucratic system which has now been evolved, civil servants are left with a free hand to make policy.' (*Manchester Guardian*, 20 July 1954.)

5. 'The New Despotism'
'The ownership of land is important and ought to be discussed — but at some other time. Parliament is met today to settle a far more important matter — something of direct concern to every man, woman and child in these islands whether they have ever owned a blade of grass or not. It is the abuse of power by civil servants.'

'They were not only careless with public money: they were careless of the public trust. They had made a little kingdom for themselves, and we, the humble citizens who pay their salaries, were to be their even humbler subjects. . . . They are corrupt with power. . . . They were filled with fury when Commander Marten tried to assert his rights against them. . . . This is the heart of the matter. This is the core of the evil. This is the New Despotism at work.' (Editorial, *News Chronicle*, 20 July 1954.)

6. 'The primary issue, and the one which has aroused so much public indignation, is the irresponsibility of a few Civil servants.'

'The conclusions of SIR ANDREW CLARK'S report are stern enough in their observations on the offending Civil servants, but the full story which precedes them is almost unbelievable in its catalogue of errors of judgement and misleading advice and in the arrogant temper which it discloses among those who are meant to be public servants.'

'However unfair the constitutional position may seem, he (the Minister) will today be the only person whom the House of Commons can hold to account. . . . '

'The redress of Commander Marten's private grievance may be one of the issues before the House today. But first and last, the House must seek the redress of the wider public grievance against the actions of presumptuous authority.' (Editorial, *The Times*, 20 July 1954.)

7. 'What could happen once could happen again. The battle is not between Farmer Marten and Farmer Tozer — indeed they are friendly enough. It is between you and me, and all the petty dictators in officialdom.' (James Derriman in *News Chronicle*, 20 July 1954.)

8. 'The men responsible for the shocking affair of Crichel Down are not fit to serve the British people. They ought to be dismissed.' (Editorial, *News Chronicle*, 20 July 1954.)

9. 'Secrecy was the main evil in the Crichel Down case. All the more honour to the man who had the good sense and determination to make the matter public, and to a public opinion which still had enough essential liberalism in it to back him up.' (*Spectator*, 23 July 1954.)

10. 'What is needed is a new principle of government, to be applied right through the whole body of delegated powers: that no Minister and no department shall take any decision affecting the rights of property of any individual without the papers being referred — not necessarily for decision, but at least for report — to some wholly independent scrutiny.' (*The Economist*, 24 July 1954.)

11. 'In the end . . . the only sure bulwark of liberty is the existence of enough men of sufficient property and wealth to be able to challenge authority by every means possible.' (Henry Fairlie, letter to the editor, *Spectator*, 30 July 1954.)

12. 'The capital revelation of the Crichel Down enquiry is how entirely defenceless the normal citizen is in England today against a Ministry acting within the ambit of its enormous powers.' (Professor C. J. Hamson, BBC Third Programme, *Listener*, 19 Aug. 1954.)

13. 'The actions of the civil servants concerned were not those of a group of men trying to do their best in difficult circumstances but rather of officials wielding the powers of the State and spending public money in an irresponsible way and with little regard to economy, efficiency or the fair treatment of individual citizens.' (Professor W. A. Robson, BBC Third Programme, *Listener*, 27 Jan. 1955.)

14. 'This discreditable story seemed to focus on itself the long pent up irritation of an over-controlled public against 'bossiness' in official places. No one believed that "Crichel Down" was unique; they suspected that the country was swarming with mute inglorious Crichels. As for the fact that these civil servants had not been bribed, no one had suggested that they had been. There are other kinds of corruption besides the passing of money. Lord Acton's dictum — "Power corrupts" — proved a useful quotation.' (*Annual Register of World Events*, 1954, ed. I. S. Macadam, 1955, pp. 38–9.)

15. 'Crichel Down had been compulsorily acquired in 1937 as a bombing site. When it was no longer needed for that purpose the hereditary owners of the land sought to buy it back. Their request met with a curt refusal.' (From the dust-jacket of *The Battle of Crichel Down*, by R. Douglas Brown (completed December, 1954, published 1955.))

16. [Officials prepared] 'reports that were carelessly inaccurate in highly relevant facts, secretively withheld vital information from one another, ignored significant factors, and skimped analysis in reaching an improvident and indefensible conclusion.'

'They took evasive action designed to give an impression of fairness where the substance of fairness was obviously lacking, and showed throughout a hostile and destructive attitude towards the former owner. Several of them clearly enjoyed the idea of shaping the destiny of Crichel Down and resented the attempt of the former owner to take this role away from them. The enemies of bureaucracy would have regarded the result as a very satisfactory model of incompetence, confusion and dissimulation. The officials misled the Minister in important particulars.' 'No civil servant was dismissed for his share in the affair, but during and after the inquiry, several were quietly transferred to other departments.' (Extracts from a 1955 presidential address to the Canadian Political Science Association by Professor J. A. Corry, treating the case as one where 'the former owner of the bulk of the area' wanted to get it back — reproduced in Stankiewicz, W. J., ed. *Crisis in British Government*, 1964.)

17. 'Extra-legal, political agitation may at times, and in hard cases, prove most effective, as was proved in the Crichel Down affair in 1953/54 (see Cmd. 9176); Mr. Pilgrim's suicide when his parcel of land was compulsorily acquired by the local authority caused so much political argument that the Government of the day agreed to add the clause which is now s.35 of the T.P. and C.P.A., 1954, when the Bill was before the House.' (Footnote, p. 9, in Garner, J. F., *The Public Control of Land*, 1956; this note, by juxtaposition of Crichel Down and the quite separate Pilgrim tragedy, may be the innocent source of the otherwise inexplicable impression, in the minds of lawyers and others, that a 'former owner' of Crichel Down was driven to suicide.)

18. 'Difficulties arose in relation to subjects outside the main clash of political controversy, such as commercial television, Members' salaries, and, above all, Crichel Down.' (p. 222.) 'Television and Members' pay paled into insignificance beside Crichel Down. This incident had so much influence on the thought of all political parties, including even the Socialists, on the position of the individual in the modern State, that it is worth a moment's consideration.' (p. 227.) 'The effect of the Report and of Dugdale's resignation was to reorientate the views of all towards improving the rights of individuals. It will be a long time before "There is an echo of Crichel Down in this case" will not flutter the administrative dovecots. Moreover the Socialists saw that, if they wanted to be returned, they must try and get rid of the idea that their all-powerful state would be erected on the ruins of individual rights.' (p. 228.) (*Political Adventure: the Memoirs of the Earl of Kilmuir*, 1962.)

19. 'The story of Crichel Down provides us with such a warning against the extension of Government power that I shall here break my journey to recall it for the benefit of all those who may be interested in the history

of British agriculture since the war.' (p. 147.) 'Whatever the Socialists may think of returning land once nationalized to private owners both they and the Conservatives desire some efficiency on the part of the officials the Government employs, and the fact that efficiency did not exist is the whole essence of the Crichel Down scandal. In fact, no officials could have been more inept than those who now proceeded to deal with Crichel Down.' p. 150.) 'They visited the property in groups, looked it swiftly over, and put forward a very different proposition.' (p. 150.) 'Never has a Minister of the Crown been so badly served by his officials as was Sir Thomas Dugdale. The information they gave him was worthless; most of it was false and all of it was misleading.' (p. 154.) 'Of all the officials who had so misled the Minister none was seriously punished. Three senior London officers were required to change their jobs. Certain officials who had made serious errors, and then to protect themselves had dodged the enquiry, should have been dismissed, but nothing happened to them. Yet these are typical of the kind of official who would wield unprecedented power under a State-controlled agriculture. We owe much to Commander Marten, for his fight certainly helped to check the growth of an agricultural bureaucracy.

'Only one man suffered for all the errors of Crichel Down. This was the one man who in the whole of the transaction was entirely innocent, and who had courageously and honourably ordered the enquiry, knowing that it might ruin his political career. Sir Thomas Dugdale, now Lord Crathorne, most unfairly was the man upon whom the lot of the scapegoat was cast, and it led him into the political wilderness.' (pp. 156–7.) (George Winder, *Modern Rural Rides*, 1964.)

20. 'The "aggrieved parties" (described as "three previous owners or tenants, two of whom were still farming in the neighbourhood and one, deceased, who was represented by a son so farming" who were given "no opportunity of re-purchasing or leasing" land acquired by the Air Ministry in 1937 — although they had been told that their claim to buy or lease would be considered . . .) had in addition some cause to suspect something worse than muddle, so they promoted a political agitation which led to the Minister of Agriculture setting up a statutory enquiry. The examiner in his report (1954, Cmd. 9176) sets out an incredible story of incompetence, folly and misjudgement.' (Professor G. Sawer, *Ombudsmen*, 1964, pp. 20–2.)

21. 'While Crichel Down was given undue prominence, it did serve to demonstrate the deep-seated unrest over the way in which civil servants could — and sometimes did — ride roughshod over the ordinary citizen's rights. The Franks Committee was ostensibly set up to review the unwholesome picture presented by the report on Crichel Down, but its terms of reference precluded it from discussing problems of administration other than those arising out of the powers exercised by administrative tribunals.' (Professor D. C. Rowatt, *The Ombudsman*, 1965, p. 268.)

22. 'Finally, in 1954, there was Crichel Down (that now all-but-forgotten place!). At the time it occurred, Crichel Down was looked upon as the bright dawn, another Runnymede. It was the victory of the individual, Lieut.-Commander George Marten, over an arrogant and unscrupulous bureaucracy: the victory of Parliament, a single parliamentarian, the late Robert Crouch, Member for North Dorset (an historically individualist county) over a somewhat lackadaisical Minister of Agriculture, Sir Thomas Dugdale, who resigned as a consequence of this incident.' (Dr Donald McI. Johnson, MP *A Cassandra at Westminster*, 1967, p. 52.)

23. What nobody could explain in any of the numerous cases that from time to time arose was the cause of the obstinacy and determination that those in charge of the spoliation of the land brought to their unlovely work. In countries with a lower standard of integrity in elected public servants and their professional advisers it would have been easy to explain it in terms of corruption, but such lapses were genuinely rare in Britain. Yet the determination to persist in a decision once arrived at, however high the cost in logic, natural justice, and damage to the interests of others, and however, low the return, seemed so great that a kind of madness appeared to possess those responsible. . . . This at times seemed true in the literal sense, as a study of the Crichel Down affair of the Fifties revealed.' (Bernard Levin, *The Pendulum Years: Britain and the Sixties*, 1970, p. 196.)

24. 'In the past the minister was held responsible for things he knew nothing about: Austen Chamberlain resigned over the medical supplies to Mesopotamia, and Sir Thomas Dugdale resigned over the Crichel Down affair.' (Anthony Sampson, *the New Anatomy of Britain*, 1971, p. 259.)

25. 'The most recent case was the resignation of Sir Thomas Dugdale, when officials of his ministry were censured over the Crichel Down Case in 1954. Sir Thomas Dugdale was a popular Minister who had the support of the Premier and there was no question of the latter asking for his resignation. He decided to leave because he felt that if he stayed, the whole matter would be smoothed over, whereas a ministerial resignation would administer a profound and salutary shock to the whole Civil Service. There is the added point that this was not a matter in dispute between the parties and Sir Thomas could act without fear of any political repercussion.' (Professor J. P. Mackintosh, MP, *The British Cabinet*, 3rd edn, 1977 (1st edn 1961), p. 530. (At p. 531, Mackintosh also refers to Dugdale's desire 'to give his officials a jolt.'))

26. 'Sir Thomas Dugdale assumed moral responsibility and as a result of pressure from his own political backbenchers he resigned his office. It should be noted that Sir Thomas Dugdale had not forfeited the Prime Minister's confidence.' (C. F. Padfield, *British Constitution Made Simple*, 5th edn 1981 (1st edn 1972), p. 147.)

27. 'The Crichel Down affair of 1954 provides a good example . . . (of the probably better grounds for complaining that civil servants are excessively protected than for criticising their defencelessness in law.')

'This was one of the rare cases where serious complaints against the conduct of officials were investigated in a public proceeding. The charge was that they had not given proper attention to a land-owner's claims for the restoration of land taken under compulsory powers before the war. There was no infringement of legal rights, but clearly there had been bad administration. A public enquiry was ordered by the Minister of Agriculture and all the correspondence was published — a most unusual opportunity for the public to see the contents of official files. But despite the strong criticism which the report contained, there were no dismissals, and in the civil service the result of all the upheaval was no more than some arrangement of duties. The Minister of Agriculture, however, resigned — although he personally was entirely free from blame, and had shown magnanimity in ordering the enquiry. There could hardly be a better illustration of the rock-like solidarity of the civil service and, in contrast, of the irrational vicissitudes of politics. The doctrine of ministerial responsibility does not, indeed, require a minister to resign if his officials have done something which is not in accordance with his orders or his policy, and of which he does not approve. But, when the choice had to be made, it was in fact the Minister who elected to pay the penalty.' (Professor H. W. R. Wade, *Administrative Law*, 5th edn, 1982 (1st edn 1971).)

28. ' . . . I must deal with what was undoubtedly the most traumatic event of my first two years, in terms of its impact on the conduct of business in Whitehall: the Crichel Down affair of 1954 (Public Inquiry into the Disposal of Land at Crichel Down 1954). The name is remembered now as the form of procedure that has to be observed when disposing of land originally acquired under compulsory powers (in most cases it has to be offered back to the former owner). But for those who were around at the time, it made a profound impression and has probably had more influence on official attitudes than any other single event in the past thirty years.'

' . . . those who were in their formative years at the time of Crichel Down will have had it in mind for the rest of their career and it seems reasonable to suppose that it has influenced the collective consciousness of the civil service ever since: how not to treat the public and what can happen if you do.' (John Delafons, Chairman of the Royal Institute of Public Administration, '*Working* in Whitehall: Changes in Public Administration 1952–1982', in *Public Administration*, vol. 60, Autumn 1982.)

29. 'Public anxiety about the accountability of senior officials has manifested itself at many times since the end of the War. Perhaps one of the most celebrated instances was that of the Crichel Down affair, when arbitrary and, in the eyes of many, inequitable behaviour on the part of civil servants

gave rise to disquiet about the adequacy of the opportunities open to the citizen for the redress of grievance often caused by the unperceived acts of officials. . . .

'Since Crichel Down, the convention has gradually been changed and it would now be unusual for Parliament to expect a minister to resign over some relatively detailed failure on the part of his department, certainly if it was a failure to which he positively contributed nothing.' (Sir Douglas Wass, Permanent Secretary to the Treasury and Joint Head of the Civil Service, Address to the Royal Institute of Public Administration, 2 Dec. 1982, on 'The Public Service and Modern Society' (*Public Administration*, vol. 61, Spring 1983).)

30. 'In 1954, a report into the sale of land at Crichel Down made serious accusations of maladministration against certain civil servants. The minister in charge of the relevant department, Sir Thomas Dugdale, accepted responsibility and resigned, though he had had nothing to do with the affair. The only other postwar incident remotely comparable was in 1982, when the Falklands invasion led to the resignation of Lord Carrington and two junior foreign office ministers—one of whom, Sir Humphrey Atkins, was wholly unconnected with the matter. None the less, ever since Crichel Down civil servants have basked in the principle that ministers, not they, are responsible for their mistakes.' (*The Economist*, 4–10 Feb, 1984, p. 25.)

31. 'Thirty years ago this summer the Conservative Minister of Agriculture told the House of Commons that he had resigned. The reason was slack and reprehensible conduct by several of his officials on the letting and use of some farm land at Crichel Down in Dorset. No one had suggested that the Minister, Sir Thomas Dugdale, was personally to blame. His resignation was a symbol of his officials' failure: he said that his "stewardship" of the ministry was involved.'

'The officials took against Marten, who was being a nuisance, and arbitrarily excluded him and the other locals from consideration as possible tenants of the land. Worst of all, they deceived the local farmers into thinking that their offer to rent the land would be properly considered.' (Anthony Barker, Reader in Government, Essex University, in the *Listener*, 13 Sept. 1984.)

32. 'RED FACES ON CRICHEL DOWN'
'The extent of the Government's embarrassment over the Crichel Down affair which culminated in the resignation of Sir Thomas Dugdale, the Minister of Agriculture, in 1954 is disclosed in the Cabinet papers.'

'Sir Andrew Clark's report, which singled out five civil servants for severe criticism, came as a bombshell to the Cabinet.

Sir Thomas initially accepted the Clark proposals, but amid mounting pressure from the Civil Service the Government decided on a compromise of establishing a three-man committee to investigate whether the civil servants concerned should be transferred.

But this delaying device worried Mr. Churchill.

On July 20 the special committee recommended to the Cabinet that three civil servants should be transferred to other duties. Sir Thomas felt he had no option but to resign.' (*Daily Telegraph*, 2 Jan. 1985.)

APPENDIX 2

The Clark Report (Cmd. 9176) HMSO, June 1954

To The Right Honourable SIR THOMAS DUGDALE, Bt., M.P.

Sir,

I was appointed by you on 6th November, 1953, with the following terms of reference:—

'To enquire into the procedure adopted (*a*) in reaching the decision that land at Crichel Down should be sold to the Commissioners of Crown Lands; (*b*) in the selection of a tenant by them; and the circumstances in which those decisions were made, but excluding from the enquiry all questions of governmental policy and, in particular, any question of whether preferential treatment should have been given to any applicant on the ground of previous ownership or occupation of the land.'

I have now the honour to submit my Report which I propose to divide into two Parts:

1. Factual Narrative

2. Conclusions.

2. In accordance with my terms of reference I duly held a Public Inquiry at the Corn Exchange, Blandford, into the circumstances in which it was decided to sell 725 acres of land at Crichel Down to the Commissioners of Crown Lands and the procedure adopted in coming to such decision, and also the method adopted in selecting a tenant for the land and the circumstances surrounding such selection. The Inquiry opened at 10.30 a.m. on Wednesday, 21st April, and the hearing lasted for 7 working days, ending at 1 p.m. on Wednesday, 28th April.

3. I heard the oral evidence of 28 witnesses and examined in detail a large number of letters, minutes and other documents. A list of the witnesses is set out at Annexures 1 and 2 to this Report. I am satisfied that all relevant documents were fully disclosed and that (with two exceptions hereinafter mentioned) all persons who could have materially assisted me in the Inquiry were present and gave evidence before me.

Having heard the evidence and examined the documents I find the facts to be as follows:—

1. FACTUAL NARRATIVE

4. In or about the year 1937 some 725 acres of land at Crichel Down in the County of Dorset (hereinafter called 'Crichel Down') were compulsorily

acquired by the Air Ministry for use as a bombing range at a total cost to the Government of £12,106 including compensation for injurious affection.

5. At the time of such acquisition 328 acres (hereinafter called the 'Crichel Area') formed part of a farm on the late Lord Alington's Crichel Estate which at all material times was occupied by Mr. Robin Harding and his nephew Mr. John Harding (hereinafter called 'the Hardings') as tenant farmers. 382 acres (hereinafter called 'the Strange Area') formed part of Mr. Farquharson's Langton Estate and were being farmed as part of Launceston Farm which was originally occupied by Mr. Jim Strange and his brother as tenant farmers, and was later purchased by them when the Langton Estate was broken up in 1940. The remaining 15 acres (hereinafter called 'The Hooper Area') were owned and farmed by the late Mr. Hooper as part of Manor Farm which is at present owned by the Trustees of his will and farmed by his son Mr. Hugh Hooper. At that time approximately 114 acres of the Crichel Area, 56 acres of the Strange Area and the whole of the Hooper Area were under cultivation. The remainder of Crichel Down was typical chalk downland used mainly for sheep grazing.

6. After the land was acquired by the Air Ministry cultivation necessarily ceased and the land deteriorated rapidly becoming covered in places with gorse and infested with rabbits.

7. After the War Crichel Down ceased to be used as a bombing range and in 1949 it was decided that the Air Ministry no longer required to retain it. It was then decided that the land should be transferred to the Ministry pursuant to Section 88 of the Agriculture Act, 1947. The requisite order under that Section formally transferring the land to the Ministry was never in fact made; but in anticipation that such order would be made in due course the Ministry assumed the control and management of Crichel Down in January 1950.

8. The Ministry in accordance with normal practice handed over the management of Crichel Down to the Agricultural Land Commission (hereinafter called 'the Land Commission'), a body corporate established by Section 68 of the Agriculture Act, 1947 for the express purposes of managing and farming land vested in the Ministry. The Land Commission have no power to buy or sell land, but may grant tenancies which are not normally to be more than a year to year tenancy. Although the Land Commission was responsible for the management of the land, they in fact were advised by and carried out their executive functions through the medium of the Lands Service. The Lands Service is an integral part of the Ministry, to which it acts as technical advisers and its officers are all civil servants. In this case, the Lands Service in turn carried out their executive functions through the medium of the Dorset Agricultural Executive Committee (hereinafter called 'The Agricultural Committee').

9. Some confusion is liable to be caused between the Land Commission and the Lands Service by reason of the fact that officers of the Lands Service are called Land Commissioners. To avoid this I refer to them hereinafter as 'Land Service Officers'.

10. In December, 1949, Colonel Norton-Fagge (who was the Land Service Officer for Somerset and Dorset), anticipating the handing over of Crichel Down to the Ministry, wrote to the Dorset County Agricultural Officer, a Mr. Ferris, asking for advice as to how the land should be dealt with. On 10th December, 1949, Mr. Ferris replied stating that he was fairly certain that each of the farmers who had previously farmed Crichel Down would be willing to take over the parts formerly attached to their respective farms and work the land. Mr. Ferris went on to say that he was quite sure that this would be a better method of dealing with the land than by attempting to farm it as one holding. In March, 1950, the Agent for the Crichel Estate wrote to the Ministry asking for an opportunity to negotiate for Crichel Down if it should be for sale, and Colonel Norton-Fagge replied that it was not then possible to give any definite reply. On the 1st April, 1950, the Minister made an Order under Section 68 of the Agriculture Act, 1947, placing Crichel Down under the control of the Land Commission. At this time part of the land was being cultivated by the Hardings and also by Mr. Strange under some nebulous arrangement with the Air Ministry, but they had no tenancy and paid no rent. The land had no water supply of its own, but water was obtained under a licence from the Crichel Estate from the Estate reservoir.

11. Early in May, 1950, Colonel Norton-Fagge inspected Crichel Down accompanied by his immediate superior, Mr. Hole, who was the Provincial Chief Officer of the Lands Service. As a result of this inspection Colonel Norton-Fagge made a written report which was sent to the Land Commission. In this report Colonel Norton-Fagge suggested three possible ways of dealing with the land, namely:—

(a) By letting in blocks to neighbouring farmers.
(b) By division into two or more independent fully equipped holdings.
(c) By the formation of a single fully equipped holding.

He discarded (b) as being unsuitable and economically unsound, and there can be no doubt that he was right in so doing. He advised contrary to the view previously expressed by Mr. Ferris, that (c) would be the best solution, and estimated the cost of equipping the land at £18,500, and that so equipped a rent of £2 per acre should be readily obtainable. He stated that the objection to (a) was that the adjoining farmers might be disinclined to deal satisfactorily with the centre of the land; when cross-examined as to this he admitted that it was pure guesswork on his part and not based on any information he had received or any enquiries he had made. He agreed that the farmers concerned were all first class farmers. He went on to make recommendations as to temporary arrangements for reclamation and cropping, pending equipment of the land as a single unit, which were in fact substantially implemented. There are no material inaccuracies in the facts set out in this report, save that the value of the land was placed at £7,500, as to which see later. The whole report was expressly subject to satisfactory arrangements being made for an adequate supply of water. This was in fact subsequently obtained by agreement with the Crichel Estate who provided a water supply from the estate reservoir.

12. On 20th June, 1950, the Land Commission resolved that one of their members, Mr. Bourke, should inspect Crichel Down as soon as possible. Mr. Bourke duly visited Crichel Down on 11th August, 1950, and reported in writing to the Land Commission. He recommended that the Agricultural Committee should farm the land and carry out reclamation work until Michaelmas, 1951, and that thereafter the land should be equipped as a single unit and let. He stated that he had discussed the matter with Colonel Norton-Fagge and considered the proposals in his report to be quite sound and adequate and recommended that they be adopted. He placed the estimated cost of equipment at £20,000, and the value of the land at £7,500. He estimated the rent obtainable at 35s. per acre which, he said, after allowing for depreciation and repairs would show a net return of 2½ per cent on capital outlay. When cross-examined as to the value of the land he admitted that he did not know where he had got the figure of £7,500 from, and that it was nothing more than a rough guess. In fact it was a mere arbitrary figure which appeared in the Ministry books for audit purposes and had been repeated in Colonel Norton-Fagge's report. It is clear from the evidence before me that the true value of the land unequipped and unrestricted was at least £20,000. Even apart from this mistake, however, it should have been clear even at this stage that from a purely financial aspect the proposal to equip Crichel Down as a single unit was probably unsound.

13. On 16th August, 1950, the Land Commission formally resolved that the proposals to equip Crichel Down as a single unit, subject to slight modification, be approved in principle. The next day Mr. Edwards, who was the Chief Technical Officer to the Land Commission, wrote to Colonel Norton-Fagge notifying him of the decision and stating that the economics of the proposal did not show up very well, even at a rent of 35s. to 40s. per acre.

14. By October, 1950, the Land Commission's proposals for dealing with Crichel Down began to be known in the neighbourhood and from then onwards applications were received from time to time by the Lands Service, either direct or through the Agricultural Committee, from a number of farmers desirous of being considered as tenants. Among the earliest

applicants was a Mr. C. T. Tozer, a member of a well known farming family at Woodyates, with whom I shall have to deal more fully later in this report. There were some 13 or 14 applicants in all, and the Lands Service acting as agents for the Land Commission answered them all in more or less similar form, stating that the property was not at that time being offered to let but their names had been recorded and that as soon as the property was available for letting they would be sent particulars; the tenancy it was stated would be advertised for tender in the public Press and any application they might then make would be carefully considered. Among the applicants was a Captain D. W. Taylor, who offered to rent the land as it was and erect any necessary buildings himself.

15. On 28th August, 1951, Mr. Lofthouse, who had succeeded Colonel Norton-Fagge as Land Service Officer for Somerset and Dorset, wrote to Mr. Hole pointing out that the water supply was then secure (an agreement for water supply had in fact been entered into with the Crichel Estate in June 1951) and saying that all now seemed ready to advertise for a tenant and asking for authority to proceed. To this Mr. Hole replied that the Chairman of the Land Commission, Sir Frederick Burrows, considered the farming of Crichel Down by the Agricultural Committee was very satisfactory, and that Mr. Edwards felt that the decision to advertise should be deferred for the time being. In September Mr. Lofthouse wrote to one of the applicants stating 'I have on record a great many persons who are definitely interested and must be given an opportunity to make an offer. . . . I regret therefore that I must not negotiate with you in advance of any of the other offers'.

16. On 31st October, 1951, a full dress inspection of Crichel Down by the Land Commission took place. Sir Frederick Burrows (the Chairman) Mr. Watson Jones (a member), Mr. Edwards (Chief Technical Officer and Land Agent) and Mr. Smith (Secretary) were present as representing the Land Commission and were accompanied by Mr. Ferris, Mr. Hole, Mr. Lofthouse and other officers of the Lands Service in an advisory capacity. The arrangements for equipping Crichel Down as a single self-contained unit were then settled and it was agreed that certain local farmers, including the Hardings, should be, and subsequently they in fact were, consulted as to the details of siting the buildings and of the necessary equipment generally. It was also decided that the Agricultural Committee should continue to farm the land until Michaelmas, 1952, as from which date the tenancy should be offered for tender.

17. On 25th May, 1952, Captain Taylor wrote to Mr. Lofthouse making a firm offer to rent Crichel down unequipped as it then stood at a rental of £2,000 per annum (i.e. approximately £3 per acre), subject to review every three years with adjustment for provision by the Land Commission of any

buildings or other assets and in the light of then existing conditions. From a purely financial point of view this was in marked contrast to and on the face of it appeared considerably more attractive than the Land Commission's proposal to spend approximately £20,000 in equipping the land with a view to obtaining a rental after it had been equipped of £2 per acre (i.e. approximately £1,400).

18. It is a little strange to see the way in which this offer was dealt with. On 5th June, 1952, Mr. Lofthouse forwarded Captain Taylor's letter to Mr. Hole with a covering letter in which he stated that as it was a serious offer he felt bound to put it up, but recommended adhering to the original plan. On 13th June, 1952, Mr. Hole forwarded Captain Taylor's letter to the Land Commission with a covering letter asking them to confirm that the Commission had no intention of letting without first equipping the land, and strongly recommending them NOT to do so. On 20th June, 1952, the Land Commission replied that they were not prepared to let the land without equipment, and Captain Taylor's offer was duly turned down.

19. There was some suggestion both in the correspondence and in the evidence that Captain Taylor would not have been a satisfactory tenant in any event, but it was clear that the real reason for turning down his application was that it had already been decided as a matter of policy that it was desirable in the interests of food production to equip Crichel Down as a single self contained unit before letting it, and accordingly, as Sir Frederick Burrows himself stated, Captain Taylor's offer was never given any serious consideration. Meanwhile on 26th May, 1952, the Agent to the Crichel Estate, Major Seymour, wrote to Mr. Lofthouse referring to the previous letter from the Crichel Estate of 24th March, 1950, asking for information as to the present situation and asking whether it would be possible to buy back the Crichel Area in order that it might be restored to the Hardings' farm to which it originally belonged and of which, he contended, it formed an important integral part.

20. Mr. Lofthouse forwarded the letter to Mr. Hole with a covering letter in which he stated that he had heard that the Crichel Estate would be willing to purchase the whole of Crichel Down. He stated his belief (which the evidence showed to be correct) that the Estate intended to add any land acquired to the Hardings' farm, and that no fixed equipment would be necessary as existing buildings would be adequate. He further stated that the Hardings were first class farmers and there was no doubt that if the land was sold to the Crichel Estate it would be well farmed. The evidence showed that this view was fully justified. Mr. Hole forwarded both letters to the Land Commission under a covering letter stating that he had not gone into the merits of the proposition as he imagined the Commission would not wish to recommend the Minister to sell the property. Mr. Edwards stated

in evidence that he never pursued the matter any further as he thought the Ministry had no power to sell land. Sir Frederick Burrows stated in evidence that the proposal was never investigated or considered, presumably for the same reason.

21. It appears difficult at first sight to see how such a misconception could ever have arisen in view of the provisions of Section 90 of the Agriculture Act, 1947, which expressly empowers the Minister (inter alia) to sell any land acquired by him in such manner as he may think expedient for the purpose for which the land was acquired (in this case, of course, agriculture) and for any other purpose provided it appears to him expedient so to do having regard to the use proposed to be made of the land. It had, however, been the fixed policy of the Socialist Government never to sell any land that had been acquired by the Government, whether compulsorily or otherwise, except under very special circumstances, and presumably this policy had become so firmly established that many civil servants were under the impression that there was no power to sell. No notification of any change in this policy was received by any of the permanent staff of the Ministry until some time in the summer of 1952, when, according to the evidence of Sir Reginald Franklin, the Minister first expressed his view that if possible a number of properties acquired by the Ministry ought to be sold. Then for some reason, which I find it difficult to understand in face of the unusually clear wording of Section 90 of the Agriculture Act, 1947, which I should have thought made it plain (not only to a lawyer but to any intelligent layman) that the Minister had a complete discretion to sell any land which he had acquired if he came to the conclusion that it was expedient so to do, the Minsiter was advised by the legal department of the Ministry that there were grave doubts whether he had any power to sell land acquired by him. As a result of this advice the opinion of the Law Officers of the Crown was obtained on this question; but it was not until November, 1952, that their opinion was received, stating clearly that the Minister had the requisite power.

22. On 10th June, 1952, Mr. Smith, the Secretary to the Land Commission, replied to Major Seymour's letter of 26th May, stating that it had been decided to equip Crichel Down as a single self-contained unit and when this had been done to advertise it for letting in accordance with the usual practice. Mr. Smith went on to say that although the management of Crichel Down had become the responsibility of the Land Commission, the freehold was still owned by the Air Ministry and so far as the Commission were aware there was no intention of transferring it to the Ministry of Agriculture and Fisheries. How Mr. Smith (and presumably the members of the Land Commission) could have been in complete ignorance of the decision to transfer Crichel Down to the Ministry, especially in view of the Order of the Minister dated 1st April, 1950, vesting the management of the

land in the Land Commission under Section 68 (1) (*a*) of the Agriculture
Act, 1947, as being land vested in the Minister or for the management of
farming of which he had become responsible, is again difficult to appreciate.
Unfortunately Mr. Smith is abroad and was unable to attend the Inquiry
to explain this and other matters. As a result of this letter Lieut. Commander
Marten (whose wife had succeeded to the Crichel Estate on the death of
her father Lord Alington) wrote to Mr. Crouch, the Member of Parliament
for the Wimborne Division of Dorset, asking him to take up the matter with
the Minister on his behalf, pointing out that the Crichel Area had been
compulsorily acquired from Lord Alington, that it formed an important
and integral part of one of the farms on the Crichel Estate, and setting
out his objections to the proposals to equip and let Crichel Down as a
single self-contained unit. On 13th June, 1952, Mr. Crouch forwarded
Lieut. Commander Marten's letter to Mr. Nugent, Parliamentary Secretary
(Commons) to the Minister. As a result Mr. Nugent directed that a report
should be obtained from the Land Commission as to the desirability of selling
the Crichel Area back to the Crichel Estate, he, of course, being then aware
from Lieut. Commander Marten's letter that this area had been acquired
under compulsory powers.

23. On 14th July, Mr. Payne, an Assistant Secretary at the Ministry, wrote
to Mr. Smith asking for the necessary report. It further appears from his
letter that Mr. Nugent's private secretary had sent direct to Mr. Smith the
correspondence with Mr. Crouch and Lieut. Commander Marten, so that
Mr. Smith must also have been aware that the Crichel Area had been acquired
under compulsory powers.

24. On 15th July, 1952, Mr. Smith wrote to Mr. Hole calling for the
requisite report and saying 'I think what the Commission must do is to give
the Minister a considered opinion on the whole question of sale versus
equipment as one unit'. He also asked for a plan showing the previous
ownerships of Crichel Down, and information as to what sort of people
the previous owners are 'and (if you are able to form a view without
approaching the people concerned) whether they would be willing and able
to buy back their various portions'. Mr. Hole passed this on to Mr. Lofthouse
to report. In his letter he asked Mr. Lofthouse to 'obtain all further
information you can without, of course, approaching the various owners'.
This it will be noted is an extension of the ban on approaching previous
owners originally imposed by Mr. Smith. Mr. Hole also expressly directed
Mr. Lofthouse 'to obtain from the Air Ministry Land Agent information
as to whether the land was purchased voluntarily or compulsorily'.

25. Mr. Lofthouse was about to go on leave and handed over the matter
to a young and comparatively inexperienced subordinate, Mr. Brown, with
instructions to prepare the necessary report. The instructions given by

Mr. Lofthouse to Mr. Brown were, according to the evidence given by Mr. Brown, which I entirely accept, somewhat extraordinary in the circumstances. Mr. Brown was told (for no apparent reason) that 'the job was extremely confidential' and that on no account was he to approach the Hardings or any of the previous owners or anyone else connected with the land. He was also forbidden to inspect the Hardings' land or anybody else's holding, and was to rely exclusively on such information as he 'could get from the office organisation'. In this respect he was further told only to consult Mr. Ferris, and any further information was only to be obtained from the office files. In fact no office files were available to him except the Agricultural Committee file (which when produced and examined contained nothing of any relevance to his subsequent report) and certain farm survey statistics of the various farmers in the neighbourhood. He was never told to consult the Air Ministry Land Agent as to whether the purchase had been voluntary or compulsory and was never shown Mr. Hole's letter to Mr. Lofthouse in which such inquiry was directed. This is all the more strange since he was supplied with Mr. Smith's letter to Mr. Hole. This was the first report Mr. Brown had ever been called upon to make and, in view of the conditions referred to above, he was left to make it almost entirely in the dark. I cannot do better than quote his own words 'I had to work completely in the dark. I was working completely blindfolded apart from what Mr. Ferris could tell me'. Under these circumstances it is hardly surprising to find that his report, when made, was riddled with inaccuracies. Although he was never instructed to favour one view more than another, and I am satisfied that he did his best to make a perfectly fair and unbiased report, he started with the knowledge, which he had had for the past 15 months, that the Land Commission's accepted policy was to equip and develop the land as one unit, and that all his superiors were extremely keen on the project. Under these circumstances it would have been expecting too much of human nature to suppose that, however unconsciously, a very junior official such as Mr. Brown would not approach his task with at least a leaning in favour of supporting his Department's already settled policy.

26. On 7th August, 1952, Mr. Brown sent his draft report to Mr. Hole, and at the same time sent a copy to Mr. Lofthouse. The report starts by stating that Crichel Down was purchased by the Air Ministry in 1940. In fact it was compulsorily acquired in 1937, as is abundantly clear from the Conveyance of the Hooper area. I mention this for two reasons, first because it may explain a later error as to the condition of the land when it was taken over, and secondly because Mr. Brown stated that he relied exclusively on the Conveyances for his information as to the circumstances in which the land was acquired. 1940 is in fact the date of the actual Conveyances themselves.

27. The report states that the whole area (with the exception of some 114 acres) was at the date of purchase virgin downland in a very rough condition, covered with much scrub and gorse, infested with rabbits and used as a sheep run. The statement that the land was covered with much scrub and gorse and infested with rabbits was quite untrue, though such may well have been the position in 1940, which was 3 years after the Air Ministry took it over. A statement that as far as could be ascertained the land had never been under plough before was also incorrect in fact, though of course Mr. Brown had no means of discovering that fact. There was at least another 72 acres of arable land in addition to the 114 acres mentioned in the report, and large areas were fenced, watered, and used for grazing cattle. Mr. Brown stated quite frankly that he was under the impression that the whole down had been just an open stretch, apart from the 114 acres he mentioned.

28. The report states that the Hooper area was purchased compulsorily, but that the Crichel and Strange areas were acquired voluntarily by agreement. Mr. Brown said in evidence that he came to this conclusion by looking at the Conveyances. Having examined the Conveyances I am satisfied that it is quite reasonable and understandable that anyone, having no other source of information available, should have come to such a conclusion. The Hooper Conveyance makes it clear on the face of it that it is made in pursuance of a compulsory purchase, the other two Conveyances do not, and are in a form which is much more consistent with a voluntary purchase. This mistake was particularly unfortunate as it is clearly one of great importance, as was generally admitted, and it would never have occurred if Mr. Hole's direction to make enquiries of the Air Ministry Land Agent had been communicated to Mr. Brown and carried out. The Report continues with a statement that the prices paid by the Air Ministry give an indication of the condition of the land at the time of purchase and show that the two larger owners were not unwilling to part with it at a low price. This again is quite untrue, and the early correspondence, which was not available to Mr. Brown and could only have been discovered by an application to the Air Ministry Land Agent, makes it quite clear that in fact they strenuously resisted the compulsory acquisition of their land, but without avail.

29. In the report, Mr. Brown states that he understands that the Land Commission's policy is to equip the land as a single unit at a cost of approximately £20,000, and in evidence he stated that this policy had been well known to him since he joined the Land Service some 15 months previously, and that he agreed with it. He also states that if Crichel Estate should obtain possession of the Crichel Area it would almost certainly be added to the Hardings' farm, the buildings of which are inadequate for the existing acreage. The statement that the Hardings' buildings were inadequate for the existing acreage was incorrect, and in direct contradiction of the view expressed by Mr. Lofthouse in his letter of 27th May, 1952, to Mr. Hole,

in which he stated that if the Crichel Area was added to the Hardings' farm
no new equipment would be necessary and there would be a properly
balanced unit between buildings and acreage. Mr. Brown was never shown
a copy of this letter, and had never seen the Hardings' buildings, and he
said that he based his statement on what he was told by Mr. Ferris. He also
states that the Hardings already had 170 acres of rough downland which
could well be reclaimed before they were given any more land. This figure,
which Mr. Brown obtained from obsolete records, was inaccurate. The total
amount of unreclaimed land on the Hardings' farm at that time being about
60 acres, which they were then in the course of, or about to commence,
ploughing up. Later in the report, Mr. Brown states that the Crichel Estate
are much more interested in the Crichel Area than they are in some of the
land at present in their ownership. This statement was quite unjustified, and
it was common ground throughout the Inquiry that the whole of the Crichel
Estate is and always has been very well farmed. He goes on to say that the
opportunity presented by these 726 acres of bare land is an unparalleled
one for the erection of a modern farming unit on a scale which will be of
interest and example to the farming community for many miles around. In
evidence he said that the Land Service were responsible for advisory work
and that this was a very unusual opportunity to show what could be done
and that he was really enthusiastic about the idea.

30. Finally in his report Mr. Brown came to the conclusion that if the
Crichel Area was sold back to the Crichel Estate it would not be possible
to equip the remainder of Crichel Down as a self-contained unit, and that
therefore the choice lay between either selling back the whole of Crichel
Down to the previous owners or other adjoining owners or else proceeding
with the scheme to equip the whole as one self-contained unit. The evidence
clearly showed that these were in fact the only two practical alternatives,
apart from letting the land as bare land without equipping it. He stated
that he felt certain that the neighbouring farmers would be willing to
buy back the land but that difficulty might well be experienced over price.
The possibility of difficulty over price was of necessity pure guesswork on
his part and was not based on any enquiry he had made or information
he had received. He concludes by expressing the view that, as only rough
off-lying land attached to large farms was taken and all but 15 acres of
that by agreement, there was no case for a sale of the Crichel area or
any other part of the land, and the best course was to go ahead with the
existing scheme. After the errors in his report had all been pointed out to
him, Mr. Brown stated in evidence that had the true facts been fully before
him he would still have come to the same conclusion. The point, however,
is that those who had subsequently to come to their own conclusion on his
report might have come to a different conclusion if the facts had been
correctly stated in it.

31. Mr. Brown further stated that Mr. Ferris had seen his draft report and fully concurred in it. When his attention was drawn to Mr. Ferris's letter of 10th December, 1949, expressing a directly contrary view, he said he had never seen that letter, but he was quite satisfied that Mr. Ferris had entirely revised his original opinion. It was, therefore, particularly unfortunate that Mr. Ferris declined to give any evidence at the Inquiry, although (I was informed) he had been requested to do so both by the Ministry and by Lieut.-Commander Marten and was still living and working in the neighbourhood. It would have been of great assistance to know exactly why Mr. Ferris had completely changed his opinion as to the best method of dealing with the land, and also how he came to approve the inaccuracies in Mr. Brown's report, some at least of which ought to have been evident to him.

32. On 10th August, 1952, Lieut.-Commander Marten wrote direct to the Minister saying that the Crichel Estate would be willing to buy the whole of Crichel Down if this would assist in overcoming any objection to the resale of the Crichel Area alone, but it appears that the Minister was already aware of that fact.

33. On 3rd August, 1952, Mr. Watson-Jones, a farmer member of the Land Commission, inspected Crichel Down accompanied by Mr. Ferris. He said in evidence that his primary object was to see whether, if the Crichel Area was sold back to the Crichel Estate, the remaining land could be satisfactorily equipped as a single unit. On 13th August, he made a written report to the Land commission in which he said that if the Crichel Area was sold it would seriously interfere with existing plans to farm Crichel Down and he considered that it should be retained. His report goes on to say that Crichel Estate have no farm buildings reasonably near this area. When it was pointed out to him in cross-examination that the Hardings' farm buildings are within a few hundred yards of Crichel Down he said that what he meant was that there were no farm buildings reasonably near the centre of the land. He also stated that he was convinced Mr. Ferris had abandoned the view expressed by him in his letter of 10th December, 1949.

34. On 13th August, 1952, Mr. Hole sent Mr. Brown's report to the Land Commission with a covering letter in which he expressed his own views to the following effect:—

(a) If Crichel Down is equipped as a single unit greater production of crops and livestock is likely.

(b) The cost of equipping will be in the order of £20,000 and he very much doubts if the increase in production would justify such a heavy outlay on the short term view—whether it would do so on the long term view depends on the future prosperity of agriculture.

(c) If the Crichel Area was sold back the remaining land could not be equipped as a single unit.

(*d*) All the adjoining owners are competent farmers who would probably be quite pleased to have their land back.

Mr. Hole ends by saying that although the proposal to create one fully equipped farm is most attractive from many points of view the high cost of doing so makes him wonder whether the project should be undertaken.

35. Sir Frederick Burrows stated that this letter was never passed on to the Ministry, though Mr. Brown's report was.

36. On 20th August, 1952, the Land Commission held a meeting at which Mr. Hole's letter and Mr. Brown's report were considered, and as a result of that meeting Mr. Smith wrote to Mr. Payne at the Ministry setting out the Land Commission's view to the effect that, if the Crichel Area was sold, it would not be possible to develop the remainder of the land as a self contained unit and therefore the only course reasonably open would be to offer the remainder back to the previous owners. The evidence showed that this advice was undoubtedly sound. The letter then went on to state other factors which it was suggested the Minister might wish to have in mind. These were apparently taken from Mr. Brown's report and were substantially incorrect in the following respects:—

(*a*) It was stated that both the Crichel and Strange areas were acquired by agreement, although as noted above Mr. Smith (who signed the letter) must at least have known that Lieut.-Commander Marten had specifically stated that the Crichel Area was acquired compulsorily. Mr. Smith unfortunately was not available to explain this.

(*b*) It was stated that there were still 170 acres of rough unimproved downland on the Crichel Estate adjacent to the S.E. boundary of the Crichel Area.

(*c*) It was stated that the buildings on the Hardings' farm were inadequate for the existing acreage.

(*d*) It was stated that if the Strange Area was sold back there was no doubt in the Land Commission's view that it would not be fully and efficiently used, but would tend to go back to a sheep run. There appears to have been nothing on which such an opinion could have been based, and it is contrary to the view expressed by Mr. Hole and to the accepted fact that Mr. Strange was a first class farmer.

37. In the penultimate paragraph of the letter Mr. Smith says, 'Finally, I would say that the purchase and equipment of the Crichel property as one unit would be a satisfactory proposition from the financial point of view . . . ' This appears to be the personal view of Mr. Smith rather than a view taken by the Land Commission. It is somewhat strange that Mr. Smith, who apparently is not an agricultural expert but merely the Secretary to the Commission, should take upon himself to express such a view to the Ministry in face of Mr. Hole's letter which contains a grave

warning to the contrary—which warning was never passed on to the Ministry.

38. The Land Commission's final advice to the Minister is 'that the whole area should be retained and equipped as a unit in the interests of full and efficient production'.

39. It is to be noted that no mention was made in this letter of Captain Taylor's offer to rent the land unequipped at a rent of £2,000 per annum, nor was the existence of such an offer ever brought to the notice of the Ministry.

40. In September, 1952, a policy letter was drafted by Mr. Payne at the Ministry for Mr. Nugent to send to Mr. Crouch, based on the recommendations of the Land Commission. Mr Nugent, however, wished to make further enquiries and the letter was not sent though the draft was later used as the basis of a subsequent letter in March, 1953, with which I deal later. At the instigation of Mr. Nugent further enquiries were made by Mr. Payne through the Lands Service, as a result of which Mr. Hole wrote to Mr. Payne on 14th October, stating (inter alia) that if Crichel Down was resold to previous owners he would expect to get a total of £25,480 for the land. It would appear from the evidence that this was an over-estimate and that the true value of the land in its then condition was probably about £21,000.

41. On 15th November, 1952, at the request of the Minister, Lord Carrington, Parliamentary Secretary (Lords) to the Ministry, visited Crichel Down for the purpose of inspecting the land and reporting direct to the Minister. Lord Carrington was accompanied by Mr. Ferris but he did not visit any of the adjoining owners or inspect any of the adjoining land. For some reason which I did not appreciate he seemed to think it would have been improper for him to do so. Before going to inspect the land Lord Carrington had read Mr. Brown's report and he stated that he assumed the statements of fact in it to be true for the purposes of his own report.

42. On 19th November, 1952, Lord Carrington reported the result of his inspection in writing to the Minister. In it he stated that from the agricultural point of view he felt convinced that Crichel Down should be equipped and farmed as a single unit. He then gave five reasons for that view, but they all appear to be based on the disadvantages of selling the Crichel Area and retaining the remainder, and none of them really touches the question of the advisability of selling the whole.

43. On 11th December, 1952, Mr. Wilcox, an Under-Secretary at the Ministry, wrote to Mr. Hole stating that Lord Carrington had advised that if Crichel Down was to be sold, it should be sold as one unit and not split up, and asking for advice as to whether if sold as one unit it would be better to sell the bare land or to equip it as a self-contained unit before sale. On

the 16th December, Mr. Hole replied reducing his original estimate of the value of the bare land from £25,000 to £20,000, which from the evidence appears to have been substantially correct, and that after expending an estimated figure of £22,500 in equipping Crichel Down it might be expected to realise about £41,000 with vacant possession or £31,000 with a sitting tenant paying a rent of 43s. 6d. per acre.

44. Mr. Hole's letter was given careful consideration at the Ministry. Sir Reginald Franklin, Deputy Secretary to the Ministry, expressed the view that the interests of food production could best be served by equipping the land and selling with vacant possession by private treaty to some person selected as a good farmer. Mr. Manktelow, the Principal Finance Officer suggested very naturally that from a financial point of view it would be better to sell the land in its present condition, but said that he would not press this if provision of equipment before sale was considered desirable on the grounds of food production policy so long as it was sold with vacant possession. He further stated that he would prefer a sale by auction to ensure getting the best price and to disarm financial criticism. Mr. Nugent stated that equipping the land was right in the interests of production but some thought would be needed to justify selling the equipped holding at a loss. The legal department advised quite correctly that it would not be possible in law, on a sale of the bare land, to impose an effective obligation on the purchaser to equip the land or to farm it as one unit.

45. It is at this stage that the Commissioners of Crown Lands (hereinafter called 'Crown Lands') first come upon the scene, and it is necessary to appreciate their organisation. There are three Commissioners, namely a Permanent Commissioner and two ex-officio Commissioners. The Permanent Commissioner at all material times was Mr. Eastwood, who was first appointed in October, 1952, having previously been an Assistant Under-Secretary of State in the Colonial Office, where he dealt with tropical agriculture, apart from which he had no special agricultural knowledge or experience. The two ex-officio Commissioners are the Minister of Agriculture and the Secretary of State for Scotland for the time being. The Commissioners never meet as a body and their business is conducted by the Permanent Commissioner, who refers at his discretion on matters of major policy to the Minister or, in the case of land in Scotland, to the Secretary of State for Scotland. Crown Lands own at the present time some 370,000 acres of land and are under a statutory obligation to invest any moneys in their hands in the purchase of land, Treasury sanction being necessary to any expenditure. Their estates are managed in some cases by a local full time staff of their own, and in others by local firms of Estate Agents employed on a part time basis for the purpose of the terms of written agreements, which vary from case to case, and who are known as Crown Receivers.

46. On 8th January, 1953, Mr. Wilcox met Mr. Eastwood and they lunched together at a Club of which they were both members. Crown Lands had at that time a large amount of money available for investment and Mr. Wilcox told Mr. Eastwood about Crichel Down, suggesting that it might be a suitable property for Crown Lands to acquire. Mr. Wilcox made it clear that the property would have to be equipped and farmed as a single unit, but at that stage it was not known whether the Ministry would equip it prior to the sale or whether Crown Lands would be required to undertake to equip it themselves if they bought it.

47. Crown Lands already owned the Bryanston Estate in Dorset which was managed by Messrs. Sanctuary and Son, a firm of Estate Agents at Bridport, as Crown Receivers under the terms of an agreement dated 6th March, 1951.

48. On 18th January, 1953, Mr. Wilcox wrote to Mr. Eastwood saying that he thought the Ministry would prefer to transfer the land to Crown Lands as bare land in its present state. On 24th January, Mr. Eastwood inspected Crichel Down accompanied by an employee of Sanctuary and Son. On 3rd February, Mr. Thomson, a partner in Sanctuary and Son, who had meanwhile inspected Crichel Down himself wrote a full report to Mr. Eastwood, in which he set out his own scheme for equipping the land with his estimate of cost which amounted to £40,000 — which was nearly double the Land Commission estimate. He assumes the land would be acquired for £15,000 making the total expenditure £55,000, which he frankly states seems to him much too high for a farm of that kind. He states that the absolute maximum rent would be £2,100 (£3 per acre) and that he would have great difficulty in getting it, and taking a long term view he would probably have to be content with a rent of £1,400, which would give a capital value of about £30,000. He concludes by advising that Crown Lands ought not to consider the purchase of the land unless it can be acquired for a good deal less than the price originally suggested, and even then Crown Lands should not commit themselves until they had had about two months in which to find a suitable tenant and agree with him a minimum rent. The next day Mr. Thomson wrote again (after consulting Mr. Middleton of the Lands Service) saying that he could make economies in his estimate for equipping Crichel Down but that Crown Lands should not consider buying the land unless they could get it for £15,000.

49. On 16th February, 1953, a meeting took place at the Ministry between Mr. Wilcox and Mr. Eastwood at which Mr. Hole, Mr. Thomson and certain other gentlemen were present. The conclusions reached were that it would cost about £32,000 to equip Crichel Down and Crown Lands could do nothing until they had ascertained what rent a tenant would be prepared to pay. It was agreed that if, as a result of a meeting the next day between

the Minister and Sir Frederick Burrows, the Minister was prepared to authorise a sale, Mr. Thomson would then be authorised to start local inquiries as to the rent obtainable and if these were satisfactory Mr. Thomson, Mr. Hole and the District Valuer should meet on the site and endeavour to agree a price for the sale of Crichel Down as bare land.

50. It is to be noted that no one at this meeting, except Mr. Hole, was aware that a number of applications had been received by the Lands Service for tenancies of Crichel Down, and that the applicants had been told that their applications would be considered and that in due course it was proposed to advertise the tenancy for public tender. Mr. Hole never mentioned this at the meeting.

51. After the meeting Mr. Thomson told Mr. Eastwood that he had a possible tenant in mind, namely Mr. Tozer. Mr. Thomson did not know that Mr. Tozer had already made several applications to the Lands Service for a tenancy of Crichel Down and had him in mind solely because he had applied for the tenancy of a farm on the Bryanston Estate in January, 1951, which had already been let and was no longer available. Mr. Thomson's only personal knowledge of Mr. Tozer was that he had met him in the Spring of 1948 when Mr. Thomson was negotiating the purchase of an estate on which Mr. Tozer was a tenant of one of the farms. Mr. Thomson said he had spent a lot of time going over Mr. Tozer's farm and formed the opinion that he was a very good farmer. Mr. Thomson's partner knew something of the Tozer family, however, as the firm of Sanctuary and Son (in which Mr. Thomson was not then a partner) had acted as advisory agents to the Pitt-Rivers Estate from 1925 to 1935, and the Tozer family were at that time tenant farmers on that estate.

52. On 17th February, 1953, Sir Frederick Burrows saw the Minister who informed him of the proposal to sell Crichel Down unequipped to Crown Lands. Sir Frederick agreed to the proposal but asked that a firm decision might be made within two months, since if the land was not to be sold the Land Commission would have to proceed with equipping it as speedily as possible so that it could be let at Michaelmas. Sir Frederick stressed that the Land Commission were most anxious to avoid having to continue to farm Crichel Down themselves after Michaelmas. Neither the Minister nor Sir Frederick were aware of the existing applications for tenancies. Mr. Wilcox duly informed Mr. Eastwood of the two months' time limit.

53. On 19th February, 1953, Mr. Eastwood telephoned Mr. Thomson authorising him to start looking for a suitable tenant but giving him clear instructions that no definite arrangements were to be made until the whole scheme had been referred to Mr. Eastwood and approved by him. Mr. Thomson at once telephoned Mr. Tozer and asked him if he would be interested in the tenancy. Mr. Tozer was interested, and Mr. Thomson

went to see him on 22nd February. At that meeting Mr. Thomson explained his ideas for equipping the farm, and asked Mr. Tozer if he would be willing to take a tenancy of it when it was equipped at a rent of £3 per acre. Mr. Tozer said he wanted to discuss it with his father and brother and would let Mr. Thomson know later. On 27th February, Mr. Tozer wrote to Mr. Thomson saying that he would very much like to go forward with the proposition.

54. On 2nd March, 1953, Mr. Nugent wrote to Mr. Crouch explaining the position. The letter was drafted by Mr. Wilcox from the draft prepared by Mr. Payne in September, 1952, which has been previously mentioned. The letter states that the buildings on Hardings' farm would not be adequate if the Crichel Area was added to the farm, and that there were still some 170 acres of rough land on the farm which could well be reclaimed. In fact even the 60 acres, which were rough land in September, had by then been ploughed up. These inaccuracies not unnaturally annoyed Lieut.-Commander Marten when the letter was sent to him by Mr. Crouch, especially as no enquiries had ever been made of the Hardings or the Crichel Estate with regard to these matters.

55. On 11th March, 1953, Mr. Middleton, who had succeeded Mr. Lofthouse in December, 1952, as Land Service Officer for Somerset and Dorset discovered for the first time the file containing the previous applications for tenancies and thereupon wrote to Mr. Hole pointing out that if Crown Lands should finally decide to purchase Crichel Down the existing applicants for tenancies might feel that the Ministry had broken faith with them and asking whether Crown Lands should be told of the position and sent a list of applicants.

56. Mr. Hole replied that the situation was awkward since it was not known whether Crown Lands would definitely buy the property or not and all that Mr. Middleton could do would be to send the list of applicants to Mr. Thomson and ask him if he would consider any of them. This Mr. Middleton did on the 19th March, stating that in most cases applicants had been promised that they would have an opportunity to tender and that letting would be by public tender. He further suggested in his letter that Mr. Thomson should give this some thought before making definite arrangements with Mr. Tozer.

57. Mr. Thomson replied the next day saying he would pass the letter on to Crown Lands and adding that if the sale went through there was no doubt that Mr. Tozer would get the farm, but asking Mr. Middleton to treat this as confidential until matters were finally settled.

58. Mr. Thomson admitted in evidence that at the time of writing this letter he had already made up his mind that, if Crown Lands purchased

Crichel Down, Mr. Tozer and no-one else was going to get the tenancy. He was unable to give any satisfactory explanation of why he asked Mr. Middleton to treat this as confidential.

59. On the same day Sanctuary & Son (i.e. Mr. Thomson) wrote to Crown Lands enclosing Mr. Middleton's letter but not a copy of Mr. Thomson's reply. In this letter they stated that it was rather late in the day for the information to be given to them as they had already spent a great deal of time with Mr. Tozer, and in view of the rent of £3 per acre which he was prepared to pay they very much hoped the sale would go through. In fact all that had been done with Mr. Tozer was to visit some five or six farms in the vicinity for the purpose of seeing what sort of equipment would be necessary.

60. On 23rd March, Mr. Eastwood replied and I quote verbatim from this extraordinary letter:—

'I quite appreciate that you have gone too far with Tozer to make it easy to give the land to anybody else and I am not suggesting that we should, in fact, do so. But I think it would be well that you should ask Middleton to send you particulars of all those who have applied for the land and exactly what promises have been made to them. You may then be able to judge whether any of them are likely to have been serious competitors and we can then decide, in conjunction with the Ministry of Agriculture, what if anything we need to do, at least to appear to implement the promises made to them. Meanwhile I do not think you need hold up your discussions with Tozer or recommendations to us on this account.'

Mr. Eastwood admitted that he had not made any inquiry and did not know at all how far Mr. Thomson had gone with Mr. Tozer when he wrote this letter. Mr. Eastwood sent a copy of this letter and the correspondence leading up to it to Mr. Wilcox.

61. On 25th March, Mr. Wilcox replied and again I quote verbatim from his letter:—

'It is of course a pity that Middleton did not let Thomson have earlier information about the promises given to various farmers on behalf of the A.L.C. that they would be given an opportunity for tendering if it were being let by the Agricultural Land Commission.
Clearly if you buy a property then you are in no way bound by these promises, and I appreciate it may be too late for Thomson to go back on anything he may have aranged provisionally with Tozer but I am very glad that you asked Thomson to get hold of the list of names from Middleton so that we can consider whether there is anything that could be done with a view at any rate to appear to be implementing any past promises. I imagine that you and Thomson for your part will be anxious to avoid doing anything that may leave a bad taste in the mouths of

any of the disappointed applicants, which might, e.g., prejudice your chance of getting them as tenants for other of your properties on your Bryanston Estate at some future date.'

At the time Mr. Wilcox wrote this letter his immediate superior at the Ministry, Sir Reginald Franklin, was away on urgent work connected with the floods in East Anglia, and Mr. Wilcox took upon himself to write this very important letter without consulting any higher authority. Mr. Nugent told me in evidence that if he had seen it he would not have allowed it to be sent.

62. Mr. Eastwood not unnaturally took the statement 'Clearly if you buy a property then you are in no way bound by these promises' as being express authority from the Ministry to go ahead and disregard the previous applicants.

63. In fairness to Mr. Wilcox I should say that I am not entirely satisfied that he realised at the time of writing the letter the full significance of these words, though he readily admitted in evidence that they bore that implication and that such a decision ought clearly to have been referred to higher authority. He also admitted that the idea of doing something to appear to be implementing promises which there was no intention to implement was so improper that it ought never to have been considered for a moment.

64. It may be that this was more a case of failing to give proper consideration to what he was writing, than of any deliberate intention to devise some scheme to mislead the other applicants. It is to be noted that the relevant passage in the letter is quoted almost verbatim from Mr. Eastwood's letter to Mr. Thomson. I found Mr. Wilcox a very nervous witness and not very clear in his explanations, but I am satisfied that he was doing his best to be frank and to tell the truth.

65. In fact the applicants were never informed of the true position, but nothing was ever done by the Ministry to mislead them.

66. On 26th March, 1953, Mr. Thomson replied to Mr. Eastwood saying that, in view of the distance he had gone with Mr. Tozer and because of his suitability, he did not think anyone else should be allowed to think that they had any chance of renting Crichel Down, and suggesting that a tactful letter be written to the various applicants turning down their offers. This advice unfortunately was not followed, and the strange thing is that after expressing this perfectly correct view Messrs. Sanctuary & Son received on 18th May 1953 a new application for a tenancy of Crichel Down from a Mr. Longman, which was forwarded to them by Mr. Middleton with a request that they would give him a proper reply, and on the next day Sanctuary & Son wrote to Mr. Longman stating that if Crichel Down was acquired by Crown Lands his application would be considered with the others which had already been received. Mr. Thomson admitted in evidence that they had no intention of considering Mr. Longman's application or any of

the other applications if Crown Lands acquired Crichel Down, as both he and Mr. Eastwood had already made up their minds that Mr. Tozer was to have the tenancy. He was quite unable to give any explanation as to why such a letter was written to Mr. Longman, and merely said that it was the usual common-form letter to write, an explanation which I could not accept. Mr. Thomson's evidence generally and his attitude in the witness box was unsatisfactory. He was obviously a man accustomed to having his own way and strongly resented anyone questioning anything that he had done or querying any decision that he had come to or advice that he had given.

67. On 1st April, 1953, Messrs. Sanctuary & Son wrote a long letter to Crown Lands giving a revised detailed estimate of the cost of equipping Crichel Down, amounting to a total expenditure of £34,632. This estimate included the following item—'Fees and expenses. Minimum . . . £2,160'. Mr. Thomson explained that this represented Messrs. Sanctuary & Son's scale fees as Architects and Surveyors in respect of the planning and supervision of the work, calculated at 6 per cent. on the cost. He said the word 'minimum' was inserted because 6 per cent. is the minimum scale fee allowed under the R.I.B.A. Scale of Professional Charges. A print of the R.I.B.A. Scale was put in evidence, and shows that 6 per cent is the fixed fee for an architect employed on new work if the contract or order exceeds £4,000. Mr. Thomson then said the word 'minimum' was used because he might have charged separately for each item, and on individual items under £4,000 the fee could be scaled up to a maximum of 10 per cent. for small items, and 'minimum' meant he was not going to charge in this way. It is to be noted that the R.I.B.A. Scale expressly provides that the charge may be reduced to 5 per cent. in the case of extensive works of a simple character which involve repetition of units. It is also to be noted that 6 per cent. on the total expenditure (excluding of course the fee itself) amounted to £1,950 and that £150 was estimated travelling expenses. It is at least very doubtful whether Sanctuary & Son would be entitled to charge travelling expenses in addition to the R.I.B.A. Scale fee. The items on which the fee was charged included *inter alia* the following:—

	£
Two Dutch Barns	2,000
Electricity	600
Roads...	3,150
Fencing	1,500
Gates...	300
Water Supply	1,811
Total	£9,361

Mr. Thomson admitted that an architect would not normally be employed or entitled to charge a fee in respect of any of the above items.

68. Under Messrs. Sanctuary & Son's contract with Crown Lands their remuneration is fixed at 10 per cent. on all moneys received by them on account of rents and such fees as may be mutually agreed upon for any work carried out by them and not covered by their commission. The Treasury had agreed that Messrs. Sanctuary & Son should receive the R.I.B.A. Scale fee for any new buildings or improvement work they undertook on behalf of Crown Lands.

69. Mr. Eastwood stated that he had tacitly accepted and would have authorised payment of the estimated fee of £2,160 on the assumption that it was the correct minimum R.I.B.A. Scale fee. In fairness to Mr. Thomson it must be clearly stated that the figure of £2,160 was only an estimate, and it may well be that when the claim for fees was finally put forward it would have been correctly calculated.

70. Meanwhile on the 27th March, 1953, Lieut.-Commander Marten had had an interview with Mr. Nugent at the Ministry. Mr. Nugent said that the most important part of that meeting was that Lieut.-Commander Marten made an entirely new proposal that he should himself be allowed to become the tenant of the whole of Crichel Down and farm it from his existing holding as one of his own farms. He explained exactly how this could be done with little or no new permanent equipment, and Mr. Nugent promised him that the proposal would be carefully considered. Mr. Nugent said that he was quite unaware at the time of this interview that Crown Lands were contending that they were already committed to Mr. Tozer and would not be prepared to consider any other tenant. As this fact was of course well known to Mr. Wilcox it is strange that Mr. Nugent was not apprised of it before he saw Lieut.-Commander Marten, but it is quite clear that he was not; and Mr. Wilcox could not explain why not. Mr. Nugent subsequently saw the Minister about Lieut.-Commander Marten's new offer and then learnt of the position with regard to Crown Lands. On 16th April, he wrote to Mr. Crouch saying that the sale to Crown Lands was the right course and that it was too late to go back on it now. He did not, however, explain that Crown Lands had already decided on a tenant.

71. On 21st April, Lieut.-Commander Marten wrote to the Minister direct saying that he felt the Minister could not have had a fair presentation of the facts. As a result, on 5th May, 1953, the Minister had a private meeting with certain Members of Parliament at which Mr. Crouch was present. The position was fully explained to them by the Minister — as appears from Mr. Crouch's letter to the Minister of 5th May, 1953, but the Minister regarded the meeting as confidential and no evidence was given as to what took place at it.

72. On 24th April, 1953, a meeting took place on Crichel Down between the District Valuer, Mr. Hole, and Mr. Thomson, at which a price of £15,000 for the bare land subject to an obligation to equip it as a self contained unit was agreed and approved by the District Valuer. It was clear from the evidence that this was a fair price if the land was burdened with the obligation to equip it, though if it had been sold free from such obligation it would have been worth probably about £21,000.

73. On 25th April, Sanctuary & Son reported the result to Crown Lands strongly recommending the purchase of the land at the agreed price of £15,000, and saying that if offered back to the original owners it would fetch about £21,000 adding 'Please do not let the Ministry know this'. Since to use Mr. Eastwood's own words 'The money will only be transferred from one public or quasi-public pocket to another' it is a little difficult to see why Sanctuary & Son were so anxious that the full facts should not be disclosed to the Ministry. In point of fact however, the Ministry must already have been well aware that they could get a substantially higher price than £15,000 by selling back to the original owners.

74. On 14th May, 1953, Lieut.-Commander Marten wrote to Crown Lands saying that he would like to buy Crichel Down if an opportunity occurred and if Crown Lands decided not to buy themselves he would be grateful if they would let him know so that he could again approach the Ministry. This letter was never answered.

75. On the same day Mr. Eastwood wrote to Mr. Wood at the Treasury asking for Treasury approval to the purchase of Crichel Down by Crown Lands at the price of £15,000 and to the expenditure of up to £34,000 in equipping it. The draft of this letter had previously been approved by Mr. Wilcox on behalf of the Ministry. In this letter he stated that a suitable tenant had been found prepared to pay £2,100 p.a. rent and that on that basis the return would be about 3½ per cent. He pointed out that the return was low but Crown Lands would be doing a service to the Ministry and would gain a lot of very interesting experience. (The underlining is mine.)

76. To this Mr. Wood replied that he felt some doubt about the proposal and asked whether it was intended to put the farm up for auction when available for letting in order to test the market. Finally he stated that as the property was near the Bryanston Estate he would approve the transaction. To this Mr. Eastwood replied that he was not going to put the farm up for auction as Crown Lands had already decided on a tenant. He went on to say that the tenant was selected after a good deal of enquiry by their Local Agent and that he was satisfied that the rent of £3 per acre was a very good one for the land, which was not worth much more than 7s. 6d. before the war.

77. Mr. Eastwood admitted that he made no enquiry of Mr. Thomson before writing this letter as to what enquiries he had made before selecting Mr. Tozer as a tenant. In fact Mr. Thomson had made none. He never at any time considered the possibility of any other tenant, and the only enquiries he had ever made about Mr. Tozer were in 1948. Mr. Eastwood also admitted that he made no enquiries as to the value of the land before the war and thought that he had got the figure of 7s. 6d. per acre from something Sir Reginald Franklin had said about the value of that type of land generally.

78. It is regrettable that a responsible official in the position of a Trustee, as Mr. Eastwood undoubtedly was, should have answered questions relating to authority for the expenditure of Trust moneys in this light-hearted manner. In point of fact, however, no harm can have been done since the evidence clearly showed that Mr. Tozer was a first class farmer, and the rent of £3 per acre was a very good one. It also appeared that the estimated rental value of the land pre-war at 7s. 6d. per acre, though low was not altogether unreasonable.

79. The question now arose as to the basis on which Mr. Tozer was to take over and in particular whether he was to be entitled to any claim for dilapidations in respect of overcropping and foul land. The Land Commission contended that no claim for dilapidations should be allowed. For some reason, which Mr. Thomson was unable to explain satisfactorily, Sanctuary and Son took up the cudgels on behalf of Mr. Tozer and insisted that he should be allowed a claim for dilapidations on the ordinary basis as between an incoming and outgoing tenant. In point of fact this was not a transaction between incoming and outgoing tenants at all, but a simple sale by an owner-occupier of the freehold (i.e. the Ministry occupying and farming through their agents the Land Commission) to a new owner (Crown Lands) who was subsequently going to let on an entirely new tenancy to a new tenant (Mr. Tozer).

80. I am satisfied, after hearing expert evidence on the subject, that no claim for dilapidations should have been allowed. That Sanctuary and Son were fully aware of this position is clear from their letter to Crown Lands dated 8th June, 1953, in which they say dilapidations form part of the landlord's counterclaim against the tenant's title to be paid for unexhausted values etc. and there is no legal right to such a counterclaim against a vendor any more than there is a legal right for a vendor to claim Tenant Right unless specifically provided for by the Contract of Sale. They go on to say that therefore Crown Lands should obtain an undertaking from the Ministry that they will pay compensation. In these circumstances the Land Commission obtained the advice of an independent expert, Mr. Ingram, a partner in Messrs. Senior and Godwin, Estate Agents and Surveyors, of Sturminster Newton, who was well acquainted with Crichel Down. Mr. Ingram

Appendix 2

strongly recommended that other than a valuation of hay, straw, fixtures and the like, there should be no valuation of any kind (i.e. neither Tenant Right nor dilapidations). This he states is the usual position between vendor and purchaser and he could see no reason why the Land Commission should allow any sums for dilapidations on the one hand or claim for unexhausted manurial values on the others. He ends by saying 'Unless there is some specific undertaking to the contrary I recommend this should be strictly followed'. Following this the Ministry wrote to Crown Lands on 15th July, 1953, in the terms of Mr. Ingram's advice.

81. Again Mr. Thomson took up the cudgels on the part of Mr. Tozer. On 27th July, he wrote to Crown Lands recommending that they should press for a full scale valuation. On the same day he sent a copy of this report to Mr. Tozer with a covering letter in which he says 'I am afraid the Land Commission are in a fairly strong position and will refuse to agree to our suggestions'. Finally, however, under pressure from Crown Lands, supported by a letter from the Ministry dated 19th August, 1953, signed J. S. Hill and stated to have been written at the request of Mr. Garside, a Principal in the Lands Division of the Ministry, the Land Commission gave way, and a full valuation was taken on the basis of incoming and outgoing tenants. When the Land Commission were themselves proposing to put the tenancy up for public tender their form of tender expressly excluded any right to dilapidations.

82. The result of this valuation was that the amount of dilapidations exceeded the value of the tenant right by £1,624. This sum was paid by the Ministry, or the Land Commission as their agents to Crown Lands, who passed it on to Mr. Tozer. It is difficult to find any excuse for the adoption of this unusual procedure which resulted in putting this large sum of public money into Mr. Tozer's pocket. Mr. Thomson attempted to justify it by saying that it was a term of Mr. Tozer's tenancy agreement that Mr. Tozer should be entitled to claim dilapidations and that this was the common form agreement adopted by Crown Lands. He admitted, however, that it was only common form in the case of incoming and outgoing tenants and that Mr. Tozer's agreement, being for a very unusual type of new tenancy, was being specially negotiated and had not been signed or even finally settled at that time. The provision in the agreement with regard to dilapidations was not agreed until after the Land Commission had agreed to pay dilapidations, and the final settling of the form of Mr. Tozer's agreement and the signing of it were expressly held up until the consent of the Land Commission had been obtained.

83. Mr. Thomson then attempted to justify this procedure by saying that if the Land Commission had not paid for dilapidations, Crown Lands would have had to pay Mr. Tozer for them. In face of the correspondence and

in the light of the expert evidence I cannot accept this contention, and I was not satisfied that Mr. Thomson was being truthful about it. Mr. Thomson then said that if Mr. Tozer had not been paid for dilapidations Crown Lands Lands would have had to accept a lower rent than £3 per acre. In face of the evidence and considering the fact that nothing whatever had been said about dilapidations when the amount of the rent was agreed, and that the question never arose until several months later, I cannot accept this contention either. In the Land Commission's letter of 25th June, 1953, to Mr. Ingram Mr. Brown says 'Obviously from Mr. Thomson's letters he anticipates making as good a bargain for Mr. Tozer as possible'. I find that statement was fully justified.

84. On 6th July, 1953, Lieut.-Commander Marten wrote again to Crown Lands pointing out that he had had no reply to his previous letter and saying that he was keeping farm cottages free for farm workers in case he should have the opportunity to buy or farm Crichel Down, and therefore wished to be informed of its disposal so that he might plan accordingly. On 9th July, Crown Lands replied that completion of the purchase was taking longer than expected but there was no reason to suppose it would not go through, and it was unlikely that the land would become available for resale. To this Lieut.-Commander Marten replied that he had ear-marked four cottages in Long Crichel to house farm workers and was prepared to rent the land with no additional equipment whatever. He asked that his proposition for farming the land should be considered by Crown Lands.

85. On 23rd July, 1953, Sanctuary & Son wrote to Crown Lands stating 'Both the Commissioners and Mr. Tozer are irretrievably committed to the present proposal'. This was not strictly true, but it would undoubtedly have been difficult for Crown Lands to back out at that stage. On 24th July, Mr. Nugent's Private Secretary wrote to Mr. Crouch saying 'It is true that the Crown Lands Commissioners are proposing to let Crichel Down to Mr. Tozer, though the negotiations have not yet been completed'. This accurately stated the true position. On 27th July, Mr. Eastwood wrote to Lieut.-Commander Marten saying there was no chance of Crown Lands being able to resell the land to him; but entirely ignoring his offer to rent it.

86. On 29th July, Mr. Nugent's Private Secretary wrote to Crown Lands asking them to set out the justification for their present policy with particular reference to Crichel Down. On 31st July, Crown Lands replied at length. The letter correctly sets out the sequence of events up to that time, and it is important to note that when dealing with the question of the original applications it said 'Mr. Wilcox was informed of the position and he confirmed that the Ministry did not regard us as in any way bound by the promises made by your Land Service people or by the Agricultural Land Commission'. This in my opinion was a fair interpretation to put

upon the passage in Mr. Wilcox's letter of 25th March, 1953, to which
I have already referred.

87. On 3rd August, Lieut.-Commander Marten wrote to Mr. Eastwood
saying that it had come as a considerable shock to him to learn that Crichel
Down had been sold to Crown Lands on terms that they were to equip
it as a single unit and that they were already committed to a tenant so
that there would be no opportunity to tender for it. He also asked if he
could be told the name of the tenant. It appears that this letter, together
with previous correspondence with Lieut.-Commander Marten, was then
sent to Mr. Thomson for advice and on 13th August, 1953, he wrote to
Crown Lands on the subject. His letter opens with the statement 'From the
correspondence alone I should say that Commander Marten was the last
person we should want as a tenant'. The letter went on to say that everything
possible would be done by Lieut.-Commander Marten to embarrass both
Crown Lands and Mr. Tozer and the intention to obtain permission to use
the Crichel Estate water had better be abandoned as he doubted if any
approach for permission would be favourably considered. In fact as I have
already stated an agreement with the Crichel Estate for the supply of water
had been signed in June 1951. I did not have a chance to ask Mr. Thomson
about this, but I assume either he must have been unaware of that fact or
else for some reason Crown Lands were not going to obtain the benefit of
this agreement. Further on in the letter Mr. Thomson writes 'You certainly
could not have Commander Marten (i.e. as a tenant) after the way he has
behaved'. Up to that time Mr. Thomson had never met Lieut.-Commander
Marten. When asked on what he based these statements he replied that they
were based on what he had read in the Press and seen in the correspondence.
Nothing at all about Crichel Down or about Lieut.-Commander Marten in
relation thereto had up to that time appeared in the Press. When this was
pointed out to Mr. Thomson he said he must have based his statements solely
on the correspondence. When asked to point out anything in any letter or
other document that he had seen which induced him to make these statements
he was unable to do so. I gave him until the next day to see if he could
find anything to justify his statements about Lieut.-Commander Marten in
this letter. Next day he referred me to a minute made by Mr. Eastwood in
which Mr. Eastwood recorded that Lieut.-Commander Marten 'was talking
of pressing for a public inquiry', and said that his statements were based
solely on that. Mr. Thomson then said that he thought now that his language
had been intemperate, and made a very proper apology to Lieut.-Commander
Marten.

88. On 20th August, 1953, Mr. Wilcox wrote to Mr. Eastwood regarding
a proposed meeting on 4th September, with Mr. Nugent, at which Lieut.-
Commander Marten and Mr. Eastwood were to be present. In that letter
Mr. Wilcox writes 'Commander Marten it is thought will continue to make

himself as much of a nuisance as he can both to you and to us so long as he thinks there is any chance of getting either of us to change our minds'. When asked in what way Lieut.-Commander Marten was 'making a nuisance of himself' Mr. Wilcox said by his repeated requests to be allowed to buy or rent Crichel Down. He went on to say that Mr. Eastwood was afraid that Lieut.-Commander Marten might by local agitation upset the arrangements with Mr. Tozer and that he was anxious to help Mr. Eastwood.

89. In his reply to this letter Mr. Eastwood added a postscript as follows. 'Gifford, Chairman of the A.E.C., is a tenant of ours at Bryanston and a good chap. I am sure we can settle him'. The significance was that objections had been taken to the letting of Crichel Down to Mr. Tozer on the grounds that Mr. Tozer already had a farm and the Tozer family were already farming a great deal of land in the County, and Mr. Gifford as Chairman of the Agricultural Committee would almost certainly be consulted about this. Mr. Eastwood stated in evidence that he had never tried to settle Mr. Gifford as there had been no occasion to do so. When it was put to him that Mr. Gifford had expressed certain views on the matter he did not answer.

90. On 4th September, 1953, Lieut.-Commander Marten, Mr. Eastwood, Mr. Wilcox and others attended a meeting with Mr. Nugent at the Ministry. At this meeting Lieut.-Commander Marten urged that Crown Lands should withdraw from their negotiations with Mr. Tozer and proceed to advertise the tenancy for public tender. Mr. Eastwood stated quite correctly that although Crown Lands had not entered into any legally binding agreement with Mr. Tozer they nevertheless felt morally bound to him. I am satisfied that by that time Crown Lands were under a strong moral obligation to Mr. Tozer since he was expecting to take over the tenancy of the bare land at Michaelmas at a reduced rent pending the erection of buildings and equipment. Mr. Eastwood agreed under pressure to see whether in the light of local feeling Mr. Tozer would be willing to withdraw from the tenancy offered to him, but made it clear that Crown Lands could not themselves withdraw. Mr. Eastwood made it clear to the Ministry that if Mr. Tozer did withdraw, Crown Lands would not go on with the purchase. This struck me as a somewhat strange attitude for Mr. Eastwood to adopt and he was quite unable to give any satisfactory explanation of it. Mr. Eastwood subsequently saw Mr. Tozer and gave him an opportunity to withdraw, but Mr. Tozer did not wish to avail himself of it.

91. On 8th September, 1953, Mr. Wilcox wrote to Mr. Hole reporting the result of the meeting and at the end of his letter he asks if Mr. Hole can throw any light on the circumstances in which Lieut.-Commander Marten was able to get a licence for building farm cottages in 1950, apparently rather 'on spec.' with the idea of enabling him to farm Crichel Down later on.

In fact Lieut.-Commander Marten had never done anything of the sort, and Mr. Wilcox was unable to explain where he got the idea from. He admitted that it was no concern of the Ministry how Lieut.-Commander Marten had got a licence in 1950, and when I pressed him as to why he made this enquiry he answered that he did so simply out of idle curiosity. That answer I cannot accept. It is quite clear that he did so in an attempt to find something that he could bring up to the detriment of Lieut.-Commander Marten.

92. Mr. Hole not unnaturally took this letter to mean that Lieut.-Commander Marten had said he built the cottages for the express purpose of farming Crichel Down and had got a licence on that basis and was using this in support of his argument that he should be granted a tenancy. This was of course quite incorrect. Full enquiries were made by the Lands Service into the circumstances under which Lieut.-Commander Marten obtained a licence for the erection of the cottages. Everything was found to be perfectly in order and at no stage was there any indication whatever that the cottages were to be used for the future farming of any part of Crichel Down. In his report on the matter Mr. Middleton concludes by saying 'I cannot understand Commander Marten's alleged remarks and can only infer that the mention of the cottages was rather a "swift" one.' It is clear that Lieut.-Commander Marten had never made any statement to the effect that the cottages were built for the purpose of farming any part of Crichel Down, and that Mr. Wilcox's inquiry into the matter was wholly unjustified and created an entirely false impression in the Lands Service highly detrimental to Lieut.-Commander Marten.

93. On 11th September, 1953, a tenancy agreement with Mr. Tozer was signed under which he became a yearly tenant of Crichel Down as from 29th September, 1953, at a rent of £1,000 for the first year plus an additional £20 for sporting rights, and £2,100 per annum thereafter plus £50 for sporting rights, there being a provision for reduction of rent if the land was not fully equipped by 29th September 1954.

94. On 20th September, 1953, Mr. Trumper, Liaison Officer to the Minister at Exeter, wrote a letter to the Ministry commencing 'Herewith a long tale of woe from one Commander Marten' and going on to say that it seemed trouble was going to be stirred up. In this letter Mr. Trumper states that the Agricultural Committee had always taken the view that the land owners concerned had neither the will nor the ability to farm the land and that they held this view strongly. Mr. Trumper did NOT give evidence, and it was impossible to ascertain whence he had obtained this wholly erroneous information. The one thing on which every witness at the Inquiry was fully agreed was that the land owners concerned were all first class farmers and that if they had obtained their land back they would have farmed it well.

95. An argument then ensued between Crown Lands and the Lands Service as to who was to write to the original applicants to explain the

position. In fact no one ever did write to them, and by this time owing to publicity in the Press there was no particular necessity to do so.

96. On 28th September, 1953, a Petition signed by a large number of farmers and landowners farming between them some 167,000 acres in the district was sent by Lieut.-Commander Marten to the Minister asking for a Public Inquiry.

97. On 9th October, the Minister personally replied at length to Lieut.-Commander Marten. The letter was drafted for the Minister by Sir Reginald Franklin and was very unfortunately worded. On its natural construction the letter gave the impression that the Minister still thought that part of Crichel Down had been acquired voluntarily by agreement. Sir Reginald explained that he only meant that apart from the Hooper area the actual price had been arrived at by agreement, and whilst it is just possible to put such a construction on the letter, it is not what anyone reading it without any oral explanation would ever have understood it to mean. It also repeated the error in Mr. Brown's report that at the date of acquisition the land was for the most part rough sheep run, infested by rabbits and covered with scrub and gorse. These unfortunate mistakes were not calculated to allay Lieut.-Commander Marten's fears that the Minister himself had never really been told the true facts.

98. Lieut.-Commander Marten replied at length to this letter on 10th October, 1953, saying in substance that whilst entirely satisfied that the Minister had acted in all sincerity on the advice he had received and the facts placed before him, he (Lieut.-Commander Marten) was firmly convinced that the Minister had been wilfully ill-advised and had never been told the true facts.

99. After further correspondence the Minister saw Lieut.-Commander Marten on 22nd October, 1953, and as a result of that interview decided to direct that a Public Inquiry be held.

100. On 23rd October, 1953, Mr. Wilcox wrote to the Agricultural Committee referring to Mr. Brown's report of August 1952, in which it was stated that the Crichel Area and Strange Area were acquired voluntarily by agreement and saying that they were now told by the Air Ministry that a notice to treat was served in respect of both these areas and that it was only the price that was fixed by negotiation. He goes on to say that the statement in Brown's report was passed on to the Minister, and asks if the Agricultural Committee can throw any light on how Brown came to make this mistake. From this letter it looks very much as though the Ministry never really appreciated that the Crichel Area and the Strange Area had been compulsorily acquired until Lieut.-Commander Marten's visit to the Ministry on 22nd October, though why this should be so in view of Lieut.-Commander Marten's previous statements I cannot think.

101. By an Order of the Minister dated 10th November, 1953, Crichel Down was formally withdrawn from the control of the Land Commission as from 29th September, 1953.

102. All the professional estate agents who gave evidence, including Mr. Ingram and Mr. Thomson himself, agreed that the proposal to equip Crichel Down as a self-contained unit was so unattractive financially that they would never have recommended it to a private client; but there was a marked divergence of opinion as to whether it would or would not result in increased production.

103. After hearing and considering the evidence given at the Inquiry and taking into consideration the demeanor of the witnesses when giving their evidence and the weight that ought to be attached thereto, and after re-reading all the material correspondence and other documents I have come to the following:

2. CONCLUSIONS

1. The decision of the Land Commission in August 1950 to equip and let Crichel Down as a single self-contained unit was, from a purely financial point of view, unsound. There was a sharp divergence of expert opinion as to whether or not this method of dealing with the land would result in increased production, but there were undoubtedly ample grounds for coming to the conclusion that it would do so. Whether the advantages of increased production were such as to outweigh the financial disadvantages is a question of Government policy outside the scope of my inquiry.

2. Captain Taylor's offer in May, 1952, to pay a rent of £2,000 per annum for the bare land unequipped brought into striking relief the financial disadvantages of the proposal to spend some £20,000 of public money in equipping the land, and the question of whether the desirability of increased production was nevertheless sufficient to justify this expenditure should have been carefully reconsidered as a policy question at the highest level. Captain Taylor's offer was shelved by the Land Commission and no reconsideration at all was given to the original decision. It was clear that by this time both the Lands Service and the Land Commission had become so infatuated with the idea of creating a new model farm that they were determined not to abandon the scheme for financial reasons.

3. Lieut.-Commander Marten's offer to purchase the Crichel Area in May, 1952, was never considered by the Land Commissionas they had no power to sell, and was never passed on to the Ministry because the Land Commission at that time were under the erroneous impression that the Minister had no power to sell the land or that at any rate it was a fixed Government policy not to sell any land.

4. When the Land Commission were required by the Ministry in July, 1952, to submit a report as to the desirability of selling the Crichel Area back to the Crichel Estate, the Lands Service, whom they asked to supply the necessary report, failed to take the necessary steps to ensure that an accurate and objective report was supplied. Mr. Brown was too junior and inexperienced to have been entrusted with such an important task. He was never supplied with the full correspondence and documents relating to the matters on which he had to report and the ridiculous and wholly unnecessary restrictions placed upon him made it impossible for him accurately to ascertain the necessary facts. Furthermore, so junior an official could not fail to be influenced by the decisions which had already been made and it would have been far more satisfactory if an independent expert who was well acquainted with the district had been employed. As a result Mr. Brown's report was inaccurate in the respects stated above under the Factual Narrative and was not only of little value, but definitely misleading, for the purpose for which it was required. Under the circumstances, however, no blame whatsoever can be attached to Mr. Brown for this. There was no improper motive in the restrictions placed on Mr. Brown and they arose solely from the passionate love of secrecy inherent in so many minor officials.

5. No steps can have been taken to check the accuracy of Mr. Brown's report before it was submitted to the Ministry. Mr. Smith knew that the statement that the Crichel Area had been acquired voluntarily by agreement was at any rate denied by Lieut.-Commander Marten, and it ought therefore to have been re-checked with the Air Ministry; and Mr. Hole knew that the statement that the buildings on Hardings' farm were inadequate for the existing acreage was contrary to Mr. Lofthouse's report and should therefore have been rechecked by visiting the Hardings' farm.

6. I cannot help inferring that the omission by the Land Commission to supply the Ministry with a copy of Mr. Hole's qualifying letter, in which he specifically drew attention to the financial objections, when submitting Mr. Brown's report was deliberate and was due to reluctance to call attention to the financial unsoundness of their decision to equip and let Crichel Down as a self-contained unit. This inference is irresistible in view of Mr. Smith's letter to the Ministry giving the recommendations of the Land Commission after considering Mr. Hole's letter and Mr. Brown's report, in which Mr. Smith expressly states that the equipment of Crichel Down as one unit is a satisfactory proposition from a financial point of view.

7. When the Minister came to his decision in December, 1952, that as a matter of policy Crichel Down ought to be equipped and farmed as one unit the true facts and considerations were not fully brought to his notice. The facts were assumed by the Ministry to have been correctly stated in Mr. Brown's report which as I have pointed out they were not. Among other

things it was assumed that the whole of Crichel Down except the Hooper Area (15 acres) had been acquired by voluntary agreement, and although Mr. Manktelow and Mr. Nugent both sounded a warning note about the financial aspect the true financial position had never been brought to the notice of anyone in the Ministry.

8. In order to enable a proper decision to be made as to whether Crichel Down ought to be equipped and farmed as one unit or whether it ought to be sold back to the original owners the following facts should have been clearly presented to the Minister in a proper brief:—

(a) The whole of Crichel Down had been compulsorily acquired for Defence purposes in the face of strenuous opposition by the owners at a total cost to the Government of £12,106.

(b) The previous owners were anxious to repurchase their respective holdings and would have paid a total of about £21,000 for the land in its then condition.

(c) The previous owners were all first class farmers and could have been relied upon to farm their respective areas properly from their existing buildings which were adequate for the purpose.

(d) It would cost approximately £32,000 to equip Crichel Down as a self-contained unit and when so equipped the maximum rent which could possibly be obtained would be about £2,100 per annum (£3 per acre) gross without allowing for repairs or depreciation, which would provide not more than £1,400 net, and that whether or not this rent could be maintained would depend on the future of agriculture generally.

(e) A detailed statement by the Ministry's expert advisers setting out the respects in which and the extent to which they estimated that food production would be increased by equipping Crichel Down and farming it as a single self-contained unit.

Whether it is likely that the Minister's decision would have been any different if the full facts and circumstances had been brought clearly and correctly to his notice is a matter wholly outside the scope of my inquiry.

9. Once it was determined as a matter of policy that Crichel Down ought in the national interest be equipped and farmed as one unit there were various ways in which this policy could be implemented, namely:—

(a) By the Ministry itself equipping the land and continuing to farm it through the Land Commission.

(b) By the Ministry itself through the Land Commission equipping the land and then letting it to a tenant.

(c) By the Ministry itself equipping the land and then selling it to someone who could be relied upon to retain and farm it as one unit.

(d) By the Ministry selling the bare land to someone who could be relied upon to equip it and retain and farm it as one unit.

The first course (a) was never considered because it was never the policy of the Land Commission themselves to engage in farming operations if it could possibly be avoided.

The second course (b), although the one originally determined upon by the Land Commission when the possibility of a sale was thought to be excluded, was financially unsound and a sale of the land was clearly preferable.

The difficulty in the case of both the other courses (c) and (d) was that it is not possible in law effectively to ensure that a purchaser would either equip the land or retain it or farm it. It became necessary, therefore, if the land was to be sold, to ensure that the purchaser was a person who could be relied upon to implement the policy. With an individual this was virtually impossible since, however trustworthy he might be, human life inevitably comes to an end and what would happen after his death could only be a matter of speculation. In these circumstances certainly the best, and probably the only certain way of ensuring that the purchaser implemented the Government Policy was by a sale to Crown Lands, whose policy the Minister himself was in a position to control by virtue of his office as an ex-officio Commissioner.

10. Although the proposition of purchasing and equipping the land and then letting it to a tenant was not a very sound one financially from Crown Lands' point of view, yet, accepting (as of course I must) the policy decision that the land must be equipped and farmed as one unit, it may well have been justified as the only feasible method of implementing that policy. This again however appears to me to have been a policy decision for the Minister in his capacity of ex-officio Commissioner of Crown Lands and therefore something which is excluded from the scope of my inquiry.

11. £15,000 was a fair price for the sale of Crichel Down to Crown Lands saddled as it was with the obligation to equip it as a unit; and the time limit of two months in which to decide whether to purchase or not, imposed on Crown Lands at the request of Sir Frederick Burrows, was a necessary and reasonable one.

12. Neither Crown Lands nor Sanctuary & Son were aware of the previous applications for tenancies until Sanctuary & Son received Mr. Middleton's letter of 19th March 1953. The failure previously to notify Crown Lands of the position with regard to these applicants was due to Mr. Lofthouse having vacated the post of Land Service Office for Somerset and Dorset before Crown Lands came on the scene, and his successor, Mr. Middleton,

being himself unaware of the position until he received a further application in March 1953, when the old file was brought to his notice for the first time. In these circumstances the selection of Mr. Tozer as a prospective tenant by Mr. Thomson in February 1953 was perfectly bona fide and, though it would have been more in accord with normal practice and more satisfactory generally if the tenancy had been offered for public tender, the time limit imposed was probably sufficient to justify the course adopted.

13. When Crown Lands were informed of the true position regarding previous applicants Mr. Thomson was in no way committed to Mr. Tozer even on the strictest moral view, and Mr. Tozer should at once have been informed of the position and told that any further negotiations could only be regarded as purely tentative pending a ruling from the Ministry as to the procedure to be adopted. The attitude adopted by Mr. Thomson and Mr. Eastwood that they were already too far committed to Mr. Tozer to break off negotiations with him was wholly unjustified, and was dictated solely by a determination not to allow anything to interfere with the plans they had in mind. There is no suspicion of any dishonesty. Mr. Eastwood's highly improper suggestion that something might be done to mislead the applicants into thinking that their applications had received due consideration speaks for itself and calls for no further comment.

14. When Crown Lands first learnt of the previous applications there would have been no difficulty whatever in then advertising the tenancy for public tender and so keeping faith with the applicants. When Mr. Wilcox received Mr. Eastwood's letter showing that Crown Lands did not intend to do this, the matter should at once have been referred to the Minister for his directions. Mr. Wilcox was guilty of a grave error of judgment in taking upon himself to tell Crown Lands that they would not be expected to implement any promises the Lands Service had made. His ready acceptance of Mr. Eastwood's improper suggestion that something might be done to mislead the applicants was equally improper, and had he not thought that there might be some such way out of the difficulty it is very unlikely that he would have been so ready to tell Mr. Eastwood that Crown Lands could ignore the previous applicants.

15. It is inevitable that with over 370,000 acres of land to manage the Permanent Commissioner must rely to a very great extent on information and advice from his local officials or Crown Receivers, but Mr. Eastwood was particularly handicapped in this respect by being new to his appointment and comparatively inexperienced. Mr. Thomson is obviously a strong character and determined to the extent of obstinacy in upholding his own views, and I am convinced that Mr. Eastwood was completely dominated by him over the Crichel Down project.

16. Although strictly outside the scope of this Inquiry, I cannot help feeling that it is a matter for consideration by the appropriate authorities whether the present system of employing local firms of Estate Agents and Surveyors as Crown Receivers on a part-time basis is satisfactory, and if so whether the method of fixing their remuneration for special work such as the Crichel Down project should be revised.

17. Mr. Tozer should never have been allowed to claim dilapidations in the circumstances of this case, and I can find no reason why Mr. Thomson should have pressed the claim so energetically on his behalf or why it was ultimately allowed. When the Land Commission were proposing to offer the tenancy for public tender any claim for dilapidations was expressly excluded in the form of tender which had already been prepared.

18. Mr. Wilcox's unnecessary enquiry into the circumstances in which Lieut.-Commander Marten obtained licences to build certain cottages three years previously was a regrettable lapse from the standard of conduct the public is entitled to expect from responsible civil servants, and had the unfortunate result of making it appear to the Lands Service that Lieut.-Commander Marten had been attempting to deceive the Ministry.

19. Mr. Tozer is a first class farmer and in every way a desirable tenant. The rent of £3 per acre which he has agreed to pay for the land when fully equipped is a high one and there is no reason to suppose that any better rent would have been obtained if the tenancy had been advertised for public tender.

20. There was a certain amount of lack of liaison between officials at the Ministry, and some letters were not drafted as clearly or as tactfully as they might have been, but apart from this and the specific matters concerning Mr. Wilcox to which I have already drawn attention there was nothing done at the Ministry itself which calls for comment.

21. The Land Commission were a comparatively new body very anxious to gain experience by trying their hand at a new and interesting venture such as equipping Crichel Down as a model farm, and in their eagerness to ensure that they were not deprived of the opportunity they adopted an irresponsible attitude towards the expenditure of public money, and they were not always as frank with the Ministry as they might have been. The responsibility for this lack of frankness appears to fall primarily, at any rate, on Mr. Smith, and it is unfortunate that he was not available to give evidence as I hesitate to lay the responsibility at his door without having heard his explanation.

22. The Lands Service were equally filled with enthusiasm for this unusual opportunity, though Mr. Hole at any rate adopted a more conscientious attitude towards the public purse. There was a lamentable exhibition of muddle and inefficiency over obtaining the report that was called for in

July 1952 when Mr. Lofthouse was about to go on leave, and a complete failure by Mr. Lofthouse properly to instruct Mr. Brown or to make a proper hand over when he did go on leave. Again Mr. Lofthouse does not appear to have put Mr. Middleton fully in the picture when Mr. Middleton took over from him in December 1952. Apart from this and the failure of Mr. Hole to check Mr. Brown's report I have no criticism to make of the Lands Service.

23. In Crown Lands there is a lack of adequate control over the activities of Crown Receivers and a tendency, at any rate in this particular case, to leave everything to the Crown Receiver and to accept without question everything that he says or does. It is a matter for the consideration of the Minister whether he is consulted sufficiently frequently by the Permanent Commissioner on policy matters.

24. A most regrettable attitude of hostility to Lieut.-Commander Marten was evinced by Mr. Eastwood, Mr. Wilcox and Mr. Thomson and to a lesser degree by certain other junior officials. There was no excuse whatever for this attitude. Lieut.-Commander Marten acted perfectly properly throughout and was merely endeavouring to stand up for what he conceived to be his moral rights. This attitude was engendered solely by a feeling of irritation that any member of the public should have the temerity to oppose or even question the acts or decisions of officials of a Government or State Department. This attitude is in marked distinction to the courtesy and care with which Lieut.-Commander Marten's complaints were treated and investigated by the Minister himself and Mr. Nugent and also (naturally so perhaps) by Mr. Crouch.

25. There was no trace in this case of anything in the nature of bribery, corruption or personal dishonesty; and once the Ministerial decision that as a matter of policy Crichel Down must be equipped and farmed as a single self-contained unit and must be so maintained for the future is accepted, the sale to Crown Lands and the subsequent letting to Mr. Tozer cannot of themselves give rise to any legitimate complaint. The procedure adopted, however, was such that it inevitably gave rise to misgivings among local farmers and landowners, and I am satisfied that Lieut.-Commander Marten was fully justified in the circumstances in pressing for a Public Inquiry.

At the close of his case Mr. Melford Stevenson, Q.C., leading counsel for Lieut.-Commander Marten and the Honourable Mrs. Marten, Mr. Strange, and Mr. Hooper, asked me to recommend to the Minister that the costs which his clients had incurred by being represented at the Inquiry ought to be defrayed — presumably out of the public purse. As I pointed out to Mr. Melford Stevenson at the time, it would be wholly outside the scope of my authority to deal in any way with a question of costs. The question is one that can only be considered by the Minister himself, and I consider that it would be improper for me to make any recommendation.

ANDREW CLARK,

Queen's Counsel.

13th May, 1954.

ANNEXURE (1)

Crichel Down Public Inquiry

List of Witnesses (Alphabetical)

No.	Name	Party	Status
1.	Mr. D. S. Brown	Ministry of Agriculture.	Assistant Land Commissioner.
2.	The Hon. G. Bourke	Ministry of Agriculture.	Agricultural Land Commission Member.
3.	Sir F. Burrows	Ministry of Agriculture.	Agricultural Land Commission Chairman.
4.	Mr. H. E. Bush	Ministry of Agriculture.	Air Ministry. Deputy Chief Lands Officer.
5.	Lord Carrington	Ministry of Agriculture.	Parliamentary Secretary (Lords).
6.	Mr. R. C. Carter	Ministry of Agriculture.	District Valuer.
7.	Mr. C. G. Eastwood	Commissioners of Crown Lands.	Permanent Commissioner.
8.	Mr. G. F. Edwards	Ministry of Agriculture.	Agricultural Land Commission. Land Agent.
9.	Mr. J. G. Eve	Lieut. Cmdr. Marten.	Surveyor and Valuer.
10.	Sir R. Franklin	Ministry of Agriculture.	Deputy Secretary.
11.	Mr. B. S. Furneaux	Lieut. Cmdr. Marten.	Soil Surveyor.
12.	Mr. R. Harding	Lieut. Cmdr, Marten.	Petitioner.
13.	Mr. D. A. Hole	Ministry of Agriculture.	Provincial Land Commissioner.
14.	Mr. H. A. Hooper	Lieut. Cmdr. Marten.	Petitioner.
15.	Mr. C. E. Ingram	Ministry of Agriculture.	Auctioneer and Valuer.
16.	Mr. R. G. A. Lofthouse	Ministry of Agriculture.	Provincial Land Commissioner.

No.	Name	Party	Status
17.	Lieut. Cmdr. Marten	Lieut. Cmdr. Marten.	Petitioner.
18.	Mr. A. C. Middleton	Ministry of Agriculture.	Land Commissioner.
19.	Col. F. G. Norton-Fagge	Ministry of Agriculture.	Provincial Land Commissioner.
20.	Mr. G. R. H. Nugent	Ministry of Agriculture.	Parliamentary Secretary (Commons)
21.	Mr. J. A. Payne	Ministry of Agriculture.	Assistant Secretary.
22.	Mr. G. N. Rawlence	Lieut. Cmdr. Marten.	Surveyor and Auctioneer.
23.	Mr. G. H. Richards	Lieut. Cmdr. Marten.	Farmer.
24.	Mr. J. Strange	Lieut. Cmdr. Marten.	Petitioner.
25.	Mr. H. A. R. Thomson	Commissioners of Crown Lands	Crown Receiver.
26.	Mr. C. Tozer	Commissioners of Crown Lands.	Tenant Farmer.
27.	Mr. E. Watson-Jones	Ministry of Agriculture.	Agricultural Land Commission. Member.
28.	Mr. C. H. M. Wilcox	Ministry of Agriculture.	Under Secretary.

ANNEXURE (2)

Crichel Down Public Inquiry

List of Witnesses (1st–7th Day)

Day	No.	Name	Party	Status
1st	—	—	—	—
2nd	1.	Mr. H. E. Bush	Ministry of Agriculture.	Air Ministry. Deputy Chief Lands Officer.
2nd	2.	Mr. E. Watson-Jones	Ministry of Agriculture.	Agricultural Land Commission. Member.
2nd	3.	Sir F. Burrows	Ministry of Agriculture.	Agricultural Land Commission. Chairman.
2nd	4.	The Hon. G. Bourke	Ministry of Agriculture.	Agricultural Land Commission. Member.
2nd	5.	Mr. E. C. Ingram	Ministry of Agriculture.	Auctioneer and Valuer.
2nd	6.	Mr. G. F. Edwards	Ministry of Agriculture.	Agricultural Land Commission. Land Agent.
2nd	7.	Col. F. G. Norton-Fagge	Ministry of Agriculture.	Provincial Land Commissioner.

Day	No.	Name	Party	Status
2nd	8.	Mr. D. A. Hole	Ministry of Agriculture.	Provincial Land Commissioner.
2nd	9.	Mr. R. G. A. Lofthouse	Ministry of Agriculture.	Provincial Land Commissioner.
2nd	10.	Mr. R. C. Carter	Ministry of Agriculture.	District Valuer
3rd	11.	Mr. A. C. Middleton	Ministry of Agriculture.	Land Commissioner
3rd	12.	Mr. D. S. Brown	Ministry of Agriculture.	Assistant Land Commissioner.
3rd	13.	Lord Carrington	Ministry of Agriculture.	Parliamentary Secretary (Lords)
3rd	14.	Mr. G. R. H. Nugent	Ministry of Agriculture.	Parliamentary Secretary (Commons).
3rd	15.	Sir R. Franklin	Ministry of Agriculture.	Deputy Secretary.
3rd	16.	Mr. C. H. M. Wilcox	Ministry of Agriculture.	Under Secretary.
4th	17.	Mr. G. N. Rawlence	Lieut. Cmdr. Marten	Surveyor and Auctioneer
4th	18.	Mr. J. A. Payne	Ministry of Agriculture.	Assistant Secretary.
4th	19.	Mr. C. G. Eastwood	Commissioners of Crown Lands.	Permanent Commissioner.
5th		Mr. C. G. Eastwood	Commissioners of Crown Lands.	Permanent Commissioner
5th	20.	Mr. H. A. R. Thomson	Commissioners of Crown Lands.	Crown Receiver
5th	21.	Mr. T. C. Tozer	Commissioners of Crown Lands.	Tenant Farmer.
6th	20.	Mr. H. A. R. Thomson	Commissioners of Crown Lands.	Crown Receiver.
6th	22.	Mr. B. S. Furneaux	Lieut. Cmdr. Marten.	Soil Surveyor.
6th	23.	Mr. J. G. Eve	Lieut. Cmdr. Marten.	Surveyor and Valuer.
6th	24.	Mr. G. H. Richards	Lieut. Cmdr. Marten.	Farmer.
6th	25.	Mr. R. Harding	Lieut. Cmdr. Marten.	Petitioner
6th	26.	Mr. J. Strange	Lieut. Cmdr. Marten.	Petitioner.
6th	27.	Mr. H. A. Hooper	Lieut. Cmdr. Marten.	Petitioner.
6th	28.	Lieut. Cmdr. Marten	Lieut. Cmdr. Marten.	Petitioner.
7th	—	—	—	—

Address by Lt.-Com. G. G. Marten to the Assembled Farmers and Landowners at a Meeting Held at More Crichel Village Hall on Saturday 26 Sept. 1953

No one could regret more than I do the necessity for this meeting. If any of you had told me a year ago that what *has* happened was going to happen I should have said, 'Nonsense. In England that is quite impossible,' but it *has* happened.

I have used every channel I knew to bring local feeling to the notice of the Authorities, without recourse to this public meeting.

I told the Parliamentary Secretary to the Ministry of Agriculture, and the Commissioner of Crown Lands, three weeks ago that there would inevitably be a *wave* of indignation against them if they persisted in their present attitude.

At least we cannot be reproached with having nursed our grievances in silence.

I would like to say this to Mr. Christopher Tozer — at present the prospective tenant of Crichel Down. 'If an impartial enquiry decides that you are the right man to come and farm in our midst — then so far as the Crichel Estate is concerned you will receive a warm welcome — but until that has been established I, and the Committee of protest of which I am Chairman, will oppose the project with all the strength we can command'.

Let me tell you the history of the land.

This area of over 700 acres was acquired by compulsory purchase by the Air Ministry for a bombing range, in 1939 and early 1940. 330 acres was taken from my wife's estate, and this formed more than half of one of our tenants farms — the Middle Farm, Long Crichel. The best part of 400 acres was taken from Mr. Strange's farm at Tarrant Launceston. At the time of the Air Ministry purchase, Mr. Strange was in the process of buying his farm from the old Langton Estate, which was being broken up. As the Air Ministry was already negotiating to acquire this particular 400 acres of his farm, he did not buy it, and it was sold direct by the Executors of the Langton Estate to the Air Ministry. The remaining small portion of about 15 acres was taken from Mr. Hooper, of Tarrant Hinton.

A few years after the War the R.A.F. were still slowly clearing away the bombs they had dropped on it. Due very largely to the initiative of Captain David Taylor, of Pimperne, the process was speeded up, as you will hear from him shortly.

Then about 3 years ago the Air Ministry *sold* the land to the Ministry of Agriculture, and it was then taken in hand and has since been farmed by the Dorset A.E.C.

When I saw the land being ploughed, my wife and I — she being a previous owner — set about trying to buy back the land which had been taken from us — in Wartime, for essential defence purposes — and which we now saw being returned to Agriculture.

I wrote to the Ministry of Agriculture, and my application was dealt with by the Land Commissioner for this district, who appears to have been the Authority responsible for the administration of the land under the Minister.

I heard he was quite upset that a previous owner should want to buy back what had been his own land. He had other plans — plans to build a magnificent new holding, and bother the expense. A plan, I should call it — 'To the greater glory of Land Commissioners.'

Anyway my application was refused.

My next approach, just about two years ago, was to my member of parliament, Mr. Crouch. Ever since that time he has taken endless trouble on my behalf, and given me his wise advice. As I know he would to any of us.

In my letter I said that I wished to buy back the land that had been ours; to incorporate it in the farm it had previously been part of, and to let it to the sitting tenants — Mr. Robin and Mr. John Harding. I gave an assurance that there were the necessary dwellings and buildings available, and that I was prepared to lay on water all over the area, from our own estate system — which in fact at this very moment is still supplying the water to that land.

Shortly after, Mr. Crouch informed me that it was the Minister's intention to deal with the whole 700 odd acres as one unit. I wrote immediately to the Minister and offered to bid for that too.

During the next year and a quarter Mr. Crouch informed me, from time to time that the matter was receiving attention. Then in March this year he forwarded to me another letter refusing my application. Any moral claim that we might have had to the land was dismissed in a few lines, and the major portion of the letter was devoted to disparagement of the Hardings as farmers. This will astonish you who know them. It astonished me.

I should like to explain how the Ministry arrived at this incredible conclusion. The accusation was that the Hardings had 170 acres of rough grazing on their 1300 acre farm — a figure that was presumably dug out of some old Agricultural return.

Now when we let them land we drew a line round the perimeter and said to them, 'That is so many acres, and we want so many shillings per acre.' This perimeter included two areas of Woodland clear felled during the war, and not yet part of our replanting programme, a copse, a brook, gardens, allotments, rights of way, orchards, three houses, numerous cottages, and of course hedges. In addition, included in the accusation there were 54 acres recently let to the Hardings, which they had already ploughed up, but which in the earlier return had been shown as rough grazing. John Harding, when making his return had worked out his cultivations, leys and so on, subtracted the total from his acreage, and lumped the rest in his return as rough grazing. Wrong perhaps—but I understand it is a common practice of which the Ministry are well aware, and it certainly should not be used as a stick to beat one of the best downland and dairy farmers in the South West.

Why, we feel entitled to ask, on an issue of such importance, didn't someone come and find out the facts? I have been told Lord Carrington *did* come down. He never saw any of us who had applied for the land.

The attitude of who ever did show him round must be open to question. Why wasn't he shown the Hardings land. It is a masterpiece of good farming. All that came out of this visit was the refusal of our case, and this sordid and untruthful accusation.

I realized from this letter that we were not just dealing with bureaucracy, but with someone—somewhere—who was definitely hostile to our case. I rebutted the charges most vigorously in a letter to the Minister, and I asked him for a personal interview in order to bring under his direct observation the state of affairs.

With Mr. Crouch I went to see his Parliamentary Secretary, Mr. Nugent, I offered to buy, publicly or privately, what had previously been ours— OR the whole area—OR to rent it. I showed him how this could be done with the existing facilities—Four modern cottages here, a modernised bothy for a further three single men there, the farmhouse, the means of bringing water, the building for corn drying and storing—in fact everything necessary to farm the land efficiently.

Mr. Nugent seemed quite impressed. He offered on behalf of the Minister to give my proposals sympathetic consideration. And how much sympathetic consideration do you suppose they received from the Minister—if indeed he ever knew I'd been there—About as much as a Colorado Beetle might expect.

Mr. Nugent admitted to me at a later meeting that he had been uninformed. When he looked into the matter he found that the Ministry was already committed in January to sell the land to the Commissioner of Crown Lands. He did not inform me of this, but merely that my application had once more been declined.

Mr. Crouch was as incensed as I was at this senseless decision, and with the support of two other local M.P.'s—Lord Hinchingbrooke, and Major Morrison—he sought an interview with the Minister himself. In early May he saw them and he *told* them—so I understand—that his Ministry were committed to the Commissioners of Crown Lands. This was the first any of *us* had heard of it.

In case anyone is in doubt about Crown Lands I can explain them briefly as follows. King George III exchanged a large portion of his private lands for a fixed annual income called 'The Civil List'. The lands have since been administered by Commissioners of Crown Lands. There is one permanent Commissioner and two others — the Secretary of State for Scotland, and the Minister of Agriculture of the moment.

The Minister regretted that owing to this previous commitment he was unable to entertain my case, BUT, he said, so far as the Ministry was concerned there was no obstacle to my acquiring the land from the Commissioners. Once again I wrote off — this time to the Commissioners — and I offered for the land. I had an acknowledgement to the effect that my letter was receiving attention. In fact it received little or none.

I waited a fortnight. I waited a month. I waited six weeks. No answer. So I wrote again, and I asked Lord Hinchingbrooke to write too. That produced a reply at last — from the Permanent Commissioner himself. It was now the end of July and I had written in mid-May. He regretted he would not let me have the land. He was committed, he said, to the *Ministry* to erect a farmhouse, cottages and buildings. Compare that with the Minister's statement two months earlier that so far as the Ministry was concerned there was no obstacle to my acquiring the land. The Commissioner also said — though at this time he hadn't even bought the land — that he was committed to a prospective tenant. Where should we be, I wonder, if as landowners we went and committed our land to tenants, before we had even bought it? I think we should be where the Commissioners are now — that is in the very devil of a hole.

I rang up the Permanent Commissioner — he was on his holiday — and I told him that the news was out about his tenant, and that I, and a large body of local opinion, were very perturbed at what had happened — that unless something could be done to rectify the situation there would be a row. He was clearly concerned at this and offered to arrange a meeting between the Minister, himself and myself, to sort this matter out. Due to their holidays it was impossible to find a date until 4th September — three weeks ago, and as the Minister was still away, Mr. Nugent again took his place. Mr. Crouch again came with me.

With all the strength I could I protested at the treatment that was being handed out to all of us. I said to Mr. Nugent 'But I applied for our land back, or if you wished, the whole 700 acres, nearly two years ago'. 'Yes', he said, 'but your application was to buy, and the land isn't being sold publicly'. 'But', I said, 'I applied to buy the land to instal the Hardings as tenants'. 'Ah', he said, 'That hardly constitutes an application on *their* part'. I thought to myself — 'you smooth creature, you're so slippery, you'd slide through the kitchen key-hole'. With Mr. Crouch's aid I pressed — certainly beyond the limits of civility — that they should reconsider the matter. I told them that there would inevitably be a wave of indignation if they continued to flaunt our rights in this way. They said they would consider the position.

Ten days ago I heard that the Permanent Commissioner considered himself morally committed to Mr. Tozer, and that he was going ahead with plans for a tenancy to begin at Michaelmas.

I should like to say this to the Commissioner. I believe he has a much wider moral commitment than that. It is to all of us — the public — to see that when the public's land is disposed of, it is done absolutely fairly and openly. He must have been aware after our meeting that a great injustice had been done to a number of people — though this was not by any means all his fault. Still it's no good saying to the Ministry — to use a Naval expression — 'To Hell with you Jack. I'm alright'.

If another government department was responsible for this injustice I maintain it was his moral commitment to put the matter right, and not blunder on to perpetrate an even deeper injustice.

Crown Lands have now taken over, in lieu of death duties the late Lord Portman's estate at Bryanston, and so they are very much in our midst. Whether we are their tenants or just their neighbours we should all like to feel that we are dealing with a body whose conduct and standards are above reproach. I don't believe we can feel any assurance of that, either now or in the future, unless the Commissioners re-examine their consciences and join us in asking for an impartial enquiry.

When I had this further refusal to reconsider the case I at once laid the matter before a meeting of landowners, and formed a Committee of landowners and farmers to take immediate action. A week ago we sent a telegram to Sir Thomas Dugdale personally, asking for an impartial enquiry. Three days ago he replied that he could not withdraw from the present arrangement without a *breach of faith*, and in the circumstances he does not think an enquiry will serve any useful purpose.

Well now, Ladies and Gentlemen, it is axiomatic in public life that the man at the top is responsible for all the official actions of his subordinates. In the light of that let us examine the official conduct of Sir Thomas Dugdale since about mid-January, in his capacities as Minister on the one hand, and a Commissioner of Crown Lands on the other.

There he is as Minister, owning 700 acres of land, for which he has a number of applications to buy or to rent. He ignores these applications. And, as Minister, he turns to himself, as a Commissioner of Crown Lands, and says to himself — 'Provided you put up a lot of buildings, and find your *own* tenant, I, as Minister, will sell this land to you.' Then, as a Commissioner, he turns to himself as Minister and says to himself — 'Alright, I'll buy it'. Thus is formed a commitment between himself, as Minister, and himself, as a Commissioner, to sell himself the land — and vice versa. Six weeks later when things are nicely settled he turns to me, as Minister, and says, 'you can't have the land.'

Not long after, in mid-May, three M.P.'s go to see him, as Minister. As Minister he tells them that he regrets he is committed to himself, as

Commissioner, to sell himself the land. 'But', he says, as Minister, 'There would be no obstacle from his point of view, as Minister, to my approaching him as Commissioner, to buy the land from himself. So I write to him, as Commissioner, and offer for the land. After a long delay he writes back and says — 'He regrets, as Commissioner, that he is committed to himself, as Minister, to put up all these buildings. Moreover, as Commissioner, he committed himself to a prospective tenant — although he hasn't yet bought the land from himself'.

This is a silly game. You would have thought that the Minister was made an ex officio Commissioner with the very purpose of avoiding this 'crazy gang' performance. We shall not worry if Sir Thomas Dugdale lies awake at night because, as Minister, he breaks faith with himself as Commissioner. What worries us is that he has broken faith with us — in the most flagrant fashion.

Let me read you this extract from a letter to a local farmer, dated 9th August 1951. 'As soon as the land at Crichel Down is likely to be available for letting it will be advertised in the public press, and any application you may make at that time will be carefully considered'.

Signed J. R. Marriott, For Land Commissioner.

There has been no such advertisement. The next thing this farmer knew was that the land was being let to another man. A breach of faith? Or do you think that we shall be told that this is no more than a departmental error?

Let me present the case for the previous owners or occupiers of the land. Firstly, ourselves. As soon as I knew that it was being returned to Agriculture, I applied to buy back what had been ours in order to let it to the Hardings. I subsequently applied to buy or rent, the entire 700 acres, and since my original applications two years ago I have continued to press my case by every means I knew.

Take the Hardings case. Over half the acreage has been taken from the Middle Farm at Long Crichel. They rested content with my application on their behalf. I assured them of the necessary cottages to accommodate extra men. They have already been deprived of their farm at Tarrant Rushton, which has been submerged beneath an aerodrome. That also was the property of my wife's estate.

Mr. Strange, at Tarrant Launceston, applied to the County Agricultural Officer to know whether there was any chance of his farming what had been part of his original holding. The County Agricultural Officer was unable to tell him how he should apply. He waited, as many others did, for some public announcement about the future. In the twenty years Mr. Strange has been at Tarrant Launceston his farm has been nearly cut in half by Ministries acquisition of land. He has lost 800 acres — on one side to the War Office, and here — on the other — to the Air Ministry.

Then there is Mr. Hooper at Tarrant Hinton. His farm too has been cut into. He has lost 60 acres to the War Office, and a further 15 to the Air

Ministry. He applied to the Land Commissioner to farm some of this land, and like everyone else his application has been shelved.

All these three are, as you know, excellent farmers, and they have the necessary farmhouses, cottages, and buildings for cultivating the land in the most efficient manner. They are now told they are not going to be allowed to do so — not, as we once heard, because the land was going to be taken to form a number of smaller holdings. We might not have agreed that this was feasible on this poor, bare land — but at least we would have sympathised with the motive. No. It was to be granted to a man from some miles away, whose family's holding is already about 1300 acres in extent. And what have they lost to the Ministries in recent years? Nothing. On the contrary I understand their acreage has been greatly increased since the beginning of the War by the grant of tenancies of public land. Now they are being granted a further large tenancy — and that in the most questionable manner. You have to stand on your head for a very long time to see the justice in this one.

As to the finance of the business we are told nothing — but, as it is our own money that is to be spent, I think we are entitled to speculate. Am I not right in thinking the official price to be paid is £25 per acre? But in fact is this the amount of cash that is going to change hands? I understand that, since that price was agreed the land has been surveyed, and that it has been decided to make a considerable reduction. Why?

Due to the Ministry's sloth in deciding the future of the land — they have had three and a half seasons — the A.E.C. have had to take three straw crops straight off this rather poor land. The result is it is in terribly bad condition — a thing the Ministry tell us we must never allow to happen, on pain of expulsion from our own farms. And what a way to assess land values. To look at — set an official figure, and then subtract from it because the land isn't what it ought to be.

Now this adds up to a very bad bargain for the country — I know there are people who would give £25 per acre for the land as it stands and no reduction. You may say — 'What does the price matter between one government department and another.' It matters to this extent. It means Crown Lands can charge a lower rent, and make it appear economic. But the country will get less interest on its money than by a straightforward sale. Even selling at this cut price — with the burden of this entirely unnecessary farmhouse, cottages and buildings, the rent, so I understand, is going to have to be over double what the surrounding, well equipped land is let for.

If there is one thing more than another that holds Landowners back from jumping up their rents, it is the knowledge that this can only lead to increased costs to the farmer, increased prices and dearer food. Yet here we have the State, as landlords wedging themselves into our lands, and setting up a rent standard of over double the present level. Can the Landowners be blamed if they follow suit?

These totally superfluous buildings they talk of erecting not only fulfil no existing need, but with the house, and *its* garden, and the cottages and *their* gardens, and the roads, and the whole paraphernalia of the farmstead, there will be actually *less* land available for production. Why don't they build these houses where they are needed? They are shouting out for them over at Ferndown.

The question that faces us is this, as previous owners and occupiers, or as neighbouring landowners and farmers, are we going to stand by and watch this folly being built up, brick by brick — an ever present reminder — a permanent memorial — to the extravagance and bad faith of the State. Or are we going to protest, and go on protesting with all the vigour that we can.

I should like to say to everyone who is looking towards greater freedom in this country — if we are going to fight this creeping disease of Land Nationalisation, now is the time to stand. Never in 100 years will ordinary country people like ourselves, have a better case against the State.

Address by Lt.-Com. G. G. Marten to the National Liberal Club (Wednesday 30 June 1954)

When I went to live at Crichel in 1950 I took the first opportunity of going round the Estate and in the course of my tour I saw a large uncultivated expanse of rough downland on our boundary. I found out that this was a disused R.A.F. bombing range, a large part of which had formerly belonged to the Crichel Estate and formed the better half of one of its farms. I heard that the land might shortly be returned to agriculture and therefore made application in March 1950, now nearly 4½ years ago, to buy back what had originally been part of my wife's property.

This request was dealt with by the Land Commissioner for Somerset and Dorset, Col. Norton-Fagge. He replied in a non-committal manner saying that it was too soon to give a considered reply to our enquiry, and I therefore wrote again to ask if he would let us know as soon as he was able to give us more definite news. It is interesting to note what happened to this request. It was not forwarded to higher authority, as in my view it certainly should have been. It was not docketed for further action, and it was not mentioned in a subsequent report in which Col. Norton-Fagge discusses the future of the land. In fact it remained neglected in the file until unearthed for the Inquiry.

It is also interesting to see what else was going on behind the scenes at this period. A month or two before, Col. Norton-Fagge had asked Mr. Ferris, the County Agricultural officer, for his opinion as to what to do with the land. Mr. Ferris had said,

'I am fairly certain that each of the farmers will be prepared to take over occupation of the area which was formerly attached to their respective farms and work the land in conjunction with their farms. I am quite sure this would be a better method of dealing with the land than by attempting to farm as a holding, as the land is not of any considerable fertility and production will be much higher if it is associated with established farms.'

In May 1950 armed with this advice Col. Norton-Fagge inspected the Down and wrote his report. He proposed two alternative methods of dealing with the land which merit closer scrutiny.

(1) Letting the land in blocks to neighbouring farmers.
(2) Making a single fully equipped holding.

He chose the latter course in preference to letting the land to neighbouring farmers and the reason he gave was as follows.

'The objection to this solution might be the disinclination of these farmers to deal satisfactorily with the core of the range. From the long term aspect it seems a likelihood that if any recession in farm profits occurs such off land would be the first to be given up by these farmers who already have considerable areas of their own.'

When Col. Norton-Fagge cast this doubt on the willingness of local farmers to deal satisfactorily with the land he had the following facts to go on.

1. — Mr. Ferris the only official who had knowledge of local farms and their farmers had said that he was fairly certain that each of the farmers would be prepared to take over occupation of the area and farm it as part of their farms.

2. — He knew we were anxious to buy our land back.

3. — He knew, so he said at the Inquiry, that all the farmers concerned were excellent farmers.

With this knowledge and without any further inquiry he was prepared to put forward as an objection to returning the land to neighbouring farmers the possibility of their disinclination to deal with it.

I cannot help thinking that if his mind had not been clouded by other considerations he would have said,

'An advantage of this solution is the probable willingness of these farmers to deal satisfactorily with the core of the range.'

He goes on to consider the possibility of a farming recession.

The Minister is, as we know, responsible for seeing that agriculture does not suffer a recession, and it can give the farmers little confidence to see a high placed official basing a course of action on this possibility. It is however a point of view which every sensible farmer takes into consideration and you may therefore think it legitimate that an official should do so too.

It is not so much the consideration of this possibility that startles me as the conclusion that Col. Norton-Fagge drew from it. He is suggesting that the possibility of a farming recession — inevitably the result of overproduction and falling prices — is a good reason for spending £20,000. This would of course immediately add a burden of overhead expense to the land which would make it much less capable of economic production if the recession came.

In the Autumn of 1951 Sir Frederick Burrows, the Chairman of the Land Commission, was saying that the decision to let could be deferred a little longer so satisfactory was the state of affairs at Crichel Down.

I thought if they carried on their activities into the life of a Conservative Government I should catch them with their trousers down and have a sympathetic hearing for my claim for the return of the land.

In May 1952 after the new administration had had a few months to settle into their chairs I told my Agent to write once again and apply to buy back our land. His letter was dealt with by the Land Commission who replied that it had already been decided to equip the land as a new holding and anyway so far as they were aware the Air Ministry were going to retain the freehold, and even if they did not, the Ministry of Agriculture powers of selling were very limited. This was of course an extremely inept reply. I immediately became aware that I was up against a body definitely hostile to my proposition and who were not prepared to examine it on its merits but preferred to prevaricate with the intention of frustrating my wishes.

My previous experience of the Civil Service had been only very slight, but my impressions in the Navy had been of a meticulous, painstaking and careful body of men particularly in regard to the spending of public money. It therefore came as all the more of a shock and a surprise to realise that I was dealing with a very different type of authority.

I wrote at once to Mr. Crouch, my Member of Parliament, and asked him to lay the matter before the Minister. He forwarded my letter to Mr. Nugent who set enquiries in motion to look into the matter. There then began that build up of inaccurate and misleading information, part deliberate and part careless, for which the A.E.C., the Land Service and the Land Commission must all bear their share of responsibility. This whole disgraceful proceeding is carefully recorded in Sir Andrew Clark's report and I will not enlarge upon it. There is however one point I should like to make in fairness to the Minister.

The impression he got out of all this was of an indifferent landlord wanting to buy a piece of land which he had neglected before the War, and had been only too pleased to part with at a low price—wanting it in order to instal an indifferent tenant with insufficient buildings to farm it properly and who already had a lot of uncultivated land on his hands.

He was told that in these hands the land would inevitably return to its original state of rough sheep grazing. He was told the alternative of creating a new farm would not only produce more food but be a satisfactory financial proposition.

Believing as he did that all this false information was true I do not see how the Minister could have reconciled his statutory obligations for full and efficient production with the return of the land to us. He has been criticised for not upholding the principle that land compulsorily acquired by the State should be offered back to its original owners when no longer required for the purpose for which it was originally taken. Even if the Minister had realised that our land had been taken compulsorily he had no power, so far as I know, to return the land to us unless such a course fell in with his statutory obligations for full and efficient production. Even if the policy of returning land to private owners had been decided and followed it would have been the Minister's duty, if the facts he had been told were true, to take the land back again because we would have failed to farm it fully and efficiently. The Minister's careful observance of his obligation under the Act is a complete contrast to the attitude under Mr. Williams' administration, when the possibility of selling land was not even examined even where it might be in the best interests of full and efficient production.

My letter of May 1952 to Mr. Crouch did not receive a considered reply until March 1953. This reply was in some respects inaccurate and once again gave me an impression of hostility. It was as a result of my protests that I had a meeting with Mr. Nugent to which I have already referred. When he refused to consider our application to buy I offered as an alternative to rent the land for several years to show the Minister what we could do and subsequently if they approved of our methods, to buy it.

It was an unsatisfactory meeting because Mr. Nugent was improperly briefed. He left me with the impression that our request would be given sympathetic consideration whereas when he went into the matter he found that the Minister had already promised the land to the Commissioner of Crown Lands who were already committed to a tenant of their own choosing. He wrote to Mr. Crouch turning down our latest offer and mentioning the commitment to the Commissioner of Crown Lands. He omitted however to mention that the Commissioner had found a tenant. This was a curious omission, particularly as Mr. Nugent was aware of my desire to rent the land myself. Perhaps he hoped to smooth over any little unpleasantness that might arise between us.

I have seen it suggested that official letters written by officials to officials on official business should not be subjected to public scrutiny in this way. Like the old fashioned methods of bringing up children it is said to stifle free expression.

I must say I think this is the most pernicious doctrine. I am sure a good precedent has been established here, and moreover this Inquiry emphasises the vital need that, in the public interest, every proposal and every action by Civil Servants should be committed to paper officially. It is equally important from the point of view of the Civil Servants themselves that the letters should refer only to official business. This always was the way things were conducted, but they seem to have become intolerably slack in the Ministry of Agriculture.

The decision not to disclose minutes meant that it is virtually impossible to apportion responsibility fairly for all the deceits and omissions which took place, purely on the strength of Sir Andrew's report. Let me take again the example of the honest mistake about whether the land was compulsorily acquired or not.

We know this was due to lack of care among relatively junior officials in Dorset. Where dishonesty began to creep in was when the Minister was not told immediately the mistake was discovered.

We know that Sir Reginald Franklin, the Head of the Civil Service at the Ministry, was aware of this mistake by early October last year.

He wrote a letter for the Minister's signature which appeared to the casual observer to confirm the statement that we had sold our land willingly. If the Minister was by this time aware that it had in fact been taken by compulsion he must bear responsibility for this rather tricky statement.

If on the other hand he was kept in ignorance of the fact, the burden of guilt that lies with Sir Reginald Franklin is a very grave one. He was deliberately withholding vital information from his Minister, and placing before him for his signature a letter framed to deceive the Minister as to the truth. I do not accuse Sir Reginald. It may be that the Minister must bear responsibility for this rather artful piece of prose. If not however, one must ask oneself why Sir Reginald should stoop to this deceit. The only logical answer appears to be that he intended to impose a policy of retaining the land in State ownership in conflict with the Minister's expressed desire.

Again there is the matter of promises to advertise the land for letting. The failure to inform Crown Lands of this was an unfortunate piece of inefficiency by local officials. It only became really serious when it was withheld from the Minister. We know Mr. Eastwood and Mr. Wilcox knew about it in March. We know Mr. Nugent knew about it before the lease was signed with Tozer on 11th September.

We don't know when the Minister learned about it. My guess is not until he read my speech delivered to local farmers and landowners at the end of September, after the lease was signed.

These are only two examples of the difficulty of looking on the Inquiry, with its narrow terms of reference, voluntary attendance of witnesses and only partial disclosure of documents, as any substitute for a court of law, or court martial.

The effect however of *no* disciplinary action is to shake the confidence of the entire county, not only in this Ministry, but in the entire Civil Service.

I went down to watch our local village cricket match last Saturday week. I was talking to one of our tenant's tractor drivers who summed up the general feeling as follows:—

'Them bastards up in Whitehall can't keep a straight bat. You go and bowl 'em and they won't leave the field — where's the bloody umpire?'

The umpire has given them out, and I'm sure it would be wrong for him to change his decision. May I however give you two examples of how deep and far reaching the effects of this decision may be.

Take the example of the Dorset A.E.C., whose misdemeanours take up only a few lines in the report, and consider the effects on farmers in the county.

An official has said of some of the most respected farming families, that:—

'they have neither the will, nor the ability to farm the land.'

This statement was made without any form of official inspection or inquiry, uttered without the knowledge of any of those concerned, and now admitted to be completely untrue.

Again an A.E.C. official — Mr. Brown — writing a report to his superior, says:—

'The Crichel Estate, having got wind of our official views over the large area of rough pasture have ploughed a large amount of the area.'

Apart from the fact that we never got wind of anything, nor ploughed up any land, this sentence reveals the most horrifying state of affairs in the A.E.C.

When Mr. Brown says:—'got wind of our official views' he makes it abundantly clear that it is quite customary for official views of an adverse nature to be held about a farmer, and used against him, without his ever knowing such views are held. When I also tell you that these official views were formed without any official inquiry or inspection, and were not recorded in any official document, and were in any case based on incorrect information, you will realise how deep and dirty are some of the roots which have to be unearthed.

Similar criticisms apply even more forcibly to the Land Commission and to Crown Lands, controlling as they do, over half a million acres of land between them, and having tenants running into thousands.

If there was confidence before in these bodies, recent events have now certainly punctured the bottom of the drum.

The Alington 'former owners' of 328 acres of Crichel Down

Robert Crouch's observation (p. 54) that the Alingtons' estate had been 'well run for generations' seems never to have been investigated officially, the Minister's decision not to sell land back to the Crichel Estate having turned not on past performance but on current expert advice for maximum future food production. Nevertheless, the history is of interest, although there is no evidence that the government's decisions were influenced by it.

To quarrel with the claim of good management for generations is to be a real 'spoil-sport', because 'sport' was the chief lifelong interest of the first and second Barons, and dissipation the chief vocation of the third. No more should be said, therefore, than is needed to show the three generations of the ennobled Sturt family as, successively, more and more dedicated to the pleasures and privileges of their station in life than to its duties. No great effort in public service was made in return for great inherited wealth, even if one includes the years of undistinguished Commons membership of the first and second Lords, before they became peers.

The Sturt family fortune derived from a joining, in the eighteenth century by successive marriages, of three estates. Two neighbouring estates in Dorset, the Napier estate at Crichel (founded on the fortune of a rich seventeenth century lawyer) and the Sturt estate at nearby Horton (founded on the fortune of, as Douglas Brown puts it, 'a rich alderman of the City of London who was Victualler to the Navy in the time of Pepys') were joined by marriage in 1717. The Sturt heir, according to Brown (*The Battle of Crichel Down*, p. 13), married 'the heiress of a Hoxton man with extensive land in what is now central London, land which rapidly increased in value as the city developed. In this way, in two generations, three great estates were united and the finances of the family consolidated to face the shocks of the 200 years to follow.' The family remained well cushioned from financial shocks. Successive manor houses and mansions with parks and lakes were constructed, superseded, or accidentally set on fire, and eventually replaced by the still-standing stately Crichel House, looking out over a large artificial lake in which, it is said, a village and a parsonage were submerged during construction in the eighteenth century.

The first Baron Alington, Henry Gerard Sturt (1825–1904) described simply as 'sportsman' in his Dictionary of National Biography entry, was a Dorset Conservative MP for almost thirty years, from 1847, soon after leaving Christ Church, Oxford, until 1876, when raised to the peerage. In his day he was famous as an owner of racehorses (trained at Woodyates, and Pimperne), as a great gambler, as a friend of the Prince of Wales (later King Edward VII), and sharer of his interests — as was his son, Humphrey Napier, the second Lord Alington. One of the better stories about the first Lord Alington's interest in the Turf is told in the 1908 edition of the Victoria County History: when an Eton boy in 1839–40, he was said to have 'backed Lord George Bentinck's famous filly, Crucifix, for all her races as a two-year-old, and wound up by landing a treble event bet, when, in 1840, she won the Two Thousand Guineas, One Thousand Guineas, and Oaks'. Later successes included the Derby (twice), the St Leger (twice), and other classics. The rent-roll of the estate brought in an estimated £24,000 a year at that period. There is evidence, however, amidst the records of the wealthy nobleman's sporting exploits, and the dispensing of 'liberal hospitality' at Crichel, that he was a considerate landlord and gave thought and attention to the estate. But throughout his period the Dorset labourer was generally amongst the worst paid in the whole country (5*s*. to 10*s*. per week), there being little local alternative to farm labour for men, and little choice of employer, even in farming.

Much has been written about the Tolpuddle martyrs, sent to Australia from Dorset for daring to disobey, but in the second half of the nineteenth century legal compulsion to go was scarcely necessary. At Wimborne Minster, for instance, the small district town nearest to Crichel, a business flourished of 'Passage Broker, Emigration and Shipping Agent', and 'local agent of the Queensland Government' supplying free and assisted passages, and Land Order Warrants to paying passengers. There was a great gulf between wealthy and immensely self-indulgent country landowners like the Alingtons and the wretched poverty of those around them.

The second Lord Alington continued life in the opulent style from his succession in 1904 (entertaining the King and the Kaiser on occasion) until his death in 1919 — or at least until World War I hastened the ending of the old order of social deference and dependence on the landed proprietor. The style of the second Lord Alington and Lady Alington was more *outré* than that of the previous generation, narrowly avoiding open scandal. The great shoots and shooting parties continued, and lavish hospitality for royal visitors went on: the slaughter of birds and animals, the 'memorable bags' continued to astonish.

At the urban end of the Alington estate, however, the Hoxton properties in London, the regular sport was of a different kind, presumably unknown to Crouch. There, according to Jeffrey, fifth Lord Amherst (an Eton 'crony' of Napier or 'Naps' Sturt, the third and last Lord Alington) the second Lord Alington and his lady were regularly burned in effigy:

The family owned a large section of Hoxton, where there were some of the worst of London's East End [*sic*] slums. I do not think the family could have been very good landlords as I remember feeling a sense of shame for them when I first heard the story of how the denizens of Hoxton would burn effigies of Lord and Lady Alington on their street bonfires on Guy Fawkes night and New Year's nights.

(Amherst, Jeffrey, *Wandering Abroad*, 1976, p. 65.)

Of the third and last Lord Alington, who succeeded in 1919 and died in 1940, there are many published stories, by supposed friends, mostly scandalous, some scabrous. None is more terrible, however, than Amherst's account of the death of his elder brother, who, had he survived, might well have made a more conscientious landlord:

Naps had an elder brother Gerard of considerable, if conventional good looks, totally different from Naps himself, who was a strange Faun, an almost Pan-like creature, surely a drawing for one of the Diaghilev Ballets. A near caricature, of considerable magnetism and charm. The boys were said not to have the same father and one could well believe it. Brother Gerard had been badly wounded serving with the Coldstream Guards in Flanders. Critically ill in a London hospital they sent word to his mother that he was dying and wanted to see her. She sent word that she couldn't come at once as she had an engagement to go to the opera, but would come when it was over. When it was over, so was Brother Gerard. He was dead.

(Amherst, op. cit. p. 65.)

The relatively short life of the younger brother, Napier, third Lord Alington, seems to have been a melancholy sort of rake's progress, from Bright Young Thing in New York, London and Paris in the 1920s, through episodes recalling P. G. Wodehouse's Drones' Club, through drink, drugs, and debauchery to a miserable death in a Cairo hospital in 1940, broken in health:

His frail carcass had been wracked with appalling tubercular coughs for many years. Yet his system was of such ironlike strength that, whereas most other people would have succumbed long before, he had hung on. Sometimes he looked desperately ill, like a pathetic wastrel, but he was always courageously ready for fun.

(Beaton, Cecil, *The Years Between: Diaries 1939–44*, 1965, p. 71)

There would be little merit in rehearsing all the sad details: they can be found in Lord Amherst's memoirs, and in those of another Eton friend, James Stuart, Viscount Findhorn, cabinet colleague and close friend of Sir Thomas Dugdale also (*Within the Fringe*, 1967). There is a good deal more about him, not entirely to his discredit, in the diaries of another friend, Cecil Beaton (*The Years Between: Diaries 1939–44*, 1965). There is much about his 'charm' as well as more dubious tributes such as 'however much pitch he wallowed in, it never stuck', and 'He appreciated the nuances of luxury but could put up with any squalor.' (Beaton, op. cit. pp. 71–3).

Other sources of gossipy comment on 'Naps' include racy biographies of the actress Tallulah Bankhead (Israel, Lee, *Miss Tallulah Bankhead*, 1972; Gill, Brendan, *Tallulah*, 1973; Tunney, Kieran, *Tallulah, Darling of the*

Gods: an intimate portrait, 1972). In Tunney's book (p. 154) Amherst is cited in aid of the proposition, attributed by Lord Berners to Mrs Gloria Vanderbilt, that Naps Alington was 'naughty, spoilt rotten to use a common expression': Amherst is quoted by Tunney thus:

I knew him well — we were at school together — and though there's no denying the charm he was certainly spoilt. Quite absurdly so. It's not unfair to say that he and his sister Lois were victims of such an utter lack of discipline that they would have needed the combined strength of Shaw, Peter the Great and Elizabeth the First to emerge unscathed. Think of their upbringing, every wilful thought, action condoned by a hopelessly indulgent mother and with that beautiful, wonderful house as a playground for any prank they thought up!

Amherst's later assessments of Napier Alington's character differ from the earlier only in their starkness:

I had known him ever since Eton days. I do not think I have ever met anyone before or since who so completely lacked any kind of discipline in respect of himself, his family or even workwise. From all I ever heard the blame for this belongs mostly to his mother, the Lady Feodorovna Alington, Feo to her friends.

(Amherst, *Wandering Abroad*, 1976, p. 65.)

Amherst also relates Alington's death, almost as pathetic as his brother's, but not so heroic. Despite being tubercular, and unfit after what Amherst calls 'the endless wallow through life from one dishevelled party to another', Alington somehow managed to get himself commissioned in the Royal Air Force, in Egypt, and given an office job, although the habits of a lifetime made it impossible for him to give up late nights and get up in the mornings in time to be at his desk by 8.30 a.m.:

He was posted to a squadron in the desert on some ground job, which delighted him and where he was very popular. One day he was invited to join in a personal capacity the crew of a bomber that was to go on a mission over Benghazi. At 10,000 feet and over the temperature falls quite low. Naps had disregarded all warnings to put on thick flying clothes. So when he landed after the mission he rapidly developed pneumonia from which he died, very peacefully as far as I could judge and I was with him until a short time before he finally stopped breathing. But he did die more or less on active service and in uniform which I think was what he wanted.

(Amherst, op. cit. p. 150)

Amherst's final grim assessment of his friend seems to leave no possibility of any real contribution by him to the good management of a large landed estate:

Naps Allington [*sic*] was another of my friends who had this quality ('charm'), but born with a surfeit of silver spoons in the mouth, lacking any kind of discipline, parental, self or professional, with an automatic entree to most of the highest in the land he traded, I think almost without being conscious of it, on the good will this charm engendered to be forgiven every kind of rude, selfish and amoral behaviour. His particular Pied Piper led him not too happily, as I have described, through years of self-indulgence, drink, drugs, sex — the lot — to a needless death at a comparatively early age in Cairo during the Second World War.

(Amherst, op. cit. p. 213)

The names of both brothers are inscribed on the village war memorial in the Witchampton churchyard, near the gates of Crichel House. How much of the family's history was known to members of the government of the day, in 1953 and 1954, one cannot say. James Stuart must have known much of it, as also Brigadier Head, Mrs Marten's uncle. Dugdale himself, a near contemporary of Napier Sturt at Eton, would have known something of it, in all probability, as would Etonian Sir Andrew Clark, and some at least of the several Etonians and others in the highest political and civil sevice posts. Scandal such as the Alingtons generated is lively enough to be remembered.

Yet there is no trace of evidence that the history of the estate, urban or rural, was adduced by anyone in the Government, whether to support a case for restoration of land, or to destroy it. On balance, the history strengthens rather than weakens the case for retention in public ownership of land bought from great landowners, even without bringing in vexed questions of socialism or land nationalization. Pity for the Alington family seems the appropriate feeling, rather than envy or admiration for the way the estate was run by them over the generations.

The Battle of Crichel Down,
by R. Douglas Brown, 1958

As noted on p. 19, the speed with which the first and very readable account of the Crichel Down affair was written, in 1954 (and published early in 1955) made for mistakes. Most of these were quite inconsequential, but one in particular had the unfortunate and unintended consequence of imprinting and reinforcing in the public mind some of the worst aspects of the Clark report.

One of these (Appendix 2, para. 25) was Clark's finding that D. S. Brown, 'a very junior official' made a report 'riddled with inaccuracies', these inaccuracies tending to support 'his Department's already settled policy'. What the journalist author R. Douglas Brown wrote about the draft report by the official D. S. Brown was not uncharitable, but showed his acceptance of Clark's verdict (p. 47, *The Battle of Crichel Down*): 'It read well. It sounded convincing. But for reasons about which Mr. Brown could do little, it was loaded with inaccuracies and debatable contentions.'

Douglas Brown's own book is entitled to the same charitable judgement. It too read well, and sounded convincing, but in the absence of better facilities for investigation it had the effect of spreading and perpetuating the Clark error. The chief mistake which both Browns made, the insider as well as the outsider, was to accept Clark's findings about the condition of the land without the requisite grain of salt. But then, so did nearly everyone else, including the Minister for whom the findings were written.

Other less consequential errors in the book should also be mentioned, not because they are of great significance in the story, but because they show the impossibility of combining speed with accuracy, easy reading with hard fact. One can sympathize with Brown's wish to give readers pleasure as well as instruction, to entertain those he was guiding, not merely to inform them in a dry-as-dust factual manner, as if he were an official. The following not very significant errors seem to arise from a laudable desire to enliven the story, to add 'human interest':

(a) At p. 73 Marten is said to have pursued the Permanent Commissioner of Crown Lands to his holiday retreat in Devonshire: in fact the course he pursued was slightly less dramatic, he contented himself with telephoning Eastwood (whom he had not met, and who was on holiday in Cornwall) to express dissatisfaction and to threaten (in italics if Brown was right) that *there would be a row*:

277

(b) At p. 105 there is a vivid picture of Dugdale striding into his office 'one mid-May morning in 1954, his usual genial self' to find on his desk 'a thick wad of foolscap', the Clark report: but the archives suggest that Clark called in person to hand over the report and covering letter to the Minister directly, with no civil service intermediary involved:

(c) At p. 121 Dugdale is said to have been given the important post of Colonial Secretary 'after only two years in the House of Commons': Dugdale was never Colonial Secretary, but did become Parliamentary Private Secretary to Sir Philip Cunliffe-Lister (Lord Swinton), whose appointments included a period as Colonial Secretary: after that Dugdale became PPS to the Prime Minister, Stanley Baldwin:

(d) At p. 122 Lady Dugdale and Lady Churchill are depicted as sitting together in the Speaker's gallery during the Crichel Down debate: according to a marginal correction by Lady Dugdale in the Crathorne copy of the book, she was not present at all on that occasion: if only because of the close Baldwin–Dugdale pre-war association, there was nothing very close in the relations between the Churchills and the Dugdales.

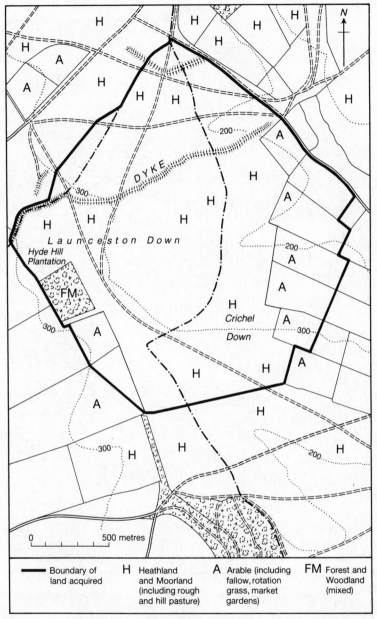

1. Pre-war (1931–2) land utilization (from map in the London School
of Economics Library) for the area of Launceston Down and Crichel
Down acquired by the Air Ministry in 1938 as a practice
bombing-range

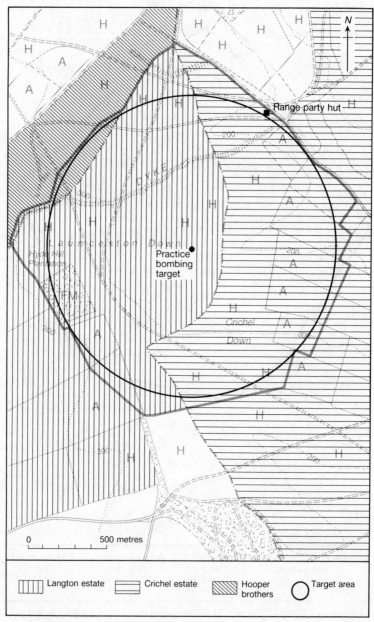

2. Ownerships of Launceston Down and Crichel Down area in 1938, before acquisition of practice bombing-range site by the Air Ministry

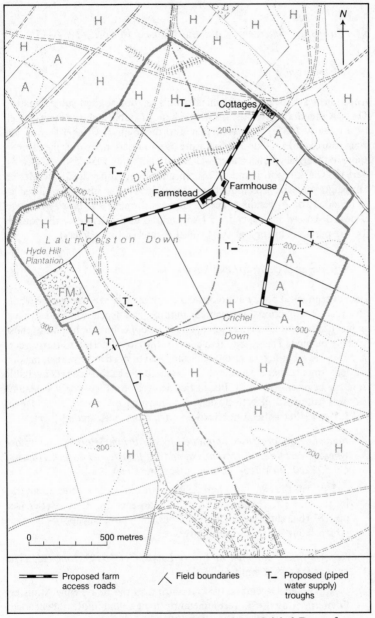

3. Proposed field layout and water supply at Crichel Down for Commissioners of Crown Lands

Bibliographical Notes

1. Published Sources within the 'Closed Period', 1954–85

A. Mythography

Appendices 1–6 give bibliographical details relevant to their subject matter. Thus, Appendix 1 gives details of the kind of published comments, from 1954 to early 1985, which contributed to the myth of Crichel Down. The main sources for that kind of literature (ignoring, as many did, the cabinet-approved Dugdale parliamentary statement on 20 July 1954, 530 HC Deb.5s) were the Clark report (Cmd. 9176) reproduced as Appendix 2; the Marten campaign material exemplified in the addresses by him reproduced as Appendix 3 and Appendix 4; and R. Douglas Brown's *The Battle of Crichel Down*, discussed in Appendix 5 (Appendix 6 details some of the sources for the previous history of the Crichel Estate and its owners).

B. Official and Quasi-official Sources before 1984–6

The governmental policy of non-disclosure was meant to last for the whole fifty-year closed period then generally in force, and depended for its survival on much sustained loyalty, stoicism, and 'stiff upper lip' on the part of those wrongly blamed. The general reduction of the closed period to thirty years (in 1966) was a big step towards the distant goal of open government, making the departmental papers available in 1984 and the cabinet papers available from the beginning of 1985. But justice delayed for thirty years instead of fifty was still justice effectively denied, to most participants. Crichel Down had led to earlier official publications of importance, among them:

> *Report of a Committee appointed by the Prime Minister to consider whether certain civil servants should be transferred to other duties, Cmd. 9220, July 1954* (The WOODS committee).
>
> This was the two and a half page report of the committee appointed by the cabinet, chaired in Churchill's absence by R. A. Butler (see pp. 187 ff.), in the expectation of Churchill's covering approval on his return from American, duly given.

> *Report of the Committee on Crown Lands, Cmd. 9483, June 1955* (The TRUSTRAM EVE committee).
>
> Appointed December 1954, reporting to the new Prime Minister, Eden, in May 1955, recommending a new and more independent statutory board of trustees (see p. 174 f.).

Report of the Committee appointed to review the Provincial and Local Organisation and Procedures of the Ministry of Agriculture, Fisheries and Food, Cmd. 9732, 1956 (The ARTON WILSON committee).

See pp. 202 ff.

Report of the Defence Lands Committee 1971–73, 1973.

Chairman, Lord Nugent of Guildford, committee appointed by and reporting to Lord Carrington as Minister of Defence.

Another most important committee, appointed by Maxwell Fyfe in 1955 soon after becoming Lord Chancellor, was the FRANKS Committee on Tribunals and Enquiries (Cmd. 218, 1957). It was generally believed to have been appointed in response to public concern over arbitrary officialdom in general and Crichel Down in particular. It was therefore a puzzle, not least to the committee itself, that their terms of reference did not permit an examination of the Crichel Down case. The answer to that puzzle must lie in the fact that the appointing Lord Chancellor had no wish to have Crichel Down publicly examined, especially by a committee whose report turned out to be very emphatic on the need for 'openness, fairness and impartiality' in tribunals and inquiries — the very qualities notably lacking in the Crichel Down Inquiry and its aftermath, and in Maxwell Fyfe's own contribution to both. (See DE SMITH, S.A., *Constitutional and Administrative Law*, 2nd edn, 1973, and WADE, H.W.R., *Administrative Law*, 3rd edn, 1971, for the belief that the Franks Committee was the result, however illogical, of Crichel Down; also Maxwell Fyfe's own *Political Adventure* at p. 301 and p. 321.)

Among the official sources must be included (although not strictly an official publication) the best available internal account of the Ministry of Agriculture of the period:

Winnifrith, Sir John, *The Ministry of Agriculture, Fisheries and Food*, 1962.

This book, written by Sir Alan Hitchman's successor as permanent secretary and by some of his colleagues in the ministry, is a clear account of the ministry's history, its rapid growth in World War II, and the wide range of its problems. In regard to Crichel Down it is a mandarin masterpiece of accurate but reticent understatement. The biggest crisis in the Ministry's history is mentioned only in the context of the resultant reversal of policy, i.e. the decisions to sell as much as possible of the nearly 200,000 acres of agricultural land acquired under previous policies (p. 31), and to offer such land back so far as reasonably practicable 'to the former owner or his successors' (p. 121). The repeal, in the Agriculture Act, 1958, of powers to place under supervision and in the last resort to dispossess farmers and landowners 'disregarding the rules of good husbandry or good estate management', is also mentioned (p. 31). That complete abdication of power is treated as a matter of detail, and as the result of the 1957 report of the

Franks Committee, with the comment: 'the use of these powers had become increasingly difficult and out of line with public opinion as time went on.' At p. 243 occurs the rueful observation that although 'Public Relations' and 'Press Officer' tend to be regarded as 'rather dirty words', government departments need an organization to explain publicly what they are doing.

C. *Political Memoirs*

In the absence during the closed period of accounts characterized by 'openness, fairness and impartiality' the memoirs of politicians are of value and interest. They include:

Brown, George (Lord George-Brown) *In My Way*, 1971.

Fyfe, David Patrick Maxwell (Earl of Kilmuir) *Political Adventure*, 1964.

Johnson, Donald McI. *A Cassandra at Westminster*, 1967.

Moran (Lord Moran of Manton) *Winston Churchill, the Struggle for Survival*, 1966.

Stuart, James (Viscount Findhorn) *Within the Fringe*, 1967.

Williams, Tom (Lord Williams of Barnburgh) *Digging for Britain*, 1965.

D. *Academic Articles on Crichel Down*

Much of the mass of references in academic writings about Crichel Down, especially in text-books, is vitiated by lack of scepticism about the Clark version and the political transactions before and after the inquiry (cf. Appendix 1). The following is a selection of some of the more thoughtful and more researched learned articles published in the closed period:

Chester, D. N. 'The Crichel Down Case'
  Public Administration, vol. xxxii, winter 1954.

Hamson, C. J. 'The Real Lesson of Crichel Down'
  Public Administration, vol. xxxii, winter 1954.

Roche, D. 'Crichel Down Surveyed'
  Administration (Dublin) vol. 3, nos 2–3, summer–autumn 1955.

Finer, S. E. 'The Individual Responsibility of Ministers'
  Public Administration, vol. xxxiv, 1956.

Wheare, K. C. 'Crichel Down Revisited'
  Political Studies, vol. xxiii, no. 2, 1974.

E. *Books on Agricultural Policy and Land Use*

The following books on the wider aspects of agricultural policy and politics, and land use in Britain, provide useful background material:

Tavener, L. E. *The Land of Britain: Dorset, Land Utilization Survey Pt. 88*, 1940.

Tavener, L. E. *Aspects of the agricultural geography of Dorset*, 1952.

Parsons, K. H., ed. *Land Tenure*, 1956.

Contains at pp. 505 ff. an address at a Wisconsin international conference, on the British experience in estate management and husbandry, by J. S. Hill, Chief Land Commissioner of the Ministry of Agriculture at the time of Crichel Down.

Williams, H. T. (ed.) *Principles for Agricultural Policy*, 1960.

Self, P., and Storing, H. J., *The State and the Farmer*, 1962.

Stamp, L. Dudley, *The Land of Britain, its Use and Misuse*, 3rd ed. 1962.

McCrone, Gavin, *The Economics of subsidising Agriculture*, 1962.

HMSO, *A Century of Agricultural Statistics*, 1866–1966, 1968.

Stacey, Frank, *The Government of Modern Britain*, 1968.

Bellerby, J. R. ed., *Factory Farming: a Symposium*, 1970.

Douglas, R. *Land, People and Politics, a History of the Land Question in the United Kingdom, 1878–1952*, 1976.

Mackintosh, J. P. *The British Cabinet*, 3rd ed., 1977.

Body, R. *Agriculture, The Triumph and the Shame*, 1982.

F.   *The Literature of Dorset*

The literature of Dorset is very rich; a good guide is the Dorset County Library Catalogue:

Carter, Kenneth, ed. Pitman, Elizabeth, *Dorset Collection, 1975; a Catalogue of the books and other printed materials on the history, topography, geology, archeology, natural history and biography of Dorset*, 1974.

2.   *Primary Sources, 1984–5*

Apart from the cabinet papers for 1953 and 1954 relating to Crichel Down, now, since the beginning of 1985, in bound voumes on the open shelves of the Public Record Office, and apart from the pre-World War II papers in the AM or Air Ministry series, relating to the acquisition of Crichel Down in 1938, the chief primary sources used in this study since the closed period ended in 1984 have been the files listed below in the MAF or Ministry of Agriculture series. It might be expected of Claude Wilcox's envisaged 'earnest research workers' in pursuit of Ph.D.s (see p. 181) that they should extend their researches to include all the departmental papers of all the departments which became involved in the Crichel Down deliberations, and should probe further into such records as might be opened to them by the other organizations taking part, such as the Country Landowners' Association, the National Farmers' Union, both sides of the National Whitley Council, the political party secretaries, the Press, and the BBC. In official records alone, it might be necessary to study the contributions of every department participating in the cabinet and cabinet committee deliberations, including the Lord Chancellor's and the Law Officers' departments as well as the Prime Minister's and Cabinet offices, and HM Treasury. That would amount to many man-years of exhaustive and exhausting work not needed for the simpler purposes of this book, to demythologize the Crichel Down story and to demonstrate the grave injustice done to the Blandford martyrs. *Ars longa, vita brevis*, and there is plenty of rich ore left for a team of 'earnest research workers' to mine, given strength and patience.

MAF (Ministry of Agriculture) files in the Public Record Office of use for this study included:

109/174	1949–53 ALC, Crichel Down, Dorset: equipping and farming the land; building quotations
109/175	1953–5 Ditto: farming accounts; correspondence
140/41	1945–51 Air Ministry, Crichel Down bombing range, Dorset: transfer of management of land to Ministry of Agriculture and Fisheries: search of land for unexploded missiles
142/148	1950–3 Crichel Down Bombing Range: acquisition and transfer to ALC and proposed sale to Crown Lands
142/149	1953–4 Ditto: preparation for public inquiry
142/150	1954–5 Ditto: proceeds from sale of land
142/241	1953–4 Disposal of compulsorily purchased land: proposals to sell back to former owners: Minister's draft memorandum to Home Affairs Committee (Cabinet case)
142/242	1953–7 Ditto: memorandum to Crichel Down Committee from Minister, on disposal of land other than airfields (Cabinet case)
142/271	1954 Report of Crichel Down Inquiry
142/276	1954 Crichel Down Inquiry: payment of costs
142/277	1954 Report of Crichel Down Inquiry: miscellaneous correspondence
142/278	1954–5 Future of land at Crichel Down
142/280	1954–5 Crichel Down: correspondence with Dorset CAEC
142/295	1954 Crichel Down; dilapidations: reports
142/308	1955–6 Question of arbitration over price of Crichel Down and on resale of land generally
148/6	1949–52 Crichel Down, Dorset: equipping and farming the land
148/7	1952–3 Ditto: tenant right valuation
148/8	1953–5 Ditto: tenant right valuation and claim for dilapidations: farming accounts: arrangements for public inquiry into disposal of land

148/9	1949–51 ALC, Crichel Down, Dorset: equipping and farming the land
148/10	1951–2 Ditto
148/11	1952–3 Ditto: sale to Crown Lands: tenant right valuation: request to return land to former owners
227/35	1954 Inquiry into disposal of land at Crichel Down, Dorset: publication of report CMD9176: comments by officials concerned: Minister's first statement to Parliament
227/36	1954 Ditto: absence of Mr L. J. Smith (Secretary ALC): correspondence
227/37	1954 Notes and briefs for Minister on future policy on disposal of land compulsorily acquired (Cabinet case)
236/1	1937–53 Copies of correspondence used in public inquiry, notated by the Hon. Charles Russell QC, bundle 1
236/2	Ditto: bundle 2
236/3	1954 Public inquiry, transcripts of evidence, day 1
236/4	1954 Ditto: day 2
236/5	1954 Ditto: day 3
236/6	1954 Ditto: day 4
236/7	1954 Ditto: day 5
236/8	1954 Ditto: day 6
236/9	1954 Ditto: day 7
236/10	1954 List of persons mentioned in the correspondence and of persons involved in transfer of land
236/11	1954 Maps and plans

Minister's Private Office Papers

236/12	1953 Submissions to Prime Minister: Prime Minister's personal minute
236/13	1954 Notes for Minister's interview with Sir Frederick Burrows, Chairman ALC
236/14	1954 Departmental observations on report of Crichel Down inquiry
236/15	1954 Allowance for dilapidations: report by R. C. Walmsley FRICS, FLAS, comments by C. G. Eastwood
236/16	1954 Report on Crichel Down inquiry: comments by officials concerned
236/17	1954 House of Commons debate, July 20: supporting notes
236/18	1954 Minister's meeting with Food and Agriculture Committee
236/19	1954 Negotiations on purchase of Crichel Down after public inquiry
236/20	1954 Notes on report of public inquiry: disclosure of documents: conduct of civil servants: grounds for less unfavourable view

236/21 1954 Miscellaneous correspondence from general public

236/22 1954 Loose papers including briefs for meetings of the Minister, Parliamentary Secretary, Mr Crouch (MP Dorset North) and Lt. Cmdr. G. G. Marten (Claimant for Crichel Down)

236/23 1954 Committee on transfer of officials concerned following report of public inquiry: note by Minister

Permanent Secretary's Papers

236/24 1954 Minister's briefs for Crichel Down debate

236/25 1954 Notes and briefs including notes for Home Secretary's meeting with 1922 Committee

236/26 1954 Conduct of civil servants and ministerial responsibilities

236/27 1954 Report on Crichel Down inquiry: comments by those concerned: letter from Dorset AEC

236/28 1954 Future of Crichel Down land

236/29 1954 Remedial action in civil service following Crichel Down Inquiry

236/30 1954 Crichel Down inquiry: absence of L. J. Smith (Secretary ALC)

236/31 1954 Dilapidations report: notes and correspondence

Land Division Papers

236/32 1953–4 Payment for dilapidations on Crichel Down

236/33 1955 Inquiry into the organisation of Crown Lands

Legal Department Papers

236/36 1952–4 Post-mortem folder on report of Crichel Down inquiry: papers originally belonging to F. P. R. Mallows, Senior Legal Assistant

236/37 1953–4 Crichel Down inquiry: preparation of evidence

236/38 1953–4 Ditto: notes, minutes and statements

236/39 1953–4 Solicitors for Lt. Cdr. Marten: correspondence

236/40 1953–4 Papers originally belonging to E. C. Harris, assistant solicitor: disposal of state-owned land other than airfields (Cabinet case)

236/41 1953–4 Ditto: negotiations on the future of Crichel Down

236/42 1954–5 Ditto

236/43 1954 Lists of applicants for Crichel Down

236/44 1954 Crichel Down inquiry: list of mistakes by persons concerned: absence from inquiry of L. J. Smith, Secretary ALC

236/45 1954 personal papers originally belonging to F. P. R. Mallows, Senior Legal Assistant

236/46   1954 Lists and précis of correspondence and rough notes originally belonging to H. P. Hall, Legal Assistant, and F. P. R. Mallows

236/47   1953 Instructions to Counsel to attend preliminary meeting of 29 December 1953

236/48   1953 Instructions to Counsel and legal opinion

236/49   1954 Statement of case on behalf of Lt.-Com. Marten and the Hon. Mrs Marten and also J. Strange and H. A. Hooper

236/50   1954 Summary prepared by Ministry for Sir Andrew Clark

236/51   1954 Questionnaire submitted by Sir Andrew Clark, with answers

236/52   1954 Commissioner of Lands: draft brief

236/53   1954 Ditto: instructions to Counsel

236/54   1954 Draft brief for MAF (version A)

236/55   1954 Brief for MAF including brief, expanded version B, supplementary notes and instructions

236/56   1954 Original draft statements of Ministry and Crown Lands witnesses

236/57   1954 Draft statement by T. R. Ferris . . . not used as Mr Ferris not called as witness

236/58   1953 Brief for MAF: Hon. Charles Russell QC

236/59   1953 Ditto: B. S. Wingate-Saul, barrister

236/60   1953 Brief for Crown Lands: J. P. Widgery, barrister

236/61   1954 Instructions to advice on evidence, B. S. Wingate-Saul

236/62   1954 Ditto: J. P. Widgery

236/63   1954 Supplementary instructions on brief, B. S. Wingate-Saul

236/64   1954 Ditto: J. P. Widgery

236/65   1954 Proof of evidence of H. E. Bush, Deputy Chief Lands Officer, Air Ministry

236/66   1948–53 Crichel Estate: building licence applications

236/67   1951–3 Land Commissioner's Office, Taunton: applications for Crichel Down

236/68   1953–4 Correspondence between Legal Department and D. S. Brown, Assistant Land Commissioner

236/69   1954–70 Letter from H. C. M. Wilcox, Under Secretary, MAF, to R. J. Vile, Chairman of First Division Civil Servants

Index

Abercrombie, Sir Patrick (1879–1957), Professor of Town Planning, London; agreed Crichel Down acquisition, 13

Acland, Sir Richard, Bt, MP Greenwich 1947–55 Second Church Estates Commissioner 1950–1, 173, 181, 199

Agricultural Land Commission (ALC), control of Crichel Down transferred to, 30; 31; Hole sends proposals to, 34; 35, 36, 39, 41; asked to reply to Seymour 47; 48, 51, 52, 55, 56, 57, 61, 64, 68; advice, 70–1; rejects Taylor's offer, 72–3; confidentiality tangle, 79; 83, 86–7, 89, 90; agrees price, 94; 104, 105, 107, 109. 110–11, 112, 123, 124, 134, 137, 157, 158, 163, 176, 180, 182, 185; detailed refutation of Report charges, 186, 187, 196, 198; Arton Wilson recommendations, 204; see also Appendix 2

Agriculture, Ministry of, Order charging Crichel Estate with costs in favour of Alington, 11; post-war consideration of Crichel Down range, 20; interpretation of 'clearance', 23; transfer of land to, 25; 26; growth and spread of, 27; Ryan Committee, 28; policy, 29; transfers Crichel Down to ALC, 34; 41, 47, 52; twin issues of policy, 54–5; 56, 75, 79, 81, 83, 88, 90, 92; agrees price, 94; 95, 99, 102, 104–5, 107; 'stand by our guns', 108; 112, 124, 127, 128, 129, 131, 134, 135, 158, 163; legal department's strategy for conduct of case, 167; rejects offer to abandon inquiry, 168; 169, 173, 180–1, 182; Smith's farewell to, 189; 199, 203; Arton Wilson Committee recommendations, 204

Agriculture Act 1947, 59, 60–1, 84, 109, 121, 126, 127–9, 155

Air Ministry, 1, 10, 13; terms not yet definitely agreed, 17; covenant to erect rabbit-proof fence, 18; no further use for Crichel Down, 21; meaning of 'clearance', 23; 25, 30; water from Crichel Estate, 32; 46, 52, 58, 61, 62, 63, 75; 93, 104, 121, 125, 138, 158

Alington, Napier George Henry Sturt, 3rd Lord (1896–1940), 6, 8; objection to selection of Crichel Down, 10; suggests Pond Bottom, 10–11; ceased to 'own' Crichel Estate 1928, 11; dispute with Hardings, 11–12; 13; Notice to Treat, 14; anxious for settlement, 17; 54, 110, 134, 193; see also Appendices 2 and 5

Applications for land, 24–5, 26, 31–2, 35, 36, 37, 39, 40, 41, 45, 46, 49–50, 52–3, 54, 64, 66, 67, 71, 72–3, 79, 80, 81, 82, 85, 87–9, 90, 92–4, 96, 97, 99, 100, 103, 104–5, 110–11, 114, 117, 131, 134, 137, 138, 142; Clark's suggested solution, 143; 144, 149; 'disregarded', 158; 168, 183, 184–5, 197; see also Appendix 2

Askew, Rev. Mr., Langton Estate trustee, 64, 71

Association of First Division Civil Servants see Buxton, Leonard; Vile, Robert; Wilcox, Claude

Atkinson, A. K. H., Assistant Principal, Ministry of Agriculture, Private Secretary to Parliamentary Secretary Nugent, 86, 97

Badbury Rings, Dorset, 2

Blandford Forum, Dorset, 2–3, 11, 13; Inquiry opened in Corn Exchange, 135

Blandford Martyrs, 120, 121, 123, 136, 145; headings, 174, 180; 181; heading, 187; 206–7

Boards: Crown Estate Board, 176; ALC Board, 176, 186

Bourke, Hon. Geoffrey, FRICS, FLAS, Member ALC, inspects Crichel Down, 35; 77

Bournemouth, 3

Boyle, Squadron-Leader, RAF. Boscombe Down, 21, 22

Bridges, Sir Edward, KG PC GCB GCVO MC FRS, 1st Baron Bridges (1892–1969), Head of Civil Service, Eton, Magdalen College Oxford, Fellow of All Souls, HM Treasury 1919–38, Cabinet Secretary 1938–46, Permanent Secretary, Treasury 1945–56, 164